Sex in Public

Sex in Public

THE INCARNATION OF
EARLY SOVIET IDEOLOGY

Eric Naiman

PRINCETON UNIVERSITY PRESS

PRINCETON, NEW JERSEY

Copyright © 1997 by Princeton University Press
Published by Princeton University Press, 41 William Street,
Princeton, New Jersey 08540
In the United Kingdom: Princeton University Press, Chichester, West Sussex

Library of Congress Cataloging-in-Publication Data
Naiman, Eric, 1958–
    Sex in public : the incarnation of early Soviet ideology / Eric
Naiman.
        p.   cm.
    Includes bibliographical references and index.
    ISBN 0-691-02626-2 (cloth : alk. paper)
    1. Soviet Union—History—1917–1936. 2. Communism and sex—Soviet
Union. I. Title.
DK266.N22   1997
947.084—dc20   96-43642
                                                                   CIP

This book has been composed in Times Roman

Princeton University Press books are printed on acid-free paper
and meet the guidelines for permanence and durability of the
Committee on Production Guidelines for Book Longevity of the Council on Library Resources

Printed in the United States of America by Princeton Academic Press
1 3 5 7 9 10 8 6 4 2

For Gregory Freidin,
Boris Gasparov,
and
Anne Nesbet

in awe

_____

CONTENTS

ACKNOWLEDGMENTS

ANNA SURASKY and Julius Bass made me want to learn Russian. Among their many gifts to me, the greatest may have been their attachment to the language and literature of the country they left behind. Jane Taubman, Stanley Rabinowitz, and Viktoria Shweitzer taught me that language and conveyed to me their enthusiasm for it. Along the road to and from the Amherst College Russian Department there were many other influences on the development of the interests and sensibilities that have led, among other places, to the production of this book. I would like to thank my first readers, Robert and Lee Naiman, as well as later ones, including Hortense Tyroler, Susan Semel, Nancy Pollak, Susan Amert, and Rya Zobel. No less than ideology, academic interest is an "affective" category, and the attraction of Russia has been sustained for me at important times by the friendship of Leslie Litzky, David Shengold, Alexander Papachristou and Carroll Bogert, Nikolai Zhemchuzhin and Natalia Zhemchuzhina, and Yury and Natalia Goroshko. The last six friends named above have fed and sheltered me in Russia, thus providing the material conditions essential to this book's research.

My work on this project has been facilitated by the staffs of the Saltykov-Shchedrin Public Library (and, particularly, of its *Gazetnyi zal*), the Lenin Library, and the Pacific Film Archive, where I have often benefited from the assistance of Nancy Goldman. Financial support has been provided by Leningrad State University and the University of California. I have also received funding from the U.S. Department of State's discretionary grant program for Studies of Eastern Europe and the Independent States of the former Soviet Union, as provided by the Hoover Institution and the Soviet–Eastern European Research and Training Act. The Social Science Research Council has funded my work several times, and I am deeply appreciative of its continued interest and support.

I am grateful to the editors at *Novoe literaturnoe obozrenie*, *Russian History*, *Signs*, and *Slavic and East European Journal* who published earlier versions of work that has been revised for this book. I am particularly indebted to Jane Costlow, Stephanie Sandler, and Judith Vowles, the editors of *Sexuality and the Body in Russian Culture* (Stanford: Stanford University Press, 1993), for expressing an early interest in this project and publishing material that in expanded form has found its way into my first chapter.

Both author and readers of *Sex in Public* are fortunate that in its various incarnations this text has had demanding, forgiving, and blessedly quirky critics. Let me mention, without publicly assigning them to any of the foregoing types, Victoria Bonnell, Helen Deutsch, Robert Hughes, Simon Karlinsky, Ronald LeBlanc, William Nickell, Sarah Pratt, Daniel Rancour-Laferriere, and Susan Ryan. I am especially appreciative of a thorough critique of this project provided at an intermediate stage by Irina Paperno. Recent readings of the manuscript by Svetlana Boym, Caryl Emerson, Katerina Clark, Laura Engelstein, Leonard Helfgott, Yuri Slezkine, and Mark von Hagen have been insightful, skeptical, and otherwise invaluable. (Lisa Little is, doubtless, responsible for any mistakes that Yuri Slezkine missed.) Lee Naiman's suggestions have substantially improved the quality of my writing; this book's readers are the beneficiaries of her careful, patient work.

Frances Bernstein, Julie Cassiday, Ian Christie, Christina Kiaer, Naum Kleiman, Natalia Lebina, and Elizabeth Wood have furnished me with important information and sources at various points in this project. Robert Wessling was a stunningly effective research assistant in Moscow. Russell Merritt, probably the most frequently acknowledged person in American academic publishing, has been extraordinarily generous with his time, camera, and expertise. Mary Murrell has been an enthusiastic and efficient editor. I thank Lauren Lepow for the wonderful job she has done in the final stages of preparing the manuscript.

I am most grateful to the three to whom I dedicate this book. The pleasure they have brought to my life and the impact they have had on this project have been enormous. I hope they find this book a worthy distortion of their scholarship, affection, and ideas.

NOTE ON TRANSLITERATION, CITATION, AND TRANSLATION

WITHIN THE TEXT, I have used the transliteration system of the Library of Congress but have altered it slightly to render the endings of first and last names familiar to, or at least less unpronounceable for, readers unfamiliar with Russian (e.g., Trotskii becomes Trotsky, Evgenii Preobrazhenskii becomes Evgeny Preobrazhensky). In the notes I adhere strictly to the Library of Congress system throughout.

A bibliography would have substantially increased the length and price of this volume. In the notes to each chapter, a full reference is provided upon the first citation in that chapter of a given work. To facilitate the task of obtaining items on interlibrary loan, for references to works published in periodicals or in anthologies of works by more than one author, I have provided in parentheses the page numbers for the entire item. The index includes references to all authors cited in the notes. If no parenthesis is given, the page(s) cited in the note constitute the entire item. The following abbreviations for places of publication have been used: L.—Leningrad; M.—Moscow; Pb.—Petersburg; Pg.—Petrograd; SPb.—Saint Petersburg. (In each case I have adhered to the place-name specified by the title page regardless of the official name of the city at the time.) IMLI signifies the archive of the Institute of World Literature in Moscow; RGALI refers to the Russian State Archive for Literature and Art. Unless otherwise noted, all emphasis belongs to quoted authors, as do all ellipses unless they are enclosed in brackets, in which case they have been supplied by me.

For readers unfamiliar with Russian I note that the word "komsomolets" refers to a young man who has joined the Komsomol (Communist Youth League). "Komsomolka" refers to a woman—and "komsomolki" to women—in that organization. "Komsomol'tsy" refers either to more than one man or to a mixed group of Komsomol adherents.

Except where otherwise noted, all translations are mine.

Sex in Public

INTRODUCTION

MENSTRUATION AND A NEW PAIR OF GLASSES

On 1 January 1925, *Izvestiia* published an attack on a new book by Martyn Liadov, the rector of Sverdlov Communist University, the highest Party school.[1] In this work, based on a series of lectures to communist cadres under his tutelage, the rector had revealed that nonseasonal sexual desire and, implicitly, menstruation had been inflicted by capitalism on the female body. "In no animal," he had explained, "is sexuality a dominant emotion throughout the whole year. It appears only at a specific time, during the female's spring heat. [. . .] For a prolonged historical period (and this is clear from a wide range of historical sources) man, like all other animals, mated only once a year. [. . .] When a market economy developed, when private property began to be accumulated, then woman, too, was transformed into private property and had to be prepared to satisfy her master's demand at any time."[2] Refuting Liadov (a noted Party historian) and Aron Zalkind (a "psychoneurologist" who frequently published articles about sex in the Komsomol press), the Soviet health commissar, Nikolai Semashko, charged in *Izvestiia* that they were turning Marx "inside out" in their ignorance of basic biological and historical facts. Many animals menstruate, he pointed out, as had women prior to the development of capitalism. The Romans, for example, had referred to women's periods as "menses," an indication that their women bled monthly and were sexually available throughout the year.

Why were future Party leaders being instructed about female physiology and human sexual desire as part of their political education, and why was this subject deemed sufficiently significant to merit space in the Soviet government's central press organ? We are accustomed to viewing early Soviet culture through the lenses of a few well-worn pairs of glasses that, depending upon our mood, enable us to spy retrospectively on political machinations, plunge us into a world of widespread artistic and social innovation, or allow us to savor the edifying spectacle of a lonely individual's heroic refusal to submit to conformity and oppression. Usually we are not bothered by the divergent ways in which these eyeglasses refract the past any more

---

[1] N. Semashko, "Kak ne nado pisat' o polovom voprose," *Izvestiia*, 1 January 1925, 5.

[2] M. N. Liadov, *Voprosy byta* (M.: Kommunisticheskii universitet, 1925), 30. Despite the book's official publication date of 1925, the publication of Semashko's attack on 1 January of that year indicates that the book was available in the previous year.

than, as readers, we are disturbed by the different worldviews found in the detective novel, the romance, or other genres available for the price of an old paperback. They have helped us categorize—and cope with the existence of—a powerful neighbor whose presence might otherwise have roused in us an uncomfortable level of fear or desire. However, as the stakes of research into the Soviet experience change and as scholars liberate themselves from the oppressive weight of judging the past through its consequences in the present, wearers of old glasses ought to feel less nervous about the dangers of trying on new visual aids. The collapse of the Soviet Empire has profoundly affected the contemporary political relevance of Soviet studies; it should also encourage scholars to engage in imaginative reconceptualization and methodological experimentation that may substantially broaden our understanding of the Soviet past.

The following pages attempt to reshape accepted narratives of early Soviet history. I will consider the manner in which ideological fictions during the 1920s led political discourse to become preoccupied with sexuality and the body. As I focus attention on the early Soviet projection of ideological and political anxieties onto a corporal canvas, my primary goal will not be to catalog the historical, moral, and political failings—or, to use the terminology of ideology theory, the contradictions—of Bolshevism during the New Economic Policy, but to examine the way in which ideological problems were imaginatively or affectively handled. This book is both a historical study and an analysis of ideological poetics.

The title, *Sex in Public*, is meant to suggest the ideological importance of sex as a topic of public discussion. I will argue that talk about sex was a means of popular mobilization and, at the same time, a process of ideological entrapment (and self-entrapment) of which the Party and Komsomol were never in total control. The subtitle of the book, *The Incarnation of Early Soviet Ideology*, requires more explanation. In 1925, in the midst of Party discussions about the extent to which the Party had delayed the achievement of the Revolution's goals, Grigory Zinov'ev, simultaneously the chief executive of the Comintern and the head of the Leningrad Party organization, declared that during the preceding few years Soviet society had witnessed the "gradual incarnation [*voploshchenie*] of the October Revolution's program." Responding to charges that in an excess of pragmatism the Party had "liquidat[ed] the Revolution's 'flight'" and had "ceased to breathe with a common breast with the poor," he contended that the Party was becoming "ever more intimate with the new masses of workers and poor in order to help them incarnate their dream [*voplotit' mechtu*] of a new order, a classless society, and genuine socialism."[3] Zinov'ev's defense of Bolshevik

---

[3] G. Zinov'ev, *Filosofiia epokhi* (M. and L.: Moskovskii rabochii, 1925), 27.

policy implicitly rejected the notion that the Revolution in its concrete, incarnated form would inevitably fall short of pre-Revolutionary goals. In the
near term, Soviet leaders would contend, Soviet reality merely *looked* different from its earlier bloodless and theoretical projection onto the future. But
many Party members were unable to achieve Zinov'ev's level of confidence,
and Zinov'ev himself would soon stand accused of the sin of ideological
pessimism. Just as—to quote one of Russian poetry's most famous lines—
"the thought, once spoken, becomes a lie," the dream of utopia is apt to
display disturbing defects when compelled to assume political and economic
flesh.[4] This book will examine the ideological uses made of the body at a
concrete historical moment when theory is put into practice; the chapters to
come will explore the discursive marks made on the flesh when it is forced
to "mediate" between the Ideal and the Real.[5]

Approaching NEP: Ideological Anxieties and the "Unarmed Eye"

Sex in Public takes as its object Soviet ideology during the years of the New
Economic Policy (NEP), a period (from 1921 to, roughly, 1928) in which the
Party asked its followers to defer ideological expectations for the sake of
economic efficiency and the consolidation of power. The Civil War that followed the 1917 Bolshevik Revolution was essentially over by late 1920, and
one of NEP's defining features was its status as communist Russia's first
experience with peace. Following the turmoil, starvation, and forced labor of
the Civil War, NEP would seem to have offered a welcome respite to a
nation that, according to its leader, had "never been so exhausted, so worn
out, as now."[6] Yet remarkably soon after the conclusion of the Civil War,
many citizens and leaders intent on revolutionizing politics, literature, and
the recalcitrant category of "everyday life" (*byt*) were to view the preceding
four years with nostalgia, as a time of uncompromising—and thus comforting—purity, as a Golden Age of physical and ideological chastity when triv-
ial but annoyingly importunate spheres of human activity had been splendidly eclipsed by an all-consuming cause. Trotsky expressed a defining
concern of the period when he worried that "without revolutionary perspectives, or a broad historical framework," the young, especially, might "ossify
in an atmosphere of Soviet petty deeds," that "one awful day it might turn

---

[4] F. Tiutchev, *Polnoe sobranie stikhotvorenii* (L.: Sovetskii pisatel', 1987), 105.

[5] I take the term "mediation" from Ludmilla Jordanova, who uses it to discuss the way in
which medical and scientific images "speak to and contain implications about matters beyond
their explicit content." *Sexual Visions: Images of Gender in Science and Medicine between the
Eighteenth and Twentieth Centuries* (Madison: University of Wisconsin Press, 1989), 2.

[6] V. I. Lenin, "Rech' na vserossiiskom s"ezde transportnykh rabochikh" (27 March 1921),
Polnoe sobranie sochinenii, 5th ed., 45 vols. (M.: Gos. izd., 1958–1965), 43:104.

out that we and [our youth] are speaking different languages."[7] For all its justly deserved reputation as a period of relative tolerance and cultural experimentation, the era of NEP was a profoundly *anxious* time; many Russians deriving retrospective pleasure from the sacrifices demanded by the Civil War had difficulty reconciling themselves to the prospect of life in a world no longer blessed by adherence to absolute categories of human interaction.

NEP began as it would end—with a whimper rather than a rhetorical or propagandistic bang. The Tenth Party Congress, lasting from 8 to 16 March 1921, is generally considered NEP's birthplace. Only one of the policy's planks, however—the replacement of grain requisitions by a tax in kind—was proposed at that gathering, and this proposal was overshadowed by the struggle with the "Workers' Opposition," a Party faction insisting on greater unity between the Party's bureaucracy and the factory workers whom the Party claimed to represent. Furthermore, the entire assembly was diminished in importance by the uprising of disaffected sailors on Kronstadt and its suppression. Not until the ensuing spring and summer were the further proposals that would become the core of NEP enshrined into law. On 23 March, a decree permitting free trade in grain surpluses at markets and bazaars went into effect; in May, the Soviet government began permitting cooperatives and private managers to lease previously nationalized enterprises. Government industries were organized into trusts and placed on *khozraschet*, which meant that their production decisions were to be determined by commercial principles. Finally, in July 1921, a decree was issued permitting anyone over sixteen years of age to participate in retail trade. Within a year, small private businesses were flourishing and a class of entrepreneurs had arisen, a group indispensable to the new market-oriented economy but despised by many whose lives it was indirectly helping to improve.[8]

Exactly when these measures, obviously part of *a* new economic policy, became *The* New Economic Policy is difficult to determine, but by fall 1921 the Party and its press had grouped these new directives together and had begun to interpret them as the unified sign of a new era. Resistance to NEP also started to surface among communists reluctant to abandon the militaristic, uncompromising positions adopted during the Civil War toward the peasantry and private enterprise. Initially there were few direct attacks on the new policy; rather, a certain confusion and unease were apparent among Party members and ideologically committed citizens who did not hold Party membership. Nikolai Bukharin, who was later to be one of NEP's most consistent supporters, complained in a much reprinted 1921 essay that

---

[7] L. Trotskii, "Mysli o Partii," in his *Zadachi XII s"ezda RKP* (M.: Deviatoe ianvaria, 1923), 48.

[8] The preceding paragraph is based upon the overview of NEP provided by Edward Hallett Carr in his *The Bolshevik Revolution 1917–1923*, 3 vols. (New York: W. W. Norton, 1980), 2:269–360.

"many of our comrades in the Party lack vision: it's as if their vision has been lost, as if clear and distinct lines have become blurred, lost in something murky and highly indistinct."[9] This sense of drift gave way to outright hostility in many quarters by fall of 1922, when a good harvest had begun to create economic inequality in the countryside. As early as March 1922, Evgeny Preobrazhensky, coauthor with Bukharin of the highly popular *The ABCs of Communism*, had warned the Central Committee:

> The leveling of class contradictions in our country has come to a halt. The process of differentiation has begun anew and grown; it is strongest in places where the revival of the peasant economy has been most successful and where the area of land under cultivation is increasing. . . . An agricultural bourgeoisie is emerging, but the peasant economy as a whole is in marked decline and the countryside is generally becoming impoverished.[10]

Hostility toward NEP would take various forms and align itself with different fears.[11] We will examine several of its manifestations in the following chapters, but at this point it is worth noting that even those whose job was the propagandizing of NEP—who knew they must sell this economic and cultural hybrid to wary, ideologically steadfast supporters—even these salesmen had doubts about their product. Speaking to the Comintern in 1924, Bukharin frankly admitted the discomfort many communists had first experienced with NEP:

> After the introduction of NEP, we Russian communists, and to some degree our friends from foreign parties as well, almost without exception felt that we were doing something that was not entirely correct, as if we had to apologize for NEP. In its most subtle form, this "apologetic" attitude amounted to our regarding NEP exclusively from the point of view of political expediency, as a political concession to the bourgeoisie. We did not think that NEP was expedient and rational in and of itself, but we believed that we should introduce it out of political considerations.[12]

---

[9] "Novyi kurs ekonomicheskoi politiki," in N. I. Bukharin, *Izbrannye proizvedeniia* (M.: Politizdat, 1988), 29. In 1921 and 1922 the speech was published as a separate brochure and included in several collections of essays devoted to NEP.

[10] Quoted in Carr, *The Bolshevik Revolution*, 2:292. Preobrazhenskii's comments represented a significant evolution from his position just seven months earlier, when he had warned that the expression of doubt about the Party's line was tantamount to "sabotage of thought." "Bol'she vnimaniia partii," *Pravda*, 27 August 1921, 1. Even here, though, Preobrazhenskii had cautioned that the Party was menaced by "a deviation toward bourgeois liquidationism" and "more retreating than we actually need."

[11] Alan Ball's study of private enterpreneurs during NEP examines the vicissitudes in the Party's implementation of its new course and discusses the hostilities that these fluctuations generated. *Russia's Last Capitalists: The Nepmen, 1921–1929* (Berkeley and Los Angeles: University of California Press, 1990).

[12] "Doklad tov. Bukharina po programmnomu voprosu," *Pravda*, 1 July 1924, 3.

It is important to note the manner in which Bukharin presented this description of anxiety. The Bolsheviks charged with implementing NEP were beset by uneasiness that could not be rationalized; they were troubled, even ashamed, by the Party's authorization to violate ideological taboos internalized in an earlier period of political life. In the speech quoted above, Bukharin would claim that Soviet communists had overcome their initial discomfort. But this assertion was belied by his too frequent protestations of members' newly acquired but now unflagging certitude. Bukharin's rhetoric exposes his difficulties in abandoning his earlier "apologetic" stance: "*I beg your pardon* for the detail with which I will be dwelling on this question [of NEP]."[13]

If Bukharin's colleagues reacted to NEP with unease, members of the younger generation and of the proletariat often responded with outright hostility. Refusing to renounce his adherence to the apocalyptic rhetoric and utopian dreams of War Communism, twenty-three-year-old Andrei Platonov, a fledgling journalist descended from railway workers and miners, complained bitterly when the editor of a local paper refused to print his hymns to the industrial promise of global Revolution. In October 1922, he dispatched his imitative poems to another editor with the following note:

> [. . .] I am sending you the rhythm of beautiful dynamite and of shots of explosively bright summer lightning. By the way, in the offices of *Kineshma Convulsions* (*Kineshma Life*) an extremely responsible and serious editor evaluated the enclosed as follows:
> —"The time for this has passed. Now it's NEPO"[14]—(a disgusting word reminding one of chocolate perfumed with cheap pomade).
> But for you (I think) Rebellion—as an idea—will always be alive regardless of all sorts of new economic and other policies.[15]

Lenin and Bukharin treated the exponents of such views with slightly less condescension than did Platonov's dismissive editor. They portrayed impatient supporters of communist ideals as children, and, indeed, the metaphor of childhood was consistently attached to War Communism, a period with an infantile psychology, when all questions had been resolved in accordance with the immediate fulfillment of needs. During War Communism the watchword had been "not '*produce*' but '*take*,' 'take' in order to supply the Red Army and munitions workers as quickly as possible. This and *only* this stood at the center of attention."[16] Now the childhood stage and its needs had been left behind forever. In 1924 Bukharin wrote in the Party journal *Bol'shevik*:

---

[13] Ibid. (emphasis added).

[14] Platonov was using the early acronym "NEPO"; "NEP" did not become the generally accepted shorthand until later in 1922.

[15] RGALI, fond 602, opis' 1, ed. khran. 853.

[16] Bukharin, "Novyi kurs," 24.

In the fire of . . . self-criticism the *illusions* of the childhood period are consumed and disappear *without a trace*, real relations appear in all their sober nakedness, and proletarian policy acquires in appearance sometimes a less emotional, but therefore a more assured, character—a solid one, adhering closely to reality and therefore much more truly changing this reality.

From this point of view, the transition to the new economic policies represented the collapse of our *illusions*.[17]

For Bukharin, NEP was a coming of age, when childish fantasies about a perfect world and unlimited power had to be put aside like the dolls with which, according to an earlier comment by Lenin, utopians were wont to play.[18] Unfortunately, Bukharin's statement collapses when viewed with anything more rigorous than the most superficial gaze. Have the illusions really been so totally obliterated, or are they being reinstated at the conclusion of his first paragraph ("adhering closely to reality and therefore much more truly changing this reality"), vanquishing reality through the wonders of dialectical rhetoric?

Platonov's transformation of the New Economic Policy to a repugnantly connotative verbal sign was typical of the era that came to bear the policy's name. NEP was a period that came to be identified with and defined by the class enemies regarded by the Bolsheviks as the era's most disturbing denizens. The fluctuations of the Party's economic policies between 1921 and 1928 did not fundamentally affect "NEP"'s ideological identity, for that identity signified something far broader than the execution of a particular economic program. In his survey of the language of "the Revolutionary epoch" (1917–1927), Afanasy Selishchev drew on speeches of two authoritative Bolsheviks in providing the following gloss:

With the word "NEP" another meaning has become associated: (1) "speculation," (2) "new bourgeois elements": "When we say NEP [*kogda my govorim NEP*], we often mean by this word speculation, self-seeking greed [*rvachestvo*] and NEPmanism [i.e., the phenomenon and characteristics of the "new" bourgeoisie]." (Zinov'ev, *Pravda*, 28 May 1924). "When people say NEP in informal speech [*kogda govoriat v prostorechii NEP*], they mean by this not our economic

---

[17] Quoted in Stephen F. Cohen, *Bukharin and the Bolshevik Revolution* (New York: Oxford University Press, 1980), 139.

[18] Lenin, "Uspekhi i trudnosti sovetskoi vlasti" (17 April 1919), *Polnoe sobranie*, 38:53–54. See also his "Detskaia bolezn' 'levizny' v kommunizme" (April–May 1920), *Polnoe sobranie*, 41:3–104, where he applied the diagnosis of "infantile leftism" to communists abroad who failed to understand that concrete historical situations frequently necessitate pragmatic departures from political ideals. In that pamphlet Lenin also used the term "children" to refer to Russian communists who had failed to understand the necessity of tactical compromises during the decade preceding the Revolution.

policy as a whole and not even the economic order as a whole, but new bourgeois elements, the new bourgeoisie." (Bukharin, *Pravda*, No. 2, 1926).[19]

Tension is implicit in these two quotations. One Bolshevik is willing to attribute to "us" ("when we say NEP") a hostile attitude that another, less
antagonistically inclined, attributes to others' everyday speech ("when people say"). In both cases a pernicious synecdoche threatens to render repugnant the country's current ideological experience: NEP—and the communists who live it—are reduced to NEP's most negative elements. Discussions
of NEP frequently employed a rhetoric of negation, as if the era could be
present as a conversational object only if the speaker simultaneously expressed a desire to deny the object's existence. In 1925, in the midst of intra-
Party struggles that will be examined in chapter 7, Zinov'ev declared in
Izvestiia that since the New Economic Policy had little new in it, it might
more accurately be labeled "Not-NEP" (*ne-Nep*). "If we really want to keep
the same word 'NEP,'" he added, then it was necessary "to say that this
word is derived from the phrase 'Necessary' Economic Policy [*Neobkho-
dimaia ekonomicheskaia politika*] or 'Inevitable' Economic Policy [*Neiz-
bezhnaia ekonomicheskaia politika*]."[20]

It was important for Party leaders to sell NEP as a legitimate policy—the
ideological "Real Thing"—and to portray War Communism as an aberration
necessitated by the exigencies of Civil War.[21] Through temporal legerdemain
"War Communism" became "nothing other than a correction to NEP" rather
than an originary and disgracefully abandoned path.[22] This point was crucial
because NEP had more in common with purgatory, a place for shedding the
mentalities and actions of the past, than with paradise. There was always a
danger that communists who had believed themselves on the brink of entering ideological heaven would, seeing similarities between NEP and the pre-
Revolutionary past, believe they were headed *down* Purgatory's mountain
rather than upward toward Marx's Beatrice.

NEP, the Party continually cautioned, did not entail struggle's cessation
but its complication. Defining the "philosophy of the epoch" in 1925,
Zinov'ev wrote:

[19] A. M. Selishchev, *Iazyk revoliutsionnoi epokhi: iz nabliudenii nad russkim iazykom posled-
nikh let 1917–1926*, 2d ed. (M.: Rabotnik prosveshcheniia, 1928), 196. Reprinted by Prideaux
Press (Russian Titles for the Specialist, No. 30), Letchworth, England, 1971.

[20] Ibid.

[21] See, for example, the assertion made in 1921 by the head of the Red Army's Political
Administration, that "had there been no Civil War, we would have introduced essentially this
same 'New Economic Policy' in 1919–1921. [. . .] The 'New Economic Policy' is the direct
continuation of the October Revolution." S. Gusev, "Eshche o novoi ekonomicheskoi politike (k
chetvertoi godovshchine oktiabr'skoi revoliutsii), *Krasnaia nov'*, no. 3 (1921): 329–330 (326–
330).

[22] Bukharin, "Doklad tov. Bukharina," 3.

The battles that will decide the fate of the Revolution continue, although they are "bloodless," silent, and without the accompanying roar of cannon fire. These battles differ from those we knew earlier on the fronts of the Civil War precisely in their quietness, in their being drawn out in time and fragmented among a whole series of almost petty episodes; they differ in that they occur in the quotidian economy and in everyday life, in that their development is hidden and without external effects, in that sometimes they are even invisible to the naked [or, more literally, "unarmed" (*nevooruzhennyi glaz*)] eye.[23]

Committed communists needed to know how to arm their eyes; they had to pay close attention and learn to find and read the "red thread" that ran through the confusing world of NEP.[24] Given the hidden nature of conflict during NEP, Zinov'ev continued, "the proletarian avant garde must look all the more attentively, all the more searchingly at the road upon which we walk; it is all the more essential that one repeatedly measure the path already covered and analyze the dangers lying in wait for the Revolution in the future."[25] This kind of close and repeated reading of the Revolution's course was predicated on a sense of heightened caution and danger in which painstaking analysis and verification could easily shade into mild paranoia or, at least, lead to the triumph of imagination over intellect. Without using the term "imagination," the constructivist dramatist and theorist Sergei Tret'iakov more or less made that category a prerequisite for the development of correct political perspective:

> [Representatives of the Party] always remember that they are in the trenches and that the enemy's muzzles are in front of them. Even when they grow potatoes around this trench and stretch out their cots beneath the ramparts, they never allow themselves the illusion that the trench is not a trench but a dacha [. . .] or that their enemies are simply the neighbors in the dacha next door.[26]

To help them "remember" that the enemy was always near, the Bolsheviks and their supporters employed various ideological narratives that will be examined from several perspectives in this book. Presented as scientifically proven antidotes to illusions, these narratives were—like all narratives— illusions themselves; they presented a satisfyingly convenient, but simplified and incomplete, view of the world and of the proletariat's place in it. In her

---

[23] Zinov'ev, *Filosofiia epokhi*, 5. The reader should note the tension implicit in Zinov'ev's reference to "bloodless" battles during a time of Revolutionary incarnation. In chapter 6, I will return to this question of the problematic relationship between "blood" and "flesh" in ideological anxieties about NEP.

[24] Ibid., 4.

[25] Ibid., 6.

[26] S. Tret'iakov, "LEF i NEP," *LEF*, no. 2 (1923): 72 (70–78). Tret'iakov was a member of the Left Front group, which explored the potential for artistic practices to play a role in the shaping of a new, communist everyday life.

important work on "the Bolsheviks' dilemma," Sheila Fitzpatrick has captured the quandary faced by the Party during and immediately after the Civil
War, when the working class had begun to evaporate into the army and the
village.[27] In 1920 there were only half as many "workers" in Russia as there
had been in 1913;[28] the urban population had been decimated by the collapse
of networks of distribution, and, by 1921, less than 40 percent of Party
members were workers.[29] Lenin admitted in March 1921: "Our proletariat is
in large measure déclassé; unprecedented crises and factory closures have
led our people to flee from hunger. Our workers have abandoned their factories and been forced to settle in villages; they cease to be workers."[30]
"Against the odds," writes Fitzpatrick, the Bolsheviks "had made a workers'
revolution. Then, in the hour of victory, the Russian proletariat had disappeared, leaving only its vanguard, like the smile of the Cheshire Cat, behind."[31] Fitzpatrick's Cheshire cat is an elegant but inapt image. Smiles were
foreign to the terrifying tales and images to which the Bolsheviks resorted to
keep their dilemmas at bay; in addition, in these stories the *body* (unlike that
of Carroll's feline) never disappeared—it remained disturbingly present and,
for reasons that will be examined, became central to the tales and pictures
that expressed and sought to defuse ideological anxiety.

Utopia and Its Infections

NEP was an exercise in patience, a period of learning and maturing for an
ideology that had hitherto not contemplated the possibility of so strange an
animal as eschatological adolescence. To many communists, NEP essentially
meant Utopia Postponed. The age was regarded as a necessary compromise
with reality, a period that would eventually lead to the evolution of the ideal
society. The shining goal of Socialism would be reached via a decidedly
dimmer, if temporary, market-based detour.[32] There was a fundamental problem with NEP's self-definition, however. In his tragicomic novel, *The Sugar
German* (1925), Sergei Klychkov tells of a powerful but ridiculous king,
Akhlamon, the lord of a fantastically rich fool's paradise.

---

[27] Sheila Fitzpatrick, *The Cultural Front: Power and Culture in Revolutionary Russia* (Ithaca:
Cornell University Press, 1992), 16–36.

[28] V. M. Selunskaia, ed., *Izmeneniia sotsial'noi struktury sovetskogo obshchestva 1921—ser-
edina 30-x godov* (M.: Mysl', 1979), 23.

[29] Ibid., 33.

[30] Lenin, "Zakliuchitel'noe slovo po otchetu TsK RKP(b) [Desiatyi s"ezd RKP(b)]" (9 March
1921), *Polnoe sobranie*, 43:42.

[31] Fitzpatrick, *The Cultural Front*, 19.

[32] The word "utopia" is often applied quite loosely to Soviet culture, frequently sarcastically
or without proper justification. I use it to refer to maximalist or chiliastic aspirations rather than
to specific blueprints for the building of perfect societies. The term is not intended—at least not
primarily—as a value judgment about communism in twentieth-century Russia.

No one has been to the World's end,
No one has seen Akhlamon's land,
And whoever has seen it, though he set out alive,
        returned dead.[33]

These playful lines, describing even as they seek to destroy the possibility of description, wisely point to a paradox that plagues all utopian mentalities, including the one that tried to reconcile itself to the wisdom of NEP. A constant feature in the construction of a would-be perfect world is the isolation of the ideal society; millenarian communities strive to wall themselves off from the rest of the world, and authors of utopian projects frequently seek to bracket their descriptions with protective narratives and framing devices that serve as a moat's narratological equivalent.[34] In the fact of description, however, lies the seed of the utopia's disintegration. The hermetic seal between the ideal, sacred land and the contagious imperfection of the reality known to and constituting the reader is necessarily broken by the mere fact of the text's existence and *transmission*. In the act of communicative intercourse between the dreamer/author/planner and his audience, both parties are fatally infected: the utopian's ideal by contact with an unsatisfactory and intrusive "real world," the "reader" by the desire for a state of purity that he cannot avoid contaminating. There is no such thing as "safe speech." The utopian enterprise is doomed by the necessity of being expressed and limited through the nonutopian, historically determined communicative instrument of language. The perfect utopia—a utopia immune to linguistically transmitted diseases—would be like the perfect crime: we would be ignorant of its existence.

Utopias are contaminated not only by linguistic but also by historical transmission. The question of how one gets from here to there requires the establishment of a link between the flawed present and the unflawed future (or past). If the utopian, or utopian-inclined, mentality producing a text does not opt for the solution of an unexplored planet or continent but seeks to ground the utopia's genesis in the present, it must deal with the problem of transition.[35] Here two concerns clash: on one hand the future must be ideal; on the other, it must not be utopian in the second sense of the word (a community that will never exist)—on some level the consciousness creating the utopia believes that it can be attained.[36] Since the present is so imperfect,

---

[33] Sergei Klychkov, *Chertukhinskii balakir'* (M.: Sovetskii pisatel', 1988), 24.

[34] For a discussion of framing in utopian narratives that does not consider the device's apotropaic function, see Gary Saul Morson, *The Boundaries of Genre: Dostoevsky's Diary of a Writer and the Traditions of Literary Utopia* (Evanston, Ill.: Northwestern University Press, 1981), 138–142, 162–175.

[35] In cases of interplanetary or intercontinental travel the problem of historical transmission does not, of course, disappear; it simply assumes a spatial disguise.

[36] Raymond Ruyer argues that a distinctive feature in utopian thought is the combination of

however, that it must be rejected for "another" reality, the process of transition is fraught with danger and necessarily becomes a period of purging, in which all imperfections of the here and now must be destroyed. The persecution of the present is, in part, a campaign against origins, against the germ from which the utopia springs, lest later, after germination, the utopia might be traced to its source and destroyed at and by its roots. Yet no matter how fierce the effort to purge, attempts to describe (or effect) a historical transmission are bound to fail, for historical—like linguistic—transmission necessarily shatters the pure isolation required by utopias for their continued survival as ideals.

As the persistence of utopian projects since at least classical times attests, the impossibility of utopian description does not squelch utopian impulses, and in this century the desire for a perfect world has been central to many ideologies. The impossibility of description, however, does play a role in structuring the necessarily contradictory utopian text or in the manner in which ideologies obsessed with imagined proximity to utopian ideals read and model the world. As if conscious of the paradoxical nature of their undertaking, texts describing utopias and transitions thereto are obsessed with their own impurities. They seem to circle around themselves, looking for every imperfection, as they endeavor to maintain a state of ideological chastity that was lost when they embarked on the enterprise of transmission. Historical epochs can also be read as texts, and those marked by the pathos of utopian yearnings are as preoccupied as their literary brothers with remaining pure. The era of the New Economic Policy is especially instructive in this regard, for the history of its discourse is one of discomfort with and hostility toward the impurities by which the period was defined.

In its fascination with flaws of ideological incarnation, discourse about NEP focused on several categories that may be called "metonymic" (i.e., relating to contiguity) in that they rely on imagery of symbolic and physical penetration and contact. We have already discussed utopian hostility toward language and history, but there are other categories of human experience that may symbolize the interference with and corruption of the Ideal by the Real.

One of these preoccupations is crime. In many societies crime is viewed at least partially, if not primarily, as a violation of the private sphere surrounding and protecting the individual; it is dreaded as a brutal intrusion into the individual citizen's illusion of isolation and independence. Seen as a social problem, crime may signify the vulnerability and penetration of the *composite* social body. As such the punishment of crime may become a matter of fundamental importance in utopian texts, where even the idea of criminality

---

fantasy with belief. "L'utopiste doit croire à demi à ses constructions, de même d'ailleurs qu'un joueur doit croir à son jeu[. . . .] Sinon, l'utopie devient pur exercice de la fantaisie poétique." *L'utopie et les utopies* (Saint-Pierre-de-Salerne: Gérard Monfort, 1988), 25.

threatens the fantasies of isolation and cohesion upon which the utopian project rests. Campanella's *City of the Sun* is so concerned with neutralizing the dangerously intrusive category of crime that it requires its narrator initially to deny that serious crime exists within the City and, later, to describe exactly how grave crimes committed within the metropolis's walls are punished. (A condemned man, the reader learns, may always appeal to the Metaphysician for mercy.)[37]

Communicable disease is another common focus of utopian fears. Plato's *Timaeus* begins with a curious, brief frame in which Socrates, longing to hear the ideal society described in action, asks where one of his desired interlocutors is, and is told, "He has been taken ill, Socrates, for he would not willingly have been absent from this gathering."[38] The story of how utopia came to be thus begins with the act of excluding illness. Socrates' brief reference to a sick acquaintance is all that remains of the idea of disease, but its verbal trace is the point against which the Ideal repulses itself into being. The significance of the opening extends beyond the mere exclusion of illness. It should be read as a symptomatic and constitutive moment of absence; the utopia is described only after a ritualistic gesture toward an absence has been made. Such a defensive gesture is indicative, I would argue, of utopia's necessary definition through absence, through the description of what it is not. Insistently excising sources of contamination, utopia reveals its metonymic core.

Sex, in particular, presents problems for utopian mentalities, for sexual desire is relentlessly metonymic, predicated upon fantasies of contact and contiguity. Frequently dependent on imagery of penetration, possession, and difference, sexuality may become a utopian obsession. Since sexual desire and activity are so fraught with vulnerability, and since sexuality often operates around the notion of the (at least figured) presence of an Other, utopian integrative aspirations and fears frequently manifest a particular dread of erotic urges. Copulation is controlled with mathematical precision or must be obliterated by monastic rules or self-mutilating strategies of defense. Moreover, sex is so evidently an avenue for contamination that other metonymic categories tend to become equated with it. It may be bound with language as equivalent agents of pollution,[39] it may be depicted—by virtue of its role in procreation—as the embodiment of historical and therefore antiutopian forces, and it may combine easily with disease or crime to produce cultural

---

[37] Tommaso Campanella, *The City of the Sun*, trans. Daniel J. Donno (Berkeley and Los Angeles: University of California Press, 1981), 41, 97.

[38] Plato, *Timaeus and Critias*, trans. Desmond Lee (Harmondsworth: Penguin, 1977), 29.

[39] Andrei Platonov's "The Potudan' River" and Andrei Belyi's *The Silver Dove* provide particularly striking instances of this combination. Andrei Platonov, "Reka Potudan'" (1937), in his *Gosudarstvennyi zhitel'* (M.: Sovetskii pisatel', 1988), 354–376; Andrei Belyi, *Serebrianyi golub'* (*Slavische Propylaen*, Band 38) (Munich: Wilhelm Fink, 1967 [1909]).

events and themes capable of holding a society spellbound. We need not decide now whether other anxieties—linguistic, historical, legal, or epidemiological—are at bottom masked anxieties *about* sexuality. At this point we need only note their similar functions and recognize that sex may act as symbolic shorthand for all forms of contamination feared by mentalities that produce utopian texts.

Sacrificing Culture / Reading Ideology

When I began this investigation of the meaning of sex during NEP, I envisioned my project as a case study of the place of sex in a "utopian culture." I gradually grew dissatisfied with this phrase. "Culture," meaning the way various segments of a population live, was not my study's object; if anything, culture was the object whose repression—or at least absence—was becoming a unifying theme of the book. Utopianism is all about the *denial* of culture, for culture, which the early-twentieth-century Russian philosopher Nikolai Berdiaev once defined in the best utopian tradition as everything that makes man fail,[40] would seem to serve as a conservative bulwark against efforts to create new societies and to transcend the limitations placed by nature upon humankind. The utopian impulse may be "Faustian" or "regressive," to use Jacques Catteau's terms;[41] it may seek to accelerate or to reverse the course of time, but in either case it manifests a deep dissatisfaction with prevailing social institutions, values, and modes of thought, although inextricably and agonizingly bound up in all these realia.

The desire for a perfect, untainted state of being, whether envisioned in political or metaphysical terms, implies the rejection of the imperfections that surround us. And while many of our endeavors are aimed at ameliorating the human condition, utopian aspirations, with their yearning for maximal transformations, seek a better life in a qualitatively different way. The emphasis is no longer only on improving one's present world but also on exchanging it irreversibly for another. At every step accompanying the utopian desire for something radically better comes a loathing for the unpleasant details one would like to replace and forget. Indeed, the "repression" of biological, historical, or personal "facts" may be the originary inspiration for utopianism, and elaborate descriptions of buildings, mores, and ontological transcendence mere camouflage.

The unpleasant facts that utopian aspirations aim to repress may be corporal—disgust with the body or with sexual desire. They may be political—repugnance at or terror of prevailing forms of social interaction. Moreover,

---

[40] Nikolai Berdiaev, *Smysl tvorchestva* (Paris: YMCA Press, 1985), 358, 434.

[41] Jacques Catteau, "De la métaphorique des utopies dans la littérature russe et de son traitement chez Andrej Platonov," *Revue des études slaves*, tome 56, fasc. 1 (1984): 41 (39–50).

since the Ideal often springs from passionate rejection of the Real, it is not surprising that the utopian text tends to reinscribe that which it attempts to purge. The detested object may disappear, but its indented characteristics leave a visible and ineffaceable mark on the world that has defined itself by that object's banishment. Utopian aspirations are profoundly—but unsuccessfully—apotropaic; they create structures to protect themselves against anxieties that nevertheless leave traces in paradise's soil. The *study* of a "utopian culture," therefore, might be a story of how a culture obsessed with self-purification struggles at a specific historical moment to repress (and reinscribe) its essential metonymic anxieties.

Such an enterprise sounds more like an analysis of discourse than one of culture. This book will be a study of sex in early Soviet *ideology*, that discursive arena concerned with culture's legitimacy, rather than an exploration of sex in early Soviet culture per se. Ideology has been described and employed in a multitude of ways.[42] I will use "culture" to refer to how people live and "ideology" to refer to how people talk about their lives in relation to questions of political legitimacy. This definition, which owes much to Louis Althusser's treatment of ideology as an imaginative, psychological category[43] and to Pavel Medvedev's and Valentin Voloshinov's insistence on the relationship of ideology to language,[44] has serious consequences for historians. Insufficiently theorized, "culture" has often served in the field of Soviet studies as an infinitely expandable "kitchen sink" into which virtually anything can fit, particularly when the analyst wants to present some aspect of life as more "real" or more valuable than officially sponsored fictions. Repelled by the language and mentality of Soviet power, scholars have sometimes forgotten that they inevitably must deal principally with discourse, albeit discourse that may well have an impact on the reality it addresses and seeks to alter.

Defining ideology as *discourse* entails approaching ideology as an object to be *read*. It means treating it with all the gentle interpretive care (or tender paranoia) that important texts merit. Ideology must be read both poetically and analytically and must be understood as a symbolic, even symptomatic, category as well as a cognitive one. As Althusser writes:

[42] For a summary of these ways and their history, see Terry Eagleton's *Ideology: An Introduction* (London: Verso, 1991), especially 1–31.

[43] Louis Althusser, "Ideology and Ideological State Apparatuses," in his *Essays on Ideology* (London: Verso, 1984), 1–60, and "Marxism and Humanism," in his *For Marx*, trans. Ben Brewster (London: Verso, 1969), 221–247.

[44] See M. M. Bakhtin (*sic!?*) and P. N. Medvedev, *The Formal Method in Literary Scholarship*, trans. Albert J. Wehrle (Cambridge: Harvard University Press, 1978 [1928]), and V. N. Voloshinov, *Marxism and the Philosophy of Language*, trans. Ladislav Matejka and I. R. Titunik (Cambridge: Harvard University Press, 1973 [1929]). The question of whether these books were written by Bakhtin (rather than by the members of his circle whose names appeared on the original title pages) is a matter of intense, but for present purposes irrelevant, dispute.

in ideology the real relation [between men and their world] is inevitably invested in the imaginary relation, a relation that expresses a will (conservative, conformist, reformist or revolutionary), a hope or a nostalgia, rather than describing a reality. It is in this overdetermination of the real by the imaginary and of the imaginary by the real that ideology is active in principle.[45]

It is one thing to formulate a definition and another to apply it in a historical study. Implicit in the work of students of ideology such as Althusser, Terry Eagleton, or Fredric Jameson is the view that ideology often is the covert, unacknowledged object of the writing of history. Yet theorists of ideology, while they have incited the march of literary studies into the domain of the historian, have been loath to take part in the incursion themselves. They do not provide a model for what it might mean to explore the "overdetermination of the real by the imaginary and of the imaginary by the real" in the context of detailed consideration of a specific topic in a specific historical epoch, a consideration, moreover, that would not take literary texts as its primary objects of analysis. Such an exercise would entail a sensitive dialogue between the disciplines of history and literature that has hitherto been lacking in Soviet studies and would appear natural in the context of Russia, where the enormous importance of literature and literary models ought to render methods developed to analyze literature particularly suitable for the reading of ideology. The rigidity of Russian political and social structures in the nineteenth century and the control exerted over these spheres from above allowed literature to serve "as a replacement for those political, social, legal and even economic phenomena that could not develop fully in Russian society."[46] Consequently, the line between society's life in art and its life in the "real world" was blurred, and both nineteenth-century positivists and twentieth-century Symbolists would have a great deal of trouble determining where the text ended and where extratextual existence began.

Scholars focusing on the extraordinary importance of literature in Russia have operated on the assumption that Russian literature should be read allegorically—as political discourse in code. Students of Russian history have been loath to draw a parallel conclusion, namely, that the unfolding of historical events (and the perception of that unfolding) in Russia may be uniquely dependent on literary models. Yet it is precisely the tremendous significance of literature in Russia that makes Russian history an ideal staging ground for assaults on traditional historical methodologies. Dominick LaCapra has writ-

---

[45] Althusser, "Marxism and Humanism," 234. Fredric Jameson modifies Althusser's definition of ideology to a "representational structure which allows the individual subject to conceive or imagine his or her lived relationship to transpersonal realities such as the social structure or the collective logic of History." *The Political Unconscious: Narrative as a Socially Symbolic Act* (Ithaca: Cornell University Press, 1981), 30.

[46] Boris Gasparov, introduction to *The Semiotics of Russian Cultural History*, ed. Alexander D. and Alice Stone Nakhimovsky (Ithaca: Cornell University Press, 1985), 13 (13–29).

ten eloquently of literature's "second-class status" in history. Often, literature is used as an example, to "give us a 'feel' for life in the past," rather than as a resource for analytical tools that may fundamentally shape the historian's endeavor.[47] Historians "covering" a historical period may devote a few pages to its fiction; capacious anthologies of scholarly articles devoted to an epoch tend to include one or two articles on literature to round out the picture.[48] An essential premise underlying the present work is Fredric Jameson's insight that since history "is inaccessible to us except in textual form, [. . .] our approach to it and to the Real itself necessarily passes through its prior textualization."[49] An explicit acceptance of ideology as discourse ought to produce a new approach to Soviet history. Such an approach would insist that questions of vocabulary, rhetorical figures, narrative, and genre are crucial to an understanding of ideology; these categories must not be forgotten even in the reading of the most "aesthetically challenged" texts.

I am not arguing that literature is the primary force controlling historical events. The occurrence of events depends on various material conditions, on "real people and their relations," as Marx and Engels argue in *The German Ideology*, which is surely one of the most hostile texts discourse theorists can imagine.[50] A fundamental premise of my reading of NEP, however, is that ideology and the literature that can shape it are not purely reflective of material realities but affect the perception of those realities in ways that then have an impact on the development of material realities themselves. In the course of their critique of the wayward Hegelian Max Stirner, Marx and Engels write that "ideologists [. . .] inevitably put the thing upside-down and regard their ideology both as the creative force and as the aim of all social relations, whereas it is only an expression and symptom of these relations."[51] Here I will be insisting that the process of symptomatization is not a one-way street, that each symptom can be a cause as well as an effect. How people perceive reality has a historical impact upon that reality; this book will argue that the perception of reality and the unfolding of history are not only inescapably discursive but rest to a significant extent on representational and rhetorical models developed in literature. Most of my readers probably do not need convincing that the history of Russia in the twentieth century demonstrates

[47] Dominick LaCapra, *History and Criticism* (Ithaca: Cornell University Press, 1982), 126.

[48] See, e.g., Sheila Fitzpatrick, ed., *Cultural Revolution in Russia, 1928–1931* (Bloomington: Indiana University Press, 1978), and Sheila Fitzpatrick, Alexander Rabinowitch, and Richard Stites, eds., *Russia in the Era of NEP* (Bloomington: Indiana University Press, 1991).

[49] Jameson, *The Political Unconscious*, 35.

[50] Karl Marx and Frederick Engels, *Collected Works*, 45 vols. (New York: International Publishers, 1975–1991), 5:99. The use of the term "real" or even "extremely real" by Marx is problematic; often, it is repeated with such frequency that it seems to perform as a lexical, even incantatory, crutch necessary for the proper functioning of a materialist worldview. I will return in chapter 4 to the question of Marxism's troubled stance on the recognition of the "real."

[51] Ibid., 420.

the real-world consequences of ideology; indeed, much work on Soviet Russia (including, to some extent, this one) may be read as appropriating one of the more vivid images in *The Communist Manifesto*, with various groups—the Old Bolsheviks, the artistic avant-garde, the intelligentsia—assuming the role of the bourgeois sorcerer who has conjured up forces beyond his control. Yet while histories of Russia have stressed the importance of ideology, they have been inattentive to ideology's inherently textual nature. Immersing myself and my readers in the discourse of NEP, I intend to provide a historically grounded *reading* of Soviet communism's ideological spell.

There are distinct problems with reading ideology as a particular epoch's text. First, how do we know where the boundaries of a given ideology lie? When we analyze a work of literature, textual boundaries seem distinct. To a degree, this clarity is a fiction. Students of textological problems know that the establishment of an authoritative text is a difficult task, and, as editors expand or contract a text's bulk, interpretations of it as an integral work may change.[52] In ideological analysis it is much more difficult to fix textual boundaries. I will be dealing with only a fraction of the material published (this word itself introduces a limit) in the Soviet Union during NEP. This study will encompass primarily the discourse generated by what the author of the first linguistic study of Soviet speech termed "the wide circles of Soviet public society [*obshchestvennost'*]";[53] its focus will be texts in which the topic of sex is bound up with Bolshevik legitimacy.

The public discourse that I will be analyzing was largely the product of the extreme discursive centralization that occurred in the Soviet Union during the 1920s. To be sure, to speak of centralization during NEP is somewhat paradoxical: after all, during NEP the Soviet center's physical, institutional presence was diminished throughout the land; libraries, clubs, reading rooms, universities, and orphanages were forced to close by the hard economic realities of the new mixed economy. Most of the materials I will be considering were published in large cities, yet more than two-thirds of Soviet citizens lived in villages, where central publications were scarce.[54] Yet while there may have been only a limited amount of interaction between city and country, there was a great deal of *idealized* urban-rural interaction within the parameters of the centralizing, urban ideological discourse.

---

[52] See, e.g., Morson's discussion of the textology and interpretations of More's *Utopia* in *The Boundaries of Genre*, 164–175.

[53] Selishchev, *Iazyk revoliutsionnoi epokhi*, 63.

[54] Roger Pethybridge, *One Step Backwards, Two Steps Forward: Soviet Society and Politics in the New Economic Policy* (Oxford: Clarendon Press, 1990), 24; Jeffrey Brooks, "The Breakdown in Production and Distribution of Printed Material, 1917–1927," in *Bolshevik Culture: Experiment and Order in the Russian Revolution*, ed. Abbott Gleason, Peter Kenez, and Richard Stites (Bloomington: Indiana University Press, 1985), 153–155 (151–174).

From the beginning of Bolshevik rule, Lenin identified centralization as "our primary thought, which has been put into effect in all our decrees."[55] Centralization was essential if Communism was "to penetrate profoundly into the consciousness of all,"[56] and the texts of the 1920s must be read with this orientation toward centralization in mind. As Katerina Clark has observed, the contraction of the Party's physical reach resulted in greater centralization and control of intellectual life, since intellectuals found it necessary to travel to the capital or one or two other large cities to work in their professions. "In publishing," Clark continues, "the problem of reduced funding for the provinces was compounded by chronic shortages of paper and operable printing presses, problems of distribution, and the high cost of publications. In consequence, official (and even private) publishing organs were largely servicing only the capitals: Moscow and Leningrad."[57] At the center of my study will be primarily texts emanating from the urban centers, texts phantasmatically representative of the entire nation but produced largely by the Party and individuals sympathetic to it. The era's centralizing orientation is especially important in the pedagogically inclined writing that we will consider below about the life of Soviet youth. Authors were acutely conscious that they were attempting to shape women and men, intellectuals and workers of the future, who would preside over a more unified culture than the existing one.

The question of textual boundaries aside, another objection to reading ideology as an interpretably coherent text is that public discourse has no author and, therefore, is not susceptible to analytical methods that assume a single organizing, intentional consciousness. An oblique, postmodern answer to this legitimate cavil would be that the idea of an author is problematic and that intention certainly does not account for every detail in a text. In the context of the early Soviet period, however, the ideal centralizing tendencies underlying public discourse render problematic both broad generalizations about the author's death and Foucault's approach to discourse as "a series of discontinuous segments whose tactical function is neither uniform or stable."[58] In early Soviet public discourse author-ity was more vibrant—and the segments of discourse more unified—than in most other European countries at the time. While the texts we will be reading were not literally scripted by a single, all-powerful author, the authority of the Central Committee and, in

[55] Lenin, "Doklad o bor'be s golodom [Ob"edinennoe zasedanie VTsIK, Moskovskogo soveta rabochikh, krest'ianskikh i krasnoarmeiskikh deputatov i professional'nykh soiuzov]," (4 June 1918), *Polnoe sobranie*, 36:408.

[56] Ibid.

[57] Katerina Clark, "The 'Quiet Revolution' in Soviet Intellectual Life," in Fitzpatrick, Rabinowitch, and Stites, *Russia in the Era of NEP*, 218 (210–230).

[58] Michel Foucault, *The History of Sexuality*, 3 vols. trans. Robert Hurley (New York: Vintage, 1980), 1:100.

particular, of Lenin, exerted a powerful influence on the composition of other, subordinate texts, many of which applied Bolshevik ideology to spheres of interest where the presence of political and economic concerns was mediated by other (e.g., scientific, pedagogic) issues. This application entailed not only the employment of the political content of authoritative pronouncements but also the utilization of authoritative words, images, and narrative. A decade after the Revolution, the linguist Selishchev marveled at the amazing rapidity with which a single "language" had emerged in post-Revolutionary Russia. In an era of extreme social change, he explained, interpersonal communication becomes remarkably intense, providing fertile soil for the emergence of shared discursive forms. In the case of early Soviet Russia, these forms arose through a process of "imitation" or "inspiration" in which influential statements of the center were "attentively studied and worked through in the localities."[59] As Illarion Vardin, a prolific and influential journalist of the time, wrote in 1923, newspapers were playing a crucial role in the dissemination of the new language: "At the present, it is with a special fury that our press is pushing into prominence fundamental slogans, key points, urgent matters, and hammering away at them importunately, stubbornly, systematically, 'tediously'—as our enemies would have it."[60] A basic premise of this book is that not only words and slogans were "beaten into the heads of the masses" but also images and genres.

Nevertheless, the Foucaultian argument concerning discourse's textual discontinuity cannot be dismissed entirely. Two factors demand consideration. First, the text offered to the reader as NEP's ideology is not composed exclusively of utterances by Party officials and members. The reader will hear from a range of speakers, many of whom lacked Party affiliation or whose affiliation is in doubt. All these voices, however, will be addressing the concerns of Bolshevik legitimacy; in speaking about sexual reproduction, menstruation, sex crimes, promiscuity, or masturbation they will also be saying something about the ideology of NEP and staking a claim to the political importance of sexual matters. Moreover, as they engage themselves with the ideological significance of these issues, they will often be concerned implicitly with their own position vis-à-vis the Party and the operation of Soviet power. In speaking ideology, the language of legitimacy, our heroes frequently seek to legitimate themselves. I do not believe that these speakers were doomed to parrot ideology. Ideological utterances not only repeat but shape and respond. I offer quoted texts both as examples of ideological discourse and as statements that, when uttered, may themselves have had an impact on Soviet ideology's development.[61]

---

[59] Selishchev, *Iazyk revoliutsionnoi epokhi*, 99.

[60] Cited in ibid., 24–25.

[61] In other words, just as discourse has an impact on reality, so *"parole"* can effect the evolu-

We must keep a second factor in mind when considering the question of the authorship of an era's text and when answering the question: Who is speaking? Just as an author is not in total conscious control of his text, so the Party was not the absolute master of early Soviet ideology. A text is the product not of a single consciousness, nor of the hermetic interaction between a single consciousness and a single unconscious, but of the searing battles of consciousness and unconscious with each other *and* with the moment, location, and language of the text's writing. "A speaker," Mikhail Bakhtin reminds us, "is not Adam, and therefore the subject of his speech itself inevitably becomes the arena where his opinions meet those of his partners (in a conversation or dispute about some everyday event) or other viewpoints, world views, trends, theories, and so forth (in the sphere of cultural communication)."[62] These clashes, which Jameson in his revision of Saussure's "langue" locates in "the political unconscious,"[63] can be examined at several levels. We will pay close attention to the contestation occurring on the "metalinguistic" level to which Bakhtin would have listened most closely. We will also consider the more traditional domain of factions and policies, for we must remember that in the 1920s the Party was riven by internal conflict; any notion of monolithic authorship of discourse cannot withstand an attentive reading of congress and conference transcripts. Finally, even if the Party had been totally unified, it would not have been the absolute master of its own discourse; every text is to some extent the product of fears and desires that remain unacknowledged by the author or author-ity producing the text. We should not discard the concept of a textual subconscious, or, at the least, of a text's superfluousness or inadequacy to its apparent object. As Terry Eagleton says with characteristic flair:

> The neurotic symptom, like the dream text, [. . .] reveals and conceals at once.
> [. . .] The truth of [an] ideology, as with the neurotic symptom, lies neither in the
> revelation nor the concealment alone, but in the contradictory unity they compose. It is not just a matter of stripping off some outer disguise to expose the
> truth, any more than an individual's self-deception is just a 'guise' he assumes. It
> is rather that what is revealed takes place in terms of what is concealed, and *vice
> versa*.[64]

---

tion of "*langue*," and so the publication of a work in a particular genre has the potential to shape that genre's future evolution. See Voloshinov's discussions entitled "Language, Speech and Utterance" and "Verbal Interaction" in his *Marxism and the Philosophy of Language*, 65–98.

[62] M. M. Bakhtin, "The Problem of Speech Genres," in his *Speech Genres and Other Late Essays*, trans. Vern W. McGee (Austin: University of Texas Press, 1986), 94.

[63] Jameson, *The Political Unconscious*. Jameson's revision of Saussure occurs most explicitly on 89.

[64] Eagleton, *Ideology*, 134.

Ideology is never "purely *instrumental*; the men who would use an ideology purely as a means of action, as a tool, find that they have been caught by it, implicated by it, just when they are using it and believe themselves to be absolute masters of it."[65]

It might (and should) be objected that the actors, or, rather, speakers, of the New Economic Policy would never have used the analytical models employed below to describe the intricate tapestry woven of their desires and fears. Late in his life, Mikhail Bakhtin dealt with a similar, but more general, methodological objection:

> Antiquity itself did not know the antiquity that we know now. There used to be a school joke: the ancient Greeks did not know the main thing about themselves, that they were *ancient* Greeks, and they never called themselves that. But in fact that temporal distance that transformed the Greeks into *ancient* Greeks had an immense transformational significance: it was filled with increasing discoveries of new *semantic* values in antiquity, values of which the Greeks were in fact unaware, although they themselves created them. [. . .] In the realm of culture, outsideness [*vnenakhodimost'*] is a most powerful factor in understanding. It is only in the eyes of *another* culture that foreign culture reveals itself fully and profoundly (but not maximally fully, because there will be cultures that see and understand even more).[66]

Bakhtin would probably have admitted that this advice can be abused. In the following pages, I will pay close attention to the voices of early Soviet ideology; I will study their speech and listen attentively to their contorted attempts at self-analysis. I will also propose more modern interpretive models as provisional, heuristic vehicles for understanding the world of NEP. I will respect that world's language but suggest new ways in which that language might be heard.

This book is by an outsider who has tried to turn his foreignness to the advantage of his work. My study is foreign to its object not only in that it is the work of an American, but also in that it employs methods and operates on the basis of assumptions alien to those held by contemporary and past Russian and Western historians. I seek productively to defamiliarize early Soviet history, to bring into relief—through a new set of glasses—aspects of early Soviet history that have heretofore been largely ignored. "Defamiliarization" (*ostranenie*), as readers of the Russian Formalists know, has traditionally been the task of the artist or—as in Viktor Shklovsky's critical and metacritical work—the goal of the literary scholar.[67] In my text, defamiliar-

---

[65] Althusser, "Marxism and Humanism," 234.

[66] M. M. Bakhtin, "Response to a Question from the *Novy[i] Mir* Editorial Staff" (1970), in his *Speech Genres and Other Late Essays*, 6–7.

[67] See Viktor Shklovskii, *Theory of Prose*, trans. Benjamin Sher (Elmwood Park, Ill.: Dalkey Press, 1991), 1–14.

ization will jostle its way into the workshop of the writing of history. Readers apt to take offense at interdisciplinary transgressions are referred to the words of one of Shklovsky's modernist contemporaries and urged to remember that these pages are meant to be taken "for signposts, and are not to blame if, in our weaknesses, we mistake these signposts for the destination."[68]

The destination toward which I want this study to point has a dual nature. As it poses the questions of literary scholarship to the objects of historiography, *Sex in Public* seeks to uncover new semantic depths not only in Soviet Russia but in the discipline of history itself. The result, I hope, will be a mutually productive dialogue that does not replace history with literature but enriches our understanding of both. Ultimately the success of this study will probably depend on its ability to satisfy readers' demands for traditional historiographic authenticity. While the text of NEP presented here is—unavoidably—an object both found and created, both echoed and authored, in the final analysis my book's impact will depend on the extent to which it is accepted as a product of the Soviet 1920s; it will have merit only if it says more about that era's discursive pathologies than about my own.

THINGS TO COME

The first chapter should be read differently from the six that follow. Rather than attempting to reach broad conclusions about the ideological meaning of sex in War Communist or pre-Revolutionary Russia, it introduces the reader to heroes and villains of these periods who exerted considerable influence on the post-Revolutionary narratives of NEP offered in subsequent chapters. As such, the opening chapter is more traditional in its methodology than the rest of the book; its intent is primarily to "put on the table" names and ideas that will be more fully digested in the material that follows. In particular, the focus in the first chapter is twofold: the intelligentsia's preoccupation with the social significance of sex and personal life, and the pernicious gender dynamics at work in the uses of sex in early-twentieth-century utopian, spiritual philosophy. Chapters 2 through 7 deal with NEP and arrive at relatively far-reaching interpretations of ideology. They represent different ways of looking at a single topic: the importance of sex in understanding the ideology of NEP.

Finally, a few words about the tone of this study. What follows is part history and part horror story. NEP has often been regarded as a flash of light preceding the Stalinist darkness. In his wide-ranging study of early Soviet utopianism, Richard Stites celebrates the years before 1929 as a time of great innovation and tolerance: "The N.E.P. system played a dual role in sustain-

---

[68] E. M. Forster. *Howards End* (New York: Signet, 1992), 96.

ing utopianism: the relative laxity and pluralism on the social landscape protected it; the more loathsome features of a revived bourgeois culture in the cities helped to fuel it as a counterweight to 'Soviet capitalism.' The emergence of the Stalinist system put an end to N.E.P. and its social pluralism."[69] There is great tension, however, between "pluralism" and the tarring of ideological opponents as "loathsome." For many of the figures who speak in Stites's book (and in this one), NEP was a time of revulsion and of political and economic disgust with the pluralism that many Western and, now, Russian historians have come to celebrate. *Sex in Public* will examine some of the more curious—and, occasionally, hideous—forms assumed by utopian intolerance in a time of enforced ideological laxity.

As they plunge into deeper and more unsettling intimacy with the strange world of the Soviet 1920s, few readers of the coming pages will probably feel inclined to react with "empathic laughter, sympathetic tears and an occasional burst of applause."[70] The view of NEP proffered here may be rejected by some readers as unnecessarily bleak; they may even ward off the horror of this vision by returning to time-honored myths of tolerance and cultural renaissance. Nevertheless, they are encouraged to dwell on the morbid images presented and to follow attentively the sensationalistic discourse of NEP that sets the tone for much of this study. The tone is not mere ornamentation; it seeks to reproduce the anxiety that was the most characteristic trait of the epoch and that helped shape the evolution of Soviet ideology toward the "bright," violent decade that followed.

[69] Richard Stites, *Revolutionary Dreams: Utopian Vision and Experimental Life in the Russian Revolution* (New York: Oxford University Press, 1989), 225.

[70] Ibid., 10.

Chapter One

THE CREATION OF THE COLLECTIVE BODY

Utopia, Misogyny, and the Russian Philosophical Tradition

In the spring of 1925, *Izvestiia* reported on a murder trial that was arousing much interest in the northern Ukraine. A peasant, Iosif Tsimbaliuk, was accused of braining his four children with a set of tongs. Apparently, he had acted from religious conviction. He had recently joined a sect inspired by the teachings of a local prophet, Kornei Kalamarchuk, who had been attracting followers throughout the Ukraine since well before the October Revolution. According to *Izvestiia*, Kalamarchuk's followers believed their leader was Christ and were certain that when the "virgin" with whom he lived gave birth to a son, their lives would be prolonged by a thousand years and Kalamarchuk would sit in judgment on all mankind. There was, however, one catch, a detail in Kalamarchuk's gospel of which Tsimbaliuk claimed to have been ignorant when he had signed on:

> Kalamarchuk's sect considers monogamy a sin and children "evil spirits" [*nechist'*] who must be gotten rid of. Only those who are childless will receive "grace."[1]

On the stand, Kalamarchuk, also a defendant, justified this tenet by explaining that during the Last Judgment marriage and childbirth would be prohibited. Both defendants were sentenced to eight years in jail.[2]

Kalamarchuk's religious teachings were portrayed by *Izvestiia* as "fanatical cruelty" not to be tolerated, even on the margins of Soviet social life.[3] Events evoking strong repugnance, however, are rarely as marginal as the outraged subject would suggest, and, indeed, within the broad contours of Russian millennial thought, Tsimbaliuk did not act alone. His mistake was in putting into action the technique that literary masters of the 1920s such as Andrei Platonov and Mikhail Zoshchenko were then employing as a stylistic, philosophical, or even comic device. Tsimbaliuk erred in taking language literally, in "realizing" infanticidal metaphors that had rarely crossed the gulf separating philosophically totalitarian aspirations from what the Russians call *byt*: the category of nitty-gritty detail and everyday life.[4]

---

[1] "Delo sektanta Tsimbaliuka," *Izvestiia*, 26 February 1925, 4.

[2] V. Tkachuk, "Delo religioznykh izuverov," *Izvestiia*, 5 March 1926, 4.

[3] Ibid.

[4] Sects had a rich tradition in Russia and were active well into the twentieth century; they were capable of serving writers sympathetic to the Revolution as a premodern (positive or

In turn-of-the-century Russia there had been a rich tradition of spiritual thinkers—noumenal revolutionaries—devouring prospective children in their philosophies. For these men, whose influence extended well beyond the 1917 Revolution, the begetting of children embodied all that prevented humanity from attaining their utopian goal of absolute integral purity: immortality.[5] I will use the statements of these philosophers about chastity and reproduction as a point of entry into the intellectual discourse about sex in early-twentieth-century Russia. None were communists; indeed, the one among them who survived into the 1920s (Nikolai Berdiaev) was to be banished from Russia by the Bolsheviks. Nevertheless, an understanding of the function of sex (and its political and utopian ramifications) in post-Revolutionary discourse requires at least a preliminary acquaintance with their views, for these views would be echoed at various points in the words and images in which post-Revolutionary ideology manifested both sexual and political wishes and fears. These philosophers were extremely influential but not typical in their views about the place of sex in the ideal community; to the extent that they were *representative* thinkers, they represented an undercurrent of maximalist or "absolutist" thinking that was by and large repressed or significantly muted in pre-Revolutionary professional (medical, legal) discourse about sex.[6] In the course of this study I hope it will become apparent that the fundamental preoccupations of these thinkers who devoted their writing to the perfectibility and immortality of man were to a significant and quite paradoxical extent legitimized by the Revolution. In the maximalist context of the Revolution's promise of radical human and social transformation, currents of discourse that had previously seemed almost entirely the property of religion or metaphysics earned a new ideological respectability and were able to combine in strange ways with other, newly legitimated ideas about the shape of ideal community.[7]

---

negative) model of the nonreligious community to come. Although some sects practiced various types of self-mutilation, infanticide does not appear to have ever been widely practiced by members of a Russian sect.

[5] These thinkers were not utopians in the classical sense; they did not provide elaborate outlines for the structure of an ideal society. Rather, their work falls squarely into the "absolutist" or "totalitarian" (*totalitarnaia*) and eschatological tradition that Nikolai Berdiaev was later to claim played a crucial role in the development of Russian thought. Nikolai Berdiaev, *Russkaia ideia* (Paris: YMCA Press, 1970 [1946]), 33, 195. By the word "utopian" I here refer to thinkers who believed or strongly implied belief in the possibility of human spiritual perfection and in the consequent literal ability of man to achieve immortality.

[6] The medical and legal pre-Revolutionary discourses about sex are the subject of Laura Engelstein's *The Keys to Happiness: Sex and the Search for Modernity in Fin-de-Siècle Russia* (Ithaca: Cornell University Press, 1992).

[7] In the early twentieth century, religious philosophy occupied a much more central place in Russian intellectual discourse than in most other European countries or the United States. For a

The ostensible rationale for religious-utopian hostility to progeny is not difficult to understand. For the philosophers Vladimir Solov'ev (1853–1900) and Nikolai Berdiaev (1874–1948), birth represented the "bad infinity of physical reproduction";[8] it was a reminder of the change of generations and of the seeming inevitability of human decay. Berdiaev, who believed that "the opposition between love and childbirth is profound," declared: "birth is always the sign of the failure of the personality to attain perfection, of falling short of eternity. The one giving birth and the one who is born are subject to decay and imperfect."[9] Nikolai Fedorov (1829–1903), whose influence on Solov'ev and Berdiaev (and throughout the intelligentsia) was considerable, tended to depict the fatal consequences of childbirth in a more biological vein.[10] Agreeing with the proposition that "death [. . .] is the transition of one creature (or of two uniting in a single flesh) into another by means of birth," he explained:

> In lower animals this is clear, obvious: within one cell embryos of new cells appear; as they grow, these latter cells rupture the mother cell and go out into the world. Here it is evident that the birth of children is also the mother's death. [. . .] In this example the cell enters the world fully mature,—but man is born immature; during feeding and upbringing he devours his parents' strength, feeding, so to speak, on their body and blood [. . .]; so that, by the time parents have finished bringing up their children, their strength has been absolutely depleted and they die or enter a state of fatal senile decrepitude. The fact that this murderous process does not occur within the organism, as with the single cell, but within the family, does not mitigate the criminality of the affair.[11]

book-length study of the Russian preoccupation with immortality in the decades before and after the Revolution, see Irene Masing-Delich, *Abolishing Death: A Salvation Myth of Russian Twentieth-Century Literature* (Stanford: Stanford University Press, 1992).

[8] Vladimir Solov'ev, "Smysl liubvi," in his *Sochineniia v dvukh tomakh*, 2 vols. (M.: Mysl', 1988), 2:547. The essay was first published in 1892–1894. The term "bad infinity" was borrowed from Hegel, who used it to refer to an endless succession of finite entities that never undergo sublation. Georg Wilhelm Friedrich Hegel, *Encyklopädie der philosophischen Wissenschaften im Grundrisse* (Berlin: L. Heimann, 1870), 115 (sec. 94).

[9] Nikolai Berdiaev, *Smysl tvorchestva* (Paris: YMCA Press, 1983 [1916]), 229.

[10] Fedorov gained prominence in part through his work as a librarian at the Rumiantsev Museum, where he served from 1874 to 1898. *The Philosophy of the Common Cause*, his epic, programmatic work for the transformation of mankind, was begun as a long philosophical letter to Fedor Dostoevskii but kept growing and was not finished until after Dostoevskii's death. For the most thorough survey of his life and work and a discussion of his relations with his intellectual contemporaries, as well as a brief consideration of his impact on Tolstoi, Dostoevskii, and Solov'ev, see Svetlana Semenova, *Nikolai Fedorov: Tvorchestvo zhizni* (M.: Sovetskii pisatel', 1900).

[11] Nikolai Fedorov, *Filosofiia obshchego dela*, 2 vols. (Vernyi, 1906; M., 1913), 1:313.

Part of the problem was that, in procreating, man was surrendering to nature. The philosophies of Solov'ev, Berdiaev, and Fedorov depended upon man's distinguishing himself from all other animals. Solov'ev contended that man existed on several levels: natural, social, and divine. Procreation tended to occur on the first or second of these planes, and only by transcending procreation and infusing sexuality with the divine would man achieve immortality.[12] "As long as man reproduces like an animal," Solov'ev asserted, "he will die like one."[13] Fedorov was obsessed with the conquest of nature, and he saw sexuality as part of the "blind force" that had placed man at the elements' mercy.[14] Attacking Schopenhauer's celebratory assertion that this force was the key to immortality—Fedorov renamed Schopenhauer's major work "The World as Lust"[15]—Fedorov argued that man's task was to respond by an assertion of will assuming several forms: science would aid in overcoming droughts, for example, but the most impressive act of will would be the renunciation of sexual reproduction.

If Solov'ev, Berdiaev, and Fedorov were attacking sexual reproduction rather than sexual relations per se, were sexual relations without reproduction an option for them? The naive reader here might be tempted to interject that birth control might have been a mundane solution to their woes. In late-nineteenth-century Western Europe contraception was heralded as part of man's conquest of nature and proof of the rationalization of human passion.[16] Russian society in the early twentieth century, however, was, on the whole, reluctant to let birth control infiltrate its language.[17] The prevailing view at the turn of the century was expressed by Professor Vladimir Bekhterev of the Imperial Military Medical Academy, when, in his introduction to a Russian translation of August Forel's extremely popular *The Sexual Question*, he took issue with the Swiss psychologist's advocacy of birth control: "Neither the law nor society, in our opinion, should support sexual pleasure, if it has as its goal only pleasure and is not aimed at the production of offspring."[18]

While our early-twentieth-century Russian religious philosophers did not subscribe to Bekhterev's justification of sex as a means of reproduction, neither did they go against the prevailing tide and seek to liberate human pleasure. Solov'ev, Berdiaev, and Fedorov endorsed the widely held view of

[12] Solov'ev, "Smysl liubvi," 2:527.

[13] Ibid., 522.

[14] Fedorov, *Filosofiia*, 1:314.

[15] Ibid., 405.

[16] Peter Gay, *Education of the Senses* (New York: Oxford University Press, 1984), 256.

[17] In her survey of medical and legal professional journals, Laura Engelstein finds only "sporadic" consideration of contraception before 1905. By 1908 the topic was more openly and frequently discussed, and contraceptive devices were advertised in newspapers. *The Keys to Happiness*, 335, 345–349.

[18] V. Bekhterev, "Predislovie," in Avgust Forel, *Polovoi vopros* (SPb.: Osvobozhdenie, 1908), vii (i–xviii).

love as an activity that should somehow bind the individual together with his fellow men, but they saw sexual intercourse as an unsatisfactory way of achieving this unity. Copulation divided as much as—if not more than—it unified. Present in much utopian thought is a striving for wholeness, and in sexual congress "difference" becomes most apparent at the very moment when the drive to obliterate it becomes most intense. For Berdiaev, in each act of intercourse the participants essentially took one step forward and two steps back: "The flesh of two should merge together into a single flesh; they should completely [*do kontsa*] penetrate each other. Instead of this an act of illusory union occurs, too temporary and too superficial. The price that must be paid for fleeting union is still greater disunity. [. . .] In the differentiated sexual act itself there is already present a certain defectiveness and morbidity."[19]

For the Russian intelligentsia sexual relations were frequently the source of discomfort precisely because they were deemed insufficiently communal. Bekhterev, for instance, viewed sexuality through a prism that insisted on the juxtaposition of privacy (a negative, antisocial category) and societal concerns: "Sexual liaisons arranged only for the sake of sexual pleasures, satisfying only personal goals, [. . .] should be limited by all means, and if the law cannot prosecute mutually consenting sexual partners whose health does not suffer [from their sexual relations], then in any case measures are wholly appropriate that tend to protect society as a whole from such forms of sexual relations."[20] Even when society was not being injured by intercourse, Bekhterev here implied, it still needed to be protected from sex; the contamination of social relations by pleasure had to be kept to a minimum.

Pleasure served political commentators of varying stripes as a metaphor for distasteful, *individualistic* phenomena exerting a negative influence on contemporary life. According to Vladimir Friche, an early adherent to the Bolshevik Party and later the editor of the first edition of the *Great Soviet Encyclopedia*, the Western European intellectual had developed in a climate of frenzied technological advances and capitalist growth. Witnessing nothing but an increasingly intense battle for survival, the Western European intellectual had been "crippled" in his soul, and now his characteristic features were "arousability" and "impressionability."[21] By the end of the nineteenth century, Friche continued, Europe's typical intellectual had been so weakened by his "impotent battle with impressions received from external reality" that he could "no longer cope with impressions made upon him by woman": "at the sight of every woman he meets, he loses his equilibrium and is no longer

---

[19] Berdiaev, *Smysl tvorchestva*, 228. For a similar statement, see Solov'ev, "Smysl liubvi," 2:522.

[20] Bekhterev, "Predislovie," vii.

[21] V. M. Friche, *Torzhestvo pola i gibel' tsivilizatsii. Po povodu knigi Otto Veninger [sic!] Pol i kharakter* (M.: Sovremennye problemy, 1909), 53.

his own man."[22] Vasily Rozanov, a widely read and anticlerical but, in many respects, politically conservative philosopher, also attacked the bourgeois character in terms that confounded notions of class and sex:

> The "bourgeois" is not ipso facto disgusting, but particularly disgusting is the bourgeois of the nineteenth century, self-satisfied with his notion of "progress," strikingly envious of all historical greatness and thus striving to *level* the circumstances of all men in identical filth and in a single hopeless swamp. [. . .] He has convinced his wife to castrate herself so that they have no children, and together they masturbate in bed. [. . .] They do a bit of business, have a credit account in a Jew's shop, [. . .] vacation on the Riviera [. . .], and are joined by a "friend of the family" since onanism has greater possibilities when practiced by three rather than two.[23]

Rozanov's use of "onanism" here to describe the use of birth control—as well as intercourse à trois—indicates the crucial importance of procreation to his thought, albeit as a *positive* element. Rozanov differed from our three philosophers in that for him the relevant human community was diachronic rather than synchronic; essentially, he agreed with Schopenhauer that "immortality is in the life cycle."[24] When their children engaged in sexual intercourse, parents were not dishonored, as Fedorov had maintained, but reborn, for the fabric of their blood was being passed down to succeeding generations.[25] (The unspoken assumption here was that coitus would lead to conception; as the quotation above makes clear, the use of birth control presumably reintroduced the notion of dishonoring the generational chain.) Only a person's name dies, Rozanov maintained; everything else is immortal. In the cosmic scheme of things, this self-professed antiutopian thinker claimed, what we call dying is really no different from the act of changing one's boots.[26]

Both Rozanov and Friche lumped together the use of birth control (Rozanov's female castration), homosexuality, onanism, *and* asceticism as characteristics of the bourgeois age. Their association of hedonism (frequent intercourse free of the consequence of conception) with asceticism may seem particularly odd, but Friche explained that asceticism (like homosexuality)

---

[22] Ibid.

[23] Vasilii Rozanov, "Opavshie list'ia," in his *Izbrannoe* (Munich: A. Neimanis, 1970 [1913–1915]), 205. Rozanov's views on sexuality were closely linked to his anti-Semitism and interest in Jewish ritual. Laura Engelstein provides a very interesting analysis of the relationship between Rozanov's views on sex and on Jews. *The Keys to Happiness*, 299–333.

[24] Arthur Schopenhauer, *The World as Will and Representation*, trans. E.F.J. Payne, 2 vols. (New York: Dover, 1958), 2:478.

[25] Ibid., 394.

[26] V. V. Rozanov, *Liudi lunnogo sveta: Metafizika khristianstva* (SPb., 1911), 68. Rozanov was concise and emphatic in his hatred of the concept of utopia and of all "Cities of the Sun": "It's not the future, it's death." "Opavshie list'ia," 102.

was essentially a reaction to the discomfort experienced by an intelligentsia with an unnatural propensity for arousal. "Hatred of the [hetero-]sexual act," "physiological weakness," "psychic impotence," and birth control, Friche said, were merely separate voices composing a single "melody" that would lead to the destruction of civilization.[27] Rozanov, who in his conservative political views had little in common with Friche, shared his aversion to trends in contemporary sexuality and gave the name "sodomites" to *all* who were disgusted by procreation.[28] In his use of this term, Rozanov was not particularly concerned with what today we would call homosexual "practices."[29] He used the word to speak about his philosopher colleagues, the Russian Orthodox Church, and members of the Russian intelligentsia uncomfortable with or repelled by sexual intercourse. In Solov'ev's preference for the Platonic Aphrodite who gives birth to images and thoughts rather than children, Rozanov found the basis for a charge of infanticide: "[Solov'ev] gives nothing to birth, not a grain of inspiration! That's the cry of Sodom. 'Oh, if I could beat your children to death with a stone.'"[30] Here, too, Rozanov's basic incompatibility with Solov'ev was his diachronic sense of community. Essentially, for Friche on the left and Rozanov on the right, what linked the inclinations to copulate too much, to copulate with the wrong sex, and not to copulate at all was that they viewed these tendencies as standing in stark opposition to the different types of interpersonal unity (and community) they were trying to promote.

But let us return to the antiprocreative philosophers. While a medical man like Bekhterev might propose abstinence as a temporary measure for resolving the tension between individual and social interests at times when conception was not desired,[31] Fedorov, Solov'ev, and Berdiaev viewed abstinence as the key to "reconciling" sex and immortality in the creation of an ideal collective. Fedorov, as usual, had the most literal solution. Sexual intercourse should give way to chastity, and children should set about the complicated business of finding the bits of matter into which their parents had disintegrated! Then they would be able, literally, to bring prior generations back to life. Solov'ev and Berdiaev settled upon the solution of androgyny.

---

[27] Friche, *Torzhestvo pola*, 78–81.

[28] Rozanov was certainly not alone in applying the term "sodomy" to heterosexual non-procreative sex. John Todd, an American minister and the author of books on education and self-discipline, made a similar equation in mid-nineteenth-century America. See G. J. Barker-Benfield, *The Horrors of the Half-Known Life: Male Attitudes toward Women and Sexuality in Nineteenth-Century America* (Evanston: Harper & Row, 1976), 211. However, the application of the term to both nonprocreative intercourse and *abstinence* (i.e., to all who refrained from attempting to reproduce) seems to have been unique to this Russian philosopher.

[29] For a particularly striking example of his confusion of asceticism and homosexuality, see his "Nechto iz tumana 'obrazov' i 'podobii,'" *Vesy* 6, no. 3 (1909): 56–62.

[30] Rozanov, *Liudi lunnogo sveta*, 111.

[31] Bekhterev, "Predislovie," xiii.

For Berdiaev, who spells out his theory in more detail, man's quest for the restoration of a lost androgynous ideal would culminate in an act of "creation" constituting the freely chosen union of man with God. This formulation, although elaborated more fully, was borrowed from Solov'ev, who had asserted that "the path of the highest love, perfectly uniting male and female, spirit and flesh [. . .] is the union or mutual cooperation of the divine with the human, a process of godmanhood [*bogochelovechestvo*]."[32]

As one of the foremost scholars of pre-Revolutionary culture has demonstrated, androgyny was a growth industry in turn-of-the-century Russia. "While being acutely aware of the imminent collapse of the old order," Olga Matich writes, "the Silver Age generation withdrew from traditional political activism and turned to the spiritual and private domains. As the esoteric ideal of inner personal harmony, androgyny was particularly appealing to those introspective Russian intellectuals seeking an ideal which was visionary and ahistorical."[33] On closer inspection, however, "visionary" and "ahistorical" claims may reveal themselves as politically conservative and context-determined. As we look more closely at the language in which the utopian goal of androgyny is cloaked, we may start to sense a hidden agenda that will be important to an understanding of androgynous imagery in post-Revolutionary Russia.

From the foregoing description of these philosophers' work, it would appear that the rejection of sexual intercourse in favor of androgyny or resurrection was a logical consequence of several desires impeded by the act of copulation: the elimination of childbirth, the distinction of man from animal, and the formation of what we might call "a more perfect union." Fedorov and Berdiaev, however, display so much horror when discussing the forms and processes of the flesh that their reader may wonder if this repugnance, rather than an incidental detail, is not the base of their programs and all their admitted desires mere superstructure.[34] Fedorov talks repeatedly of "the shame of birth" and compares its horror to death: "One might well guess how all the blood in a person must rush to his face when he learns of his origin, and how he must pale with horror, when he sees the end of a creature

---

[32] Vladimir Solov'ev, "Zhiznennaia drama Platona," in his *Sochineniia*, 2:619. The essay was originally published in 1898.

[33] Olga Matich, "Androgyny and the Russian Religious Renaissance," *Western Philosophical Systems in Russian Literature* (Berkeley and Los Angeles: University of California Press, 1979), 165–166 (165–175). See also her "Androgyny and the Russian Silver Age," *Pacific Coast Philology* 14 (1979): 42–50.

[34] Boris Paramonov wittily makes this same point in his pursuit of "homosexual" models in turn-of-the-century culture: "The resurrection of ancestors is a dubious affair, which in any case will require a great deal of time,—but Fedorov tells us that it is already high time we abandoned our wives." "*Chevengur* i okrestnosti," *Kontinent*, no. 54 (1987): 345 (333–372).

like himself. [. . .] If these two things do not kill a person on the spot, then it is only because he probably learns of them gradually and is not forced to appreciate the full horror and baseness of his situation all at once."[35] In his philosophical autobiography, Berdiaev confesses, "There is something hideous in the sexual act itself," and cites approvingly Leonardo's remark that "the sexual organ is so hideous that the human race would die out if people did not fall into a state of possession [when reproducing]."[36] He recalls that "repugnance at the life of the species [Schopenhauer's term] belongs to the earliest and ineffable characteristics of my being. Pregnant women have always repelled me."[37]

In their disgust with the sexual organs and sexual functioning Fedorov and Berdiaev were not alone; this theme often surfaced in Russian discourse about sex in the late nineteenth and early twentieth centuries. Parallels to Tolstoi's repugnance at sexuality in "The Kreutzer Sonata" and his disgust with pregnancy in *Resurrection* can be found in many places. Mikhail Chlenov's 1905 survey of 2,150 students at Moscow University revealed that of the 50.3 percent who did not engage in sexual intercourse, 17.9 percent (203) abstained out of "moral revulsion at the act of coitus," 4.6 percent (53) rejected sexual life "on principle," and 1.1 percent (13) expressed physical revulsion toward women.[38] A certain O. Fozi, whose brochure, *Marriage and the Moral Personality*, Rozanov subjected to scathing criticism, wrote that the only valuable aspect of sexual intercourse—a process in which man submits to nature and where "evil celebrates its complete victory"—was the shame a moral person experiences afterward. It was impossible for a person to conquer his or her shame about sex, Fozi wrote, and not destroy himself or herself as a moral personality.[39]

In *The Meaning of the Creative Act* Berdiaev pretends to glorify sex and to condemn asceticism. He may claim that "there is no getting away from sex,"[40] but that impossible escape is precisely the project of much turn-of-the-century Russian religious utopian thought. Berdiaev glorifies sex only as he redefines it: "In the depths of sex, the creative act must conquer birth, the individual personality must defeat the species, and union in the spirit must

[35] Fedorov, *Filosofiia*, 1:312–313.

[36] Nikolai Berdiaev, *Samopoznanie* (Paris: YMCA Press, 1983 [1949]), 83–84.

[37] Ibid., 89–90. Both Rozanov and Berdiaev believed that a philosopher's attitude toward the female body revealed something significant about his worldview. Rozanov confessed: "Breasts and the pregnant body excite and attract, or rather, enchant me. I have always wanted to see the entire world pregnant." "Opavshie list'ia," 157.

[38] M. A. Chlenov, *Polovaia perepis' moskovskogo studenchestva i ee obshchestvennoe znachenie* (M., 1909), 53.

[39] Quoted in Rozanov, *Liudi lunnogo sveta*, 131.

[40] Berdiaev, *Smysl tvorchestva*, 217.

triumph over natural union occurring in flesh and blood. This will be possible only with the appearance of a new, creative sex [androgyny], with the revelation of the creative mystery of man as a sexual being."[41]

While Berdiaev was not original in his ascetic beliefs, he was *speaking* about asceticism in a new way. Throughout the Western world, language about sexuality had been overrunning bourgeois and intellectual culture for decades, but the Russian intelligentsia, which absorbed this concern comparatively late, was faced with a particularly intense assault of speculation about the inner man. Berdiaev's glorification of sex permitted him to duck under the waves, to disguise a panicky, conservative cry for help as the latest fashion. His praise of sex also located him in the center of a somewhat deceitful forty-year-old tradition in the "left" Russian intelligentsia. The advent of liberal, realist fiction had led to scandal with its advocacy of "free love" and its "awareness of the details of concrete, material existence, even the petty, ugly or revolting ones,"[42] but free love for Nikolai Chernyshevsky, the preeminent nineteenth-century radical, and his intellectual heirs had, ideally, involved very little physical mating, as Berdiaev was wont to point out.[43] At the time of its publication in 1863, the failure of *What Is to Be Done?*, Chernyshevsky's scandalous and inspirational novel about "new people," to consider the possibility of his heroine's bearing a child as she switches from one husband to the next had provoked comment and led some readers to see the absence of children as part and parcel of the novel's purported depravity.[44] One might just as well, however, have read this absence of procreation as evidence of a certain impotence within the free love ideal, of a desire to promote a free love sanitized of sex and sexual parts, as an indication that Chernyshevsky's vaunted awareness of "revolting" details had not been incompatible with a wish to be rid of them. Chernyshevsky was dismayed by his own penis, noting in his diary, "it's disgusting that we've been given this thing [*Skverno, chto nam dana eta veshch'*]."[45] In *What Is to Be Done?*, a novel that, according to one source, Lenin claimed to have read five times in the course of one summer, finding "new, exciting thoughts" each time, few

[41] Ibid., 237.

[42] Irina Paperno, *Chernyshevsky and the Age of Realism* (Stanford: Stanford University Press, 1988), 44.

[43] Berdiaev, *Russkaia ideia*, 112.

[44] P. S. Reifman, "Predpolagaiutsia li deti?" *Uchenye zapiski Tartuskogo gosudarstvennogo universiteta*, no. 251 (Trudy po russkoi i slavianskoi filologii XV. Literaturovedenie) (1970): 357–363.

[45] N. G. Chernyshevskii, *Polnoe sobranie sochinenii*, 16 vols. (M.: Khudozhestvennaia literatura, 1939), 1:82. Fifty years later Rozanov had no problem placing Chernyshevskii and his famous novel within Russia's ascetic "homosexual" tradition. (*Liudi lunnogo sveta*, 160.) Rozanov found evidence of homoerotic desire in Chernyshevskii's work, but here, again, Rozanov's equation of asceticism and same-sex desire makes it difficult to understand just what he meant by this assertion.

of the earthy details that so fascinate the diary-writer Chernyshevsky are permitted to surface.[46] The novel's utopian Crystal Palace is all glass and light, save for the chambers whither the lovers disappear to make love. These rooms, with curtained doors and "luxurious carpets that devour sound,"[47] are where the realist's penetrating gaze stops. Chernyshevsky's grandchildren, the old Bolsheviks, would deny vehemently that they were ascetics, or indeed anything but materialists, while preaching the virtues of asceticism.[48] Berdiaev was part of a long tradition in the Russian intelligentsia that claimed to be redeeming "the flesh," "the real," or "matter," but that did so only by redefining these terms in order to exclude that which had once been inherent in their definitions.

Not surprisingly, progressives who seemed to be expanding their worlds to encompass the flesh also believed they were expanding the circle of socially significant beings to include women. Inclusion and exclusion often went hand in hand; what was permissible for Chernyshevsky's hero Lopukhov—a relation to woman as an equal on various levels—was not permitted to contaminate the life of his superman Rakhmetov. Our trio of turn-of-the-century philosophers did not escape the prevailing mentality of their age and the intellectual tradition equating women with "flesh." The equation was so "obvious" that it had often no need of affirmation and emerged in simple cadenced parallels. For Solov'ev, the fifth and highest path of love, the androgynous route, would unite "male with female, spirit with body."[49] Moreover, nature (*priroda*—etymologically related to *rody*, the process of birth), the other negative term that these philosophers asserted man should seek to control through the transformation of sexuality, was inevitably compared to a woman: "Through maleness the human race communes with the Word; through woman—with the natural soul of the world. [. . .] The domination of the feminine over the masculine is that of the natural elements of the world over the Word. It has ever been revealed by mystical vision and religious consciousness that the fall of man was accompanied by his subjugation to woman, for the fallen angel acted through the female element."[50]

Essentially, our three philosophers all subscribed to a dominant tendency in eighteenth- and nineteenth-century European writing about sex to view

[46] The source is a Bolshevik who first met Lenin in 1902. M. M. Essen, "Vstrechi s Leninym," in *Vospominaniia o Vladimire Il'iche Lenine*, 5 vols. (M.: Politicheskaia literatura, 1984), 2:112, On the influence of Chernyshevskii on Lenin and the Russian Left, see A. V. Lunacharskii, *Stat'i o literature*, 2 vols. (M.: Khudozhestvennaia literatura, 1988), 1:344–345 and 2:204–235.

[47] N. G. Chernyshevskii, *Chto delat'?* (L.: Nauka, 1975), 290.

[48] See, inter alia, "VI Vsesoiuznii s"ezd RLKSM," *Pravda*, 13 July 1924, 4 (Krupskaia); "Plenum TsKK. O partetike," *Pravda*, 9 October 1924, 3 (Iaroslavskii); "Uchitel'stvo i Komsomol," *Izvestiia*, 4 February 1925, 4 (Bukharin).

[49] Solov'ev, "Zhiznennaia drama," 619.

[50] Berdiaev, *Smysl tvorchestva*, 110.

female sexuality as all-encompassing, to equate sexuality with femininity per se because sexuality supposedly had a far greater impact on a woman's life than on a man's. "The male is male only at certain moments," Rousseau had written in *Emile*; "the female is female during her whole life or at least during her whole youth. Everything constantly recalls her sex to her . . ."[51] More than a century later August Forel had endorsed the same view, declaring: "man's sexual attraction is much easier than woman's to distinguish from the aggregate of his remaining mental and emotional abilities [. . .], and for all its storminess, it is much more ephemeral, exerts much less influence on his entire personal life."[52] Belief about the nature of female orgasm may have served implicitly as evidence for his subscription to this theory; Forel could not contain his amazement and disgust with lesbian sex, in which "orgasm follows orgasm, day and night, almost without a break."[53] Berdiaev and Fedorov took the old belief that a woman was "more sexual" than a man and transposed it to the realm of utopian metaphysics, making it a cornerstone of their "absolutist" philosophical endeavors. Berdiaev declared, "woman is the cosmic, global carrier of the sexual element, of all that is elemental [i.e., natural and bestial] in sex. The natural-procreative element of sex is the female element."[54] For Berdiaev, the uninterrupted nature of female sexuality was a temporal as well as a spatial phenomenon: "In man sex is more *differentiated* and *specialized*, but in woman it is spread over all the flesh in the organism, through the entire field of her soul."[55]

While the notion of woman as an undifferentiated sexual field can also be found in Western European commentary about sex, there this image was for the most part deployed in arguments glorifying (or "protecting") woman's role in procreation.[56] Berdiaev, however, was *attacking* reproduction, and in

---

[51] Jean-Jacques Rousseau, *Emile, or On Education* (New York: Basic Books, 1979), 361.

[52] Forel, *Polovoi vopros*, 95. Between 1907 and 1912, Forel's book appeared in at least four Russian translations in editions totaling at least 38,000 copies. As late as 1928, the book was published in Kharkov in another translation. *Knizhnaia letopis'* (SPb., 1908–1913; M., 1929). Part of Forel's lasting appeal to the Russian intelligentsia was his progressive views and his conversion to socialism. In 1920, when Forel sent a letter to the Soviet press recommending for translation and performance two plays that attacked bourgeois society, the education commissar Anatolii Lunacharskii hailed him as "our friend" on the pages of *Izvestiia*. "Pis'mo ot nashego druga," *Izvestiia*, 12 July 1920, 1.

[53] Forel, *Polovoi vopros*, 261.

[54] Berdiaev, *Smysl tvorchestva*, 226.

[55] Ibid. (emphasis added).

[56] See, e.g., the comments of the turn-of-the-century Berlin-based sexologist Iwan Bloch in his *The Sexual Life of Our Time*: "Women are in fact pure sex from knees to neck. [. . .] Properly speaking, they procreate unceasingly, they stand continually at the witches' cauldron, boiling and brewing; while we lend a hand merely in passing, and do no more than throw one or two fragments into the vessel." Quoted in Sheila Jeffreys, *The Spinster and Her Enemies: Feminism and Sexuality 1880–1930* (London: Pandora, 1985), 138–139. Jeffreys considers at length the views of Bloch and his colleagues and the social use to which they were put.

his hands the image of woman as undifferentiated sexual space takes its place in a virtually gynocidal text. In his—more hostile—use of the image, Berdiaev seems to have been indebted to the Austrian suicide Otto Weininger, whose book *Sex and Character* (1903) created a sensation in Russia and Europe.[57] Weininger, whose fingerprints can be found all over early-twentieth-century Russian thought, had portrayed woman as a soulless creature who, because her sexuality was neither temporally nor topographically localized, was eternally in a state of arousal, receiving sexual pleasure from every object with which she came into contact.[58] This was a substantial reworking of Rousseau's "everything constantly reveals her sex to her." In Weininger's hands this idea, smuggled into the realms of biology and psychiatry—areas he poorly understood—became a misogynistic touchstone for comprehending the universe. For him, every woman was part mother, part whore, and particular abuse was heaped upon those tending toward the former. Not only was maternal love "instinctive," "involuntary," "amoral," and "blind," it was also egotistical since directed only toward a woman's progeny, not toward all mankind.[59] Weininger's popularity in Russia may have been due to a convergence of opinion on these matters. For Fedorov, mothers were "base, sensual, and intolerant; their entire world was limited to the nursery."[60] Solov'ev was willing to admit that maternal love is based on sacrifice, but he could not forgive its role in condemning man to live among the beasts.

> To a mother her child may be dearer than all else, but this is precisely because it is her child, just as with other animals; in other words, here the purported acknowledgment of an other's unconditional significance is in reality founded upon an external, physiological connection.[61]

Significantly, Weininger, who, like Berdiaev and Solov'ev, believed in the possibility of physical immortality, began his treatise with a lengthy exposi-

---

[57] Between 1908 and 1912 Weininger's book appeared in at least 39,000 copies and four translations. The Russian literary critic Akim Volynskii recalled: "The book's appearance in 1903, soon after its author's suicide, caused an uproar in society; it was like the explosion of a grenade. All the papers, journals, people of different scholarly professions, students, everyone was in turmoil." A. K. Volynskii, "Madonna," in Otto Veininger (Weininger), *Pol i kharakter* (SPb.: Posev, 1909), xiv (xiii–xxvi). Volynskii's failure to distinguish Russian from European reaction suggests that he saw the fascination with Weininger in Russia as part of the transcontinental infatuation with the young author. The anxiety of influence is apparent in Berdiaev's treatment of Weininger. He says in a footnote, "Weininger makes remarks of intuitive genius about female psychology, but they are spoiled by his bad, weak enmity toward feminity." *Smysl tvorchestva*, 432.

[58] Weininger, *Pol i kharakter*, 279.

[59] Ibid., 268–269.

[60] Fedorov, *Filosofiia*, 1:323.

[61] Solov'ev, "Smysl liubvi," 2:510.

tion of the fundamentally bisexual nature of man, a concept he had taken from Fliess and Freud[62] but had transformed from a psychological to a metaphysical and biological notion. In Weininger's work, bisexuality was the functional equivalent of the Russian religious utopians' androgyny, and he, too, paid lip service to the need to overcome sexual difference. For Weininger, however, the most valuable aspect of bisexuality/androgyny was that it entailed the destruction of women,[63] a view Berdiaev shared. In the creative act that Berdiaev thought would presage a mystically whole, spiritually utopian "third age," women's creative act, maternity, would be "conquered" and matter would be "gotten rid of."[64] He predicted confidently: "There will come [. . .] the end of the religion of the species, the religion of maternity and of matter, and there will be no power capable of preserving the maternal, material, organic life of the species or protecting it from doom."[65]

Just as Berdiaev did not attack "paternity," Fedorov spoke nearly exclusively of the "resurrection of fathers." For both men the solution to man's mortality—whether androgyny or scientific resurrection—surreptitiously marginalized if not eliminated women; their hostility toward the female sex is frequently so marked that one begins to suspect that this antipathy was their philosophical cornerstone rather than a by-product. Solov'ev is less open to this charge than are his colleagues, but rhetorically he also suggests that it is more important that women become like men than the other way around. Once woman has been identified as matter and man as spirit, what else can the "spiritualization of matter" (*odukhotvorenie materii*)[66] mean but the molding of the essence of femininity to remove all traces of the feminine?[67]

---

[62] See David Abrahamsen, *The Mind and Death of a Genius* (New York, 1946), 43–45.

[63] Weininger, *Pol i kharakter*, 421–423.

[64] Berdiaev, *Smysl tvorchestva*, 372.

[65] Ibid., 240.

[66] Solov'ev, "Smysl liubvi," 2:540.

[67] In Solov'ev's cosmogony, "the eternal feminine" was defined as that which God both separates from himself and embraces: "in relationship to God, it is a passive unity, female, since here eternal emptiness receives the fullness of divine love" ("Smysl liubvi," 2:533). Solov'ev claimed that in perfect love the male lover would see—and not in a transitory manner—the eternal feminine in his earthly female beloved. However, the disastrous attempts of the Symbolists to infuse Solov'ev's teachings into their lives and writings reveal how easy it was for devotion to the eternal feminine to coexist with hatred for real women. See, inter alia, V. F. Khodasevich, *Nekropol'* (Brussels: Petropolis, 1939), 16–17, 68–69, and Zinaida Gippius, *Zhivye litsa*, 2 vols. (Prague: Plamia, 1925), 1:16–19. Berdiaev, perhaps with the experience of the Symbolist generation in mind, claimed that the concept of the eternal feminine was itself inherently flawed because the eternal feminine provided no escape from the female sexual element. Unless philosophers abandoned the eternal feminine for an androgynous ideal of virginity, he urged, man would never "be fully emancipated from immersion in the feminine sexual element, in magnetic and engulfing [*zasasyvaiushchaia*] sexual polarity." *Smysl tvorchestva*, 224.

The surfacing of a desire to be rid of women within the utopian project of eliminating history should remind us of the repressive nature of much utopian thought. Women were making substantial economic and political inroads into turn-of-the-century Russian society, and the student of that period should keep their progress in mind when looking for what is being absented from the aspirations of the era's texts. As early as 1909, the Bolshevik Friche charged that the "homosexual" (i.e., ascetic) ideals of Weininger and of European modernism as a whole had been born of a reaction to the female emancipation movement: "In an age where woman is striving to participate actively in the construction of culture, homosexuality is preaching the idea of a civilization created by men alone."[68] In Berdiaev's work the repressive impetus behind the author's vision of androgyny is not difficult to find:

> The holy, mystical idea of androgyny has its dangerous caricature in hermaphroditism. *Turned inside out*, androgyny in "this world" [i.e., of matter, rather than of spirit] assumes hermaphroditic form. [. . .] Androgyny is man's likeness to God, his ascent above nature. Hermaphroditism is a bestial, nature-bound mixing of the sexes that has not been transformed into a higher form of being. The women's emancipation movement is in its essence a caricature, simian and imitative; in it there is hermaphroditic deformity and not androgynous beauty. [. . .] Woman, by mechanical imitation, out of envy and enmity, appropriates masculine characteristics to herself and becomes a spiritual and physical caricature.[69]

If we read androgyny itself "inside out," we may find that Berdiaev's ideal is a fearful reaction to and a repressive *imitation* of what he calls hermaphroditism. Indeed, in all the cases we have considered thus far, imitation and appropriation help to constitute immortality, replacing woman's reproductive function by its likeness. Fedorov marginalizes "the cult of women" and of mothers (*materi*), deifying instead fathers and a paternalized concept of "matter" (*materiia*): the dust of fore*fathers*.[70] He suggests "daughterliness" as a woman's proper function, and as an appropriate role model he suggests, among others, Antigone, whose name means "in place of a mother."[71] In the work of Weininger, Berdiaev, and Solov'ev, this appropriation of maternity

---

[68] Friche, *Torzhestvo pola*, 84.

[69] Berdiaev, *Smysl tvorchestva*, 238 (emphasis added). It is comments such as this that emphasize both the proximity and the distance between Berdiaev and early Christian writers who also viewed the elimination of the feminine as a resolution of the division of the sexes. For a look at early Christian parallels, see Peter Brown, *The Body and Society: Men, Women and Sexual Renunciation in Early Christianity* (New York: Columbia University Press, 1988), 112–114. Berdiaev, Fedorov, and Solov'ev were essentially updating and elaborating religious and philosophical traditions at a moment when throughout Europe women's initial inroads into the patriarchy were generating a savage discursive backlash.

[70] Fedorov, *Filosofiia*, 1:445.

[71] Robert Graves, *The Greek Myths*, 2 vols. (Harmondsworth: Penguin, 1960), 2:380.

functions in equally metaphorical ways, but here anatomy plays a more obvious role. Weininger's answer to mortality is the male characteristic of "genius," which he portrays as a state of universal receptivity. "The ego of the
genius is universal apperception, a point in which all the infinity of space is
already contained. The outstanding man contains within himself the entire
world; genius is a living microcosm."[72] This sounds suspiciously like his
descriptions of woman as an undifferentiated sex organ, copulating to varying degrees with every object around her, capable of being impregnated even
from afar. In fact, Weininger is willing to admit that woman is a *copy* "on a
baser, physical level" of genius.[73] Here again we should seek to discover
what is an imitation of what, to read the "mechanics" of copying, or utopian
parody, "inside out."[74] Weininger builds his notion of genius on characteristics stolen from women, one of the most important of which is depth:

> Genius is identical with depth [or profundity], but just let anyone try to define
> "woman" as "deep" [or profound]. Thus female genius is a *contradictio in ad-*
> *jecto*, for genius has always been defined as the highest sort of virility, strikingly
> manifested, fully developed, and achieving full consciousness.[75]

Here Weininger goes through mighty contortions to recover depth—an aspect associated with the female reproductive system more often than with
the male—from woman. Engorged with genius, profundity becomes the
phallic property that saves man from death.[76]

The notion of genius as an all-encompassing phenomenon was an old,
Romantic one, associated in German tradition with the protean figure of

[72] Weininger, *Pol i kharakter*, 199.

[73] Ibid., 280.

[74] In his groundbreaking discussion of the poetics of parody, the Russian Formalist Iurii Tynianov accords a predominant place to "mechanization," defining it as quotation (often through
distortion or reversal of an utterance's components) in a context that undercuts or polemicizes
with the utterance's original speaker. *Dostoevskii i Gogol'* (Letchworth: Prideaux, 1975 [1921]),
23. For Tynianov, parody is essentially copying with a marked difference; it undermines its
original, regardless of whether the original and its parodic copy are comic or tragic. In the case
of these turn-of-the-century philosophers we can see how Tynianov's term functions when transposed from literature into different sites of discourse. Weininger and Berdiaev seem to be
caught up in intense *interdisciplinary* anxiety about questions of primacy and about the parodic
relationship between woman and man, and between biology (or sociology) and metaphysics.

[75] Weininger, *Pol i kharakter*, 220.

[76] Women, too, were capable of using androgyny to "parody" and overcome "hermaphroditism." According to Sandra Gilbert, modernist women writers derived power from an ideal of
androgyny that effectively reversed the misogynistic, male modernist vision of the emancipated
woman as hermaphrodite. "Costumes of the Mind: Transvestism as Metaphor in Modern Literature," *Critical Inquiry* 7 (1980): 391–417. The writing of Weininger, Berdiaev, and Fedorov (the
last called women desirous of being active outside of the home "a teratological phenomenon"—
Filosofiia obshchego dela, 1:324) shows how the misogynistic image of emancipated woman as
hermaphrodite could be "parodied" by no less misogynistic fantasies of salvation.

Goethe, in Russia with Pushkin. But in Weininger's system it was explicitly sexualized, and in this context an old metaphor became part of a metaphysical attack on and figurative robbery of women. Berdiaev's theory of immortalizing creativity was also based on a rhetoric of all-encompassing filling and incorporation:

> The universe can enter into a man, be assimilated by him; it can be comprehended only because all the elements of the universe are present in a man, all its strengths and qualities, because a man is not a fractional part of the universe but an integral small universe.[77]

Here, though, Weininger was only a minor source for Berdiaev, the most important being Solov'ev's concept of "all-encompassing unity" (*vseedinstvo*). Solov'ev's description of "*vseedinstvo*" is replete with the metaphoric language of love:

> Already in the world of nature everything belongs to the idea [of *vseedinstvo*], but her true essence demands that everything not only belong to her, that everything be included in her or embraced by her, but also *that she belong to everything herself*, that *everything*, that is, *all* private and individual creatures and, consequently, *each* of them, actually possess [*obladat'*] this ideal *vseedinstvo*, including it within themselves.[78]

It is no coincidence that *vseedinstvo* is defined as "a certain manner of perceiving [or of "taking in," *vospriniat'*] and of appropriating to oneself everything else."[79] Human activity informed by the ideal of *vseedinstvo* releases "real spiritual-bodily currents," but, Solov'ev assures us, "the strength of this spiritual-bodily creativity in man is only the *turning inward* of that same creative strength which, in nature, being turned outward, has created the bad infinity of the physical reproduction of organisms."[80] The essential dynamic underlying Solov'ev's utopian enterprise is one of appropriation; in conquering the forces of history, man makes himself immortal not only by ridding himself of woman, but by retaining her womb and making it his own.[81]

---

[77] Berdiaev, *Smysl tvorchestva*, 88. The word Berdiaev uses for "man" in this passage, "*chelovek*," is gender neutral, but throughout *Smysl tvorchestva* woman ("*zhenshchina*") is the marked member in the male/female dichotomy, and gender neutral terms should be read as those purified of femininity.

[78] Solov'ev, "Smysl liubvi," 2:542. Solov'ev's substitution of "the idea [*ideia*] of *vseedinstvo*" for "*vseedinstvo*" allows him to accord feminine gender to the concept in this passage.

[79] Ibid., 506–507.

[80] Ibid., 547.

[81] Here it is worth recalling the long history of images of male appropriation of female reproductive functions. Elaine Showalter finds that in Western culture such fantasies—which date back, of course, at least to the Greek myths—"emerged with a particular virulence in the 1880s." *Sexual Anarchy: Gender and Culture at the Fin de Siècle* (New York: Penguin, 1990), 77–78. What seems particular to the figures we have been examining is their utopian and

It should not be surprising that as Russia self-consciously entered a new century and the modern era, philosophers would attack maternity and elaborate new myths and strategies for survival in a qualitatively different future. A strong line of hostility toward maternal power runs through nineteenth-century Russian thought, even in the work of writers who have left us apparently ennobling depictions of childbirth and who have devoted considerable effort to praising good mothers while condemning bad ones. One of the central stories in Tolstoi's career is his effort to come to terms with maternity, and the lesson of much of his work may be that men are far better off when mothers do not survive into their sons' adolescence.[82] Even in Tolstoi's early diaries, woman's absorbent nature makes her the consummate sign of man's dependence on "outside circumstances" beyond his control,[83] and one

---

programmatic use. The figurative appropriation of the womb becomes essential to the achievement of immortality and to a notion of ideal community.

[82] Tolstoi's "Childhood" may be read as his clearest representation of this fantasy; read as a prescription, the story contends that the process of maturation requires the death of the mother. Childhood cannot end—and be aesthetically finalized in memory—until the mother departs. In a recent article, Hugh McLean draws attention to the near total absence of any mention of Pierre's and Andrei's mothers in *War and Peace*. "The Case of the Missing Mothers, or When Does a Beginning Begin?" in *For SK: In Celebration of the Life and Career of Simon Karlinsky*, ed. Michael S. Flier and Robert P. Hughes (Berkeley: Berkeley Slavic Specialties, 1994), 223–232. McLean suggests several narratological reasons for this absence, but one might add that Tolstoi's interest in exploring his heroes' freedom could have been a significant factor. *War and Peace* is obsessed with the proposition: "If we look at a man alone, apart from his relations to everything around him, each of his actions appears to us to be free. But if we see his relation to anything around him, if we see his connection with anything whatsoever, [. . .] we see that each of these circumstances has an influence on him and controls at least one aspect of his activity." *War and Peace*, trans. Ann Dunnigan (New York: Signet, 1968), 1444. Andrei and Pierre represent man at the first of these poles: they float through the novel, deciding how they should live their lives, as if they were not dependent on circumstances. One might juxtapose to them the example of Nikolai Rostov, whose life is determined (and, in his opinion, burdened) by his mother until the very end. Nikolai is man at the opposite pole, a man tied to his surroundings and incapable of floating through a narrative or a life. In the novel's second epilogue, in a final, oblique reference to maternity, "an unborn child" is mentioned (along with a dying man and an idiot) as an example of a case where freedom is reduced to zero.

Hostility toward figures of maternity may be found in several other classics of late-nineteenth-century Russian literature. As several critics have recently noted, Raskol'nikov's demonstration of his superhuman character comes at the expense of a mother substitute (see, inter alia, Bernard J. Paris, "Pulkheria Alexandrovna and Raskolnikov, My Mother and Me," in *Self-Analysis in Literary Study: Exploring Hidden Agendas*, ed. Daniel Rancour-Larerriere [New York: New York University Press, 1994], 111–129), but rather than reading *Crime and Punishment*'s crime through a psychoanalytic focus on Raskol'nikov, we might view his murder of the pawnbroker and the text's eventual liquidation of his mother within the pattern of philosophical hostility toward maternity that I have been sketching out. (Indeed, a major point of the much-disputed epilogue to *Crime and Punishment* may be the text's need to attest to Raskol'nikov's mother's death; the male hero's spiritual transformation must be preceded by the devaluation and elimination of maternity.)

[83] L. N. Tolstoi, *Polnoe sobranie sochinenii*, 90 vols. (M. and L.: Khudozhestvennaia literatura, 1928–1958), 46:32–33.

of Tolstoi's most controversial later works—"The Kreutzer Sonata"—targets women and, in particular, a mother, as a site where at least the symbolic overcoming of reality can occur.[84] Our philosophers transposed "The Kreutzer Sonata"'s murderous declaration of independence onto a metaphysical plane. The 1920s would witness a further transposition, as the figurative destruction of the female body and the concern with woman as a limiting origin would come to play an important role in the Soviet discourse of class identity and national survival.

The Signification of Sex

In 1934, at the Writers' Congress that enshrined Socialist Realism as the reigning force in Soviet literature, Maksim Gor'ky contrasted the coming era with the one that had immediately preceded the Revolution. "In general," he declared, "the decade 1907–1917 completely deserves the name of the most shameful and shameless decade in the history of the Russian intelligentsia."[85] While the culture of the pre-Revolutionary decade merely developed, in a heightened key, many themes present in Russian literature from the start of the century, Gor'ky's choice of 1907 was neither arbitrary nor the result of a preference for decimal calculation. That year, which began with the publication, in the left-leaning *Sovremennyi mir*, of the first installment of Mikhail Artsybashev's novel *Sanin*, was marked by intense debate over the place of sex in Russian literature and society. By 1907, the role played by sex in the relationship between the individual and society functioned throughout the Russian intelligentsia as an ideological signpost. Public statements about the importance of sex began to be perceived as an essential component of an *intelligent*'s worldview, and the interplay between sexual and political desires had become a crucial topic with which the writer depicting a better world (or the path thereto) had consciously to grapple.

Sanin appeared at a moment when the Russian intelligentsia was at a pivotal moment in its evolution. In his introduction to *Landmarks*, a widely read 1909 collection of articles that took stock of the state of the intelligentsia, the philosopher, literary historian, and publicist Mikhail Gershenzon asserted that for all their differences, the contributors were motivated by the common belief that "inner life, not the self-sufficing principles of political life, is the single lasting basis for the building of any society." This position, Gershenzon remarked, constituted a radical revision of "the ideology of the Russian intelligentsia," which had hitherto rested "entirely on a

---

[84] For a discussion of the polemic surrounding Tolstoi's novella in the 1890s, see Peter Ulf Møller, *Postlude to "The Kreutzer Sonata": Tolstoy and the Debate on Sexual Morality in Russian Literature in the 1890s*, trans. John Kendal (Leiden: E. J. Brill, 1988).

[85] *Pervyi vsesoiuznyi s"ezd sovetskikh pisatelei. 1934. Stenograficheskii otchet* (M.: Sovetskii pisatel', 1990), 12.

contrary principle—on the acknowledgment of the unconditional primacy of social forms."[86]

The inward turn of the intelligentsia was in part a facade, or, more charitably, a means to an end rather than an end itself. Gershenzon was not contending that the "building of society" was irrelevant; rather, he was arguing that society had to be built through an inward detour. There was something of a paradox to this inward turn. For at least the past fifty years, personal life had often been treated as an irrelevant, unimportant matter by the Russian intelligentsia, particularly by its more "progressive," radical members who yearned to sacrifice themselves for a larger, collective cause and were later lionized by the Bolsheviks for having done so.[87] For many of the intelligentsia, personal life had been important only in its diminution or obliteration. When the intelligentsia turned inward, it did not endorse personal life as an independent domain but brought public concerns into the personal realm as never before. As inner life and its chief standard-bearer, sex, became more significant, they lost their private character; in effect, they were exteriorized by the philosophical, political, and artistic colonists who were turning inward to explore them.

In one respect there was nothing new about the "signification" of inner life that occurred in early-twentieth-century Russia. The emotional life of extraordinary individuals had had cosmic significance for the German and Russian Romantics, and even the resolutely anti-Romantic generation of the young radicals of the 1860s had expanded the scope of relevant life, propelling political significance into the home, workshop, and factory. The new, early-twentieth-century cult of the individual (or, to put it more precisely, of the individual's collective significance), however, was born in the wake of Zola's naturalism, fascination with Nietzsche, European decadence, and the revival of mysticism. The enormous discursive impact of these influences made the examination of the personal sphere more invasive than earlier, nineteenth-century assaults, and more ready to draw sexuality and the body into its orbit. The foremost artistic movement in Russia in the early twentieth century, Symbolism, insisted on the spiritual significance not only of artistic creation but of all aspects of a Symbolist's life; the Symbolist "canon" required that the individual personality be structured entirely in accordance with "the norms of the universe," with "the law by which ties between the individual and the collective, global and divine, are animated, strengthened, and recognized."[88] The consequences of this "canon" for intimate life could

---

[86] M. Gershenzon, "Predislovie," in *Vekhi. Sbornik statei o russkoi intelligentsii*, 4th ed. (M., 1909), ii (i–iii).

[87] The eclipse of personal life is a major theme of Barbara Engel's account of Russian women radicals: *Mothers and Daughters: Women of the Intelligentsia in Nineteenth Century Russia* (Cambridge: Cambridge University Press, 1983).

[88] Viacheslav Ivanov, "O granitsakh iskusstva," in his *Sobranie sochinenii*, 4 vols. (Brussels: Foyer Oriental Chrétien, 1974), 2:640.

be terrifying, as the Symbolists discovered.[89] Decrying the burden of significance bequeathed by them to his generation, Osip Mandel'shtam would exclaim in 1922 that it had become impossible to eat dinner or light a fire without communing with the cosmos: "a person is no longer master of his own home."[90] Mandel'shtam might have added that a man (or woman) was no longer master (or mistress) of his (or her) own bed. As never before in Russian intellectual discourse, sexual activity was endowed with tremendous symbolic importance.[91] The semantic invasion (or metastasis) of intimate life would continue after the Revolution, when the boundaries between metaphysics and politics would become quite porous and pre-Revolutionary ideals of communality would be brought down to earth and put into practice.

Sanin was the text that, more than any other, served as a lightning rod for consideration of the social significance of personal life and its essential synecdoche: sex. The novel's serialized publication was a cultural event of enormous importance, sparking lectures to overflowing halls, mock trials, and the publication of several monographs refuting the novel's gospel of "free love."[92] The furor was likened to that generated by the appearance of Turgenev's *Fathers and Sons*.[93] The influential literary commentator Petr Pil'sky described a lecture on *Sanin* given by a virtually unknown critic in Moscow in 1908:

A crowd of many thousands came [to the theater]. All tickets had been sold and it was impossible to admit another soul, but those who desired—and thirsted—to enter kept forcing their way in and taking seats even though they had no tickets. They made a great deal of noise, shouting, demanding empty chairs, and insisting that the talk start soon.

People went up to them and said:

---

[89] For discussions of the ideological significance of the Symbolists' personal lives, see the essays collected in *Creating Life: The Aesthetic Utopia of Rusian Modernism*, ed. Irina Paperno and Joan Delaney Grossman (Stanford: Stanford University Press, 1994).

[90] Osip Mandel'shtam, "O prirode slova," in his *Sobranie sochinenii*, 4 vols. (New York: Inter-Language Literary Associates, 1966), 2:255.

[91] In his brilliant book on psychoanalysis in Russia, Aleksandr Etkind accounts for the limited impact of Freud on pre-Revolutionary Russian intellectul culture by suggesting that the cultural role of psychoanalysis was already occupied by Russian Symbolism, a movement that was similarly obsessed with the unconscious, language, the decoding of duplicitous, everyday signs, and the relentless organization of a worldview around a single mythological figure. *Eros nevozmozhnogo* (SPb.: Meduza, 1993), 94. Whatever the explanation, Freud's theories about the fundamental importance of sexuality had far less impact on pre-Revolutionary Russia than did those of Weininger.

[92] For a discussion of the excitement surrounding the novel's publication, see Petr Pil'skii, "Reaktsiia zamuzhem," *Voprosy pola*, no. 5 (1908): 19–24.

[93] G. S. Novopolin, *Pornograficheskii element v russkoi literature* (SPb.: Stasiulevich, 1909), 118.

—Ladies and gentlemen, all the tickets are sold out. You have no right to interfere with others who want to hear the lecture. What do you want?

—We don't give a fig about your order and your tickets. We want to hear about *Sanin*. And by what right? By a very simple one. We are Saninites ourselves.

The lecture had to be postponed, and when it took place on the following day (twice, in the morning and at night!), the hall was packed beyond capacity, a reinforced brigade of police was stationed at the door, and there were ever more and more who wanted to hear the talk.[94]

Pil'sky's point was that *Sanin* was not read simply as a novel, but also—in the great tradition of both *Fathers and Sons* and *What Is to Be Done?*—as a primer on how to live.[95] He describes the disappointment generated by a lecture he gave in Saint Petersburg on "the problem of sex." His auditors, he suddenly realized, had no interest in what he was saying about contemporary Russian literature, Nietzsche, and idealistic philosophy. The typical woman in attendance, he began to understand, did not want to hear about philosophy but about how she should behave if "a local Sanin from Ligovka or Vasilev-skii Island" (two rough districts in early-twentieth-century Petersburg) should put his hand around her waist.[96]

Why was *Sanin* so influential? By today's standards the novel, with its muted glimpses of sexual encounters, its fade-outs at appropriate moments and abstention from anatomical references below the chest, is tame. The most important factor behind *Sanin*'s appeal was probably not its eroticism but its pretense to ideological coherence. The book purported to offer a uni-fied worldview that smoothly blended changes in contemporary attitudes about morality into a new sexual ethos. Dmitry Sanin, the novel's hero, rejects all ideologies that demand the suppression of an individual's desires. He confronts an arrogant army officer as well as an exiled student with a penchant for picking up girls at Party meetings and prevails over both in competition for two well-endowed women. These struggles are portrayed as symbolic: Sanin triumphs over the Right and the Left, over a member of the aristocracy and over the latest—Marxist—incarnation of the "superfluous man." This latter victory is especially meaningful, for it signifies rejection of the entire system of values that produced the "problem" of the superfluous man, a system predicated on the notion that an individual establishes his worth (or social potency) through his contribution to society. According to Dmitry Sanin, community is superfluous. The hero's creed is the affirmation of the individual through the satisfaction of his desires.[97]

[94] Pil'skii, "Reaktsiia zamuzhem," 19.

[95] On the role of Chernyshevskii's novel in the modeling of behavior, see Paperno, *Cher-nyshevsky and the Age of Realism*, passim.

[96] Pil'skii, "Reaktsiia zamuzhem," 20.

[97] Artsybashev, *Sanin* (Berlin: Moskovskoe knigoizdatel'stvo, 1921 [1907]), 88.

Sanin's philosophy, as critics were wont to point out, owed an enormous amount to Nietzsche, and in it, as in *Thus Spoke Zarathustra* and *Beyond Good and Evil*, the will to power is decidedly male.[98] Various characters repeatedly voice their contempt for women. "Among men one can find at least one out of a thousand who merits the term human being, but no such deserving women are to be found. They are naked, pink, fat tailless apes, and no more."[99] Sexual desire in the novel frequently surfaces in self-aggrandizing male fantasies. Essential to *Sanin* is the obliteration of woman's personality in the creation of the Nietzschean man. Repeatedly the text asserts its contempt for men who despise women, yet the explicit detail it employs in describing the fantasies of such men betrays a fascination from which the narrative cannot tear itself away.

Sanin claims to respect women, and the novel seems to treat him as if he were free from the dynamic of female humiliation so persistent in the text. Sanin's love, however, and his credo, "people should take pleasure in love without fear or prohibition, without limit,"[100] do not bring happiness to Karsavina, the one woman in the novel with whom he has intercourse. The morning after her "surrender" (on a boat in the middle of a lake), Karsavina feels like a "crushed reptile."[101]

> When she thought about Sanin, she didn't see his face. There was only the memory of frenzied strength, terrifying pleasure in which suffering merged with the desire for greater, more profound intimacy and, at moments, with the desire to be tortured to death. Then there was the bright and shining memory of some sort of singing and of an inexpressibly intimate tenderness, and this last memory softened her heart.
>
> —I myself am guilty!—Karsavina said to herself:—I am a disgusting, dissolute creature![102]

A relentless policy of textual purity is at work here: Artsybashev determinedly seals his hero off from imagery of humiliation. "His" paragraph (the first of the two quoted above) is full of bliss; only in his "absence" does abasement occur. The construction of this hermetic wall around Sanin betrays *Sanin*'s implicit acknowledgment of the dynamic upon which its hero thrives. The image of a woman being humiliated and beaten may not be in the mind of Sanin the character, but the novel cannot talk about sex

---

[98] In a playful gesture to an obvious source, Sanin tries to read *Zarathustra* in bed. Quickly tiring of Nietzsche's "bombastic images," Sanin spits in disgust before casting down the book and falling asleep. Ibid., 28.

[99] Ibid., 121.

[100] Ibid., 277.

[101] Ibid., 283.

[102] Ibid., 287.

without lapsing into a rhetoric of male aggrandizement and female humiliation.[103]

A glance at the later evolution of Artsybashev's oeuvre, and in particular
at his 1917 novel *A Woman Standing in the Middle*, confirms the suspicion

[103] It is difficult to imagine that any woman reading *Sanin* would feel inclined to adopt the
hero's professed ideology. The details concerning "what happens to girls who . . ." are so relentless as to make one question the extent to which Artsybashev shared his hero's views. This does
not appear to have been the perception of Artsybashev's contemporaries, many of whom felt
that the author "adhered entirely to Sanin's views." Aleksei Achkasov, *Artsybashevskii Sanin i
Okolo polovogo voprosa* (M.: Efimov, 1908), 9. Nor have more recent readers been quick to
identify the misogynist dimensions of the text. Laura Engelstein asserts that "while exalting the
purity of natural desire, Artsybashev condemns sexual conquest for the sake of domination,
along with language and actions degrading to women." She cites approvingly the comments of
the educator A. N. Ostrogorskii, who claimed, Engelstein tells us, that "the novel could more
convincingly be read as a brief for women's sexual emancipation and equal social standing than
as a vindication of the unimpeded sexual appetite of men." *The Keys to Happiness*, 385.
Nicholas Luker insists: "Sanin's behavior is designed to demonstrate Artsybashev's conviction
that man is no longer true to his essential self and that he has become constrained by empty
conventions and false priorities, a conviction neatly expressed by the epigraph to the novel
taken from the Book of Ecclesiastes which the author often quoted: 'Lo, this only I have found,
that God hath made man upright; but they have sought out many inventions.' " Nicholas Luker,
In Defence of a Reputation: Essays on the Early Prose of Mikhail Artsybashev (Cotgrave,
England: Astra Press, 1990), 77–78.

The fault of these readings is that they treat characters in a novel as if they were real people
participating in a conversation with no intrinsic relation to the background against which the
conversation occurs. A novel ought to be read as a single, albeit complex, utterance, rather than
as a collection of independent utterances that merit individual, separate evaluation. *Sanin* is
composed of scene after scene of female humiliation, and Dmitrii Sanin's opposition to sexual
humiliation serves as a justification for (and, perhaps, is a symptom if not cause of) humiliation's insistent depiction. The novel's epigraph, cited so approvingly by Luker, comes from a
passage in Ecclesiastes that readers who detach Sanin from *Sanin* necessarily ignore. Artsybashev's selection of the last line of Ecclesiastes 7 for a novel about sex is entirely appropriate,
because the verse concludes a series of misogynistic remarks centered on the role and difference
of women:

> The wiles of a woman I find mightier than death; her heart is a trap to catch you and her
> wiles are fetters. The man who is pleasing to God may escape her, but she will catch a
> sinner. "See," says the Speaker, "this is what I have found, reasoning things out one by
> one, after searching long without success: I have found one man in a thousand worth the
> name, but I have not found one woman among them all. This alone I have found, that God,
> when he made man, made him straightforward, but man invents endless subtleties of his
> own. (*The New English Bible with the Apocrypha* [New York: Oxford University Press,
> 1971], 794)

In his isolation and recuperation of the last line of Ecclesiastes 7 Artsybashev in effect mirrors
and foreshadows the strategy of his novel, which recuperates Sanin by isolating him from his
surroundings.

In this context, it is worth noting that when Sanin first becomes attracted to Karsavina, after
seeing her naked by the river, he sings the first two lines of "Iz-za ostrova na strezhen'," a
popular song based on Dmitrii Sadovnikov's 1883 poem of the same name. The song tells of the

that in *Sanin* delight in female humiliation masquerades as a critique of sexual hypocrisy. The later and far less widely read novel is a simultaneously misogynistic and moralizing text that both revels in and condemns the humiliation of women. Artsybashev proceeds to rework in a sexual key Ivan Karamazov's cry that "If there is no God, everything is permitted." One of the novel's more odious characters proclaims:

> The helplessness of a woman who is raped does not evoke any pity or indignation in us . . . It only arouses us. When we read in the newspaper about the rape of a defenseless girl by a crowd of hooligans, we become indignant only because we are hypocrites; actually, we thirst for details and are painfully envious that we were not in that crowd, even if only as a witness . . . Oh, if prison did not exist! . . . If today they abolished all punishment for rape, by tomorrow evening not one unraped woman would remain. They would catch them everywhere, in forests, in drawing rooms, in servants' quarters, in boarding school dormitories, in classrooms and in convents . . . For why do we need women? . . . Do you really think that we could not get along without them in our art, wars, sciences, and work? Do soldiers, politicians, workers, writers, and philosophers really need the help of a woman? Take away from her her instrument of pleasure and for us a woman becomes only another mouth to feed.[104]

Particularly startling in these remarks, which the plot and imagery of the novel do little to counter or contain, is their attack on the hypocrisy of those who express "pity and indignation" about rape, for one of Artsybashev's earliest works, the short story "Horror" (1906), had done just that. Artsybashev's early stories were praised by Aleksandr Blok for their fine sympathetic understanding of collective psychology,[105] and "Horror" relates a mob's vengeance against government officials for their violation and murder of a young girl.[106] Rereading this tale after *A Woman Standing in the Middle*, however, one suspects that its political moral and criticism of a corrupt judicial system may have been introduced largely to justify the *description* of the consequences of the vicious crime, that the story's raison d'être is its vivid portrait of a woman's humiliation.

---

drowning of a captured Persian princess by the seventeenth-century rebel Sten'ka Razin. We will return to the political and gender significance of this song in the context of its quotation by Soviet authors, but here it is worth observing that this is an odd piece to sing in praise of female beauty. Sanin's eventual sexual conquest of Karsavina in the middle of a lake and her resultant feeling of humiliation may serve as a reprise of Razin's casting his lover overboard into the Volga.

[104] Mikhail Artsybashev, *Zhenshchina stoiashchaia posredi, Eroticheskii roman* (Riga: Gramatu draugs, 1930), 26–27.

[105] Aleksandr Blok, "O realistakh," in his *O literature* (M.: Khudozhestvennaia literatura, 1989), 91.

[106] "Horror" may actually have been composed after *Sanin*, which Artsybashev later claimed to have written in 1903. Luker, *In Defence of a Reputation*, 76.

The figure benefiting most from the humiliation of women in Artsy-bashev's novels was Artsybashev himself. In *A Woman Standing in the Middle*, the only remotely positive hero is a writer, obviously modeled on the author, whose topic is sex and whose mistress the chief female character becomes. Artsybashev's approach to this writer, to whom women offer themselves after they have read his work, is somewhat ironic, but nevertheless this figure is introduced as a testimony to the power wielded by those who write about sex.[107]

The centrality of sex, and, in particular, violent sex that measured the subject's social significance through his violation of a female Other, had its fullest development in the popular status accorded in the decade prior to the Revolution to the poetry of the Futurists, in which disgust with bourgeois society finds an outlet in moral and sexual épatage. In the poetry of Vladimir Maiakovsky, the entire cosmos often is in a state of sexual arousal, either lusting after the poet's body or about to be raped by him.[108] The Futurists achieved fame by understanding that the sexualization of a topic generated powerful metaphoric language which in the post-1905 cultural climate could secure the attention of a wide—and rapt—audience. Their use of sex transcended mere aesthetic marketing and could easily serve as a potent weapon in social commentary. This tendency is most evident, perhaps, in the work of Maiakovsky, which can be read both as bombastic self-promotion and as a critique of alienation and an unjust social order. It is this ambivalent characteristic of Maiakovsky's work that enabled him and his readers so effectively to transport the pre-Revolutionary, modernist aesthetic discourse of sex into the socially conscious post-Revolutionary work of the poet and his young proletarian readers and imitators.

The misogynistic intoxication with sex and power on display in the work of Artsybashev and Maiakovsky was not universally shared by Russians who wrote about sex and culture in the decade before the Revolution. A common critical reaction to the culture's obsession with sex was to read current talk and behavior as a symptom of social *disease*. The failure of the 1905 Revo-

---

[107] The appearance of a sexually attractive, writing alter ego was not limited to Artsybashev's *Woman*. The most prominent alter ego in a novel devoted to sex belonged to Aleksandr Kuprin. In *The Pit*, his phenomenally successful book about prostitution, Kuprin introduced the figure of "Platonov," a great writer with a magnetic personality who is the sole man trusted by the exploited women who are Kuprin's subject. (Platonov does not seek to abuse this trust, but the impression is created that he certainly could, if he so desired.) Kuprin's contemporaries had no trouble discerning the author's double in the novel. A literary critic in the Symbolist journal *Vesy* urged Kuprin not to flatter himself: "Neither [Platonov], nor you is an artist." Rtukh, "Ne otstupites'! (Nechto o *Iame* Kuprina)," *Vesy*, no. 6 (1909): 86 (82–86).

[108] For a detailed discussion of the treatment of women in Maiakovskii's verse, see A. K. Zholkovskii, "O genii i zlodeistve, o babe i vserossiiskom masshtabe (Progulki po Maia-kovskomu)," in A. K. Zholkovskii and Iu. K. Shcheglov, *Mir avtora i struktura teksta* (Tenafly, N.J.: Hermitage, 1986), 255–278.

lution to generate meaningful social change was seen by many Russian progressives as the origin of the culture's turn toward sex. In the representative words of one critic, "as soon as the emancipatory movement in Russian fell silent, Russian society immediately began to display indisputable signs of an extraordinary development of sensuality."[109] Sexual content seemed to possess the alarming power of filling all the old forms and fora of social debate. The question of sex had replaced questions of government in lecture halls across the land, and in a contribution to *Landmarks* that deplored the plight of intelligentsia youth, Aleksandr Izgoev, a lawyer and prominent member of the Constitutional Democrats, noted his distress that although secret reading groups still existed, their members now studied and debated *Sanin* and Otto Weininger rather than the prohibited writings of the progressive populists.[110]

There was also some concern among the intelligentsia that the 1905 Revolution had in some ways done too much rather than too little. In her study of sex and liberalism in pre-Revolutionary Russia, Laura Engelstein tells the story of doctors and lawyers who viewed the 1905 Revolution as having destroyed the moral foundations of society, corrupted the virtuous lower classes, and unleashed a dangerous wave of sexual violence throughout the land.[111] Dmitry Zhbankov, a progressive zemstvo physician and prolific social epidemiologist, viewed the 1905 Revolution and the events that had nourished it as a national trauma that had produced a precipitous increase in sex crimes and deviance. For Zhbankov, the rise in "pathological sexual violence" (rape in public places, by men who were not deprived of access to consensual sex, by groups of men, and of unattractive women), as opposed to "normal"—but "in no way justifiable"—sexual violence, was a sign of the times. Sex crimes, Zhbankov thought, could be mapped in Russia alongside the acts of horrific violence that had convulsed the country over the preceding years. Where acts of violence such as pogroms, executions, and terrorist attacks had been most prevalent, one would also find the highest incidence of sex crimes and perversion.[112]

The mentality of those outraged by the cultural interest in sex was in many respects similar to that of those who catered to it. If, for example, Blok was correct in his judgment that Artsybashev had important insight into the psychology of the Russian public—and the phenomenal success of *Sanin* would indicate that Artsybashev knew how to read his potential audience—then there is something both representative and chilling about the progression of his treatment of sex. The point is not simply that Artsybashev equated "free love" with rape, but that he was unable to find a middle

---

[109] Achkasov, *Artsybashevskii Sanin*, 5.

[110] A. S. Izgoev, "Ob intelligentnoi molodezhi (Zametki ob ee byte i nastroeniiakh)," in *Vekhi*, 104 (97–124).

[111] Engelstein, *The Keys to Happiness*, 254–299.

[112] D. Zhbankov, "Polovaia prestupnost'," *Sovremennyi mir*, no. 7, pt. 2 (1909): 54–91.

ground between the old, bourgeois morality Sanin professes to detest and a
world in which women are consistently abused and humiliated. Artsybashev
was joined by his critics in his failure to find a golden mean for sexual
behavior. The work of many other writers and commentators also revolved
around Nietzschean and sexual themes, but these authors leaned in the opposite direction, toward asceticism.

In many respects, the early work of Maksim Gor'ky himself, full of sexual
contests of wills, provided a model for Artsybashev's scandalous novel. The
young Gor'ky was fascinated by sexuality as the raw material of power and
trained his microscope on the sexual lower depths of human existence. If the
bosiak (tramp) is the essential, unadorned man, sex is nature at its most
savage, the elemental arena in which the battle for self-affirmation was
waged. By the end of the first decade of his career, Gor'ky had, however,
"castrated" his fiction, making sex yield to political message.[113] In *Mother*
(1906–1907), the novel out of the skirts of which Socialist Realism would
later claim to have issued, sexual desire is deemed incompatible with revolutionary activity. Those who would save society have no time for sex; once
again, there is no middle ground. In this second phase of Gor'ky's career,
however, sexual imagery does not disappear; it is merely raised (or sublated)
to the level of collective metaphor. At the conclusion of *Mother*, Gor'ky's
heroine is surrounded by a large crowd eager to receive the Revolutionary
pamphlets that she has begun to disseminate:

> —"Move aside!" cried the policemen, pushing the crowd out of their way.
> The people yielded unwillingly to these shoves. They pressed against the police-
> men with their mass, impeding them without, perhaps, desiring to do so. They
> were powerfully attracted to this gray-haired woman with her big honest eyes
> and kind face, and, although life had made strangers of them and torn one from
> another, they now merged into something whole, warmed by the fire of the word
> for which, perhaps, their many hearts, injured by the unfairness of life, had long
> been searching and thirsting. The closest stood silently; the Mother saw their
> greedy, attentive eyes and felt their warm breath on her face.[114]

This moment is yet another hypostasis of Solov'ev's *vseedinstvo*, the latest
specimen in a long line of sexually tinged portraits of a collective ideal.
Maiakovsky, we have noted, would employ similar imagery in his decidedly
nonascetic descriptions of women pursuing his "meat." Gor'ky's image
serves as further evidence that these orgiastic moments could be placed at
ascetic or hedonistic poles.[115] Between the antipodal portraits of collective

---

[113] Blok, "O realistakh," 77.

[114] Maxim Gor'kii, *Mat'. Vospominaniia* (M.: Khudozhestvennaia literatura, 1985), 382.

[115] There are other authors who might serve as examples of Russian writers' failure to remain
advocates of anything other than the most severely limited standards of sexual behavior. The
Bolshevik hero of Aleksandr Bogdanov's 1908 novel *Red Star* advocates polygamy for the

unity, however, there was little room for the authorization of norms for individual sexual life.

By far the most interesting case of an author's failing to find a place in his worldview for acceptable sexual norms is G. S. Novopolin's 1909 study, *The Pornographic Element in Russian Literature*, a broad survey of "pornography" that never defines its object. Instead, it tars as pornographic virtually every work that speaks about love. In the process, by portraying Russian literature (and the Russian intelligentsia) as constantly menaced by and virtuously resisting "pornography," Novopolin unwittingly makes a strong case for the centrality of sex to Russian intellectual history as a constitutive principle.

In his attacks on various authors, Novopolin's language revolves around images of slippery slopes; once a writer has begun to speak of sexuality, he is almost invariably led, in Novopolin's view, into pornography. The key word in Novopolin's diatribes is "*perekhodiashchii*," which might be translated as "becoming" or "slipping into," and describes an inexorable transition from worthy literature to pornography. Reviewing the love poetry of the 1890s, Novopolin finds in its turn toward "love" and away from social concerns the roots of society's current dissolution: "Love with all its accessories: yearning, sighs, tears, reminiscences, appeals, longings; love slipping [*perekhodiashchaia*] into erotomania and nymphomania shoves aside all that has until recently been at the very heart of and stirred the blood of the young generation: lofty interests, disinterested indignation, and a proud belief in a self preparing manfully to battle for its own ideas."[116] In this passage, as in Novopolin's attack on the Symbolist Valery Briusov's poetry ("it's not love, but passion. And not even passion, but a sort of uninterrupted lascivious delirium slipping into satyriasis"),[117] the slightest thematic contact with sexuality invariably leads writers into the depths of depravity. There is no middle ground between socially correct and dissolute themes, only a quick and irreversible transition from purity to unbridled lust potentially destructive of an entire civilization.

The difficulty of accepting sexual desire as a legitimate part of human emotions without succumbing to the worst excesses of the flesh received its clearest exposition in Leonid Andreev's 1902 story "The Abyss," which tells

---

strong-willed inhabitants of a future communist state, but in the novel's sequel, written four years later, nonprocreative sexual relations no longer exist as a normative part of life. The ideal sex life for a builder of utopia is a single encounter with a caring, fertile woman. Aleksandr Bogdanov, *Krasnaia zvezda. Inzhener Menni* (Hamburg: Helmut Buske, 1979).

[116] Novopolin, *Pornograficheskii element*, 74. Novopolin was a pseudonym used by the publicist and critic Grigorii Neifel'd. I. F. Masanov, ed., *Slovar' psevdonimov russkikh pisatelei, uchenykh i obshchestvennykh deiatelei*, 4 vols. (M: Vsesoiuznaia knizhnaia palata, 1956–1960), 4:333.

[117] Ibid., 95.

of a young woman who is attacked and gang-raped in a forest. At the story's end, the victim's young male friend, who has unsuccessfully tried to defend her, looks down at her unconscious and violated body and falls prey to the same passion that motivated her assailants. While other writers embellished their work with similar moments, "The Abyss," remained *the* symbol of the awful—and exhilarating—consequences attendant on the victory of passion over reason in the new age. Readers readily identified with the story's male protagonist. As a participant in the 1905 Moscow sex survey wrote on his questionnaire: "There is no doubt that 'The Abyss' has a sensual effect—together with its hero you mentally experience the seductiveness and dizziness of the abyss."[118]

The Russian intelligentsia's inability to find a middle ground where sexuality was concerned received especially paradoxical expression in the hands of leftists trying to reconcile Marxist attacks on bourgeois morality, and aversion to the inherently noncommunal nature of sexual relations, with their own bourgeois roots. Engels had refrained from taking a position on this matter in his *The Origin of the Family, Private Property and the State* (1884). While admitting that the abolition of private property—and with it of "the single family [as] the economic unit of society"—might lead to "the gradual growth of unconstrained sexual intercourse," Engels had opined that communist monogamy was more likely than communist polygamy, a supposition he supported with references to Europe's chivalric past and quotations from the *Niebelungenlied*.[119] As early as 1908, in an attack on *Sanin*, a doctor with Bolshevik sympathies endeavored to show that sexual relations under communism ("free love") would be monogamous but totally unlike the hypocritical monogamous ideal professed by the contemporary bourgeoisie. Defining "the highest form of free love" as monogamy that develops into marriage and lasts "to the grave," Dr. Aleksandr Omel'chenko's ruminations on this question even led him to conclude with startling precision that young communist men and women would probably abstain from sexual intercourse before age twenty-three.[120] Omel'chenko was particularly concerned with

---

[118] Chlenov, *Polovaia perepis'*, 52. Nearly 96 percent of the students surveyed said they had read "works of belles lettres specifically devoted to the sexual question," and 57 percent stated that those works had influenced their sex lives (49).

[119] Friedrich Engels, *The Origin of the Family, Private Property and the State*, trans. Michèle Barrett (Harmondsworth: Penguin, 1985), 107–112. Several years later Engels revised Marx's fourth thesis on Feuerbach. The original version, written by Marx in 1845, concludes, "once the earthly family is discovered to be the secret of the holy family, the former must then itself be destroyed in theory and in practice." In 1888, Engels amended this sentence to read, "Once the earthly family is discovered to be the secret of the holy family, the former must then itself be criticised in theory and transformed in practice." Karl Marx and Frederick Engels, *Collected Works*, 45 vols. (London: Lawrence & Wishart, 1975–1991), 5:4, 7.

[120] Dr. A. P. Omel'chenko, *Svobodnaia liubov' i sem'ia* (SPb.: Posev, 1908), 29, 46. Born in

providing advice to the young proletarian woman of the future, who, he imagined, would resemble the (aristocratic!) maidens gracing the pages of Turgenev's novels. After quoting Goethe's Mephistopheles, a "great realist," Omel'chenko told the young woman of the communist future:

> Kiss only when you believe that you are in love and beloved for your entire life; otherwise you risk shattering two lives: your own and another's. And let your first kiss be the kiss of a happy monogamous woman who gives herself to another only to receive a freely born child from her beloved. In the matter of one's first love there can be neither abortions nor condoms; if this love is to have poetry, you must choose between abstinence and kissing [only] the father of your future child.[121]

Omel'chenko's book is stunning in its sentimentalization of Marxist historical analysis, and it borders on the comical in its reinscription onto future communist society of the bourgeois, patriarchal code of sexual behavior it professes to replace. Its moral tenets about sex, however, may have been closer to those of the Old Bolsheviks who founded the Soviet state than those of any of the philosophers or writers mentioned hitherto. Solov'ev's sense of community, Artsybashev's misogyny and fascination with sexual humiliation and violence, the new insistence on the global significance of sexual life—all these elements would be shuffled and recombined in the formation of post-Revolutionary attitudes about sex, community, and physiology. Omel'chenko's attitude toward sex would also survive the Revolution, and, borne by many older Party members in positions of power, would mingle with antagonistic currents of thought in post-Revolutionary culture.

Fantasies of the War Communist Body

When one compares the texts bequeathed to us by the first four years of Soviet power with the recent assessments of that period by historians and sociologists, one is struck by the phantasmatic, delusional nature of the period's self-image. The vision of Soviet Russia that emerges from many of the era's texts is one of a unified, militant proletariat, single-mindedly struggling against fierce class enemies to establish a communist paradise. Demographic and economic data, however, depict this period, later enshrined as "War Communism," as one of fragmentation and class dissolution. Before falling under the spell of the corporal fantasies of the age, we should consider the evidence provided by present-day judgments.

For most of the four years separating the Revolution from the Tenth Party

---

1872, Omel'chenko was a specialist in mental diseases and the author of several political pamphlets.

[121] Omel'chenko, *Svobodnaia liubov' i sem'ia*, 43.

Congress, the Bolshevik government was at war. The urban population was decimated as lines of supply were blocked or obliterated. The population of Petersburg, the "cradle" of the workers' revolution, fell by 50 percent between 1917 and 1920,[122] that of Moscow by 40 percent, and overall the urban population decreased by almost a quarter.[123] The number of workers engaged in manufacturing and metallurgy fell by nearly half between 1918 and 1919.[124] Among Party members the percentage of workers dropped drastically between 1917 and 1920, from 60.2 to 43.8, while the percentage of peasant members rose from 7.6 to 25.1.[125] This statistic does not reflect an overall diminution in workers within the Party—that number climbed nearly three-fold, from 65,000 to nearly 189,000—but it shows the extent to which the Party owed its victory in the Civil War to its ability to win support outside its supposed urban power base. The Bolshevik victory was more the product of an alloyed than of a pure proletariat.

The War Communist era came to be regarded as one of great self-sacrifice and discipline in which committed communists, on the brink of starvation, battled the enemy. This picture probably is more accurate than not, but we should beware of a certain mnemonic hypocrisy that tends to color subsequent Russian depiction of the Civil War. While NEP would be the epoch most closely linked in the popular imagination to speculation and economic profiteering, those activities probably had their heyday during War Communism. The cities and the proletariat survived the Civil War—albeit barely—only by relying on illegal trade in bread and other foodstuffs.[126] The black market was often essential to the physical survival of the most ideologically devout communists.[127] By the same token, the realms of literature and the arts, although pervaded by a rhetoric of homogeneity and uniformity, showed remarkable diversity throughout the period of War Communism.

We can read the texts that we will soon encounter as an example of a necessary delusion. Cognizant of the illusory nature of the era's ideological fantasies, Leopold Haimson nevertheless argues that it would be a grave mistake "to fail to recognize the crucial significance of these representations in the shaping of political and social attitudes and patterns of collective

[122] V. M. Selunskaia, ed., *Izmeneniia sotsial'noi struktury sovetskogo obshchestva. Oktiabr' 1917–1920* (M.: Mysl', 1976), 143.

[123] Daniel R. Brower, "'The City in Danger': The Civil War and the Russian Urban Population," in *Party, State and Society in the Civil War: Explorations in Soviet History*, ed. Diane P. Koenker, William G. Rosenberg, and Ronald Grigor Suny (Bloomington: Indiana University Press, 1989), 61 (58–80).

[124] Selunskaia, *Izmeneniia. . . . 1917–1920*, 141.

[125] Ibid., 149.

[126] Mary McAuley, "Bread without the Bourgeoisie," in Koenker et al., *Party, State and Society*, 159, 167–173 (158–179).

[127] Alan M. Ball, *Russia's Last Capitalists: The Nepmen 1921–1929* (Berkeley and Los Angeles: University of California Press, 1990), 7–9.

behavior, especially during those periods of acute political and social crisis when members of various social groups had to decide who they were, in order to determine how they should feel, think, and ultimately act."[128]

The ideological fantasies of War Communism would assume a markedly nostalgic power during the subsequent era of NEP. Discussing the tasks of his university in 1925, Rector Liadov saw one of his goals as the recuperation for his students of the fondly regarded earlier age:

> Looking back at the years of War Communism one must be astonished at how unerringly class instinct functioned then among the vast majority of rank-and-file Party workers. What a harmonious orchestra was represented by our Party apparatus. How sensitively it changed the tempo and direction of its work, following the conductor's baton at the center. [. . .] Every participant of the struggle was penetrated through and through with one and the same basic idea, acted in accordance with the same basic method [revolutionary Marxism].[129]

The very term "War Communism," at least as applied to Soviet policies before 1921, was first coined by Lenin in a brochure published only in May 1921 and subtitled "The Meaning of the New Policy and Its Conditions," a detail that heightens its status as a signifier of NEP.[130]

My purpose in this section will not be to present a complete portrait of the ideological landscape of the period antedating 1921. Rather, I will focus on two discourses that would exert a powerful influence on the ideological meaning of sex during NEP. Both relied—one explicitly, the other implicitly—on sexualized political rhetoric and, quite often, on a rhetoric of rape.

The pre-Revolutionary texts already discussed suggest the extent to which sex served in the years leading up to 1917 as a sign of the speaker's point of rapport with an ideal community. After the Revolution, writers who sought, sincerely or opportunistically, to ride the crest of the wave of political change quickly made use of the existent sexual discourse. Boris Pil'niak's

---

[128] Leopold H. Haimson, "Civil War and the Problem of Social Identities in Early Twentieth-Century Russia," in Koenker et al., *Party, State and Society*, 27–8 (24–47). For a similar argument, that the importance of War Communism lay primarily in the "qualitative" changes wrought by the period in social attitudes and values, see V. P. Buldakov and V. V. Kabanov, "'Voennyi kommunizm': Ideologiia i obshchestvennoe razvitie," *Voprosy istorii*, no. 3 (1990): 56–58 (40–58).

[129] M. N. Liadov, "O zadachakh komuniversiteta imeni Ia. M. Sverdlova," *Metodika prepodavaniia obshchestvennykh nauk v komvuzakh, sovpartshkolakh i shkolakh politgramoty* (L., 1925), 68–69 (63–78).

[130] V. I. Lenin, "O prodovol'stvennom naloge (Znachenie novoi politiki i ee usloviia)" (May 1921), *Polnoe sobranie sochinenii*, 5th ed., 45 vols. (M.: Gos. izd., 1958–1965), 43:219–220. One historian goes so far as to argue that "the only reality assumed by War Communism was retrospective, that is as a foil against which could be highlighted more 'realistic,' or even 'human' policies." Lewis H. Siegelbaum, *Soviet State and Society between Revolutions, 1918–1929* (Cambridge: Cambridge University Press, 1992), 66.

The Naked Year, the most resonant literary document generated by the War Communist era, was written by a "fellow traveler" who fervently strove to turn himself into Russia's first Revolutionary Writer. The novel set the tone for many depictions of the Revolution.[131] Like Pil'niak's other fiction of the early 1920s, it portrays the Revolution as an exhilarating destructive force that strips away centuries of civilization, leaving man in the clutches of paganism, violence, and sexuality. For Pil'niak, the Revolution returns man to a nearly animal, sexually charged, state of existence. His writing frequently reduces social upheaval to a man's taking the woman he desires into virtual sexual slavery on the steppe, to a crowded train car in which the feverish brain registers only the image of women leaning out the doors and squatting over the rails as they perform bodily functions. "Sex!" cries the delirious mind in Pil'niak's revolutionary world: "one wanted to scream, to hit out, to throw oneself on the nearest woman, be strong without measure and cruel, and here, in front of everyone, rape, rape, rape! Thought, nobility, shame, stoicism—to the Devil! Beast [*zver'*]!"[132]

Lines such as these seem to justify Artsybashev's prediction that if everything is allowed, no woman will be safe. Rape becomes the single most representative revolutionary act in Pil'niak's fiction. The author, however, does not limit his contemplation of revolutionary violation to a misogynistic leer; his gaze betrays a Rozanovian exultation in "the life of the species," in pregnancy, and in the functioning of the sex organs. "Beast" is a word with positive value, one flung by an excited and horrified fellow traveler in defiance of both bourgeois hypocrisy and Solov'ev's (or Berdiaev's or Fedorov's) insistence on the distinction of man from animal. "In what respect are animals bad?" Rozanov had demanded of one of Solov'ev's disciples,[133] a question that Pil'niak rephrases in a paean to the liberation of man's animal nature.

Rozanov's worship of sex undergoes a major revision as Pil'niak transposes it into the context of the Revolution. Pil'niak wrests Rozanov's deification of sex free from its domestic, essentially bourgeois setting; put to the service of the Revolution, sex becomes a violent, transformative force. In *this* return to the "life of the species," one of the first casualties is language, which is ripped apart and reduced to primordial sounds. And as language

[131] Boris Pil'niak, *Golyi god* (M.: Khudozhestvennaia literatura, 1976 [1922]), 35. The novel was apparently written in 1920 and 1921 and, thanks to public readings, became a part of Soviet literary life well before its publication. For Pil'niak's place in the early Soviet literary establishment, see Peter Alberg Jensen, *Nature as Code: The Achievement of Boris Pilnjak, 1915–1924* (Copenhagen: Rosenkilde and Bagger, 1979).

[132] Pil'niak, *Golyi god*, 149–150. This passage was first published in a fragment entitled "Poezd No. piatdesiat' sed'moi smeshannyi. Otryvok iz romana *Golyi god*," *Dom iskusstv*, no. 2 (1921): 38 (36–43).

[133] Rozanov, *Liudi lunnogo sveta*, 112.

reels backward to its origins, Artsybashev's figure of the writer as a master of sex is no longer tenable. With the disintegration of language and the release of words from grammatical and traditional literary fetters comes the escape of sexuality from the control of a writer's textual alter ego.

In Pil'niak's early Soviet works the figure of the writer is not merely dwarfed but obliterated by the Revolution. His (or frequently her) pen falls prey to sexual forces that the old bastion of culture cannot resist. His 1923 story "Old Cheese" begins with a letter from a Russian woman extolling the virtues of Western—and particularly British—civilization; subsequently she and the story's other first person narrator are raped by a group of Kirghiz nomads emboldened by Revolutionary chaos. Once she had walked about London, kissing the stones of Parliament; now she has learned "how much more ancient, how more significant—how much more terrible—is human life."[134] Another of Pil'niak's heroines—a Chekist named Katia—describes in a letter how she lost control, uttering cries that a stenographer could not record, as she interrogated the man who had taken her virginity and how, shooting him, she experienced sexual pleasure.[135] In a passage that aroused much comment and criticism, Katia suggests modifications to Marxist doctrine:

> [Karl Marx] took into consideration only physical hunger. He didn't take into account another thing that moves the world: love, love as blood, in the name of childbirth. Sex, the family, the species—mankind did not err when it deified sex.—Oh, yes—physical hunger and sexual hunger. That's very inaccurate: better to say—sexual hunger and the religion of sex, the religion of blood . . . [. . .] Sometimes I feel acutely, to the point of real, physical pain—I begin to feel that the entire world, all culture, all mankind, all things, chairs, chests of drawers, dresses,—are permeated by sex, no, that's not right, permeated—by sex organs, [. . .] I'm not alone. Sometimes my head begins to spin and I feel that the entire Revolution—the entire Revolution smells of sex organs.[136]

In this story the Red Terror becomes sexual terror; the Cheka, organ of Revolutionary control, becomes an instrument of sexual arousal and violence that can no longer control itself.

Not only the Cheka but, through it, the entire Revolution undergoes a

[134] Boris Pil'niak, "Staryi syr," in his *Mat' syra-zemlia* (M. and SPb.: Krug, 1923), 94. The story derives its name from the pub (Ye Olde Cheshire Cheese) frequented by Samuel Johnson and other luminaries of British civilization.

[135] Boris Pil'niak, *Smertel'noe manit* (M.: Grzebin, 1922), 159.

[136] Ibid., 154. Pil'niak's remark about the origin of the Revolution's intoxicating smell became the most frequently quoted line from his works in the 1920s, but only in this edition of the story did he actually speak his thought through. In another edition published the same year the sentence was amended to read elliptically, "The Revolution has begun to smell of ————." (i.e., "вся революция пропахла"————instead of "вся революция — пахнет половыми органами"), *Ivan da Mar'ia* (Berlin, SPb., and M.: Grzhebin, 1922), 71.

process of sexualization in Pil'niak's prose. This sexualization reworks pre-Revolutionary sexual philosophy in a strange pairing of Rozanov with his archenemy Weininger, for if the Revolution is the embodiment of Schopenhauer's *World as Will* and of Rozanov's idolatry of reproduction, it also catalyzes the incarnation of Weininger's mother/whore, copulating with everything with which it comes into contact. Contemplating the bloody sexualized world, Katia finds herself in the position of the hero of Andreev's "Abyss": her head spins and she begins to topple into the pit of her own desire.

In Pil'niak's work the Russian Revolution incarnates itself in a female body, a body no longer in control of itself, possessed by the forces it has unleashed—a body without a will. But while the Revolutionary body does experience the ecstasy of sexual gratification, its climaxes—in keeping with the pre-Revolutionary intelligentsia's rejection of pleasure for the sake of pleasure—are justified solely on the basis of reproduction. For Pil'niak, the Revolution functions as a paganistic fertility rite that overpowers the consciousness of the subject, who, violated, is forced to bear and bring forth a future that has been inflicted upon—rather than chosen by—her. In "Old Cheese," Maria, the devotee of British culture, is impregnated by her rapists:

> And just think about this good Russian woman, who loved the husband murdered by her rapists, this woman who up until the very day she gave birth did not know who was the father of her child—her husband who would never return and whose son would be the only memory of him, or the rapists who had profaned her soul and body.—And she gave birth to a small slant-eyed Kirghiz child, red, like all newborns. [. . .] So how did this mother react to her child? She lay there in the torments of birth; they were afraid to show [the child] to her, they gave it to her and—she took it to her breast, like all mothers, in that wonderful joy of being which has still not worn off from the secret of birth.[137]

In Pil'niak's world the Russian Revolution is akin to a rape of the West—and of Civilization—by the "life of the species." Raped, the West is forced to bring a strange being into the world and to love it. To be sure, this was a development of the Scythian theme so prominent in the Symbolist movement. But although the threat of violation may have been implicit in the hoofbeats of the Huns galloping westward in the Symbolists' imagination, it had never been stated so clearly and in such an explicitly sexual key. Moreover, we should not fail to note the gender and class dynamics of the Revolutionary rapes staged by Pil'niak. In these sexual narratives the Old World and the intelligentsia are feminized so that they can be violated, inseminated, and, ultimately, transformed and redeemed by the Revolution and the previously oppressed classes or peoples whom the Revolution represents.

The position of the *male* intellectual producing this influential representa-

---

[137] Pil'niak, "Staryi syr," 93.

tion of the Revolution as rape remains ambiguous. On one hand, as a representative of the intelligentsia, Pil'niak places himself in the position of a female victim, masochistically redeeming himself through symbolic castration and violation. On the other hand, as a man, Pil'niak may be seen as protectively distancing himself from the raped female figure upon whom his identity as an *intelligent* has been projected. The ambivalence of this representation of rape illustrates not only the political anxieties of the intelligentsia in the post-Revolutionary age but also and more generally the potential for political anxieties in Revolutionary Russia to seek resolution in the rhetoric and imagery of sex. We will encounter further instances during NEP of the use of violent sexual imagery as a tool for shoring up vulnerable political identity.[138]

Pil'niak was not the only writer who grasped the Revolution's potential as a vehicle for exploring sexuality and sexuality's potential as a means of investigating the Revolution. The availability of these themes emerges in sharp relief when we turn our eyes to decidedly second-rate scribblers. Shortly after the Revolution, Ippolit Rappgof, a prolific novelist and screenwriter who, as "Count Amori," had built a career by catering to sensationalistic tastes and had published his own conclusion to *The Pit* when Aleksandr Kuprin had been slow in finishing the final installment of his controversial novel about prostitution,[139] wrote *The New Decameron*, a series of tales comparing the hunger and starvation of Boccaccio's Italy to that of Revolutionary Russia. For the most part, Amori's work owed much to the subject matter and style of Artsybashev and other boulevard writers—he simply added bits of topical material. For example, in the midst of a story of a girl's seduction by her stepfather the reader discovers sentences such as "Kerensky's predictions, however, came to naught."[140]

A far more integral—and earlier—linkage of sexuality and the Revolution was Veniamin Stroev's 1918 novel *The New Woman* (*Femina Nova*), which concerns a girl's loss of innocence to her mother's anarchist lover in 1917.[141]

---

[138] My views on the significance of rape in Pil'niak's work have been influenced by several conversations with Igal Halfin and by a reading of a draft of his article "The Rape of the Intelligentsiia: A Proletarian Foundational Myth," forthcoming in the *Russian Review*. For a reading of gender in Pil'niak's work that places the author within a modernist rather than distinctly Russian or Soviet context, see Mary Nicholas, "Russian Modernism and the Female Voice: A Case Study," *Russian Review* 53 (1994): 530–548.

[139] Graf Amori, *Final. Roman iz sovremennoi zhizni. Okonchanie proizvedeniia "Iama" A. Kuprina*, 3d ed. (SPb.: N. I. Kholmushin, 1914).

[140] Graf Amori, *Novyi Dekameron* (M., 1922). The novel must have been written well before its publication date, for Count Amori vanished soon after the Revolution; by one account he was executed in 1918 when the Anarchist Republic that he had helped establish in Rostov-on-the-Don collapsed just one day after it took power. See E. T. Iaborova, "Graf Amori," *Russkie pisateli 1800–1917*, 5 vols. (M.: Bol'shaia rossiiskaia entsiklopediia, 1989–), 2:12–13.

[141] Stroev, whose real last name was Proper, was a prolific and, judging by the frequency with

The heroine's seducer is a Promethean figure who defies both God and the
Bolsheviks and enflames the young heroine with his words and kisses. The
book, presented through diary entries inscribed by the heroine between May
1914 and June 1918, is virtually a *Who's Who* of philosophers and poets
influential in pre-Revolutionary discussions about sex. The anarchist is a
Nietzschean who lapsed from socially useful work into depravity after the
failure of the 1905 Revolution but who now puts his oratorical charisma to
the service of the Revolution. Professing to be a student of Schopenhauer, he
refuses to acknowledge any power other than nature and, deriding Lenin,
takes the heroine to a poetry reading by the popular Symbolist Konstantin
Bal'mont.

The significance of *The New Woman* lies primarily in its date rather than
its literary merit. As early as 1918, Stroev had grasped the usefulness (in
terms of both plot and marketability) of identifying the Revolution with sexuality. The novel, moreover, is an early advocate of taming the Revolution's
sexual potential and of politically supervising sexuality so that Bolshevism
might profitably channel its energy. Stroev's heroine differs from her anarchist lover in that she respects discipline and organization. It is natural,
therefore, that she should find sex more intense and rewarding with a Bolshevik sailor. "Every atom of my being took part in this union," Stroev's
heroine writes of her first act of intercourse with an ideologically correct
partner.[142]

---

which his novels were reprinted, relatively successful author of topical novels in the pre-Revolutionary decade. His fiction prior to 1917 included *Explosion* (*Nadryv*), a novel first published
in 1914 that ran to four editions by 1916 and was followed by two sequels: *Intoxication* (*Ugar*)
and *Rupture* (*Perelom*). In addition, his pre-Revolutionary work encompassed topical brochures,
including *The Trial of Wilhelm*, an indictment not only of the kaiser but of the economic system
that produced the prewar arms race. *Sud nad Vil'gel'mom. Dolzhna li lit'sia krov'?* (M.: Moskovskoe izdatel'stvo, 1915). Of the works written before 1917, the most interesting for our
purposes is undoubtedly *Nonna*, the story of a woman author's career. The book begins as a
boulevard tale of seduction but soon switches genres and becomes the success story of a latter-
day Anna Karenina. It concludes with a utopian vision of a women's movement triumphant all
over Europe. (The novel is notable in the Russian context for its valorization of guilt-free
pleasure and its inclusion of a satisfying, unproblematic lesbian encounter in its account of its
heroine's love life.) *Nonna*, 2d ed. (M.: Stoliar, 1917). After the Revolution Stroev wrote several brochures and works of fiction for the Soviet state: *Doloi negramotnost'. P'esa v odnom
deistvii* (M. and L.: Doloi negramotnost', 1926); *Zhizn' i smert' Nikolaia Ernestovicha Bau-
mana* (M. and L.: Gos. izd., 1930); *K otkrytiiu monumental'nogo pamiatnika Nikolaiu Baumanu*
(M.: Sovet rabochikh i krasnoarmeiskikh deputatov, 1931). A quick glance at these later publications shows that Stroev was able to recycle scenes by simply inverting a topos: compare the
conclusions of *Nonna* and *The Life and Death of Nikolai Ernestovich Bauman*, both of which
end with the funerals of their heroes: "The people standing around wiped away the tears streaming from their eyes" (*Nonna*, 179) and "Comrade Bauman's funeral exuded military readiness.
There were no tears of weakness" (*Zhizn' i smert'*, 43).

[142] Veniamin Stroev, *Sovremennaia zhenshchina. (Femina Nova)* (M.: 1918), 143. Prior to

The Revolution wrought such cataclysmic changes in Russian society that many who lived through it experienced it as a real-life apocalypse. In keeping with the expectation of total, drastic transformation of all spheres of life, many Russian writers after 1917 began to take the language of social discourse in pre-Revolutionary society to maximal conclusions, to literalize (or materialize) figures of speech. Not surprisingly, metaphors emphasizing the collective dimension of an ideal sexuality became more simple, more accessible, and much more physical. The self-professed artists of proletarian culture who saw themselves taking over the intelligentsia's role did not merely vaunt social cohesiveness, they envisioned society as a collective body. Their orderly fantasy of a unified collective body stands in marked contrast to the chaotic vision of frenzied body organs that we find in the modernist vision of Pil'niak.

The collective body was a product of different groups and tendencies, but the leading role in its constitution was played by the Proletkul't. Founded in 1917, this organization was devoted to formulating and nurturing a uniquely proletarian worldview and claimed four hundred thousand members in three hundred local organizations by 1920.[143] Sponsoring journals and clubs through its local affiliates, the Proletkul't was an enormous platform for cultural influence not limited to Moscow and Petrograd but radiating outward to provincial cities.

The first book published by the Proletkul't—Aleksei Gastev's *Poetry of the Worker's Blow*—contained many works written prior to the Revolution but which, when published together in 1918, became emblematic of the new discourse. All editions of Gastev's collection began with a poem, "We Grow from Iron," that set the physiological tone for the entire volume and for hundreds of Proletkul't verses modeled on it. The poem's lyric "I" gazes at a factory and compares the beams supporting it to a "giant's shoulders," a sight inspiring him to feel transformed into an enormous body with steel shoulders and "iron blood." The persona's body begins to merge with the body of the factory, and at the poem's conclusion Gastev emphasizes his work's collective dimension, stressing that his "I" is really a "We." Gastev's factory, in effect, furnishes the working class with a phallic cathedral in which the boundaries among workers and between workers and machines dissolve. As Gastev writes in another prose poem from his collection:

Femina Nova Stroev's work frequently used the author-as-protagonist-and-seducer trope that we have seen employed by Artsybashev and Kuprin. By 1917 Stroev had already realized that he would have to sacrifice his alter ego's sexual prowess to the Party.

[143] Lynn Mally, *Culture of the Future: The Proletkult Movement in Revolutionary Russia* (Berkeley and Los Angeles: University of California Press, 1990), xix.

The crane's tense metal grew warm, burned, and was transformed. Fused, soldered, the crane discovered its tempered metallic blood, became a single monster . . . with eyes, with a heart, with a soul, and with ideas.

In friendship it infected millions of its worker-builders with its iron thoughts.

Both the crane and the human million grew exceptionally, fantastically defiant.[144]

The impact of Gastev's book—and of its images of united corporeal power—was tremendous.[145] Soon collective bodies were appearing on the pages of Proletkul't journals across Russia. Most of the poems were undistinguished, their vocabulary limited, and their range of technical imagery narrow, features that attest to the naive sincerity motivating these unsophisticated poets and the extent to which the collective body was internalized and transformed into a staple of War Communist discourse.

In 1919, the regional committee of the Party in Nizhnii Novgorod published a thin volume by a young poet named Sergei Malashkin. The book does not stand out from countless other samples I might have chosen, except, perhaps, for the fact that one of the poems may have been the first of thousands of Russian verses dedicated over the ensuing decades to one of Stalin's premier associates, Lazar Kaganovich. In view of the important role Malashkin would play in the molding of the Soviet body during NEP, however, it is worthwhile choosing his poetry as a representative text and noting that his career began with the image of the body fostered by the Proletkul't. Malashkin's book was entitled *Muscles*; its opening poem, "The Course of Work," began as follows:

> О, мускулы сурового труда,
> О, мышцы рук, о мышцы гулких ног,
> От вас жужжит, как пчелы: провода,
> Шипят, как змеи, колени дорог.
> От вас, забыв кровавые года,
> Апофеоз костей глубокий стон,
> Кровавят небо радостью знамен
> деревни, станции и города.
> От вас заводов, фабрик корпуса,
> Нарывы гнойных шахт и рудников
> таращат яростно свои глаза
> И смотрят электричеством зрачков.
> О, мускулы, о, мышцы, жизнь от вас,

---

[144] Aleksei Gastev, *Poeziia rabochego udara* (M.: Khudozhestvennaia literatura, 1971), 127.

[145] For a more detailed consideration of Gastev and his significance, see Kendall E. Bailes, "Alexei Gastev and the Soviet Controversy over Taylorism, 1918–1924," *Soviet Studies* 19 (1977): 373–394.

О камни, о бетон и о гранит
Железом лязгая—громокипит
И славит вас и творчества экстаз.

[O muscles of stern labor, O muscles of arms, O muscles of rumbling legs, you make the wires buzz like bees, you make the bends [or knees] of the roads hiss like snakes. Villages, stations, and cities, having forgotten the bloody years, the apotheosis of bones, the deep groan, turn the sky red with the joy of banners— all because of you. It is because of you that the bodies of factories and plants, the abscesses of purulent mines and pits, goggle their eyes and gaze with the electricity of their pupils. O muscles, O muscles, life comes from you, and scraping with iron against stone, concrete, and granite, it thunderously boils and glorifies you and the ecstasy of creation.][146]

In the poem Malashkin does not find it necessary to mention to whom the muscles belong—*that* would entail excessive individuation, a violation of the collective principle. All of Russia is a body, and its eyes—body parts that observe rather than do—watch with fury as proletarian muscles empower arms and legs across the land.

Virtually all Proletkul't writing was informed by a joy of incarnation, by a delight in seeing the cosmos take new form as flesh. According to one proletarian poet, the essence of the new beauty that the Revolution was bringing into being was "the unmediated possibility for [man] to incarnate everything through himself."[147] A decade earlier, as he broke away from the spiritual chains of Symbolism for the earthbound solidity of Acmeism, Osip Mandel'shtam had rediscovered physicality and asked: "A body has been given to me. What shall I do with it, so unique and so very mine?"[148] The Proletkul't also marveled at the human form but emphasized that its awe originated in the body's being so collective, so uniquely *ours*. The individual body was beautiful for the Proletkul't only as synecdoche; Man's body, not *a* man's body, was the Proletkul't's concern.

In poetry written by poets outside the Proletkul't, one also finds this transition from a lyric "I" (a poet's concrete alter ego) to a gigantic "Everyproletarian" capable of incarnating "everything." The deeply personal "I" of Maiakovsky's longer pre-Revolutionary poems yielded its place during War Communism to the collective body of his "150,000,000," a long work in

[146] Sergei Malashkin, *Muskuly. Poemy* (Nizhnii Novgorod: Nizh.-Novgorodskii gubernskii komitet R.K.P., 1919), 5. The book contained a declaration that "all pure profit" from its sales would be donated to "the families of communists who have fallen in battle with the Counter-Revolutionaries."

[147] A. Mgebrov, "Proletarskaia kul'tura," *Griadushchee*, no. 1 (1919): 23.

[148] Osip Mandel'shtam, *Sobranie sochinenii v trekh tomakh* (Washington: Inter-Language Literary Association, 1967), 1:6.

which virtually all matter—organic and inorganic—in Russia unites into a single colossus to battle capitalism.[149]

While Mandel'shtam had attempted—through a language of physicality and incarnation—to bring poetry down from the heavens, the Proletkul't sought to send the poeticized body skyward. Proletkul't physicality was not bound by earthly desires. In Proletkul't poetry, love is not overtly sexual, nor is it cheapened by desire for a single other. Rather, desire is transformed into worship of the factory:

> Люблю я наш завод большой
> Люблю его я всей душой
> Он для меня милей всего,
> Милее матери родной,
> Милее красавицы любой,
> Люблю, люблю, люблю его (and so on)

> [I love my big factory,
> I love it with all my soul,
> It is dearer to me than anything,
> Dearer than my own mother,
> Dearer than any beauty,
> I love, I love, I love it. . . .][150]

This poem by Doronin is atypically sentimental and restrained in its use of transgressive rhetoric. Most Proletkul't verse was far more violent. Rather than simply dismissing mothers as less valued objects, many of the Proletkul't's leading figures resorted to images of symbolic sexual assault. Their approach, though, differed fundamentally from Pil'niak's. Both Pil'niak's and the Proletkul't's visions of the Revolution revolved around images of violation, but Pil'niak focused on the subjectivity of a female body upon which the Revolution violently inscribes itself, while the Proletkul't poets identified with a decisively male collective body eternally in the process of penetrating female surrogates.[151] Gastev's "Tower," reproduced in many Proletkul't journals, is a prose poem dedicated to phallic construction and to

[149] Maiakovskii, *Sochineniia v trekh tomakh* (M: Khudozhestvennaia literatura, 1965), 3:94–137. As if to stress the break with his earlier, self-aggrandizing work, Maiakovskii originally published "150,000,000" anonymously.

[150] I. Doronin, "Liubliu ia nash zavod bol'shoi," *Proletarskoe stroitel'stvo*, no. 7 (1920): 34. Since "factory" is a masculine noun in Russian, one might replace "it" with "He" and "him" in the quoted passage, a substitution that would be fully in keeping with the Proletkul't's tendency to masculinize both subject and beloved object in its rendition of Revolutionary desire.

[151] Compare Roman Jakobson's definition of verbal art as "the raped word." "O khudozhestvennom realizme," in *Readings in Russian Poetics*, ed. Ladislav Matejka, Michigan Slavic Materials, vol. 2 (Ann Arbor: University of Michigan Press, 1962), 32. Jakobson's article first appeared (in Czech) in 1921 but may be read as springing from the same tradition of sexualized aesthetic discourse (Maiakovskii, Shklovskii) that inspired War Communist rhetoric.

proletarian man's collective assault on the earth. The tower's foundation is laid only after a frantic effort to excavate the hard ground, to drill holes into it, to pour concrete supports. After the initial murderous battle with the earth has been concluded and the tower built, the pit from which the tower emerged still remains a threat:

> Those who have risen to the top, to the spire, suddenly will be burned by a horrible doubt: perhaps the tower does not exist, perhaps it's only a mirage, a fantasy of metal, granite, concrete, all dream. Suddenly the dream will be cut short, and below them will open that same bottomless gulf, the grave.[152]

This moment is Gastev's version of Andreev's "Abyss" and reveals the extent to which the Proletkul't saw its phallic self always threatened and at war with the feminine embodiment of nature, with a biological *reality* ever capable of exposing the illusory dimension of Revolutionary transformation. The observation of the most thorough student to date of the Proletkul't movement, Lynn Mally, that "women and children were minor, almost missing, themes in the factory-centered thematic of Proletkul't creation,"[153] is true only in the most literal sense, for women and the family were emphatically present in symbolic form, represented by the forces of nature and matter that the Proletkul't had yet to conquer.

Occasionally women surface in literal, less mythologized guise but are invoked only for the sake of their rejection. Pavel Arsky's 1920 poem "To a Girl Arriving in the City" pointedly rebuffs femininity's invasion of masculine, urban turf and woman's attempt to captivate the working man:

> Меня пленил румянец щек,
> Покрытых бронзовым загаром . . .
> И в сердце сплав горячий втек,
> Зажег лазоревым пожаром.
> Но в пыльной, дымной мастерской
> Струится белый блеск металла . . .
> И жгучей зацвели тоской
> На шее алые кораллы [. . .]
> Мне люб громопевучий мех,
> Удары молота и звоны.
> Тебе же — ландышевый смех,
> Лесные тихие затоны. . . .
> У голубых озер в плену
> Твоя печаль, тоска и думы.
> Тебе, влюбленной в тишину,
> Не внятны пламенные шумы.

---

[152] Gastev, *Poeziia rabochego udara*, 123.
[153] Mally, *Culture of the Future*, 176.

[I was captivated by the rosiness of your cheeks,
Covered with a bronze tan . . .
And into my heart a burning alloy flowed,
And ignited with an azure fire.
But in the dusty, smoky workshop
The white shine of metal streams. . . .
And the crimson coral beads on your neck
Bloomed with burning melancholy [. . .]
I hold the thunder-singing bellows dear,
And the blows and peals of the hammers.
While you like lily-of-the-valley laughter,
And the quiet sylvan backwaters.
Your sorrow, melancholy, and thoughts
Are in thrall to the deep lakes.
In love with quiet,
You don't heed the fiery sounds.][154]

The banishment of love—in the person of a peasant woman who, it turns out, cannot be incorporated in a Proletkul't "alloy"—had its parallel in the Proletkul't's frequent disparagement of the family, mothers, and maternity. The Proletkul't was touted as a "public hearth," designed, according to its president, "to create an atmosphere [. . .] where a person can learn to work in public life, freed from the clutches of petty family life."[155] Doronin was not alone in boasting that his factory was dearer to him than his mother; one of his colleagues proclaimed:

Здесь мы чужие, и зажигаем
Мертвую землю до конца.
Мать никакая нас не родила,
Руку невесты никто не держал.

[Here we are strangers and we ignite
The dead Earth from end to end.
No mother gave birth to us,
None of us has held the hand of a sweetheart.][156]

In the course of an attack on Futurist poetry, Pavel Bessal'ko, an editor of the Proletkul't journal *Griadushchee* (The future), declared, "As far as its content is concerned, [Futurism] is in no way innovative or original, save for a single, piquant desire of Marinetti, the father of Futurism, to give birth to a son without the help of a woman."[157] The dominant interpersonal dynamic in

[154] Pavel Arskii, "Devushke, prishedshei v gorod," *Griadushchee*, nos. 7–8 (1920): 1.
[155] Pavel Lebedev-Polianskii, quoted in Mally, *Culture of the Future*, 184, 176.
[156] Andrei Platonov, "Pakhar," *Voronezhskaia kommuna*, 7 November 1920, 5.
[157] P. Bezsalko (*sic!*) and F. Kalinin, *Problemy proletarskoi kul'tury* (SPb.: Antei, 1919), 39.

Proletkul't rhetoric was not reproduction, however, but universal production through masculine conglomeration. Rozanov, exulting in the life cycle (and, although here sotto voce, in the submissive role of women in it) had asked: "What are a grandfather, father, and grandson? A giant as big as a house who has been broken into three parts: one part sixty years old, another thirty, a third two."[158] The Proletkul't was insisting that that masculine giant be put back together again, and the eclipse of woman and her reproductive role was a price the Proletkul't—like Fedorov a generation earlier—was eager to pay for this bit of utopian reconstruction.[159] The eclipse (if not destruction) of the feminine was typical of early Soviet iconography outside as well as within the Proletkul't. War Communist imagery resolutely ignored the human female form, even allegorical representations of the sort to which the French revolutionary tradition was so indebted.[160]

So far we have been dealing with poetic images. Those of the Proletkul't were taken seriously in a way in which poetic images rarely are—they were hyperbolized and came to dominate other genres of social discourse. At a time of maximalist, utopian yearning and national conflict, genres of social discourse other than "pure" poetry were rhetorically poeticized to a heightened degree. Proletkul't literary critics were also critics of culture, and they nurtured the language of the collective body because they saw its value when projected off the page into "real" life. Fedor Kalinin, a vice president of the Proletkul't and director of the Proletkul't section of the Commissariat of Enlightenment, commended Gastev for leaving "no place for the individual I or the spirit of individualism." In Gastev's poetry there was only "a many-faced [mnogolikoe], immeasurably large, incalculable 'we,' and this 'we' inspires the proletariat, perfects and forges the 'worker-creator-man.'"[161] In writings where literature was not explicitly mentioned, the collective body still played an essential part in the Proletkul't's worldview. In their manifesto, Against Civilization, Evgeny Poletaev, a former clerk and now a

---

[158] Rozanov, Liudi lunnogo sveta, 77.

[159] The influence of the utopian (or "totalitarian") Russian religious-philosophical tradition on the Proletkul't deserves further study. In any event, the poets of the Proletkul't, like Gor'kii before them, frequently relied on Christian imagery repackaged in a proletarian, Promethean context. For Fedorov's influence on Gor'kii and the Proletkul't, see Semenova, Nikolai Fedorov, 349–363 and Masing-Delich, Abolishing Death, 123–154.

[160] For a discussion of this divergence of Russian from Western revolutionary representations, see Elizabeth Waters, "The Female Form in Soviet Political Iconography, 1917–1932," in Russia's Women: Accommodation, Resistance, Transformation, ed. Barbara Evans Clement, Barbara Alpern Engel, and Christine D. Worobec (Berkeley and Los Angeles: University of California Press, 1991), 185–207.

[161] Bezsalko and Kalinin, Problemy proletarskoi kul'tury, 126. Mally's Culture of the Future provides biographical information on these two authors and many more of the Proletkul't's more prominent participants, as does the first edition of the Literaturnaia entsiklopediia, 10 vols. (M.: Kommunisticheskaia akademiia, 1930–1939).

Proletkul't editor and poet, and Nikolai Punin, the Enlightenment Ministry's director of the Petrograd Division for Graphic Arts as well as the "commissar" of the Hermitage and the Russian Museum, predicted that the people of the future would "smile when they talk about the time when it was considered shameful to share a single heart with one's people, to breathe with the people with a single breast, to see with its eyes, to feel mechanically the clear and powerful union of one with all."[162] The genre of journalistic encomium was also affected:

> The Revolution is the biggest and the most real person on Earth. And Lunacharsky is the tenderest curve, the most formidable bend of its brain, that tensed nerve, in which a thought begins to twitch and to which it returns, laden with feelings and representations, and where for the last time [a thought] catches fire and burns with the bright flame of pure consciousness, with the light of the soul that has just begun to see.[163]

Despite the neurological extreme to which he here took physiological metaphor, Andrei Platonov, writing political-literary commentary in prose, was still confining himself to a figure of speech. The notion of a collective body was used far more literally in the work of a practicing neurologist (and psychiatrist), Vladimir Bekhterev, whom we met earlier rejecting intercourse for pleasure's sake in his introduction to the Russian edition of Forel's *Sexual Question*. Elected president of the Psychoneurological Institute in 1907 and sympathetic to the Bolsheviks since 1917, Bekhterev had founded the Institute for Brain Research and become one of the most influential figures in Soviet medicine and psychology. In 1921 he published *Collective Reflexology*, on which he claimed to have been working for a decade. We can only speculate whether the work would have appeared had there been no October Revolution; in any case its appearance in 1921 placed the book squarely within the discourse of collective corporeality.

Collective Reflexology begins with an attack on subjective, sociological notions of collectivity that use terms like "collective soul," "collective consciousness," and "collective will"; in something of a semantic sleight of hand, Bekhterev proposed to study "collective reflexology" instead. Bekhterev insisted that "the laws for the manifestation of a collective's activity are the same as the laws for the manifestation of an individual personality's activity": "in the manifestations of social life [. . .] we essentially meet with the same reflexes, in the form of social movements and their course of development, as we find in the activity of an individual personality."[164] "Each

---

[162] Evgenii Poletaev and Nikolai Punin, *Protiv tsivilizatsii* (Pg., 1918), 38. For a biographical sketch of Punin's life and work, see N. N. Punin, *Russkoe i sovetskoe iskusstvo* (M.: Sovetskii khudozhnik, 1976), 244–246.

[163] Andrei Platonov, "Lunacharskii," *Krasnaia derevnia*, 22 July 1920, 2.

[164] V. M. Bekhterev, *Kollektivnaia refleksologiia* (Pg.: Kolos, 1921), 13. For Bekhterev's ca-

collective," he contended, "is a unique collective organism with its own history, for it is conceived, grows, and develops in certain conditions only to disintegrate and die after a longer or shorter life, often being transformed into other collective forms." "As a collective organism," he continued, "a collective has its own mood, its own power of observation and of impression, its own views, judgments, and acts, which often do not correspond in all respects with those of the individual personalities who make up the collective."[165] This last point was crucial. For Bekhterev, the beauty of the collective organism was that when the individual's interests clashed with the interests of the collective, the latter took precedence.[166]

What happened when the poet most responsible for the prominence of the collective body no longer perceived that corporeal collectivity was only a trope? In summer of 1919 Aleksei Gastev published an article entitled "Tendencies of Proletarian Culture." Proceeding from the Marxist premise that material conditions determine consciousness, Gastev argued that as production became more standardized, so would all other aspects of proletarian life. "Gradually, standardizing tendencies will increase and work their way into the confrontational forms assumed by workers' movements: into wildcat strikes and sabotage, into social creativity, eating, living quarters, and, finally, even into the proletarian's intimate life, up to and including the aesthetic, mental, and sexual needs of the proletarian class."[167] Other members of the Proletkul't writing in the same issue of *Proletarskaia kul'tura* were horrified by Gastev's conclusions. Fedor Kalinin accused him of fetishizing technology. "One mustn't forget," Kalinin argued, "that the life of a worker is not limited to his profession; he also has a life outside the factory that is profoundly complex and varied and which is also determined by his class situation."[168] Proletkul't discourse, however, had *already* subsumed this life within the factory's walls; not much Proletkul't poetry existed about the conditions of everyday life. On the level of his language and imagery, Gastev was saying little new when he contended that the proletariat's psychology was shaped primarily by the conditions of its industrial life alone. Gastev's belief that standardization of production would lead to standardization of psychology and even of sexual desire flowed naturally from the tropes of Proletkul't poetry and from the assumption that the proletariat had a collec-

---

reer before and after the Revolution, see David Joravsky, *Russian Psychology: A Critical History* (Oxford: Blackwell, 1989), 83–91, 271–281, and A. S. Nikiforov, *Bekhterev* (M.: Molodaia gvardiia, 1986).

[165] Bekhterev, *Kollektivnaia refleksologiia*, 88.

[166] Ibid.

[167] Aleksei Gastev, "O tendentsiiakh proletarskoi kul'tury," *Proletarskaia kul'tura*, 1919, nos. 9–10, 43 (35–45).

[168] Fedor Kalinin, "Proletarskaia kul'tura i ee kritiki," *Proletarskaia kul'tura*, 1919, nos. 9–10, 3.

tive body. In his vision of the future, not only would the details of everyday life become standardized, but all the trappings of individual man as he then existed would fall away, leaving nameless workers whose thoughts would be directed by a common mechanism:

> The "machinization" not only of gestures, not only of productive methods, but also the "machinization" of everyday thought, in conjunction with maximal objectivity, will standardize the proletarian psychology to an astounding degree. [. . .] Perhaps there is not yet an international language, but there are international gestures and international psychological formulae possessed by millions. It is this feature which endows proletarian psychology with a striking anonymity that permits the qualification of every separate proletarian unit [*edinitsa*] as A, D, C, or even as 325, 075, 0, and so on. [. . .] From one end of the earth to the other, powerful, weighty psychological currents are in motion for which there are no longer millions of heads but one global head. In the future, this tendency will lead imperceptibly to the impossibility of individual thought, which will be transformed into the objective psychology of an entire class with systems of psychological ignition, shutdown, and circuiting.[169]

As worker psychology became more standardized and the Revolutionary body grew increasingly collective, what would happen to the concept of pleasure? We have already seen that prior to the Revolution various philosophers, artists, and even doctors had deemed pleasure an insufficient justification for sexual intercourse because it occurred between two individuals rather than "communally," or "collectively," among all members of society.[170] With the advent of the collective body, would pleasure become obsolete, or would it, too, be collectivized? In *Against Civilization*, Poletaev and Punin, while attacking pleasure as generally belonging to the individualistic category of "civilization" rather than to the collective ideal of "culture," predicted that pleasure would be redeemed in the communist future: "The society of culture will not reject pleasures and will fear neither their qualitative nor quantitative use. But this use will be regulated by an institutional structure [*apparat*] so that a simple means of relaxation does not become the goal of vital individual and societal efforts."[171] In a footnote, they added: "Love will vanish, that is, love as the cult or idealization of an individual man or woman[. . . .] Even love, simple love itself, will undergo fundamental disinfection, because often it is no more than an acute psychosis and a socially

---

[169] Gastev, "O tendentsiiakh proletarskoi kul'tury," 44.

[170] The word "*soborno*" ("catholically" or "communally") more or less disappears from social commentary after the Revolution. Often, however, Solov'ev's communal ideals echo in discussions of "collective" rather than "catholic" goals.

[171] Poletaev and Punin, *Protiv tsivilizatsii*, 44.

detrimental waste of energy. In the society of culture, love is possible only in the broadest sense of the word."[172]

The idea that sexual activity could be dangerous to the individual because it entailed a loss of vital energy (the theory of the "spermatic economy") had been widespread in nineteenth-century Europe and America.[173] Society's new status as a single entity, however, had transformed the link between sexual activity and the depletion of energy into a phenomenon that affected all areas of social and economic interaction. Moreover, since the collective body had been born in an industrial context, this conceit of intercourse as entropy lost its status as *metaphor*: Punin and Poletaev conceived of the energy lost through love as a genuinely squandered *economic* resource.

What did Poletaev and Punin mean when they said that in the future love would be possible only "in the broadest sense of the word"? Emmanuil Enchmen stepped in to provide an answer. An obscure figure, who rose by 1921 to the position of scholarly consultant to Mikhail Pokrovsky, the deputy commissar of enlightenment, Enchmen was the author of *Eighteen Theses on the "Theory of New Biology": A Project for the Organization of a Revolutionary-Scientific Council of the Republic and for the Introduction of a System of Physiological Passports*, published under Party auspices in 1919 and 1920. The brochure, claiming to be a summary of a longer work in progress, was completed in Saratov in December 1919 and was a product of War Communism. Enchmen later wrote that it had been written "on the Red Front, literally under the roar of artillery."[174] In some quarters the book was widely read. At several institutes of higher learning, circles were formed by his young adherents (known as *"TNBisty,"* from his "Theory of New Biology") to study his work.[175] Within a few years he had attracted a large enough following for Bukharin to publish a refutation of its Marxist bona fides in *Krasnaia nov'*, the leading political and cultural journal in the early 1920s.[176]

[172] Ibid.

[173] On this point, see G. J. Barker-Benfield, *The Horrors of the Half-Known Life*, 175–189.

[174] Emmanuil Enchmen, *Teoriia novoi biologii i marksizm* (Pb.: Rabochii fakul'tet peterburgskogo gos. universiteta, 1923), 29.

[175] P. V. Alekseev, ed., *Na Perelome: Filosofskie diskussii 20-kh godov* (M.: Politicheskaia literatura, 1990), 508.

[176] Nikolai Bukharin, "Enchmeniada (K voprosu ob ideologicheskom vyrozhdenii)," *Krasnaia nov'*, no. 6 (1923): 145–179. Bukharin's article was published as a separate brochure in 1923 and included in his 1924 anthology of articles *Ataka*. Enchmen and his place in early Soviet culture merit further investigation. He has been all but ignored by Western historians. Very little biographical information is provided in the commentaries accompanying two recently published fragments of his work; my statement concerning his attachment to Pokrovskii rests on a passing reference made to Enchmen in an article devoted to the evolution of the Soviet government's attitude toward Pavlov. See Viktor Topolianskii, "O golode, refleksakh i zapiatoi," *Literaturnaia*

Enchmen's brochure is replete with vague—but superficially mathematical and even Pavlovian—blueprints, and its argumentation is convoluted, but one quickly sees what made it attractive to idealistic young members of the new communist society. Coining a term, "stenism," which he defined as "joyfulness" (*radostnost'*), Enchmen tried to explain "how the epoch of communism will be regarded by communist humanity not in accordance with the temporary aesthetic formula: 'from each according to his abilities, to each according to his needs,' but as an era of complete leveling of all human organisms in a tension of 'uninterrupted joyfulness,' in a 'coefficient of uninterrupted stenism.'"[177] His still unwritten book, "The Theory of New Biology," he professed, would show how communist society could increase the level of its stenism, "using all the 'organic stimuli' [*organicheskie razdrazhiteli*] at its disposal," until "the present division of labor and consumption vanishes, merging into a general concept of 'systems of organic movements, reactions, systems of coupling, chains of reaction.'"[178] Joyfulness, however, would have to be rationed. Enchmen explained:

> The author of the Theory of New Biology [will] tell the organism [i.e., his reader] how the communist economy [of the future] will be founded on a system of "physiological passports" for all human organisms; moreover, each such passport shall numerically specify the tension and strength ("the coefficient of conservation of reactions" [*koeffitsienty konservativnosti reaktsii*]) of the most essential reactions (chains of reflexes) of the specific human organism to which the passport has been issued by a specific organ of communist consumption (the *Revnauchsovet*). The passport will also specify the coefficient of joyfulness, of stenism, for that year or for a fixed interval of time in the communist economy. The author will show how this "physiological passport" will serve the organism as—to use today's language—a ration card [*kartochka*] for both work and consumption in the widest sense of the word, how communist administration will at certain times reissue all physiological passports, as soon as data appear which lead one to presume that during the preceding period essential physiological changes have occurred in the human organism.[179]

Enchmen's language is extremely abstruse, yet his general drift is not so different from Gastev's nor from the sentiments implicit in Proletkul't verse.

---

gazeta, 22 March 1995, 5. Cf. Alekseev, *Na Perelome*, 508, and Iosif Sheiman, "Iz istorii nauki," *Khudozhestvennaia volia*, no. 7 (1993): 6–8.

[177] Emmanuil Enchmen, *Vosemnadtsat' tezisov o "teorii novoi biologii" (proekt organizatsii Revoliutsionno-Nauchnogo Soveta Respubliki i vvedeniia sistemy fiziologichesogo passporta)* (Piatigorsk: In.K.O. Severo-Kavkazskogo Revoliutsionnogo Komiteta, 1920), 34.

[178] Ibid., 34–35.

[179] Ibid., 35. The parentheses are Enchmen's. The term "Revnauchsovet" is based on an analogy with "Revvoensovet" (the Revolutionary military council) and indicates the degree to which Enchmen's collectivity is part of the War Communist ethos.

What he was advocating was not only the collectivization of the human body but also the collectivization of that body's functions, pleasures, and desires.

In Enchmen's book, names become virtually obsolete. The reader is referred to simply as "the organism," and a certain Athenian philosopher is referred to as "the organism famous in history under the name of Plato."[180] It is not so far from this language or from the numbers and letters used by Gastev to designate proletarian units to the language of "the United State" in Evgeny Zamiatin's dystopian novel, *We* (1920), in which all citizens are designated by letters and numbers.

Zamiatin's novel about the horrors of a futuristic "United State" is profoundly critical of War Communism's "scientific" language, portraying it as a type of collective insanity; his narrator-citizen owes much not only to the likes of Gastev and Enchmen but also to the narrator of Gogol's "Diary of a Madman." Bukharin was to observe that from an orthodox Marxist point of view Enchmen had pressed the biological analogy to the point where its original sociological context was virtually lost, where it became collective *individualism* on a grand corporal scale. Zamiatin appears to have understood that this critique might be made about War Communist rhetoric as a whole. Teasing out—in a sexual context—the logic of War Communist discourse, Zamiatin shows what happens when a nation does indeed collectivize love. In a scene near the end of the novel, Zamiatin exposes the true nature of the only type of sexual behavior the collective body can engage in—the only form remaining when individual differentiation and "the Other" no longer exist. As she plans a rebellion against the oppressive United State, the mysterious "I-330" instructs Zamiatin's hero-chronicler to pretend at a later time that she is with him and to lower the shade of his room—a conventional sign in the United State that sexual intercourse is occurring within.[181] This scene essentially "lays bare" one of the sexual consequences of War Communist mentality, for when all society is bound up in a collective body, the sole sexual activity that can occur is masturbation.

The importance of sex in Zamiatin's novel might strike some modern readers as an idiosyncratic curiosity, but the prominence of sexual questions in some of the more radical quarters of Russian thought in the years preceding and immediately following the Revolution made sex a virtually obligatory element in a book concerned with depicting the dystopian aspects of such thought. *We*, which pits the rigid culture of the United State and its most prominent creation, the phallic rocket, the Integral, against the chaotic forces of the virtually simian, prehistoric people who live outside the State's walls, effectively reorchestrates two of the prominent discursive currents of the War Communist era: the Proletkul't's phallic vision of unanimity, which

---

[180] Ibid., 22.

[181] Evgenii Zamiatin, *Sochineniia* (M.: Kniga, 1988), 76–77.

in its substitution of production for reproduction and in its dream of radically transforming nature in some respects echoed the utopian fantasies of Fedorov and Solov'ev, and the violently reproductive worldview that Pil'niak had composed on the basis of debts owed to Rozanov and the Symbolists. Zamiatin fantasized that these two discursive strains would come into direct conflict; in fact, they would combine in far more subtle forms in the anxiety-ridden ideology of NEP.

Chapter Two

"LET THEM PENETRATE!": STRATEGIES AGAINST DISMEMBERMENT

PARADOXICALLY, War Communism, an epoch when Russian society had been split as rarely before, soon became absorbed in cultural memory as a time of unity. As far as the retrospective mythology about the Civil War was concerned, Russian society—at least the part that mattered to the victors—had been unified during War Communism, bound up in a cataclysmic struggle with an absolutely evil enemy whose defeat had demanded a great degree of ideological purity. In effect, many communists during NEP took elements of War Communist discourse "at their word" and unquestioningly accepted as fact the rhetoric of purity and homogeneity that had been a hallmark of many of the previous era's programmatic texts.

Writing in 1918, Punin and Poletaev had taken aim at the notion that diversity strengthens society. This Darwinist view, they had contended, was a "harmful and dangerous delusion": "[Diversity] violates the principle of the concentration of culture and the law of the concentration of energy; it simultaneously lowers the social machine's coefficient of useful activity and increases striving for personal happiness."[1]

NEP, however, as Lenin emphasized in one of many attempts by Party leaders to "sell" the Party's new course, was all about diversity since it required the reintroduction to the Soviet economy of a wide variety of economic activities: "The capitalists will be right next to you," he had warned; "next to you there will also be foreign entrepreneurs, operators of concessions, and lessees."[2] The proletariat would have to learn from these "new" neighbors so that it might compete with them successfully. Their presence within the would-be communist state was distasteful but necessary to the state's continued survival and eventual success.

Not surprisingly, the reintroduction of diversity to the Soviet economy made many in the Party nervous and provoked fits of semantic juggling intended to prove that this diversity was *not* what it seemed, that there was something not *so* diverse about it, that above it stood a new unifying scheme. Bukharin explained to foreign communists in 1924:

[1] Evgenii Poletaev and Nikolai Punin, *Protiv tsivilizatsii* (Pg.: 1918), 54.
[2] V. I. Lenin, "Novaia ekonomicheskaia politika i zadachi politprosvetov" (17 October 1921), *Polnoe sobranie sochinenii*, 5th ed., 45 vols. (M.: Gos. izd., 1958–1965), 44:167.

On one side we have gigantic enterprises with proletarian content. On the other—forms of another social character. This, perhaps, is the most important thing, and you have to master it in the proper fashion. All doubts, all dissatisfactions, all attacks on the New Economic Policy and on current Russian conditions flow from the fact that comrades do not understand the absolutely new form assumed by class struggle in the sphere of economic competition. Formally, the situation looks almost exactly the way it did under capitalism: workers receive a salary, formally the whole process flows exactly as it does in capitalist society, but the most important thing is that despite this formal similarity there is also a *principal* difference. If we examine the economy of the proletarian dictatorship, then we must keep in mind that an economic diversity of forms is paired with a [new and] different social content of [economic] enterprises.[3]

As a strategy for reassurance, this logic had its danger. It is disquieting to be told that you cannot trust your eyes, that appearances are deceiving. The Bolshevik leaders did their best to justify and explain the reemergence of difference within the Soviet economy and society, but, as Trotsky admitted, differences asserted themselves even within the supposedly homogeneous proletariat: "The proletariat consists of a powerful social unity that is revealed fully and ultimately in periods of tense revolutionary struggle for the goals of the class. But within this unity we observe extreme diversity and not a little heterogeneity."[4] Bolshevik theorists emphasized that NEP was only a transitional, albeit prolonged, period, and resorted to ingenious rhetorical constructions and imaginative forms of presentation. In 1922, for example, Evgeny Preobrazhensky, the chairman of the Central Committee's Financial Commission, published a collection of lectures from the future supposedly delivered by a certain Professor Minaev at the Moscow Polytechnic Museum in 1970 (*sic!*). From the secure standpoint of historical objectivity, Professor Minaev explained how NEP had lasted ten years, how it had originally occasioned much anxiety—"the fears of our grandfathers that under NEP the bourgeoisie would take over again now seem foolish"—but how eventually, after the failure of a kulak rebellion, NEP had culminated in the triumphant installation of true communism not only within the Soviet Union but all over Europe.[5]

The reintroduction of economic differences was a necessity that, after the Tenth and Eleventh Party Congresses (see chapter 6, below), few communists were prepared to refute. Economic heterogeneity, however, concentrated ideological attention on *other*, additional differences and on the concept of difference in general; it is in these parallel spheres that ideological fears about NEP were vocalized and played out. NEP's focus on the pres-

---

[3] "Doklad tov. Bukharina po programmnomu voprosu," *Pravda*, 1 July 1924, 3.

[4] L. Trotskii, *Voprosy byta* (M.: Krasnaia nov', 1923), 12.

[5] E. Preobrazhenskii, *Ot NEP'a k sotsializmu* (M.: Moskovskii rabochii, 1922).

ence of economic divisions created a climate in which *all* divisions were foregrounded in social discourse and in which discomfort with the necessity of a mixed economy was projected onto other manifestations of heterogeneity. It was inevitable that sexual differences would not escape this focus. Moreover, given the prevalence of physiological imagery in War Communist discourse, it is not surprising that during NEP larger ideological concerns should have found expression in talk about the body and, more particularly, about sex. Sex was a natural topic for the desperate, necessarily paradoxical thinking of a vanguard supposedly on the way to utopia and endeavoring to preserve ideological purity as it engaged in commercial intercourse with the enemy. ("We are deliberately cohabiting with the bourgeoisie," Karl Radek said in 1922.)[6]

During War Communism, the topic of sexual difference had not preoccupied the founders of the Soviet state. The Bolsheviks had grappled with pressing military concerns, and the focus of rhetoric and ideology on images of unity had not permitted questions about sexual differences and their consequences to surface—if they did, it was in antithetical, repressed, and heavily symbolic form. In 1919 Riurik Ivnev, a poet turned publicist writing in the first issue of the Agricultural Commissariat's journal, *Krasnyi pakhar'*, had confidently declared: "If women are made equal in their rights with men, it will follow that all complicated questions involving the interrelationships of the sexes will die out and fall away by themselves. And isn't it time to say that in socialist society there are neither men nor women? There are only people, comrades, and citizens with equal rights. [. . .] The women's question will cease to exist as soon as men and women receive equal rights."[7]

In our discussion of pre-Revolutionary philosophers, we saw where the language of "there will be no more men or women" can lead, and we examined briefly the relentless privileging of masculine imagery in Proletkul't poetry and prose; later, we will have occasion to investigate the development of this exclusionary logic during subsequent years. For now, let us simply accept at face value this rejection of the *relevance* of sexual differences (as opposed to the rejection of sexual difference itself!) under communism. Similar sentiments were expressed throughout the War Communist era. In his oft republished *Revolution and Woman*, the Bolshevik chronicler Vadim Bystriansky told his readers: "Life has shown that the Marxists were right when they said that the victory of the proletariat would automatically lead to the elimination of all oppression and of every form of exploitation: both the

---

[6] Karl Radek, "Oktiabr'skaia revoliutsiia i ee mesto v istorii," *Novaia ekonomicheskaia politika: sbornik materialov k kursam* (Kazan': Gos. izd. Avt. Tatarskoi S.S. Respubliki, 1922), vyp. 8, 10 (3–12).

[7] Riurik Ivnev, "Vzaimootnosheniia polov v kommunisticheskom obshchestve," *Krasnyi pakhar'*, no. 1 (1919): 12 (12–13).

exploitation of one nation by another and the exploitation of one sex by the other."[8]

With the inception of NEP, sexual differences again became explicitly relevant in social discourse. In October 1921, Valerian Kuibyshev, soon to become a secretary of the Central Committee, wrote an article defending the Party's continued reliance upon its "women's divisions," the *zhenotdely*:

> One often hears about the appropriateness of the existence of the *zhenotdely*, of a special organization for communist work among women workers.
>
> At the root of this objection lies the generally correct tenet that the proletarian movement must be unified and that both halves of working humanity have common interests, and so on; however, these people [objecting to the *zhenotdely*] have not taken into account the peculiarities of our economic situation and of the daily life with which Old Lady History has surrounded us.[9]

Here, in an early manifestation of what would become a common rhetorical figure, the defense of an institution designed for the protection of and propaganda among women was expressed by a metaphor feminizing the forces of reaction.

Attention was refocused during NEP not only on sociosexual differences but also on physiological ones. At a conference entitled "Woman and the New Everyday Life" held in the Moscow Polytechnic Museum in February 1925, the speakers agreed that to a significant degree woman's special biological function—childbirth—determined her position in society. Nevertheless, these "experts" were at odds on which differences were more important—social or physiological. While one participant insisted on the fundamental nature of psychological differences between the sexes, another contended that *other* differences were more essential: "In her psyche the woman worker much more closely approaches the man of her own class than the woman of another class[. . . .] 'Psychological particularities,' by and large, are determined by the relationships of production."[10]

Anton Vital'evich Nemilov, an endocrinologist and professor at Leningrad University who devoted great effort to explaining to the general public the consequences of the hormonal "dictatorship" exercised by a woman's sex over her brain, declared: "We cannot speak of the 'human being' as such [. . .]. We know only man and woman."[11] Legislative and economic changes, he professed, could not alter this essential fact of a woman's "biological tragedy"—that with her hormonally incapacitated body woman had paid the

---

[8] V. Bystrianskii, *Revoliutsiia i zhenshchina* (Pb.: Gos. izd., 1920), 5.

[9] V. Kuibyshev, "Novaia ekonomicheskaia politika i zadachi zhenshchin," *Kommunistka*, nos. 16–17 (1921): 10 (10–11).

[10] "Zhenshchina i novyi byt," *Izvestiia*, 20 February 1925, 5.

[11] A. V. Nemilov, *Biologicheskaia tragediia zhenshchiny*, 2d ed. (L.: Seiatel', 1925), 39.

price for the progress of human civilization and would continue to do so in the communist future.[12]

Even those who did not see sexual differences in Nemilov's "tragic" light drew attention to these differences' importance. In lectures at Sverdlov Communist University Aleksandra Kollontai, the head of the Party's Women's Division until early 1922, told students that the Soviet government was wisely making use of the "natural division" of work that had arisen between the sexes over centuries:

> Working in areas with which they are better acquainted (supervision of public nourishment, orphanages, prenatal and postnatal care), women are able to give to the building of the Revolution—ever a rushed and energy-exacting task—the maximum of their labor energy, thus helping to maximize the success of both [Revolutionary] construction and the entire workers' Republic. Less than ever should the Proletariat during the epoch of the [workers'] dictatorship admit the viewpoint of bourgeois feminism, which supports equal rights for women as a principle in and of itself. Properly understood, governmental expediency requires, rather, that one take into account the physical and spiritual particularities of women, the specificities of both sexes, their distinctive characteristics and qualities, and, accordingly, that one assign to them different spheres of work directed toward a unified goal.[13]

Ekaterina Troshchenko, who wrote frequently about women in the Komsomol press and who, like Kollontai, generally reminded her readers of woman's equal right to participate in building communist society, was less sanguine about enshrining sexual differences in society. During NEP, she complained, sex role differentiation, which had begun to disappear in the first years after the Revolution, was beginning to reassert itself. Accompanying the "renaissance of the old female psyche" was interest in family life, cosmetics, and fashion.[14]

As attention to differences on all levels grew, the notion of a healthy collective body began to split apart. In its use of figures and images of bodily mutilation Mikhail Bulgakov's retrospective portrait of the NEP years in *The Master and Margarita* (1929?–1940) is highly satiric, but, as elsewhere in his fiction, Bulgakov manages to capture the spirit of the times. That the novel begins with a decapitation and proceeds to describe the consternation occasioned by the disappearance of a severed head is not entirely a product of Bulgakov's fancy.[15] The newspapers of the 1920s delighted in covering bizarre events, particularly those describing freakish injuries and

[12] Ibid., 142. Nemilov's book will be the focus of discussion in chapter 5.

[13] A. Kollontai, *Polozhenie zhenshchiny v evoliutsii khoziaistva* (M.: Gos. izd., 1922), 205.

[14] E. Troshchenko, "Devushka v Soiuze," *Molodaia gvardiia*, no. 3 (1926): 131–135.

[15] Mikhail Bulgakov, *Sobranie sochinenii v piati tomakh* (M.: Khudozhestvennaia literatura, 1990), 5:7–384.

disfigurement. The following item is a typical document of the era; despite its lack of reference to specific historical or cultural events, it is impossible to imagine any other period in Soviet history in which it could have appeared in the Russian press:

> Information has been received that on the first of January the head of a woman, a brunette of apparently 25 to 30 years of age, was found in Leningrad in the Moika Canal. The deceased has not yet been identified. After an intensive search, the remaining parts of the body have been located in various regions of the city. The characteristics of the dismembered corpse are as follows: height— one meter, 65 centimeters; build—a moderately well nourished woman; on the toes and fingers—pedicure and manicure. It is suspected that the murdered woman was not a resident of Leningrad but a visitor. It is requested that anyone recognizing the deceased contact the authorities at once, either by telephone or in person.[16]

To a certain extent this report, which was accompanied by an artist's sketch of the severed head, is a fortuitous "find." I want to suggest, however, that this call for help be read as part of a larger, disquieting discourse of social disintegration, of a yearning that the social fabric might somehow be sewn back together. Moreover, we should not close our eyes to the sex of this dismembered body, nor to its description through foreign words for feminine adornment (*manikiur, pedikiur*). The appearance in this *fait divers* of the sexually "marked" member of the male/female dichotomy epitomizes the extent to which the disorganized collective body might be feminized—and thus, implicitly, sexualized, in sharp contrast to the unified collective body of War Communism, which had been masculine and sublimating.

Ideological discourse during NEP may be termed "desubliminal" in its use of sexual metaphors, because criticism of the distasteful social and economic heterogeneity that had been introduced into Soviet society by NEP often took a sexual tack. For a 1923 editorial in a Voronezh newspaper, the height of NEP's offensiveness was represented by the ascendancy in Moscow of Nepmen who had become so audacious in their depravity that "they have even opened houses of free love."[17] Boris Pil'niak's second major novel— *Machines and Wolves*—an extremely acerbic account of NEP, highlighted the connection of economic diversity with the forces of the past and sexual depravity:

> At night they engaged in great debauches:—several hundreds of people, people, who just yesterday had laid their traders' sacks down from their shoulders, and people, who had survived with them, "princes" and "counts," and with them

[16] "Proisshestviia," *Izvestiia*, 1 February 1925, 6.
[17] Untitled editorial, *Repeinik*, 4 March 1923, 1.

foreigners from diplomatic missions, and with them Russian actresses, writers, artists, many Jews,—last year's snow,—and in various corners of Moscow, when the theaters and restaurants had let out, in houses, like last year's snow, in old living rooms, in carpets, in parquet gleaming with electricity,—in frock coats, in plastrons, in white waistcoats, in women with bare breasts, in fox-trots,—in electricity, champagne, and warmth—they made merry, they knew how to make merry with the autumn puddles in which everything that lives by daylight was smashed to bits: they knew how to dance the fox-trot until they were utterly exhausted, they knew how not to talk about "workdays," they knew how to straighten a woman's garters in front of everybody: and the women knew how to make up every inch of their lips, to smoke cigars and English tobacco, to smoke up the nights, the rooms, themselves—[18]

In this passage, as in the newspaper item quoted above, anxiety over social heterogeneity manifests itself not only in the disquieting scene described but also in word choice. Markedly foreign words (*deboshi, missiia, frak, sham-panskoe, fokstrot, kepsten*) abound and mirror the fragmentation into which Pil'niak saw Soviet society falling. If in *The Naked Year*, a novel more "about the Revolution" than about specific characters, the effacement of writing was a formal metaphor for sexual energy's role in the destruction of pre-Revolutionary society,[19] here, in Pil'niak's novel about NEP, the verbal counterpart of sexual depravity is a new heterogeneity of language.

In *Machines and Wolves* flour is traded for abortions and alcohol swapped for barren cows, as Pil'niak does his utmost to depict sexuality's integration into the new mixed economy.[20] The story of Raia the telegraph operator serves as an example of how sexual and commercial relations merge into a single whole:

Raia, who worked at the telegraph station, had a lover: he speculated, he traveled somewhere and brought back flour and butter, then he went away again and brought back cotton textiles and kerosene. He brought Raia bread and ker-osene so that she could fry cutlets for him and curl her hair. Fisa, the landlady's daughter, was Raia's friend. She curled hair with Raia, although she was too young to have a lover. Aglaia Ivanovna—through Raia—asked Raia's lover to bring her flour and paid for it with her husband's silver watch. Raia had a brother who came to spend the night when her lover was away. Petr Kar-povich—Raia's lover—brought three hundred pounds of flour—for Raia and Aglaia—but didn't have time to say how much he had brought each one,—he

[18] Boris Pil'niak, *Mashiny i volki* (L.: Gos. izd., 1925), 180.

[19] See, in particular, the novel's opening, which begins with the communication of a "now effaced" inscription. Boris Pil'niak, *Izbrannye proizvedeniia* (M.: Khudozhestvennaia literatura, 1976), 35.

[20] Pil'niak, *Mashiny i volki*, 113.

put the flour in the pantry without weighing it and at night someone stole it by climbing through the pantry window from the yard.[21]

In Pil'niak's novel the figure who most symbolizes the sexual depravity of the early NEP years is a nun called Olga. The reader is provided with a thumbnail biography of the character, an account as much a sign of the age as Stroev's 1917 biography of a seductive anarchist:

> Somewhere in Vetluga, in a sect of Old Believers, Olga's fanatical mother and aunt had died casting anathemas,—and Olga's mother had been an abbess. But Olga, from a family of Old Believers and weavers from Ivanovo-Vosnesensk, finished the gymnasium as its best student, and she was exemplary when she studied in the department of philosophy in her first year at Gerier's women's college. During the Revolution, in October, during the days of the Uprising, she went to the headquarters of the White Guard with a Browning in her hands, and wearing a Red Cross armband she stood up for the Kremlin—only later to burn with fervor for the Communist Party, to be a fanatic, like a monk, to hate with frenzy and to love with frenzy, to shout out the "International" to the world, to hate the old Russia, to curse God and to hurl a poem to the machine out into the world,—later, remembering, Sister Olga remembered how in the Party School she had torn down the icon of Saint Nicolas and hung in its place a portrait of Karl Marx. She had been in Ivanovo-Vosnesensk, and there it had seemed to many communists that she had lost her mind when she had thought up, invented, and fervently put into effect a system of socialist record keeping where people were totally effaced [*sovsem vyshelushchivalis'*], all that remained were numbers. She had still been a virgin then: neither as a girl nor as a woman had she loved anyone. She had been sent to the front to edit a newspaper, there, retreating from Wrangel's advancing army, she had been raped in the train cars that were her office,—she had gone wild, had fallen in love, gone mad with love, had a husband who later went over to the Whites—and a half year later, having broken with the Communist Party, with the Revolution, she was already a novice in the Biuliukovskaia convent, in a black dress, like a jackdaw, at prayer and in sexual hysteria.[22]

This was Pil'niak's Sanin, circa 1923–1925, formed not by 1905 but by 1917, by the Proletkul't, and by Civil War: a hero "adjusting" through sex to the new reality of Russian life. The anxieties that Pil'niak saw as constitutive of the time demanded that the sexual symbol of the era be female rather than male, not a clone of Nietzsche's Superman, but a nymphomaniacal nun.

The concern with difference during NEP extended beyond classes and sexes—it also encompassed differences between the individual and the collective. Discussions of this larger issue, of the factors that separated a single

[21] Ibid., 114.
[22] Ibid., 174–175.

person (or a couple) from society, also revolved around notions of sex, because they called into question the idea of an established unit of sexual organization: the family.

According to received Marxist wisdom, in bourgeois society the family had been a mainstay of capitalist oppression: "The capitalists know perfectly well," Kollontai wrote in 1918, "that the family, with its enslavement of woman and with its accordance to the husband of responsibility for familial well-being and nourishment, has been the best means of checking the [proletariat's] will, of weakening the revolutionary spirit of male and female workers."[23] Under communism, Kollontai opined, the family would have no reason to exist. Families had arisen as units of economic production, she wrote, but were rapidly becoming no more than atavistic units of consumption. When the State took over the task of meeting consumer needs, when the government provided meals, health insurance, and public education, the family would no longer have a raison d'être.[24] The family's disintegration would, in addition, have an extremely positive effect on an individual's relationship to his society—egotism would give way to a sense of connection with fellow citizens. Women would learn to seek and receive support from the collective rather than from their husbands. Public schools, furthermore, would inculcate a healthy attitude toward the collective at an early age:

> The narrow, closed family—with its parental squabbles and its tendency to think only about the well-being of kin—cannot educate the New Man. The New Man can be educated only in educational institutions—playgrounds, kindergartens, and other public centers—where a child will spend the greater part of his day and where wise educators will make out of him a conscientious communist who acknowledges only one slogan: solidarity, camaraderie, mutual assistance, and loyalty to the collective.[25]

In the first communes formed after the Revolution, family and marital relationships indeed did give way to a spirit of attachment to a larger collective. In May 1919, *Krasnyi pakhar'*'s Mark Krinitsky visited a commune founded by a man now calling himself Lazar Luch. (The surname means "ray of light.") All children in the commune had taken this last name, and Luch told Krinitsky that the children of one were the children of all:

> Didn't you give your wives the best things? And didn't you pass other people's crying children by? We are born from the Spirit, and each child is the same for us, because from the Spirit's point of view all children are equals. Just so, all women, too, if you look at them from a spiritual, rather than a filthy perspective, are our sisters, and from the spiritual point of view someone else's wife is just as

[23] A. Kollontai, *Sem'ia i kommunisticheskoe gosudarstvo* (M. and L.: Kommunist, 1918), 18.
[24] Ibid., 10. See also A. Kollontai, *Obshchestvo i materinstvo* (Pg.: Zhizn' i znanie, 1916), 13.
[25] Kollontai, *Sem'ia*, 18–19.

dear to me as any other woman, and will I really begrudge her a piece of bread if she is hungry or asks for it? We say to you: "Dear brothers and sisters— abandon all divisions among people."[26]

This kind of sermon—which obviously owed more to Christianity than to Marxism—would have great difficulty surviving into the 1920s. From the start of NEP the Soviet state rapidly conceded that it could not provide for all social needs, and most Soviet educators and jurists found themselves compelled to defend the institution of marriage and the narrowly focused responsibilities it imposed on its citizens. Advocates of the family's abolition were berated for abandoning a materialist's realistic perspective. Like government, the family would *eventually* wither away, but for the time being its survival was—along with the reintroduction of capitalism—an economic necessity. Calls for its immediate abolition, the Komsomol journal *Molodaia gvardiia* claimed, often concealed "dirty little love affairs."[27]

An acknowledgment of the family's necessity did not, however, prevent the expression of anger toward or frustration with it. Writers complained that marriage and family life were dragging men and women away from socially useful work, particularly when their spouses were not members of the Party or the Komsomol.[28] Trotsky suggested that the family be rebuilt so that it would become the smallest political unit in the land, the most intimate Party cell.[29] Others were more radical. Although Kollontai had reassured her readers in 1918 that the communist collective would never forcibly separate children from their parents, Sverdlov Communist University Rector Liadov stated categorically in 1925 that a new, collective man could not be raised within the narrow, egotistical confines of the family: "Every conscientious father and mother should say: if I want my child to be free of the petty bourgeois characteristics that lie deep within each of us, he must be isolated from us."[30] Anticipating the objection that Soviet orphanages were in terrible

[26] M. K. (Mark Krinitskii), "Novyi byt," *Krasnyi pakhar'*, nos. 4–5 (1919): 13–14 (13–15).

[27] E. Lavrov, "Polovoi vopros i molodezh'," *Molodaia gvardiia*, no. 3 (1926): 142 (136–148).

[28] G. Rzhanov, "Lenintsy i voprosy sem'i," *Pravda*, 17 August 1924, 3; "Pochemu devushki ukhodiat iz soiuza," *Komsomol'skaia pravda*, 6 October 1926, 3.

[29] Trotskii, *Voprosy byta*, 54. In 1924, the Presidium of the Party's Central Control Commission proposed to the commission's Second Plenum a draft resolution on "Party ethics" that did not diverge from Trotskii's formulation of the family's relationship to the Party: "Under current conditions the communist family ought to be a cell that, founded on natural feelings of attachment, concerns itself with creating favorable conditions for the communist work of all family members, transforming the family into a working comradely commune." The portion of the draft containing this formulation was dropped from the resolution approved by the plenum. As far as I have been able to determine, no explanation was provided for the deletion. See "O partetike. Proekt predlozhenii prezidiuma TsKK II plenumu TsKK RKP(b)," in *Partiinaia etika. Diskussii 20-x godov*, ed. A. A. Guseinov, M. V. Iskrov, and R. V. Petropavlovskii (M.: Politicheskaia literatura, 1989), 154, 474 (151–170, 473–474).

[30] M. N. Liadov, *Voprosy byta* (M.: Kommun. u-t. im. Ia. Sverdlova, 1925), 25.

shape and could not cope with an influx of "isolated children," Liadov countered: "Let the mother who has such a hard time detaching herself from her child dedicate herself to the work of raising the many children alongside of whom her own child will grow. Let her extend her highly developed maternal love to all children."[31]

The heroine of one of the most discussed literary works of 1925 followed Liadov's advice. Dasha Chumalov of Fedor Gladkov's *Cement* puts her daughter in an orphanage in order to devote herself to the common good. Gladkov does not overtly condemn his heroine's action; when Dasha's child dies, the reader is left to decide whether Dasha has taken the right course.

Contemporary readers reacted in a variety of ways to Dasha's conduct. An interesting record is preserved in questionnaires distributed in the mid-1920s to factory workers who were asked for their reactions to characters and themes in the most widely discussed works of contemporary literature. Although the responses collected in no way provide a statistically significant survey, they do suggest that workers' reactions to Dasha varied widely. Some readers expressed bewilderment: "Why did Dasha abandon her family?" one seamstress asked; "Is this really necessary? Did her Party work really interfere with her family?"[32] Others felt that Dasha could not exist in the Soviet Union of the NEP era. She was more a lifeless model of what the New Woman would be like, or else, several readers suggested, the type of woman who had existed during War Communism.[33] One reader, a worker from a printing plant in Briansk, responded:

> I didn't like *Cement*, a lot of fuss has been made about this book, but when I started to read it I was disappointed. What kind of hero is this, would a real woman really have greeted her husband [Gleb] like Dasha does and would a real woman have given her child up to a shelter? She should have first concerned herself with putting the shelters in good order, and only later have given up her daughter, a child can't live without maternal affection, and Gleb is a fine one too, he just can't understand his wife, in general I didn't find what I was looking for.[34]

Almost as many workers, however, approved of Dasha's conduct. A female employee at a vodka factory in Sverdlovsk declared, "Dasha acted as any

[31] Ibid., 26. For earlier proponents of this opinion, see Wendy Z. Goldman, *Women, the State and Revolution: Soviet Family Policy and Social Life, 1917–1936* (Cambridge: Cambridge University Press, 1993), 9.

[32] IMLI, fond 51, opis' 2 (Otzyvy rabochikh. Kabinet po izucheniiu chitatel'ia). For a more general discussion of reader-response surveys conducted during NEP, see Jeffrey Brooks, "Studies of the Reader in the 1920s," *Russian History/Histoire Russe* 9 (1982): 187–202.

[33] The confusion of past and future—and their merging in a united front against the present—are discussed at length by Anne Nesbet in her dissertation, "The Aesthetics of Violence in Russian and East German Literature" (University of California, Berkeley, 1992).

[34] IMLI, Otzyvy rabochikh.

one of us would have."[35] As this statement indicates, workers read—and were encouraged to read—the novels of the time as models for their behavior: a time-honored Russian tradition. For the most part, the respondents related to Dasha not as a literary construct but as they would have to a woman living next door, and they judged her accordingly. A Moscow tailor commented:

> I consider Dasha's attitude toward her personal life perfectly correct. Why? First of all, can a woman like Dasha, active in social work,—and this goes even more for a seamstress—put her personal life first? Of course not, and in this respect Dasha is great. When Gleb came home from the front, Dasha did not do what most women would have, she didn't grab her husband and start kissing him, but she met her husband like a comrade and said, no, brother, now don't be naughty, you should not need me as a woman on whom one looks as an object, I should be a comrade with full rights, and without any question that's how it should be.[36]

As this response suggests, the significance of Dasha's conduct was not limited to her voluntary renunciation of her child. The question of the family was part of a larger category of difference—that of "personal life." This issue, which encompassed broad questions of privacy and philosophical and juridical concepts of the individual, was one of the most frequently discussed topics of the Soviet 1920s.

As Richard Stites comments in his survey of the Russian women's movement, nineteenth-century socialists had, in general, "little to say about sex."[37] While, for the most part, Proletkul't rhetoric had tended toward the complete elimination of private life, those few War Communist voices which had conceded that the sphere of private life would continue to exist under communism had generally maintained that sexual relations would *not* be controlled by the government. Ivnev had written in 1919, "The government does not interfere in intimate relations among members of the communist society, if these relations are established by the mutual consent of mature and competent members of society."[38] In Lazar Luch's commune, sexual relations were the sole sphere of personal interaction where the notion of the collective was not paramount: "As far as the intimate side of sex is concerned, I think it is not proper to go into this. This is the affair of the two people concerned."[39] Similar statements continued to be voiced in the early years of NEP. In 1923, Il'ia Lin, writing in *Molodaia gvardiia*, defended sexual activity in the Kom-

---

[35] Ibid.

[36] Ibid.

[37] Richard Stites, *The Women's Liberation Movement in Russia* (Princeton: Princeton University Press, 1978), 268.

[38] Ivnev, "Vzaimootnosheniia," 13.

[39] Krinitskii, "Novyi byt," 113–114.

somol as harmless, irrelevant behavior: "Without a doubt, all these kom-somol'tsy, male and female, have their own relationships, sexual relation-ships with someone. But all this occurs imperceptibly, occupying neither time nor place."[40] A survey of students at the Sverdlov Communist Univer-sity in January 1923 found that 91.6 percent of the "communist student body" had active sex lives. The study reported that according to 80.2 percent of the sexually active respondents, sexual relations did not interfere with their public spirit or work (obshchestvennost').[41] Trotsky cautioned that "careless, inappropriate interference by the press in the internal life of family members can only increase the number of complications, disasters, and ca-tastrophes [in private life]."[42] Dr. S. Ia. Golosovker, director of the Central Venereal Clinic in Kazan and one of the first Soviet sex researchers, ended his study of female sexuality by reaffirming the maxim that "sexual life is the private affair of each individual inasmuch as it does not impinge upon the legal rights of another."[43]

These assertions of an individual's right to sexual privacy eventually suc-cumbed to an increasingly strong discomfort with individual life outside the collective. From its infancy, the Soviet press had attempted to erase—or at least shift—the line dividing public from private life. A January 1919 article in the provincial Party organ Voronezhskaia bednota had taken stock of at-tempts to interest citizens in public affairs and observed that, unfortunately, petty private pleasures still occupied a large place in the lives of Soviet men and women. The recent staging at the local Communists' Club of a New Year's pageant devoted to "the most famous leaders of socialist movements of the past—Plato, More, Robespierre, Marat, and others" had not been a success since "our guests (alas, even the communist ones) were more inter-ested in dancing than in the history of the revolutionary movement."[44]

On the basis of similar experiences, a Voronezh delegate to the First Kom-somol Congress in 1918 had suggested that the Komsomol organize dances and even avoid using the word "communist" in order to attract young people who would not ordinarily come to their meetings. At these entertainments, young communists could draw their contemporaries to the communist cause through "internal work"—a more subtle and potentially quite effective form of covert propaganda. The Moscow and Leningrad delegates were outraged by this suggestion that "large and small" questions, public and private mat-

[40] Il'ia Lin, "Eros iz rogozhsko-simonovskogo raiona," *Molodaia gvardiia*, nos. 4–5 (1923): 153 (152–155).

[41] "Anketa o polovoi zhizni studentov Kom. Un-ta," *Zapiski kommunisticheskogo universiteta imeni Sverdlova*, no. 1 (1923): 370–371 (370–409).

[42] Trotskii, *Voprosy byta*, 84.

[43] Dr. S. Ia. Golosovker, *K voprosu o polovom byte sovremennoi zhenshchiny* (Kazan': Ka-zanskii meditsinskii zhurnal, 1925), 23.

[44] "Po Voronezhu," *Voronezhskaia bednota*, 4 January 1919, 4.

ters, politics and entertainment might be blended. "Our Union's task is not to organize parties but to put into effect a specific political program," one Moscow delegate responded. Another added: "If comrades come to our Union, they know that they are coming to do serious work. I say—down with dances, let our political work be taken care of and then everybody will say: 'Long live the Communist Youth League.' "[45]

Two years later, however, a report on the first large-scale women's conference in the Voronezh Guberniia (province) was more upbeat. It contended that great strides had been made in linking private and public spheres and that workers were willing to place politics over personal concerns:

> The peasant woman has always built her own *private personal life*. In this area she has achieved even more than a man: all household worries have fallen on her shoulders, especially now, when husbands, fathers, and children have gone off into the Red Army to fight the landowners. But in social life, in the organization of the life of the *entire government*, woman has not played a role.
>
> But now working women have come to realize that *personal* life depends entirely upon social life, that the ordering of social life is *more important* than the ordering of one's home. They understand that if the government falls apart, there will be no such thing as family comfort.[46]

By the mid-1920s, this attitude was no longer adequate; rather, it was turned on its head. Now, the Soviet press argued with increasing frequency that the life of the social organism *depended* on the course assumed by the personal lives of its members. The latter was not simply a reflection of but also exerted an influence on the former. In 1924, Nadezhda Krupskaia told the Sixth Congress of the Komsomol: "We understand perfectly well that personal life cannot be separated from social concerns. Perhaps earlier it was not clear that a division between private life and public life sooner or later leads to the betrayal of communism. We must strive to bind our private life to the struggle for and the construction of communism."[47] In October 1924, the Party's Central Control Commission, originally formed to discipline communists guilty of noncriminal abuses of power, formally declared members' personal lives to be the Party's concern. According to the commission, this decision was a fundamental distinction between the Party and the Second International.[48]

In his famous conversation with the German communist Klara Zetkin, first published in 1925, Lenin rejected the idea that sexual intercourse, like drink-

---

[45] A. S. Trainin, ed., *Pervyi s"ezd RKSM. Protokoly. Iz komsomol'skogo arkhiva* (M.: Molodaia gvardiia, 1990), 65, 68–69.

[46] E. St——vich, "Na puti k novoi zhizni," *Krasnaia derevnia* (Voronezh), 2 November 1920, 2.

[47] "VI Vsesoiuznyi s"ezd RLKSM. Rech' Tov. N.K. Krupskoi," *Pravda*, 13 July 1924, 4.

[48] "O partetike," 152–153.

ing, was an uncomplicated response to a biological need. There was, he said, a fundamental difference between the two acts: "Drinking water is truly an individual affair. But two participate in love and there arises a third, new life. This is where the public interest comes in, where a responsibility to the collective arises."[49]

The primacy of public interest over private life was the central theme of Rector Liadov's *Questions of Everyday Life*. Addressing the cadres under his tutelage at the Sverdlov Communist University, Liadov revived War Communist imagery in a sustained attack on personal life and argued—in language more radical than Lenin's or Krupskaia's—for the complete subordination of private life to the public sphere. Liadov attempted to show that the notion of privacy was a capitalist idea. It was in early bourgeois culture, with its roots in the alchemist's laboratory, in the tradesman's dwelling, and in the hut of the recently freed serf, that individual and family interests became paramount. "Here the word 'I' was born. Neither the savage, nor the hunter, nor even the proud citizen of Rome knew the word 'I.' There was no private hearth, only the public one. [. . .] Only with my clan, with my tribe could I protect *our* pastures, our cattle. [. . .] Everything belonged to 'us,' not to 'me.' "[50] The society of the future would witness the restoration of the absolute coincidence of the public and private spheres:

> We imagine the society of the future as one in which everyone will feel that his interests conform with the interests of the entire collective. Every person will feel pain, will feel burdened, if his personal interests in any way contradict the interests of the collective. [. . .]
>
> What will regulate our relations in this area? After all, there will no longer be any coercive power. In each of us inhibitive centers will be developed by life itself, by the force of collective creativity. I will not be able to experience pleasure if I see that beside me someone else cannot experience it. I will be capable of experiencing only the general pleasure, the general satisfaction, the unlimited pleasure that will reign all around me.[51]

In an atmosphere of disturbing divisions, the question of control became paramount in all areas fraught with fragmentation. It was only logical that, in 1926, as the Party began to tighten its grip on previously "apolitical" areas of social activity, Komsomol organs launched a concerted effort to penetrate privacy and organize leisure. *Smena*, the chief press organ of the Leningrad Komsomol, asked:

> Where lies the chief deficiency of our Komsomol's work? In our failure to bridge the gap between society and the individual. The Komsomol has suffi-

[49] Klara Tsetkin, *O Lenine. Vospominaniia i vstrechi* (M.: Moskovskii rabochii, 1925), 16.
[50] Liadov, *Voprosy byta*, 7.
[51] Ibid., 22.

ciently absorbed the social side of our youth's lives, but our young people's
leisure and their narrowly personal lives still lie beyond the threshold of our
collectives. Collectives should not be simply groups of people united only by
their common dependency upon a factory or plant. Our collectives should become communities uniting young people not only within plants but also outside
the factory gates, responding not only to our youth's social needs but also to
their personal, intimate attractions.[52]

The Komsomol press started to focus on judicial cases in which komsomol'tsy had committed horrible deeds because attention had not been paid
by the organization to the private affairs of its members. In the middle of
December 1925, as Zinov'ev and Stalin traded accusations at the Fourteenth
Party Congress, *Komsomol'skaia pravda* reported on the trial of a "model"
komsomolets charged with infanticide and cautioned its readers to acquaint
themselves with the private, everyday lives of fellow members.[53] The following year *Komsomol'skaia pravda* fumed about Petr Aksenov, a komsomolets
who, the press charged, had kept his wife in virtual slavery:

> As if this were the private life of komsomolets Aksenov! Must we interfere in it?
> Must we weigh all his acts? There can only be one answer. Yes. We must. We
> have the right to judge komsomolets Aksenov. He is staining our entire organiza-
> tion. We must mercilessly open our sores, however painful for us that may be.[54]

Another case, that of Konstantin Koren'kov, a student at a mining academy who had murdered a cashier during a robbery, received special attention. Prior to committing the murder, Koren'kov had been expelled by his
local Komsomol cell for driving his wife to suicide, but the regional Party
Control Commission, content merely with reprimanding Koren'kov, had reversed the decision. In the chorus of comment devoted to the affair, an important conclusion was repeated again and again: if the Party had intervened
more forcefully in Koren'kov's personal life, he might never have moved
from domestic to public misconduct. Sof'ia Smidovich, Kollontai's suc-
cessor as head of the Zhenotdel, exploded in anger: "It is far wiser, from the
social point of view, to consider 'personal life' an inseparable part of a
whole that determines a man in all his aspects than to shut one's eyes to
personal life, supposing that there is just no getting by without this or that
[dissolute komsomolets]."[55]

[52] Anat. Gorelov and V. Rozov, "Bol'ny li Eseninym?" *Smena*, 14 July 1926, 2.

[53] "O tovarishchestve," *Komsomol'skaia pravda*, 18 December 1925, 4.

[54] Il. Isbakh, "Delo komsomol'tsa Aksenova," *Komsomol'skaia pravda*, 14 August 1926, 1.

[55] S. Smidovich, "O Koren'kovshchine," *Molodaia gvardiia*, no. 7 (1926): 99 (95–101). The
Koren'kov case burst into prominence when *Pravda* put it on its front page. See L. Sosnovskii,
"Delo Koren'kova," *Pravda*, 5 June 1926, 1. Its lessons were discussed throughout the fall in
the Komsomol press. V. Kirshon and A. Uspenskii quickly used the affair as the basis for a play,
which was soon translated into English and produced, under the title *Red Rust*, in London and

To appreciate the change in attitudes about privacy in the mid-1920s we can return to *Cement* and workers' responses to it. A central figure in the novel is the chairman of the local executive committee, Bad'in, who is at once Sanin *and* an ideal Bolshevik, at least insofar as the performance of his official duties is concerned. Bad'in's personal creed is indebted to both Nietzsche and Artsybashev: he acts as he desires and is not averse to raping subordinates. He says to Dasha when she resists his vigorous advances: "I don't see any shame in what I'm doing. We are a handsome and strong couple, and it's not fitting that we pretend and utter sententious phrases. [. . .] You know that I never yield in battle, and what I want, I take."[56] Bad'in's sexual prowess overwhelms women; surrender to his sexual advances is "inevitable."[57] As she struggles against him, Dasha feels that "his blood was streaming into her body through his arms, lips, and nostrils, and in answer to these strong pulsations a wave of feminine weakness passed languorously through her veins, a wave of confused pleasure and fear." Although she tries to resist Bad'in's assault, Dasha appreciates his raw power; simultaneously she considers him both a personal threat and her salvation from the forces of counterrevolution. Accompanying Dasha on a journey through dangerous territory, Bad'in becomes a biological and political phallus, engorged with power in all its manifestations:

> Bad'in, reserved, large, full of blood, quivering from his blood's animal pulsations, with a body hard as stone, sat deep in the pillows of the phaeton, fearless and calm, but in his eyes, beneath his heavy forehead, far away, behind the dark mother-of-pearl of his corneas, excitement blazed along with the pulsations of blood. Did danger intoxicate him or was he inebriated by Dasha's proximity? And how could Comrade Egorov [the driver] fear marauding bandits when Comrade Bad'in was so inexpressibly strong and bold? Dasha sat motionless. It was stuffy, and Dasha suffered from Bad'in's stony weight, and yet it was also pleasant that this man of steel was a reliable support at a dangerous time.[58]

A figure such as Bad'in could not exist in later Soviet literature, when notions of public and private life had utterly converged. Workers discussing his role in the novel found his character troubling, but for the most part they were unable to express their discomfort in the form of a judgment securely dictated by an internalized ideological "code." The comments of two seamstresses highlighted Bad'in's duality: "I am satisfied with Bad'in as a Party

New York. Opening in both cities in 1929, it was, according to the *New York Times*, the first Soviet play ever produced in London and only the second to run in New York. *New York Times*, 17 March 1929, sec. x, 1, and 18 December 1929, 31.

[56] Fedor Gladkov, "Tsement," *Krasnaia nov'*, no. 3 (1925): 61 (no. 1, 66–110; no. 2, 73–109; no. 3, 47–81; no. 4, 57–87; no. 5, 75–111; no. 6, 39–74).

[57] Ibid., no. 5, 102.

[58] Ibid., no. 3, 61.

worker, but he treats women like animals"; "In his job Bad'in is the Party's
man [*partiinyi*], but he has wild ideas about women. A Party man cannot
look at women that way."[59] In neither case did the conclusion reached in the
second clause preclude the conclusions reached in the first. However, another young worker—significantly, a member of the Komsomol—perceived
that Bad'in had no place either within the Party or in Soviet society at large:
"Today Bad'in would be charged with rape, and appropriately so. There's
nothing good about him—he's a bureaucrat who uses the Party for his personal ends."[60] This last reader had mastered the new integrative discourse
and understood that *Cement* was already a period piece. By 1926 personal
life was the object of sustained Party attention: Sanin/Bad'in had been transformed into Koren'kov. By 1927, when *Smena* reported the results of a poll
of komsomol'tsy at a technical institute on the connections between ideological and sexual relations, it was obvious that the autonomy accorded to
sexual relations in the earlier, Communist University study was no longer
ideologically acceptable. Forty-four percent considered an ideological relationship to be essential in a sexual relationship; 20 percent answered, "It's
good with ideology but OK without"; and 36 percent responded, "What does
ideology have to do with sex with a woman?" Those in the last category
were depicted as coarse and totally devoid of appreciation for ideology's role
in a communist's life: "In general, I pay little attention to ideology, it's
enough that a woman not be sick and that she be amenable to my demands,
after all, I need only one thing and where does ideology come into the
picture?"[61] This caricature of a bad communist as one who rejected the rapport of ideology to sex was a common approach in literary feuilletons and
stories about life in the Komsomol.

How did the Party go about securing control over personal life? The
Party's approach was typically scientific: "personal life" had to be studied if
it were to be brought under greater control. Toward this end, researchers
conducted studies of sexual attitudes and behavior,[62] but the privileged vehi-

[59] IMLI, Otzyvy rabochikh.

[60] Ibid.

[61] "Adres vuzovtsa ne 'Sobachii pereulok,'" *Smena*, 9 March 1927, 2.

[62] For an analysis of several sex surveys, see Sheila Fitzpatrick, "Sex and Revolution," *The
Cultural Front: Power and Culture in Revolutionary Russia* (Ithaca: Cornell University Press,
1992), 65–90. Fitzpatrick examines four surveys: two conducted in Moscow, one each in Omsk
and Odessa: I. Gel'man, *Polovaia zhizn' sovremennoi molodezhi: Opyt sotsial'no-biologich-
eskogo obsledovaniia* (M.: 1923); G. A. Batkis, "Opyt podkhoda k izucheniiu problemy pola: Iz
rabot Gosudarstvennogo Instituta Sotsial'noi Gigieny," *Sotsial'naia gigiena*, no. 6 (1925); V. E.
Kliachkin, "Polovaia anketa sredi Omskogo studenchestva," *Sotsial'naia gigiena*, no. 6 (1925):
124–138; D. I. Lass, *Sovremennoe studenchestvo (byt, polovaia zhizn')* (M.: 1928). For other
surveys, see N. V. Gushchin, *Rezul'taty polovogo obsledovaniia molodezhi g. Iakutska* (Iakutsk:
Narkomproszdrav IaASSR, 1925); Golosovker, *K voprosu o polovom byte*; Dr. A. K. Platovskii,
Polovaia zhizn' sovremennogo studenchestva (Rostov-on-the-Don: Sovet sotsial'noi pomoshchi

cle through which control was sought and exercised was literature. The strategy of utilizing literature to gain a greater hold over youths' personal lives was outlined in a July 1926 article published in the newspaper of the Leningrad Komsomol:

> The years of direct military struggle are past. The personal and the intimate are making their claims. Our poetry, in large measure, eschews these personal, intimate themes, preferring to remain on the public squares, to sing of assemblies, theses, reports. Rarely do our Komsomol poets take Misha or Kat'ka from the intimate point of view; they do not allow us to share the thoughts, aspirations, and possible failures of young people. In the majority of cases the intimate sphere is insufficiently developed in proletarian poetry; collectivism is understood as a sort of effacement, or destruction, of personality.
>
> Thus the strength of [Sergei] Esenin, a poet alien to our working youth, lies in his success in capturing that which is most intimate. Strumming the hidden strings of his life, he conveys the image of a man, his human pain and his infrequent joys. Esenin's charm lies not so much in the dimensions of his talent as in his willingness to touch upon themes other poets more often pass by in silence.
>
> If poets who come to the fore will be able to portray the intimate from a point of view other than Esenin's, not through pain and alienation, but joyously and cheerfully, then their success will be incomparably wider and deeper, for they will capture our personal and intimate experience; they will genuinely be our bards and heralds.[63]

The authors of this article called upon young writers to invade the territory of the intimate and to "capture that which is personal and intimate within us."[64] And while they supposed that this could occur through the portrayal of personal experience in "joyous and cheerful" tones, the opposite was true. The Komsomol scored its greatest successes—and its most significant conquests of personal life—by publishing pictures of abject sexual depravity.

To understand the nature of the discourse on sex in the mid-1920s, we must first appreciate that for the Party and the Komsomol, sex was a *means* of control as much as it was a *goal* of control. At a meeting with Trotsky in 1923, one Party activist complained that the Party was ignoring marriage, the family, and sexual relations—the issues that interested workers most. "When we discuss such questions at our meetings," he reported, "and when

---

pri tuberkuleznykh i venerologicheskikh dispanserakh, 1926); Dr. L. M. Vasilevskii, "Polovoi byt uchashchikhsia," *Komsomol'skaia pravda*, 19 March 1927, 2 (on Riazan').

[63] Anat. Gorelov and V. Rozov, "Bol'ny li Eseninym?" *Smena*, 14 July 1926, 2. The article was written during the height of the Komsomol's campaign against hooliganism, several months after Esenin's suicide. The campaign and the dead poet's place in it will be discussed in chapter 7.

[64] Ibid.

workers know this will be the topic, the hall is packed."[65] When topics from private life were not discussed, attendance at meetings was dismal. In a 1925 article, "Komsomol Meetings, as They Really Are," one reporter noted that official Komsomol gatherings were depressing affairs, full of tedious, ill-prepared papers on topics of minimal public interest that were not usually followed by discussion. "Rarely, quite rarely," the reporter complained, "are questions of everyday life raised . . . , rarely are questions discussed that concern individual members of the Komsomol. In a word, questions are not raised that, by virtue of their general interest, might provoke heated discussion among the fellows and statements by as many participants as possible."[66] When *Komsomol'skaia pravda* asked in its hundredth issue for comments from its readers, many responded that they wanted more articles on questions of Komsomol ethics and sex. *Komsomol'skaia pravda* obliged. Entire pages of that large-format newspaper were given over to discussions of sex: in addition to hodgepodge collections of "scientific" articles and fiction, *Komsomol'skaia pravda* frequently published individual pieces on the topic.

Initially, it might seem as if Soviet publications had done a bit of market research and responded accordingly. In December 1924, the editorial board of *Saratovskie izvestiia*, desiring to increase its female readership, asked the local women's division "what question [was] most interesting and troubling for women workers and housewives at the present time." The women's division responded that "the topic of abortion would now have the greatest success, since this question is seriously affecting women." Accordingly, on 21 December, the paper printed an article broaching the abortion question and asking women to express their views. Soon, the editorial offices were "swamped" with letters from female readers; for several weeks, 100 to 150 lines of each issue were devoted to this question.[67]

The goal of organs like *Saratovskie izvestiia* was not to *sell* as many copies as possible. Rather, it was to attract as wide a readership as possible into the net of Party propaganda. From the Bolshevik perspective, the newspaper was equivalent to the bayonet and the rifle: "with it we will break down the front of the rule of bourgeois consciousness; we will create a new consciousness: communism."[68] Sex provided ideal ammunition for the launching of this propagandistic assault.

In late November 1925, newspapers throughout the USSR published Nikolai Bukharin's "Theses on the Work of the Komsomol," a document that

[65] Trotskii, *Voprosy byta*, 122.

[66] Vik. Rozin, "Komsomol'skie sobraniia, kak oni est'," *Komsomol'skaia pravda*, 5 November 1925, 3.

[67] S. Telegin, "Neskol'ko slov o nashei diskussii," *Abort* (Saratov: Saratovskie izvestiia, 1925), 3 (3–6).

[68] Andrei Platonov, "Gazeta i ee znachenie," *Krasnaia derevnia* (Voronezh), 23 September 1920, 2.

had been approved unanimously by the Party's Politburo. The "Theses," in effect, put the imprimatur of the nation's most powerful body on a process that had been occurring for several months in Komsomol publications throughout the land: the use of "personal life" as a tool to gain greater influence over the nation's youth. Bukharin wrote:

> We must intensify our efforts to bring to fruition the following practical under-taking: Komsomol cells in factories should use all measures to draw the entire mass of working youth into the organization. This process of attraction should not be undertaken by pure [or naked] agitation, but by having young people discuss and practically resolve vital and interesting questions of economic and cultural significance, including questions of everyday life. [. . .]
>
> The Komsomol cannot be silent about questions of everyday life, which have become more acute with the growth of our economy. We must oppose the cor-rupting influence of Nepmen and of the petty bourgeoisie by organizing a battle for the rationalization of everyday life. The Komsomol should discuss such questions widely at public meetings and should encourage the organization of voluntary Komsomol-affiliated associations that will struggle for such rationaliz-ation and raise the cultural level of the Komsomol masses and of worker and peasant youth in general.[69]

The economic contradictions that typified NEP, Bukharin continued, required that the Party "battle for [its] youth." As it turned out, this battle was to be a process of courtship and seduction. "Naked agitation" gave way to more effective agitation about sex.

In 1926 and early 1927 the publication of three literary works caused an enormous stir in the literary and Komsomol establishments. When read to-day, Pantaleimon Romanov's "Without Cherry Blossoms,"[70] Sergei Ma-lashkin's "The Moon from the Right Side,"[71] and Lev Gumilevsky's *Dog Alley*[72] seem didactic, moralizing tracts. Yet they were attacked as depraved and dangerous libels of contemporary youth. At meetings throughout the country on topics such as "Pornography and Pathology in Contemporary Literature," the authors were criticized for writing works which were por-nographic in that they had "as their goal the artificial arousal of sexual emo-tions."[73]

The attacks on Romanov, Malashkin, and Gumilevsky seem remarkable because the intentions of the writers—as voiced in memoirs and at myriad

---

[69] "O rabote RLKSM. Tezisy tov. N. I. Bukharina, odobrennye Politbiuro TsK RKP (b)," *Komsomol'skaia pravda*, 28 November 1925, 3.

[70] "Bez cheremukhi," *Molodaia gvardiia*, no. 6 (1926): 13–21.

[71] "Luna s pravoi storony," *Molodaia gvardiia*, no. 9 (1926): 3–54.

[72] *Sobachii pereulok* (L.: 1927).

[73] Val. Bronunshtein, "Otpor," *Smena*, 22 April 1927, 4.

disputes and "trials" organized around their works[74]—were in complete accord with those of their critics. In Moscow in early 1927 at a packed public meeting at which Osip Brik, Vladimir Maiakovsky, Sof'ia Smidovich, Sergei Tret'iakov, and Fedor Raskol'nikov discussed "problems of sex," Malashkin defended his story in the following terms:

> If you've read this thing, you know I didn't relish [its descriptions of depravity]. I have stated my authorial opinion rather precisely: I do not approve of this. I have seen these Smerdiakovs; I featured these people. I wanted to evoke revulsion toward them. I thought I had succeeded. Studying this life, I used the diaries of about seventeen komsomol'tsy. Eleven of them had committed suicide. My material was quite rich. Then I went to see where women and girls have abortions, to look at what kind of young people go there. And when I saw the huge line of sixteen- and seventeen-year-old girls, my heart began to bleed. What will become of this mother, of this generation that is supposed to build our communist society?[75]

Gumilevsky's memoirs, in particular, reveal the paradoxical nature of the discourse. Lacking Romanov's status as an established writer and Malashkin's close relationship with Viacheslav Molotov, Gumilevsky had difficulty finding a publisher and finally printed *Dog Alley* in a small edition at his own expense. The book probably would not have become a "success" but for the attention focused upon it by its critics:

> *Dog Alley* became extremely famous thanks to the fuss kicked up by *Komsomol'skaia pravda*, *Smena*, and other papers. Its fame was augmented by the many debates, discussions, and "trials" of the novel's heroes. The book was generally declared to have "slandered Soviet youth." But the fact is that I had followed Lenin's dictates about sexual relations as set down in his conversation with Klara Zetkin. Lenin had said the following: "We must fearlessly admit the existence of evil so that we can struggle against it decisively."
>
> The young people in Soviet society who were so offended by my book wanted to struggle against evil no less decisively than I, but without admitting its existence. And so it always happened this way: from the podium yet another orator from the ruling Komsomol circles would accuse the book's author of slander, ignorance, and invention, while from the overflowing and excited hall people would send me scraps of paper on which they had written, "Just ask what happened yesterday in the dormitory of the Technological Institute."[76]

[74] See, inter alia, "Adres Vuzovtsa ne 'Sobschii pereulok,'" 2.

[75] RGALI, fond 1328 (V. P. Polonskii), opis' 3, ed. khran. 27 (Voprosy pola i braka v zhizni i literatury [Stenogram of debate held in the Moscow Polytechnical Museum on 6 March 1927]), 27. On the Russian obsession in the 1920s with suicidal youth, see Anne Nesbet, "Suicide as Literary Fact in the 1920s," *Slavic Review* 50 (1991): 827–835.

[76] Lev Gumilevskii, "Sud'ba i zhizn'," *Volga*, no. 8 (1988): 105 (83–118).

Romanov stated his intentions in a long didactic introduction, later cut, to "Without Cherry Blossoms." Just as Gumilevsky asserted that he had followed Lenin's dictates to the letter, Romanov claimed that he had followed instructions from above:

A year or two ago it would have been crazy to think that young people all over the country would be preoccupied by moral questions—not just during a week of intensive meetings, but for months on end. *Then* such an interest would have been considered excessive and useless romanticism. But this year, that's the way it is. [. . .] The directive has come: to reexamine questions of morality, questions about our young people's everyday life and about distortions therein that have been reflected in monstrous facts.

Usually, governmental power acts as a sort of inhibition; in order to move forward, society must overcome the resistance of its rulers. But for us, governmental authority is the vanguard of society and always takes the lead in pointing out new directions to which social forces can apply their energies.

And so here, too, when it became clear that the norms of the first years of the Revolution, or, rather, the absence of such norms, had led to regrettable consequences, the government focused attention on a wing of our general front that had been lagging behind, on the elaboration of our morality.

And the first result of this new focus was the abolition of a taboo on many aspects of life that previously we had been obliged contemptuously to ignore.[77]

Obviously, none of these three writers regarded himself as a rebel; each thought he was doing the bidding of the Party and its leaders.

In 1926 Boris Zavadovsky, a biologist connected with the Sverdlov Communist University and a staunch proponent of medical enlightenment, spoke of the need to inculcate order in youth through a new proletarian, scientifically based ethics that would achieve what traditional methods of positive reinforcement and punishment had been unable to attain. "The ability to keep in check biological impulses and instincts in all cases where they conflict with the interests of the entire collective," he wrote, could be fostered only "by means of the most difficult of the neurocerebral reactions: the reaction of inhibition."[78] This reaction was not easy to provoke:

As direct physiological experimentation shows, inhibiting reactions are achieved with great effort and require continuous and multifaceted training for their simplification.[79]

We can read Soviet discourse on sexuality in 1926 and 1927 as precisely this sort of "training," a process in which discussion was first eroticized so that it could ultimately be more effectively politicized. To use Foucault's

[77] IMLI, fond 24 (P. Romanov), opis' I, ed. khran. 82.
[78] "Otvety na ankety o khuliganstve," *Molodaia gvardiia*, no. 11 (1926): 215 (210–219).
[79] Ibid.

terminology, "lines of penetration"[80] were deployed as power sought to use pleasure for its own ends. Fiction and criticism played crucial, mutually reinforcing roles in this spiral. The following pattern was established. An author would publish a work of fiction that aroused prurient interest and purported to discuss "the problem of sex." An outburst of critical letters or articles would follow close on the heels of publication, provoking in turn published "disputes" and editorial comments. Virtually all the participants in the debate would focus on sexual "excesses." The writers would first depict degenerate behavior within the Komsomol; critics would then charge them with slander or else bemoan the depravity they had unmasked. Komsomol writers made virtually no attempt to discuss in positive terms how sexual life *should* be structured, and very little attention was paid to the broader issue of sex roles in society. Rather, both "sides" attacked "depravity," using almost exactly the same terms. The real object of the debate, the destruction of the autonomy of "personal life," was achieved phatically—that is, by the very fact that sex was the "topic" of repetitive discussion for such a sustained period of time.

The repetitive nature of the discourse is particularly evident in an exchange of barbs by P. Ionov and Vladimir Ermilov. The former, in an attack on "Without Cherry Blossoms" published by *Pravda* on 4 December 1926, accused Romanov of "introducing the smell of Gogol's coachman Petrushka into the higher principles of proletarian culture." Claiming that he was introducing a new word, Ionov wrote: "Up unto the present time we have somehow been embarrassed to use the word 'depravity' [*razvrat*]. However, it's high time to use this word when discussing that which is occurring in certain circles of our student youth."[81] The word had, however, been at the center of the debate on sex for several months. Ionov's article provides a particularly blatant example of how the discourse was circling around itself; its speakers purported to add something new while engaging in more repetition.

Ermilov pounced on the lack of substance in Ionov's article—although not the same lack in the "debate" about sex as a whole—correctly arguing that Ionov had had nothing new to say and had simply voiced a sentiment with which everyone obviously agreed: that the October Revolution had been fought on behalf neither of anarchy nor of the bordello.[82] The essential point to be gleaned from Ionov's attack on Romanov and Ermilov's attack on Ionov is that *all three* men shared the same perspective on "free love"; for them the question of sex was a matter of excess and depravity. Fiction and apparently hostile criticism were cut from the same cloth. Fiction, jour-

---

[80] Michel Foucault, *The History of Sexuality*, trans. Robert Hurley, 3 vols. (New York: Vintage Books, 1980), 1:42.

[81] P. Ionov, "Bez cheremukhi," *Pravda*, 4 December 1926, 5.

[82] V. Ermilov, "O besplodnom pravouchitel'stve," *Molodaia gvardiia*, no. 3 (1927): 174 (166–176).

nalistic outrage, and public meetings functioned to excite and then control debate along lines that brought sex increasingly within the purview of a national polemic concerned with eliminating difference—not sexual difference but the difference between public and private life. An unfortunate sentence contained in the first edition of the influential editor Viacheslav Polonsky's *On Contemporary Literature*—and later cut along with other "stylistic sins" from the second—illuminates the dynamics of the discussion:

> We are being threatened by an extremely dangerous and corrupting wave of erotic literature.
> *We want to dwell on this question.*[83]

In its treatment of "The Moon from the Right Side" and "Without Cherry Blossoms," *Molodaia gvardiia* adopted a tentative, shifting position designed to "dwell" on the question as long as possible and to maximize reader participation in the debate. Excerpts from a special "dispute" organized at the Krupskaia Academy of Communist Education to discuss the treatment of sex in literature were included in the journal's December 1926 issue.[84] The journal's treatment of another story by Romanov, "The Trial of a Pioneer," was even more patently designed to produce debate. Romanov's tale expanded the scope of the sexual question, touching for the first time upon attitudes of members of the Party's children's organization (the Pioneers) toward sex. The editors published the following statement alongside the story:

> Although they welcome Comrade Romanov's attempt to reflect the daily life of Pioneers in artistic form, the editors consider it necessary to point out that in "The Trial of a Pioneer," Romanov reveals that he is inadequately acquainted with this daily life.
> The editors suggest that our reader-comrades who are interested in the work and life of the Pioneers send in their responses to Romanov's story.[85]

Six months later, Sergei Gusev, the journal's chief editor, criticized a conference of Pioneer leaders and "students" that, he said, had condemned Romanov for writing "The Trial of a Pioneer" and *Molodaia gvardiia* for publishing it. Pioneer leaders, he alleged, had wanted to hush up the question of sex among their charges. It would be a mistake, however, to ignore sex; physiological considerations, he argued, would inevitably spark Pioneers' interest in the topic.

[83] Viacheslav Polonskii, *O sovremennoi literature* (M.: Gos. izd., 1928), 193 (emphasis added). The same publisher printed the second edition a year later. This passage originally appeared in a short article by Polonskii in *Izvestiia*, "O 'problemakh pola' i 'polovoi literature,'" 4 April 1927, 3.

[84] "Disput v Akademii Kom. Vospitaniia im. Krupskoi," *Molodaia gvardiia*, no. 12 (1926): 171 (168–173).

[85] P. Romanov, "Sud nad pionerom," *Molodaia gvardiia*, no. 1 (1927): 86 (86–91).

Acute interest in the sexual problem, as well as conversations, debates, and
articles in newspapers and magazines, creates an atmosphere in which questions
about sexual relations literally hang in the air. It would be more than naive to
claim that these questions do not penetrate Pioneer circles. And the task of the
directors of the Pioneer movement is not at all to prevent that penetration. Let
them penetrate. [. . .] What is important is that such questions penetrate the
Pioneer environment not as physiological but as public questions.[86]

As Gusev's preoccupation with the rhetoric of penetration suggests, the
discussion of sex was intended by some participants to serve as a tool for the
sublimation of sexual energies. There was, however, an additional factor at
work. Prior to the Revolution, when publishing was still directed by the
market, literature about sex had often served the aim of authorial aggrandizement, a goal represented in the text by the seduction of a heroine by the
author's alter ego. (We have seen this dynamic at work in the novels of
Artsybashev and Kuprin.) A decade after the Revolution, textual seduction
operated on a more profound, metatextual level. Not authors but institutions
of power (the Party, the Komsomol)—through their literary organs—played
the leading role in an enterprise of seduction directed not at fictitious characters but at real-life readers, who fell prey to tacticians adept in what might be
called the sexology of reader response. Complimenting *Molodaia gvardiia*
on its November and December 1926 issues, *Komsomol'skaia pravda* wrote:

Both issues contain highly interesting discussions of Malashkin's "The Moon
from the Right Side" [which, it should be remembered, had itself been published
by *Molodaia gvardiia*]. It is especially commendable that throughout the maga-
zine one senses the presence and imprint of its reader on its pages. We must
recommend to *Molodaia gvardiia* that it strengthen its connection [*sviaz'*] with
its reader in all ways. This necessary task has been extremely well embarked
upon.[87]

The use here of the word *sviaz'*, which can also signify a sexual "affair,"
should not be overlooked. The Komsomol and the Party were attempting to
superimpose their insistent presence upon the sexual relationships of Soviet
youth. Intercourse *with* the reader became an essential part of intercourse
between readers. The text was an increasingly important and controlling sexual aid.

Significantly, voyeurism was central to the narratives of many texts
around which "controversy" raged. "Without Cherry Blossoms" was subtitled "From Women's Letters" and presented as a woman's confession. Malashkin's "Moon" was presented as a documentary account (recall the

---

[86] S. Gusev, "Sud pionerov nad P. Romanovym," *Molodaia gvardiia*, no. 7 (1927): 141 (140–
148).

[87] T——ov, "Bibliografiia," *Komsomol'skaia pravda*, 2 February 1927, 3.

author's "rich material"!) that exploited interviews, letters, and a diary. Malashkin's narrative tactic of imposing one layer of voyeurism over another had the effect of continually reminding readers that they were moving deeper into a private world. Readers stared over Malashkin's narrator's shoulder as he confessed, "When I read the letters of a stranger, I always have the uncanny feeling that I am standing in front of his door [. . .], shyly and inquisitively looking into the keyhole, through which I barely catch, barely sense the man, and even then only parts of his body." In essence, Malashkin's public was induced to reenact the process of penetration of which, on a different level, it was the victim. The principal heroes in these works, and in the discourse on sex in general, were the agents of penetration—the spying, eavesdropping figures who served as the readers' surrogates in the text. At the start of rehearsals for Bulgakov's *Zoia's Apartment*, which opened in October 1926 at Moscow's Vakhtangov Theater and in many respects participated in the discourse we have been exploring, the director, Aleksei Popov, told his cast: "All the types in the play are negative. The only exceptions are the criminal investigators, who should not be idealized but portrayed as workmanlike and simple. This group of characters is positive in that through them the audience is delivered of its feeling of protest [*cherez nee zritel' razreshaetsia v svoem chuvstve protesta*]."[88] In this strange metaphor, the direction in which the hands of the agents of penetration are moving is not clear; by participating in the penetration, the audience pierces the veil of secrecy surrounding Zoia's den of thieves and at the same time opens itself to the ministrations of Bulgakov's investigators.

In the sexual discourse of NEP—and not only in literature—eavesdropping and penetration play an extraordinary positive role, frequently functioning as an epistemological deus ex machina that enables knowledge to clarify, punish, and, sometimes, to cure.[89] But the use of eavesdropping never lost its essential organizing function. Malashkin's "The Moon from the Right Side" presents a fascinating study of how an author may seek to occupy simultaneously several positions, or, in this case, pseudo-positions, in a discourse. Into his work Malashkin drew apparently opposing voices within the sexual spiral. The tale begins with the narrator's justifying himself against critics who may object to his depicting the repellent side of Soviet life. As the story unfolds, peripheral characters debate whether the story is representative of all or just some segments of Soviet society. What unified these opposing voices—in the story as in real life—was that they, like Malashkin and his critics, were all on the same side of a debate in which a true opponent could

---

[88] M. A. Bulgakov, *P'esy 1920-x godov* (L.: Iskusstvo, 1989), 543.

[89] For an example of how reading a diary can help establish a medical and social diagnosis in the (supposedly nonfictional) genre of the popular medical brochure, see Dr. P. G. Bakaleinikov, *Polovoe znanie* (L.: 1927), 6–7.

neither speak nor exist. The story of the moral degeneration of Malashkin's heroine provided a vehicle for the representation in miniature—or "meta-polemic" terms—of the debate on sex. A work about sex, "Moon" is also a story about talking about sex. It is part of *and a picture of* a discursive framework in which only one side had a voice and talked with itself end-lessly.

Parody played a significant role in the discursive spiral. Periodically, the Komsomol press would publish pastiches combining elements of various "scandalous" works that earlier had appeared in the Komsomol's press or-gans. In these sketches, the building blocks of depraved works were high-lighted as elements that could be recombined in ludicrous ways:

THE MOON WITHOUT CHERRY BLOSSOMS, OR LOVE FROM DOG ALLEY

The air carried the smell of cherry blossoms and herring, of sweaty bodies and wine. In the next room, students from the workers' preparatory classes, who had been neglecting their studies for two years, were beginning an Athenian Night. They became depraved.

Peter came to Tania, having heard about her "fall." With intelligent, rock-hard, and decisive eyes he looked at her with commitment and asked tenderly, so as not to offend her, "How did all this happen?"

Tania smiled at him coquettishly, smeared her lips with powder from *Coty*, took off her dress and underwear, and put on a see-through *crepe-de-chine* dress over her naked body.

—That's how all the girls from the workers' courses dress. It's more comfort-able for discussions of the sexual question.[90]

All of the elements of the rhetoric of dissolution were present—including the use of foreign words to describe the licentious heroine. Far from under-mining the discourse of penetration, such parodies played a part in *preserv-ing* its vitality, keeping alive the notion that there was a "debate," and reaf-firming the imagery of the works they apparently targeted. One phrase, the

---

[90] My translation probably does not do justice to the original:

Луна без черемухи или любовь из собачьего переулка

Доносился аромат черемухи и селедок, потных тел и вина. В соседней комнате рабфаковцы, уже два года бросившие грызть гранит науки, начинали афинскую ночь. Разложились.

Петр зашел к Тане, услышав о ее падении. Умными, твердокаменными и решительными глазами посмотрел он стопроцентно на нее и нежно спросил, чтоб не обидеть, "Как все это произошло?"

Таня кокетливо улыбнулась ему, помазала помадой Коти губы, сняла с себя платье и белье и на голое тело надела просвечивающееся креп-де-шиновое платье.

—Так у нас ходят рабфаковки . . . Дискуссировать о половом вопросе удобнее.

(Pankrat Bul'ver, "Luna bez cheremukhi ili liubov' iz sobach'ego pereulka," *Smena*, no. 9 [1927]: 10)

"gauze dresses" Malashkin's heroines fling on "directly over their naked bodies," was quoted with particular frequency by Malashkin's critics.[91] Each time it appeared—whether in Malashkin's original or in parodies—it implied manifest disdain either for the practice of wearing such clothes or for Malashkin's "invention" of it, yet each reference reaffirmed the image's iconic force and served as a measure of its erotic charge. The "transparency" of the material is apt, for the dresses were emblematic of the heightened vision with which the reader was being simultaneously endowed and exposed.

It is important to emphasize that Malashkin's novella, Romanov's stories, and Gumilevsky's novel cannot be regarded as independent works of fiction. They should not be read as self-sufficient "utterances" but as parts of larger ones that also encompassed the disputes and editorial comments inevitably following the "literary" works. These disputes and comments were in no sense supplemental to the fiction; rather, together they composed a new, participatory, and collective genre of ideological utterance that was a distinctive feature of the Soviet 1920s. One Komsomol journalist, writing in 1926 about the propagandistic activity of public lecturers, called talks about sex "the hit" of the season: "every speaker [lektor-obshchestvennik] must have 'the problem of sex' in his repertoire; all other questions of sexual life are perceived as supplementary material that must inevitably be listened to along with the 'hit.' "[92] At least one contemporary critic explained Romanov's popularity by observing that his poetics were those of "staged, publicistic dialogues" and that his characters' words sounded "like detailed, tested, and carefully reworked reports";[93] as such, they naturally found an important place in the new, public, and participatory genre used by the Komsomol to promote disclosure and self-disclosure.

The propagandistic, integrative goal that Romanov and his fellow writers were pursuing on a (relatively!) sophisticated level was also the aim of countless public "trials" throughout the decade.[94] These trials, which in

[91] See, inter alia, RGALI, "Voprosy pola i braka," 35.

[92] Vikt. Iuz, "Na ocherednye temy. 'Problema pola,'" Zhenskii zhurnal, no. 2 (1926): 4. The word used for "hit" (boevik) has a military connotation and, in this case at least, reflects the aggressive propagandistic use to which the question of sex was being put.

[93] Zel. Shteiman, "Pobediteli, kotorykh sudiat," in Golosa protiv (L.: 1928), 110, 98 (89–114). Shteiman summed up Romanov's work as "nonstop blabber [sploshnaia govoril'nia] with a very peculiar slant: people speak principally about the biological and physiological problems of the individual, and also about how society regulates and liberates" (94). In this context, it is worth noting that Romanov achieved substantial fame earlier in the 1920s for his public readings of his work. V. Petrochenkov, Tvorcheskaia sud'ba Panteleimona Romanova (Tenafly, N.J.: Ermitazh, 1988), 113. Romanov's writing may seem flat and simplistic today, because we no longer have a vivid feeling for the audience whose participation was an intrinsic part of his work.

[94] One of Romanov's more provocative stories, "The Trial of a Pioneer" ("Sud nad pionerom"), even borrowed its title from the genre of the public, or "agitational" trial.

Artsybashev's day were confined to debates about and judgments of literary characters, were employed extensively throughout NEP for a variety of educational purposes: the battle with religion, the struggle to eradicate illiteracy, the propagation of proper hygiene.[95] Many of the plays concerned sexual issues (abortion, promiscuity, venereal disease), and here, too, the goal was a scripted entrapment of the public. Following is a typical example, from Dr. E. B. Demidovich's "Trial of Sexual Depravity," published in 1925:

> *Chairman* [addressing the audience]: I want you to remember that the decision about the defendant's—citizen Vasil'ev's—guilt or innocence will not be made by this gathering's Presidium but by a count of the voices of all those present. That is why in analyzing this case, each of us should be an active and conscientious judge. I ask you to provide yourself with paper and pencil in order to take notes. I recommend that you consider all the evidence critically so that by the time of the vote you will have reached a conscientious, well-considered decision.
>
> I ask the meeting to proceed to the election of people's judges.
>
> [Judges are elected]
>
> Does the meeting desire to become acquainted with the accused, citizen Vasil'ev?
>
> *The Public answers*: We do. [*Otvet publiki: Zhelaem.*][96]

The audience's desire is here literally co-opted. Although the audience is given a voice in the outcome, the cards are so stacked by character portrayal, plot, and the intrusion of "experts" that it is difficult to imagine a public jury speaking in an unexpected way. By its participation, the public was, in essence, assenting to the co-option of its desire and "enacting" the sexual discourse's principal goal: the infiltration of official ideology into private life. Participation was a two-way affair. The conclusion of Demidovich's play is entirely in keeping with this dynamic: the defense attorney suggests that the defendant be sentenced to being "surrounded" by "conscientious comrades who can help him return to a normal and healthy life."[97]

The theme of collective participation was emphasized to an even greater extent in other mock trials. In the script for a trial of "Free Love," a crowd gathers around komsomol'tsy debating sexual ethics. When one komsomolets asks, "Should the government interfere?" voices in the crowd respond, "The government interferes!" (*Gosudartsvo vmeshivaetsia!*)[98] And in *The

---

[95] These agitational trials are the subject of books in progress by Julie Cassiday and Elizabeth Wood. I would like to thank Julie Cassiday for sharing with me her copies of some of these trials.

[96] Dr. E. B. Demidovich, *Sud nad polovoi raspushchennost'iu* (M. and L.: Doloi negramotnost', 1927), 6.

[97] Ibid., 38.

[98] N. Bozhinskaia, *Prestuplenie Ivana Kuznetsova (Svobodnaia liubov')* (M.: Molodaia gvardiia, 1927), 60.

Trial of Anna Gorbova for Having an Abortion the individual body's owner-ship by the collective is stressed most emphatically:

> *Prosecutor*: Do you understand that a fetus is a future human being, that in it life has already begun, that you have killed a future person, a citizen who might have been useful for society?
>
> *Accused*: I was sorry that I had to have an abortion. After all it was of my own blood. I wanted a little child, but my husband was not happy, he began to de-spise me. I was so upset: what would have happened if my husband had stopped loving me? My life would have been finished.
>
> *Prosecutor*: Did you realize that each person belongs not only to himself, but to society, that a person does not have the right to injure himself in any way that might decrease his capacity for work, that abortion often leads to disease and to a work disability?
>
> *Accused*: No, I didn't know that. I thought that my body was my property, that I could do with it what I wanted and that my fetus belonged only to me.[99]

One moment in the development of the new discursive genre merits particular attention: the discussion surrounding the production of Sergei Tret'iakov's play: *I Want a Child!* (*Khochu rebenka*). Tret'iakov, who was one of the central figures in the constructivist journals *LEF* and *Novyi LEF* and in their drive to transform art into life, wrote *I Want a Child!* in 1926, at the height of the Komsomol's campaign to colonize "private life." In Sep-tember of that year he signed a contract with Vsevolod Meierkhol'd's theater for the play's production. Soon excerpts were published in *Novyi LEF*, El Lissitsky began designing sets, and the play was put into rehearsal under Meierkhol'd's direction.[100]

I Want a Child! was designed by its author to make an important and unique contribution to the debate about sex. The drama is centered on Milda, a Latvian communist from a poor rural background who is helping to build a new, communist way of life in the Soviet Union. She has never been inter-ested in sex or traditional feminine dress or behavior; in fact, when she first meets the man who becomes the father of her child, her clothes lead him to mistake her for a man. Her virtually nonexistent libido notwithstanding, Milda wants to contribute a healthy child to Soviet society, so she sets about

[99] A. E. Kanevskii, *Sud nad Annoi Gorbovoi, po obvineniiu v proizvodstve sebe vykidysha (aborta)* (Odessa: Odesskii dom sanprosveta, 1925), 7–8. The integrative and aggressive poten-tial of the dramatic trial reached a new height in a 1932 film by Mikhail Kalatozov, *A Nail in the Boot* (*Gvozd' v sapoge*). In Kalatozov's film the audience finds the defendant culpable of a deadly act of negligence and then, in a terrifyingly quick turn of events, is itself found guilty of the same offense. Kalatozov brilliantly displays how the act of passing collective judgment immediately renders each judge a potential victim.

[100] S. Tret'iakov, "Khochu rebenka!" *Novyi Lef*, no. 3 (1927): 3–11. The play was not pub-lished in its entirety until 1988. For the text of an early version, see S. Tret'iakov, "Khochu rebenka," *Sovremennaia dramaturgiia*, no. 2 (1988): 206–243.

hunting for a short-term sexual partner with impeccable class and biological credentials. Eventually, she chooses Iakov, a worker, and terminates the relationship as soon as she discovers that she is pregnant.

Almost all of Milda's dialogue is couched in ideologically correct language. Believing that "conception must be organized," she writes a note requesting "a three-day leave [from work] for the production of conception [*dlia proizvodstva zachatiia*]."[101] Control over previously elemental behavior is very much the play's central issue. One character vociferously endorses artificial insemination: "Scientific control must be established not only during a child's upbringing, not only during childbirth, but also during conception."[102]

Tret'iakov insisted that his goal was not to endorse a particular point of view but to promote discussion: "The play is intentionally problematic. The author's task is not so much the provision of a single answer as the demonstration of possible variants that can provoke a necessary, healthy social discussion around the serious and important questions touched upon by the play."[103] In addition, Tret'iakov sought to involve the audience in a novel way; from the outset he rejected and sought to "discredit" the standard technique of encouraging vicarious desire by eroticizing the topic of sex.[104] His play, he emphasized, had a radically different approach:

> *I Want a Child!* was conceived and developed with the idea that the sexual moments in it would not be perceived in accordance with sexual aesthetics but as an anatomical atlas.
>
> In the play there are didactic-propagandistic elements, a doctor's consultation, and, at the end of the play, a competition for the healthiest child.
>
> The play is meant to be a discussion piece. This means that its conclusions are variants and are suggested to the audience for discussion.
>
> Readings of the play before different audiences have already shown that it quite energetically rouses the audience's thought about the questions posed. That is the point of the play. It must not leave people indifferent.
>
> I am not a big fan of plays that conclude with an approved maxim that confers equilibrium on the powers that have been battling on stage, plays in which the plot is wrapped up, a conclusion presented, and the audience can peacefully go get its galoshes.
>
> I consider most valuable those plays where the conclusion emerges in the thick of the audience after it has left the building.
>
> Not a play that closes in an aesthetic circle, but one that begins on the aes-

---

[101] Ibid., 231, 209.

[102] Ibid., 221.

[103] From a 1927 interview quoted by A. Fevral'skii in his "S. M. Tret'iakov v teatre Meierkhol'da," in S. Tret'iakov, *Slyshish', Moskva?!* (M.: Iskusstvo, 1966), 198 (186–206).

[104] Ibid.

thetic trampoline of the stage and unfolds in a spiral, winding its way through the audience's arguments and through their extratheatrical experience.

Up until now love has been a tonic on the stage. It has held the audience in tension, transforming it into an "illusory lover."

In *I Want a Child!*, love is placed on the operating table and analyzed in all its socially significant ramifications.[105]

We have observed other writers and critics taking aim at and then participating in eroticized discourse. Tret'iakov's play—with its schematic, ideologically polarized, and parodically outrageous characters—avoids eroticizing the sexual question. Precisely its bluntness, however, made it run afoul of the authorities at Glavrepertkom, the theatrical censorship agency, which banned its production in 1927. Meierkhol'd fought the play's prohibition, arguing that Glavrepertkom should base its decision not on the play's text but on a director's vision for its staging. At a meeting at Glavrepertkom in early December 1928, discussion was heated. A representative worker invited from the Hammer and Sickle factory declared that the language was offensive; he did not want his sixteen-year-old daughter to hear such words. (The characters in the play discuss masturbation, birth control, "one-night stands," "spermatozoids," and the intrauterine rinse most useful for facilitating conception; their speech is far more explicit than that usually found on the Soviet stage or in the Komsomol press.)[106] More sophisticated commentators at the meeting also attacked the play, concentrating on its "vulgarity" and its extreme sociological generalizations. "There's more of Enchmen here than Bukharin," one dramaturge claimed. A representative from the Organization for the Protection of Mothers and Children criticized the play for improperly depicting medical consultations. On the other hand, the play was passionately defended by several speakers, including the film director Avram

---

[105] Ibid., 203–204.

[106] In the 1920s discussion of contraceptive techniques and of birth control in general was limited to special hygiene brochures or to publications intended for the medical community; the topic rarely surfaced in Party and Komsomol publications. (A rare exception was a letter published in early 1926 by the Komsomol journal *Smena* in which a Bolshevik called Nina Vel't criticized Sof'ia Smidovich, the head of the Zhenotdel, for refusing to discuss contraception in her statements on the "sexual question." Vel't's claims in support of birth control, that "nature is antiquated and poorly organized," and that "it is not fitting for revolutionaries and communists to bow down before the forces of nature," did not meet with approval from the many readers whose responses were subsequently carried by *Smena*. For the most part, the responses themselves did not mention birth control; one of the few that did noted that birth control was inappropriate for a virgin, led to female sexual deviance, and might even contradict Marxist doctrine on the indestructibility of the laws of nature. For the letter and responses, see I. Razin, ed., *Komsomol'skii byt* (M.: Molodaia gvardiia, 1927), 178–203. Unlike contraception, abortion was widely discussed in the Komsomol and popular press, and its harmful consequences were often presented in lurid terms. For a discussion of "the control of reproduction" in the 1920s, see Goldman, *Women, the State and Revolution*, 254–295.

Room, who deplored "sugarcoating" and warned that the banning of *I Want a Child!* would cause disenchantment among filmmakers. Finally, Meierkhol'd convinced Glavrepertkom to hold a special, closed session at which he and Igor' Terent'ev, another director desiring to stage the play, would present in detail their plans for production.[107]

Meierkhol'd's conception of the play may have differed from Tret'iakov's from the very start, for Meierkhol'd does not seem to have ever endorsed the idea of allowing the audience to decide for itself which position in the play was correct. At a rehearsal in 1927, Meierkhol'd had compared the play to a "mousetrap" into which even the actors in his troupe had fallen.[108] Now, at the Glavrepertkom meeting, Meierkhol'd saved the play with a passionate explanation of how its topic would be handled in his theater. The minutes of the meeting are worth quoting at length:

> *Meierkhol'd*: The performance has to be constructed as a discussion piece.
>
> I will extend the audience's section of the hall onto the stage. We will sell some places on the stage, but others will be given to organizations that will participate in discussions during or after the performance. The action will be interrupted for discussion. The characters will show themselves, like two-dimensional diagrams, to the orators; it will be similar to an anatomical theater where students cut up bodies.
>
> Therefore we will have a guarantee that all questions will be treated correctly [even if] they have been posed or resolved by the author improperly.
>
> In the roles of orators, we will place people on whom we can rely.
>
> *Richard Pikel'* [member of Glavrepertkom, affiliated with the Komintern and the Commissariat of Enlightenment]: Meierkhol'd's orientation is entirely in keeping with the nature of the play. But usually an author resolves a problem at the end of a performance. How will discussion unfold in the middle?
>
> *Meierkhol'd*: The discussion will proceed on dialectically constructed lines that will furnish a proper orientation for the discussion to come at the play's end. We will also provide provocative remarks that will unmask those who speak out against the play. And we will also organize discussions in order to collect material.
>
> *Nikolai Ravich* [dramaturge, historian]: Obviously, the discussion will be partly prepared. But each performance will have to vary.
>
> *Meierkhol'd*: Absolutely. There will be a surplus of people desiring to talk. In this performance, we will renew the genuine improvisation of the commedia dell'arte. Now everybody says that our epoch is the one most appropriate for discussions.
>
> *Ravich*: A significant portion of the creative work on the performance will belong to the theater and the director. It would be difficult to foresee how the

---

[107] Tret'iakov, "Khochu rebenka," *Sovremennaia dramaturgiia*, 238–240.
[108] Fevral'skii, "S. M. Tret'iakov v teatre Meierkhol'da," 199.

director's treatment will work. But the most ingenious orientation can be un-done. Uncertainty can enter the picture. There may be surprises.

We have to approve this production, but we should place a part of the respon-sibility on Comrade Meierkhol'd.

Meierkhol'd: Of course, but from time to time you have to send representatives to participate in the discussion. I am in complete solidarity with Glavrepertkom's opinion about the play. [. . .]

The play must be staged so as to fill in as many points as possible. Tret'iakov should come out occasionally from the stalls and say to an actor, "You are not saying it right," and he himself could pronounce a specific line. [. . .]

Pikel': Under these conditions all the author's ideas will be carefully carried out. And the public will understand the play in the way it ought. This maximally insures the correct understanding of the play. Meierkhol'd's proposal is the only solution and a most valuable experiment in the area of the renewal of traditional theater. [. . .]

Meierkhol'd: On the posters we won't write "first," "second," or "third perfor-mance," but "first," "second," and "third discussion."[109]

Igor Terent'ev, the director competing with Meierkhol'd for the right to stage the play, conceived his production along lines close to those of Meierkhol'd; the similarities reveal the extent to which the two directors understood the need to use as a model and improve upon the discursive forms of the day. Terent'ev, too, would have turned the play into a "perfor-mance-discussion," a "special form of theatrical action that might be stopped by the audience at any moment in order to receive answers to questions which arise in the course of the play." He wanted to place a suspended glass room, "a headquarters for theatrical maneuvers" (*shtab teatral'nykh deistvii*), in the center of the hall. In this room there would be a stenographer, typist, and announcer who would field questions radioed in from the audience. (Ter-ent'ev's plan was resolutely multimedia). All answers to the questions would be written before the first performance; surprise questions, presumably, would not be answered, and Terent'ev absolutely rejected the notion of im-provisation.[110] Pikel' explained why Meierkhol'd's version would be better: "Comrade Meierkhol'd's treatment is more valuable for us than Comrade Terent'ev's because discussion in the latter's version is of a didactic nature, since in his plan the general headquarters will have to prepare questions in advance. In Meierkhol'd's version there will be genuine discussion, living, acting, active thought. There is none of this in Terent'ev's version. [. . .] It's important for us that this play reach the viewer's consciousness in a manner

[109] Tret'iakov, "Khochu rebenka," *Sovremennaia dramaturgiia*, 241–242.
[110] Ig. Terent'ev, "'Khochu rebenka' (Plan postanovki)," *Novyi Lef*, no. 12 (1928): 32 (32–35).

that suits our needs."[111] Pikel''s judgment initially seems paradoxical until we consider his understanding of the dynamic of audience incorporation. The aim of the production would be to provoke "genuine discussion, vibrant, efficacious, active thought," and to capture that thought by channeling it to a predetermined conclusion. Discussion that did not "genuinely" shape the audience by encouraging and processing its involvement would risk leaving the audience cold.

Meierkhol'd received the exclusive right to stage the play in Moscow, although Glavrepertkom was still suspicious. Officially, the play remained forbidden; Meierkhol'd's production was approved as an experimental "exception" and was not authorized for inclusion in his theater's tours to other Soviet cities.[112] In the end, however, *I Want a Child!* was not produced until 1976, when it was staged in Karlsruhe, nearly forty years after both Meierkhol'd and Tret'iakov were destroyed in the Terror. After receiving authorization to stage the play, Meierkhol'd decided to wait until construction was completed on a new theater building that would more effectively permit the merger of audience and stage. This decision to delay production had the effect of ensuring that the play would not be produced, because timeliness was the play's raison d'être. Still, Meierkhol'd's vision for the play stands as a brilliant aestheticization of the integrative discourse prevailing in Soviet society. Meierkhol'd understood the theatrical, scripted character of the contemporary debate on sex, but he was disturbed by its (at least, apparent) lack of control from above. Moreover, his engagement with *I Want a Child!* was itself a convenient staging ground for his campaign for directorial control over all theatrical life. In the years to come Meierkhol'd would extend this campaign and advocate an aestheticizing control over everyday, nonartistic discourses. His 1930 article "Reconstruction of the Theater" implicitly equates directorial with dictatorial control. In it Meierkhol'd argues that the actions of the public in the streets should be better managed; in seeking to apply to the masses "a wheel and a rudder," he suggests that a lesson or two might be learned from the fascists or the Church.[113] If Boris Groys is correct and there is a direct line connecting the Russian avant-garde with Stalin's governance, that line surely runs through Meierkhol'd and *I Want a Child!*.[114]

[111] Tret'iakov, "Khochu rebenka," *Sovremennaia dramaturgiia*, 242.

[112] Ibid., 243. The Glavrepertkom resolution stated that Terent'ev's options were not entirely foreclosed. He might still reapply for permission to produce the play outside of Moscow.

[113] Vsevolod Meyerhold, *Meyerhold on Theatre*, trans. Edward Braun (New York: Hill & Wang, 1969), 253–274.

[114] Boris Groys, *The Total Art of Stalinism: Avant-Garde, Aesthetic Dictatorship, and Beyond*, trans. Charles Rougle (Princeton: Princeton University Press, 1992). Through Tret'iakov and Meierkhol'd, this line found further adherents in Western Europe, particularly in the aesthetic theory of Walter Benjamin. See his essay "The Author as Producer," in which he speaks approv-

As personal and sexual life were drawn into discursive prominence during NEP, the Soviet press could not stop talking about sex. By 1927 the sexual question was a constant topic of nondebate, a vortex that drew the reader/listener into its center as it sought to destroy his autonomy. Discourse, of course, is never simply an agent of conscious manipulation. Rather, discourse acquires power over all speaking it, gaining a momentum of its own. Klara Zetkin's interview with Lenin, first published in 1925 and frequently reprinted, provides a striking example of how even the center of power can fall under the sway of the discourse which works that power's ends. According to Zetkin, Lenin began their discussion of morality by criticizing talk of sexual mores, a topic that ought to be subordinate to larger social questions: "I don't trust those who are constantly and stubbornly devoured by questions of sex, like an Indian fakir by the contemplation of his own navel."[115] But Lenin (or Zetkin's Lenin) could not refrain from talking about sex and repeating himself on semantic and lexical levels:

Lack of restraint in one's sexual life is bourgeois; it is characteristic of decay [*razlozhenie*]. The proletariat is the ascendant class. It does not require intoxication, which might deaden it or arouse it. It needs neither the intoxication of uninhibited sexuality nor the intoxication of alcohol. [. . .] It neither dares nor wants to forget the foulness, filth, and barbarity of capitalism. It finds its strongest inducement to battle in the position of its own class, in the communist ideal. The proletariat needs clarity, clarity, and more clarity. That's why, I repeat, there must be no weakness, no squandering or destruction of strength. Self-possession, self-discipline—and not slavery; these are essential in love, too. But forgive me, Klara. I have strayed from the initial subject of our conversation. Why didn't you call me to order? Anxiety made me talk on. The future of our youth disturbs me profoundly.[116]

Zetkin was surprised by Lenin's preoccupation with this question:

Lenin spoke with animation and convincingly. I felt that each word was coming from the depth of his soul, and his expression confirmed this feeling. Sometimes his thoughts were emphasized by an energetic movement of his hand. I was amazed that along with the most important political questions Lenin accorded so much attention and analysis to problems affecting the individual.[117]

---

ingly of Tret'iakov, the Soviet press, and the use of writing to turn "readers or spectators into collaborators." Walter Benjamin, *Reflections*, trans. Edmund Jephcott (New York: Schocken, 1978), 220–238.

[115] Tsetkin, *O Lenine*, 11.

[116] Ibid., 17.

[117] Ibid., 18.

Here Lenin (or Zetkin's Lenin) spoke, as did nearly all commentators on sex in the mid-1920s, a language dominated by images of dissolution. Even on the etymological level, this language was obsessed with fears of centrifugal motion. Soviet youth was the victim of depravity (**raz**vrat), dissipation (**ras**pushchennost'), and of unbridled (**raz**nuzdannye) passions. Lenin's word for decay, (**raz**lozhenie), also means "decomposition," and his repeated use of the prefix indicating dissolution (raz/ras) points to the anatomical resonance of the struggle for the minds of Soviet youth. The collective body in NEP was putrefying, its parts coming apart in the rhetoric of the time. Fear of this figurative corruption prompted the attack on personal life and also gave rise to other discursive dynamics that we will investigate in the course of this study; all were part of an attempt to put the collective body back together again in the anatomical theater of public debate. It was appropriate that Malashkin, the singer of the collective's unified and muscular strength in 1919, should have turned his attention during NEP to the corruptions of disease and sex. One critic attacked Malashkin for showing his readers only "pieces of man," not his whole body, but this fractionalization of the body was part of a much larger ideological dynamic.[118]

One way to "recompose" the collective body was to introduce the collective into every potentially divisive activity. The suturing of the New Prometheus required the collective to play a role in every sexual act. In Soviet narratives of 1926 and 1927 intercourse often occurs in the bed of a third party, a "nonparticipating" other—as in Avram Room's 1927 film *Bed and Sofa*, where a guest moves into his absent host's bed and sleeps with his hostess, or as in "Without Cherry Blossoms," where the heroine notes with surprise as she loses her virginity that her assailant has thrown her on a comrade's bed rather than his own. N. Borisov's 1926 story "Vera" provides a particularly acute example of how in the fiction of the time descriptions of sexual intercourse or desire rely upon the implied or imagined presence of a third party who was simultaneously a specific character, all other characters, *and* the reader:

> Seized with desire, Nikolai approached Misha's bed. Vera lay on her back. Her shirt was pulled up to her stomach, baring her white splayed legs. Her silken hair was scattered about the pillow. [. . .] Nikolai carefully crawled over her, lay on his right side and began greedily to stare at her peaceful face, her evenly fluttering breast. Then he led his trembling hand over her bared, hot legs, he stroked her resilient breast and the small nipples that were looking straight up [*sic*!], and, becoming more and more infected by passion, he kissed her. Vera woke. Kissing him and passionately slapping his back, she muttered:
>
> —Oh . . . ooh . . . oh . . . My dear boy. Now come to me, come—and she pulled him onto her.

[118] V. Ermilov, "Literatura i molodezh'," *Vecherniaia Moskva*, 9 December 1927.

—Who! Who's this?!?—she suddenly cried in horror. It's not Misha! Nikolai, go away!!!

—Vera, listen to me . . . —he babbled, as if drunk.

—Go away! Go away!

But as a hungry wolf does not spare a sheep once he has caught it, so Nikolai, mad with sexual passion, did not heed poor Vera's entreaties. He overpowered her.[119]

In fiction of this period, the bed often gives way to more public places as an erotic site. The train, in particular, had a rich history in Russian and European fiction as a sexual symbol,[120] no doubt owing, partially, to its phallic shape, its role in commercial intercourse, its rocking motion, and its "carnivalesque" status as a place where conventions of everyday life might be disrupted, social strata mixed, and a certain anonymity of desire attained. Yet while the train afforded sexual partners anonymity and an exhilarating opportunity to give greater rein to repressed fantasies, it also brought into the public sphere behavior that would ordinarily be far more removed from the public eye. Aleksandra Kollontai's fiction provides a striking, post-Revolutionary example of how the train car becomes a place where intense sexual desire is both depicted and concealed. In her novella "A Great Love" (1923), set in Western Europe before 1917, the eroticizing of the heroine's relationship with her former mentor occurs as the pair travel to a political rally in a crowded train: "They had to sit pressed tightly together. [. . .] Natasha felt passing between them that sweet 'current' which both beckons and tortures."[121] Kollontai's passage is interesting because it so clearly connects the motif of public seduction with the collective ideal. This train journey is not only an interruption in daily life, it is a voyage between individual life—Semen Semenovich's home and family—and a new, "publicized" life in the collective, symbolized by the political rally.

The evolution of the insistence on public participation in personal and, above all, sexual matters can be traced on various levels. One instructive example can be found in the story of a commune founded by committed young communists in 1925. Initially the commune had decreed, in the best tradition of Russian asceticism, to forbid sexual relations because they "weaken the organism and lower one's capacity to work." Within a year or two, however, members changed their "charter," stating: "We consider that there should be no constraint on sexual relations (love). They should be open

[119] N. Borisov, "Vera," *Komsomol'skaia pravda*, 18 July 1926, 3.

[120] Peter Gay, *Education of the Senses* (New York: Oxford University Press, 1984), 63. *Anna Karenina* provides the most obvious pre-Revolutionary example, but Anatolii Kamenskii's story "Four" ("Chetyre," 1907), Evdokhiia Nagrodskaia's *The Wrath of Dionysus* (*Gnev Dionisa*, 1910), and Stroev's *Nonna* also made use of the erotic and liberating dimensions of train travel.

[121] A. Domontovich (Kollontai), *Zhenshchina na perelome (psikhologicheskie etiudy)* (M. and Pg.: Gos. izd, 1923), 27.

and we should relate to them conscientiously and seriously. An uncomradely attitude toward this question leads to a desire to hide and, as a consequence, to flirtation, dark corners, and other, similarly undesirable phenomena."[122] Sex became ideologically less undesirable when it moved out of the darkness of privacy into the light of public discourse.

Often the collective's participation in the romantic affairs of its citizens was symbolized through the direct insertion of a specific political figure into a sexual relationship. The proletarian poet Aleksandr Zharov provides a primitive example of this device in his "Poem to a Beautiful Girl":

> Вот взяла и примостилась ловко
> На широком выступе окна.
> Я люблю, когда твоя головка
> Над "Бухариным" наклонена.
>
> [Now you've gone and perched nimbly
> On the broad window ledge.
> I love it, when your little head
> Is bent over "Bukharin."][123]

We find a slightly more sophisticated instance in Kollontai's "Love of Three Generations." Zhenia, the heroine's daughter, who has no scruples about sleeping with any man who pleases her, admits to her mother that one fellow—Lenin—is different from and more important than all the rest: "Don't smile. This is very serious. I love him much more than all the others, than the men with whom I've gone to bed. When I know that I am going to hear and see him, I am not myself for several days. . . . For him I would give my life."[124] A student present at a debate on sex at the Krupskaia Academy in December 1926 drew a conclusion that manifested a keen understanding of how the prevailing discourse of penetration and collectivization operated: "It is essential to be able to love tenderly and to work, like Dzerzhinsky," he said, naming the founder of the Soviet secret police as his model.[125]

In many respects, the patched-together collective body recalls Solov'ev's social "catholicism" (*sobornost'*), and nowhere was this more apparent than in Kollontai's articles published in 1923 in *Molodaia gvardiia*. These pieces were frequently and harshly attacked for encouraging depravity, an interesting misreading whose implications we will more fully explore in a later chapter. To a significant extent, Kollontai expressed and anticipated discursive developments, but she did so in a language at once too concrete *and* too

---

[122] V. Leizerovich, ed., *Kommuna molodezhi* (M.: Molodaia gvardiia, 1929), 36–37.

[123] Aleksandr Zharov, "Stikhi krasivoi devushke," *Komsomol'skaia pravda*, 11 July 1926, 1.

[124] A. Kollontai, *Svobodnaia liubov'* (Pg.: Gos. izd., 1924), 50.

[125] "Disput v Akademii Kom. Vospitaniia," 171.

vague—she depicted a collective engaged in an ethereal orgy that, in her prose, is more sentimental metaphor than a manual for sexual practice. Her doubts about the suitability of monogamy were couched in the following terms:

Is it not important and desirable from the point of view of proletarian ideology that the feelings of people become richer, more varied in their harmonies [*mnogostrunee*]? Do not a variety of chords in one's soul and a multifaceted spirit facilitate nourishment and development of the complex, intertwined network of spiritual and emotional ties by which a collective is bound together? The more such strands are stretched from soul to soul, from heart to heart, from mind to mind—the more lastingly will a spirit of solidarity be inculcated and the more easily will the ideal of the working class—comradeship and unity—be realized.[126]

In *Dog Alley* Gumilevsky dwelt at length on the "sexual spider" entrapping Soviet youth.[127] Kollontai's "network" in the above passage should also be read as a web, an appropriate metaphor for a discourse that used sexual promiscuity—its presumed target—as bait for the souls it was supposedly trying to save.

Kollontai's network of varied "harmonies" suggests a musical model of entrapment, and it ought to recall to us Rector Liadov's nostalgic vision of War Communism as a brilliant orchestration. In this context of musical collectivity, it is worth considering for a moment the extent to which her ideal community is "polyphonic." An encouraged discourse, Foucault argues, may be a more effective form of control than censorship,[128] and Bakhtin's polyphonic model for Dostoevsky's novels, in which self-consciousness is forced to unfold "spontaneously and artistically," may owe as much to the collective form assumed by ideological discourse at the time of the writing of *Problems of Dostoevskii's Art* (mid-1920s) as to *The Brothers Karamazov*. "The freedom and independence" of Dostoevsky's heroes is, after all, both spontaneous *and* compelled:

This [independence of the heroes] does not mean, of course, that the hero falls out of the author's plan. No, this independence and freedom are themselves part of the plan. It is as if the plan predestines the hero to freedom (relative freedom, to be sure) and, as such, leads him into the strict and calculated plan for the whole.[129]

The word "relative" is key here, and one's interpretation of Bakhtin's use of it will affect the degree of proximity in which one relates Bakhtin to more

---

[126] A. Kollontai, "Dorogu krylatomu Erosu," *Molodaia gvardiia*, no. 3 (1923): 121 (111–121).
[127] Lev Gumilevskii, *Sobachii pereulok* (Riga: Gramatu draugs, 1928 [1927]), 80.
[128] Foucault, *The History of Sexuality*, 1:23 and passim.
[129] M. Bakhtin, *Problemy tvorchestva Dostoevskogo* (L.: Priboi, 1929), 19.

obvious artists of the organizational discourse like Meierkhol'd. At any rate, the argument has been convincingly made that, in one of its Marxist incarnations, the Bakhtin circle was in step with the integrative devices of Bolshevik ideology. Aleksandr Etkind places both Valentin Voloshinov's attack on the idea of an unconscious and his insistence on language's primary role in the formation of consciousness within the context of the consolidation of totalitarian power: "In the Soviet Union there can be no feelings outside of words and therefore there can be no unconscious. [. . .] Everything must be controlled by totalitarian power; and that which is not controlled cannot exist. Only that which is expressed in language is under control. That which is not expressible in words does not exist."[130] This important insight should be amended somewhat. Rather than wishing away the notion of an uncontrollable, profoundly individual realm, the Party and the Komsomol sought in the 1920s to bring the individual under control by converting silence into discourse and by making the lecture hall, the auditorium, and the courtroom (rather than the intimate setting of a doctor's office) the fora for the exposure of the individual and his implication into a new community.[131]

Escape from this ideological and discursive web was the most terrible act an individual could commit. Small wonder, then, that sexual activity conducted alone should be so disturbing to Soviet commentators on sexuality. Distress about masturbation did not, of course, begin with NEP. This virtually unmentionable sin had perturbed Dostoevsky,[132] and in *Landmarks* Izgoev had cited it as a troubling symptom of the state of the Russian intelligentsia.[133] At least some members of the pre-Revolutionary medical community had viewed masturbation as a disturbingly egoistic and antisocial act.[134] The Revolution effectively raised the ideological stakes of masturbation as a topic in public discourse; as collectivism was enshrined as society's central virtue, onanism became a particularly disturbing symbol of bourgeois alienation and of anticollective, individualistic spirit. Soviet commentators took great pride in statistics revealing that properly educated proletarian Soviet youth masturbated less than young people in less desirable national, class, or educational categories. I. Gel'man's 1923 study of sexuality in Soviet youth

[130] Aleksandr Etkind, "Kul'tura protiv prirody: psikhologiia russkogo moderna," *Oktiabr'*, no. 7 (1993): 186 (158–192).

[131] For an extended discussion of the rapport between Bakhtin's work and the integrative discourse of his day, see Anne Nesbet and Eric Naiman, "Formy vremeni v 'Formakh vremeni. . . .': Khronosomy khronotopa," *Novoe literaturnoe obozrenie*, no. 2 (1993): 90–109.

[132] F. M. Dostoevskii, *Polnoe sobranie sochinenii v tridtsati tomakh* (M.: Nauka, 1972–1988), 22:19–20.

[133] A. S. Izgoev, "Ob intelligentnoi molodezhi," *Vekhi. Sbornik statei o russkoi intelligentsii*, 4th ed. (M., 1909), 102 (97–124).

[134] See Laura Engelstein's discussion of this view in *The Keys to Happiness: Sex and the Search for Modernity in Fin-de-Siècle Russia* (Ithaca: Cornell University Press, 1992), 232–236.

proudly boasted that with the Revolution masturbation in young men had fallen from 73 to 52.8 percent and in women from 52 to 14.8 percent.[135] A 1925 Yakutsk study found that only 6 percent of Komsomol women masturbated, as compared to 28.5 percent of those studying at the local polytechnic school, a disparity the study attributed to the difference between the active, collectively oriented life of komsomol'tsy and the backward, "self-enclosed" life of the educational institution.[136]

Although some authors alleged that masturbation led to impotence and mental disease, most admitted, in conjunction with the latest research in the West, that onanism's dangers had been magnified. Still, commentators could not bring themselves to renounce the struggle with it. Dr. B. S. Sigal, author of numerous books on sexuality in the 1920s, emphasized in a brochure endorsed by the Russian Federation's Commissariat of Health that the danger of masturbation had been greatly exaggerated. Canvassing a variety of surveys, he observed that in some cases *no* harm at all had been noted.[137] Dr. L. Ia. Iakobson, the foremost Soviet expert on the subject, reached similar conclusions.[138] Nevertheless, both experts then proceeded to recommend ways of combating the phenomenon, with Sigal advocating sexual abstinence until at least twenty years of age as the "solution."

An obvious motive for the continuing preoccupation with masturbation was the reluctance of doctors and pedagogues to abandon deep-rooted and cherished ideas about so basic a form of sexual behavior. An additional factor, however, was present. Masturbation was a "deviation [*uklon*] of sexual desire"[139] because, although it might be the only sexual act possible for a truly unified, reified collective body, when practiced *outside* the collective, it was the ultimate antisocial act. G. N. Sorokhtin, in "Sexual Education in the Context of Marxist Pedagogy," declared that "all autoerotic processes, moments of self-satisfaction that do not require contact with another, occasion a pathological increase in egocentrism and produce shy loners imprisoned in themselves and unconcerned with the life of society."[140] In masturbation, moreover, sexual desire, a potent weapon in the state's campaign to weld the individual to the collective, was resolved without collective gain. While Dr. Golosovker in his survey of women in Kazan did provide the comforting datum that petty bourgeois women were twice as likely to masturbate as

---

[135] I. Gel'man, *Polovaia zhizn' sovremennoi molodezhi*, 2d ed. (M. and L.: Gos. izd., 1923), 33.

[136] Gushchin, *Rezul'taty polovogo obsledovaniia*, 44.

[137] B. S. Sigal, *Polovoi vopros* (M. and L.: Molodaia gvardiia, 1925), 36–37.

[138] L. Ia. Iakobson, "Onanizm s sovremennoi tochki zreniia i mery bor'by s nim," *Pedagogicheskaia mysl'*, nos. 9–12 (1921): 36 (29–42).

[139] Bakaleinikov, *Polovoe znanie*, 6.

[140] G. N. Sorokhtin, "Polovoe vospitanie detei v plane marksistskoi pedagogii," in *Polovoi vopros v shkole i zhizni*, ed. I. S. Simonov (L.: Brokgauz-Efron, 1925), 81 (73–94).

women from other social groups, he also quoted one woman of unspecified class origin who found the act liberating. According to this "conscientious onanist" (*soznatel'naia onanistka*):

> For women who, for some reason, do not have the opportunity to marry and who experience sexual feelings, I recommend moderate masturbation, once or twice a month. At first, this practice oppressed me, but then I began to think in a more healthy way. First of all, this practice reflects hygienic circumspection, and second, I feel that I am not obliged to anyone and bound to anyone [*nikomu ne obiazana i ni s kem ne sviazana*]. I masturbate with the middle finger of my left hand, first stimulating my clitoris with soap foam and touching my vagina just a bit. I experience complete satisfaction, and I have known no other type, since I am afraid of men. I feel healthy and satisfied. I do not experience the bitterness common to old maids, nor any nervous disorder on this account, nor any other diseases . . . I am full of energy, strength, and the desire to live.[141]

This statement is striking not only for its candor but also as an utterance resisting the discourse of corporeal collectivization. Sigal's assertion that onanism was an "absolutely abnormal act"—even though his own findings showed that more than one-half of all Soviet youths resorted to it[142]—is motivated by fear of individual independence, of an individual's reluctance to be "tied down." "Masturbation is an acute perversion of the sexual act," he wrote. "Here we have only one person, provoking in himself sexual arousal, by means of various devices that artificially arouse sexual feeling."[143] "The absence of a second participant in the sexual act requires the masturbator to waste a mass of physical and nervous energy to reach orgasm, which occurs with significantly greater ease [when attained] in the usual conditions," wrote one of Dr. Sigal's colleagues.[144] Onanism was deemed by one Soviet physician to be especially harmful to women, because it gave them access to a higher state of satisfaction than they could achieve if not acting alone.[145] Significantly, the most commonly suggested Soviet cure for masturbation utilized the same language of "bondage" that the "conscientious onanist" had used and rejected in proclaiming her liberation. An early issue of *Komsomol'skaia pravda* included a lengthy article by a leading venereologist, Dr. N. Rossiiansky, who provided the following advice on "how to combat masturbation": "If the child, and later the adolescent, is taught to transfer all his activity and all his energy to socially valuable creative work, if the adolescent is firmly tied to the communist youth movement [*krepko uviazan*

[141] Golosovker, *K voprosu o polovom byte*, 13.

[142] Sigal, *Polovoi vopros*, 34.

[143] Ibid.

[144] Ia. Golomb, *Polovaia zhizn'. Normal'naia i nenormal'naia* (Odessa: Chernomorskii meditsinsko-sanitarnyi otdel, 1926), 20.

[145] M. Mikhailov, *Bor'ba s onanizmom v sem'e i v shkole*, 2d ed. (L., 1925), 21.

s kommunisticheskim dvizheniem molodezhi], if the adolescent's mind is occupied by his studies or by social work, then that adolescent will never become an inveterate masturbator."[146] Instead of having his hands bound to the side of the bed, the young offender in these enlightened times was to be bound to something larger, albeit less concrete: the collective.

In 1923, two Voronezh writers published an undistinguished utopian tale, "Man of the Stern Morning," in which the villain, an engineer, is the only character who values privacy. "Locks had long gone out of use, doors opened automatically before anyone who desired to enter, and the engineer himself had to design and construct a locking mechanism for his laboratory."[147] Within several years, this affirmation of the "desire to enter" over the desire to be let alone was producing texts that earlier might have seemed to have sprung from the imagination of these coauthors or even from the author of *We*. Two months prior to the appearance of "Without Cherry Blossoms," *Molodaia gvardiia* published an article by Dr. S. G. Rozenberg-Epel'baum entitled "Making the Life and Work of a Komsomol Activist Healthy." In it, under the guise of combating mental fatigue and nervous disorders, the doctor provided a detailed schedule for the structuring of an activist's day.[148] August Forel, writing before the Revolution, had suggested merely that young people be kept busy,[149] but now Doctor Rozenberg-Epel'baum was telling them with precision what they should do and when. The guardians of the nation's youth were busily designing a future in which few aspects of life would lack the benevolent supervision of the state. In various areas of social interaction a supervisory campaign was being waged against the decomposition of the collective body and for the consolidation of that body. Entropic corporeal decay would be resisted when life was rendered more rational and planned. The infiltration of private life by means of a "debate" on sexuality, the conquest of Eros by his own arrows, was ironic but entirely consistent with this regulatory process.

[146] N. Rossiianskii, "Ob odnom rasprostranennom iavlenii," *Komsomol'skaia pravda*, 15 August 1925, 4.

[147] Pan and V. Keller, "Chelovek surovogo utra," *Zheleznyi put'* (Voronezh), no. 3 (1923): 9 (no. 2, 3–6; no. 3, 6–15).

[148] S. G. Rozenberg-Epel'baum, "Ozdorovlenie truda i byta komsomol'skogo aktiva," *Molodaia gvardiia*, no. 4 (1926): 147 (142–148).

[149] Avgust Forel, *Polovoi vopros* (SPb.: Osvobozhdenie, 1908), 238.

Chapter Three

THE DISCOURSE OF CASTRATION

"On 1 October 1923, at seven in the morning, Anastasia E., twenty-four years old, cut off the penis of her sleeping husband"—so begins the first case described in N. P. Brukhansky's *Materials on Sexual Psychopathology*, published in 1927.[1] The book, written by the founder of the first Soviet clinic "for the study of the criminal personality and of crime" and enthusiastically recommended by the nationally distributed journal *Pechat' i revoliutsiia*, was a collection of reports on sexually motivated crimes and on their subsequent adjudication in Soviet courts.[2] Although Brukhansky was aware that he was dealing with exceptional cases, he maintained that these instances of individual pathology were important in identifying pathological processes at work in Soviet society as a whole: "The court," he wrote, "is the mirror of our social life, and it reflects a complicated spectrum produced by the interaction of many factors that are developing dynamically not only within a socioeconomic context, but also—and consequently—within the purview of ethics, the law, philosophy, pathology, biology, and everyday life."[3] "Only by looking at this complicated judicial refraction," Brukhansky claimed, could one arrive at "a necessary synthesis" that would transcend the "horrors" described in these cases and lead to important conclusions about the nature of "normal and quotidian" Soviet existence.[4]

Brukhansky's book is preoccupied with cases of sexual violence and sex-

[1] N. P. Brukhanskii, *Materialy po seksual'noi psikhopatologii* (M.: M. & C. Sabashnikovy, 1927), 9.

[2] See Brukhanskii's description of his work in his article "Antisotsial'nye dushevno-bol'nye, psikhopaty i prinuditel'noe lechenie," *Moskovskii meditsinskii zhurnal*, no. 3 (1925): 55–68. For the review, which regretted Brukhanskii's expository "reticence," see P. Gannushkin in *Pechat' i revoliutsiia*, no. 2 (1927): 167–168.

[3] Brukhanskii, *Materialy*, 8.

[4] Ibid. This theme of the court's importance as both mirror and diagnostic tool was a common one in the NEP era. In a 1925 book of sketches on the work of the Soviet judiciary, one writer declared:

The Court and the Revolution are brother and sister, sharing a single will, a single thought, the same interests. [. . .] And the only difference between them is that the Revolution does its great deeds on the grand scale of history, moving millions of people, surrounded by the smoke of gunpowder, the noise of the barricades, and the thunder of battle.

And the Court? It does its work absorbed in the petty, quotidian, gray, unremarkable deeds of small, gray, unremarkable people, people scarcely distinguishable one from the other, people crushed by the small griefs and small wants from which the Revolution itself is born. (I. Dolinskii, *Sudebnye ocherki* [M. and L.: Novaia Moskva, 1925], 4)

ual disfigurement. Two of the first three cases discussed at length involve castration; the third deals with a lover's deocculation.

Brukhansky advocated study of "the complex social, biological, and psychopathological roots of the carrier of criminal tendencies."[5] He viewed all violent sexually related acts as socially significant and linked to recent changes in Soviet life. In his book's introduction he claimed:

> Over the last few years we have witnessed a general disorder and instability in sexual life. We have seen our young people begin their sexual lives far too early; we have observed significant increases in sexual perversion and in the rate of sex crimes[. . . .] Of course, this recent instability in sexual life is in many respects the product of the substantial economic tensions that our country is now acutely experiencing, and in particular of the economic growth that has been occurring under NEP and has been accompanied by increased speculation, easily earned money, and the desire for pleasure.[6]

It is important to note—and we shall later have occasion to return to this phenomenon—that Brukhansky here ascribes the increase in sex crimes, and depravity in general, to economic *growth* rather than to economic decline. He measured NEP's economic success by its *negative* impact on the "sexual life" of the USSR. In this context Brukhansky's recitation of the facts of the first case in his collection leaves little doubt as to why he selected it to open the book. The defendant, a peasant's daughter, came to Moscow in 1916. The Revolution provided her with the opportunity to study and become a midwife. In January 1922 (i.e., before NEP was a year old), she lost her virginity to her future husband, an event with catastrophic consequences. On the witness stand she gave the following testimony:

> Until I met my husband, I lived by my rational faculties alone. But then I began to live in accordance with my feelings. My reason declared: you have to finish your education. But all the same, my feelings won out. The life of reason faded into the background, yielding its place to something else. Mind and heart were not in harmony. I myself realized that. My mind had always been my master, until I became sexually active with my husband.[7]

By June 1922 the defendant had venereal disease. She obtained treatment, but the condition recurred frequently, for her spouse had many sexual partners. In late 1923, while suffering from a sexually transmitted uterine infection and high fever, she was forced by her husband to have intercourse twice in a single evening, an experience she found extremely painful. The next morning, upon awakening, she cut off his penis.

Anastasia E. was acquitted on grounds of temporary insanity. Although

---

[5] Brukhanskii, "Antisotsial'nye dushevno-bol'nye," 58.

[6] Brukhanskii, *Materialy*, 3.

[7] Ibid., 11.

satisfied by the court's decision, Brukhansky believed the following commentary to be essential to an adequate understanding of the case's importance:

> There can be no doubt that the defendant's reason was eclipsed. But at the same time, the very character of the crime, which, by the way, is unique in criminological practice, definitely points to the complexity of the act and to its discernible teleology. And, indeed, why not murder rather than mere amputation of the penis? [. . .] The character of the act committed by [the defendant] becomes clear. Her striving to emancipate herself, to regain her previous outlook, an orientation that had been eclipsed by the profound sexual attachment that had captured and enslaved her, all this led unconsciously to the penis as the culprit responsible for all. And it is characteristic that after the crime she felt relief. She compared her emotional state before and after to "waves on the sea after a storm."[8]

Brukhansky's presentation of castration as a symbolic and even logical event was not an isolated representative act; it crystallized discursive currents prevalent in Soviet society. The New Economic Policy had introduced a dangerously new—and yet disturbingly old—corruption into Soviet life, and the strategies advocated to combat it often relied on language with a pronounced surgical bent. Thus Aron Zalkind, one of the most prominent early Soviet commentators on sex, a psychoneurologist who attempted to synthesize the work of Pavlov and Freud, argued that the body had been "disorganized" by capitalism.[9] Zalkind attributed the "unnatural" balance

---

[8] Ibid., 17.

[9] A. B. Zalkind, *Polovoi vopros v usloviiakh sovetskoi obshchestvennosti* (L.: Gos. izd., 1926), 28. Zalkind (1831–1936) became interested in psychoanalysis early in his career. Prior to the Revolution he published several articles in *Psikhoterapiia*, the journal of the fledgling Russian psychoanalytic movement. In 1919 he became director of the Clinical Psychoneurological Institute in Petrograd and rapidly established himself as an authority on sexuality and sexual pathology. His position was enhanced by his work as a lecturer at the Sverdlov Communist University. Toward the end of the decade, Zalkind became the leading figure in Soviet "pedology," a discipline defined as a "psychophysiological synthesis" concerned with all aspects of man's life during his developmental stages. "Pedology" was juxtaposed by its advocates to pedogogy, which they deemed a lesser science since it concerned itself with the study of merely the process of education. See A. S. Zaluzhnyi, *Lzhenauka pedologiia v "trudakh" Zalkinda* (M.: Gos. uchebno-pedagogicheskoe izdatel'stvo, 1937), 12. For reasons that remain obscure, pedology was liquidated as a field of scientific research by a Central Comittee resolution on 4 July 1936. Zalkind died several days later. Aleksandr Etkind, whose *Eros nevozmozhnogo: istoriia psikhoanaliza v Rossii* (SPb.: Meduza, 1993, 326–332) contains the most detailed account of Zalkind's career to date, cites a personal communication from M. G. Iaroshevskii as authority for his claim that Zalkind died of a heart attack (456). David Joravsky, citing Zaluzhnyi's book, writes that Zalkind was "publicly cursed for killing himself as denunciations grew against him" (*Russian Psychology: A Critical History* [Oxford: Basil Blackwell, 1989], 279, 511). Zaluzhnyi's book, however, does not support this statement. Zaluzhnyi writes that Zalkind re-

currently prevailing among physiological processes to the influence of several centuries of bourgeois domination. Under capitalism, man's sexual life had "swollen" to an unnatural size, and his disorganized body now responded sexually to symbols that previously had not aroused him.[10] Over the past few centuries, Zalkind continued, the market economy had even given rise to conditions that had "sexualized the universe."[11]

According to Zalkind, capitalists had used sex as a new opiate to replace the increasingly ineffective narcotic of religion: "The striving for social interaction [*obshchenie*],—for class organization and class struggle—*weakens if it is deflected by sexual hypnosis*, by the extremely diverse temptations of contemporary art and of everyday life."[12] It was important to note, he added, that the effect of the expanded domain of sex could be found not only among the working classes; over the centuries the dominant, capitalist class also had lost some of its more egotistical and predatory members to the sexual narcotic. Nevertheless, "the principal significance of this sexual bacchanalia is its poisoning of the working class, its filling the proletariat up with a weakening, disempowering [*obessilivaiushchii*], and subtly concocted recipe, beside which the old hackwork [*topornaia rabota*] of religious deception must humbly bow its head."[13]

Zalkind's talk about sex was replete with images of emasculation. He divided human existence into three categories: "direct biological maintenance (nourishment, breathing, etc.)"; "aspirations toward socialization (contact with other people)"; and "the creation of progeny (sexual life)."[14] The "pansexualism" currently characterizing capitalist society had arisen as sexuality had infringed on man's natural tendency to identify with and interact with his social class. Sexuality was "feeding upon the drastically reduced [or "crudely cut off"] collective powers of the human organism" (*pitaetsia grubo urezannoi kollektivistskoi moshch'iu chelovecheskogo organizma*).[15] In

---

nounced pedology shortly after the Central Committee's resolution and shortly before his death. He does not mention suicide.

[10] Zalkind, *Polovoi vopros*, 23.

[11] Ibid, 28. A curious, rather Lamarckian parallel—not related, however, to the notion of the influence of capital or of the market—can be found in the writings of Annie Besant, one of the leading proponents of birth control in the late nineteenth century, who after her conversion to theosophy declared that the human sex instinct "has reached its present abnormal development by self-indulgence in the past, all sexual thoughts, desires and imaginations having created their own thought forms, into which have been wrought the brain and body molecules, which now give rise to passion on the material plane." Quoted and discussed in Sheila Jeffreys, *The Spinster and Her Enemies: Feminism and Sexuality, 1880–1930* (London: Pandora, 1985), 50–52.

[12] A. B. Zalkind, "Polovaia zhizn' i sovremennaia molodezh'," *Molodaia gvardiia*, no. 6 (1923): 247 (245–249).

[13] Ibid.

[14] Ibid., 246.

[15] Ibid., 247.

Zalkind's portrait of the disorganized body, sexuality had become a gross, engorged parasite, "swelling without limit" and "sucking the juices from other, biologically more valuable forces—more valuable but unfortunately cruelly disorganized by contemporary social reality."[16] The solution, at least in Zalkind's terms, was a countercastration: *We have to take from sexuality all that it—by the will of the deceiving class—has stolen from human creativity.* [. . .] We have to begin by tearing off from it [*otodrat' ot nego*] everything stolen by it from other [types of physical energy]."[17]

Possibly, there is a strange parallel between Zalkind's call for the emasculation of sexuality and earlier, pre-Revolutionary notions about man's ability (and woman's inability) to detach himself (herself) from his (her) sexuality. "Since a man's sexuality is only an appendage and does not take up his whole life," Weininger had written, "it gives him the opportunity of psychologically distinguishing it from the general background and thus of comprehending it." Turning castration anxieties into a virtue, Weininger had added, "A man may juxtapose himself to his sexuality and contemplate it isolated from the rest of him."[18] In essence, Zalkind's depiction of the disorganized body, in which sexuality has overrun its bounds and infused all other physiological functions as well as all culture, is similar to the pre-Revolutionary portrait of female sexuality as undifferentiated and tending to overwhelm all intrapsychic and intracorporeal divisions, "threatening and devouring, like the ocean."[19] Zalkind, in effect, inserts the bourgeoisie into woman's place as the threatening incarnation of sexuality; a concept developed in the context of gender becomes an important gauge of class relationships and exploitation. As we shall see in subsequent chapters, however, the original text of this palimpsest was never lost; women and the bourgeoisie were capable of emerging as horrific synonyms at any time.

Zalkind was not alone in believing that there were few biological givens in the human constitution. His declaration that "man eats, breathes, sleeps, and loves not as a man but as a man belonging to a specific historical epoch and a specific social group"[20] was shared by most commentators on the "sex-

[16] Zalkind, *Polovoi vopros*, 24.

[17] Zalkind, "Polovaia zhizn'," 247, 249. In his wide-ranging, savage attack on Zalkind's work and career, A. S. Zaluzhnyi singles out the quoted phrase (and the word "stolen" [*ukralo*] in particular) as an example of Zalkind's deficient writing: "It has long been clear that true science knows how to speak in intelligible language, that it has no need to resort to verbal disguise. We know how simply Lenin was able to set forth the most profound thoughts, how simply and how like clarity itself Comrade Stalin expresses his thoughts, how all the great writers of classical Marxism wrote. We do not find a hint of this in Zalkind." *Lzhenauka pedologiia v "trudakh" Zalkinda*, 33.

[18] Otto Veininger (Weininger), *Pol i kharakter* (SPb.: Posev, 1909), 107.

[19] Nikolai Berdiaev, *Smysl tvorchestva* (Paris: YMCA Press, 1983 [1916]), 225.

[20] Zalkind, "Polovaia zhizn'," 246. "There is not a single organ," he wrote, "not a single biological function, that is not extremely closely connected with man's social activity." *Ocherki kul'tury revoliutsionnogo vremeni* (M.: Rabotnik prosveshcheniia, 1924), 54.

ual question." Writing in 1923, I. Gel'man was merely restating a commonly held tenet when he claimed that sexuality was shaped by social as well as physical influences and was therefore subject to manipulation: *Sexual and instinctive attractions and experiences can be checked or stimulated by this or that social environment*; they can be replaced—in accordance with the laws of psychic and energetic equivalency—by other psychic phenomena. Finally, they may, in the interests of government or of the race, become the object of consciously exerted influence by powers that are not biological but socioeconomic."[21]

Most commentators advocated establishing a more "natural," class-conscious balance between sexuality and other physiological processes. Zalkind protested that he did not want to eliminate sexuality completely but to reduce it to a more manageable size. Here, however, he anticipated opposition: "'But,' they will say to me, 'how can you cut down on sexuality [*urezyvat' polovoe*]? After all, it has nourished human fantasy and moved creative processes forward.' [. . .] All these objections are unfounded. I do not demand the destruction of sexuality—I just want to put it in its place—in a place significantly more modest than the one it occupies now."[22]

During the 1920s—for reasons we shall examine below—in the popular press this "place" was defined almost exclusively in negative terms, often in the rhetorical gesture of a speaker denying his or her own puritanism. If sexual excess was a mark of bourgeois-dominated culture, then the dynamics of class struggle required that these excesses be relentlessly pursued—until the phenomenon of sexual behavior would disappear altogether, withering away as concepts such as ethnicity or the State were supposed eventually to do under communism. Any manifestation of sexual desire was tainted by the possibility of excess; the logic of the discourse demanded a retreat to a point where sexuality's "swollen" size would become infinitely small. Many pedagogues, doctors, and politicians entering the lists of the "debate" on sex seemed to suspect where their language was leading, for the denial of asceticism became a standard trope in discussions of sexuality. "The Government is *not* striving at all to make everyone asexual," wrote Dr. Golosovker in his study of female sexuality;[23] "the Communist Party does not want to create a sect of *skoptsy* or a society of virtuous monks out of the Man of the Future," Bukharin told a 1925 congress of teachers.[24] After each disclaimer, however, came a "but" and such a vigorous attack on sexual excess that by the end of an article or speech the denial of ascetic purpose carried virtually no weight.[25]

[21] I. Gel'man, *Polovaia zhizn' sovremennoi molodezhi* (M. and L.: Gos. izd., 1923), 11.

[22] Zalkind, *Polovoi vopros*, 48.

[23] Dr. S. Ia. Golosovker, *K voprosu o polovom byte sovremennoi zhenshchiny Kazani* (Kazan': Kazanskii meditsinskii zhurnal, 1925), 19.

[24] N. Bukharin, "Uchitel'stvo i komsomol," *Izvestiia*, 4 February 1925, 4.

[25] See Lenin's remarks to Klara Tsetkin: "I am far from a gloomy ascetic, but it often seems to me that this "new sexual life" of our youth—and of our adults, too—is purely bourgeois, a

"The majority of us are not clear what normal sexual attraction is," one doctor admitted in a typical treatment of the question in *Komsomol'skaia pravda*, "nor where the boundaries of licentiousness and chastity lie," but his ensuing attack on cosmetics and on "a sedentary way of life" attested that for him, at least, the boundary between licentiousness and chastity was situated so as to accord the latter very little space.[26] "We are fighting," Bukharin maintained, "for the realization of life in its maximal fullness. But between the fullness of life and hooliganism there is a difference, and this difference cannot be forgotten."[27] Such line drawing was a discursive preoccupation in many areas of debate in the Soviet 1920s; where sex was concerned, this rhetorical device was practiced with exceptional enthusiasm, and as a result the territory assigned to sexual behavior—the area falling between the realms of abstinence and depravity—was usually left blank. The potential existence of a middle ground, as Bukharin's statement attests, was always present in the minds of speakers, but the dynamics of the epoch's discourse tended not to permit it to be described.

Several halfhearted attempts were made during the 1920s to establish sexual norms to serve young Soviet citizens as guides. Unfortunately, the reductive nature of the discourse—with its pressure infinitely to shrink the area within which sexuality could function—did not allow for the positive affirmation of norms. When the question was phrased in the following manner, "How should sexual life transpire so that the interests of the entire society, of the entire working class, will *not* suffer,"[28] it was difficult to stake out territory within which class interests might *not* be—at least, potentially—affected adversely. Even when norms were haltingly proposed, they were proffered in negative terms. Sexual intercourse should occur *no more* frequently than three times a week or once daily;[29] it should *not* occur before age twenty-two[30] or twenty.[31] In a pamphlet entitled *What Is Normal Sexual Life?* Dr. O. Feigin could conclude only that "from a scientific point of view" men should *not* engage in sexual intercourse before age twenty-two, *nor* should women do so under twenty.[32] "Experts," such as Dr. Rikhard Fronshtein, a

---

variation on the good old bourgeois brothel." Klara Tsetkin, *O Lenine. Vospominaniia i vstrechi* (M.: Moskovskii rabochii, 1925), 15.

[26] Dr. I. Kallistov, "Polovoi vopros i fizkul'tura," *Komsomol'skaia pravda*, 29 July 1925, 3.

[27] Bukharin, "Uchitel'stvo," 4.

[28] Dr. B. S. Sigal, *Polovoi vopros* (M. and L.: Molodaia gvardiia, 1925), 4.

[29] S. A. Selitskii, "Polovaia zhizn' zhenshchiny," in *Polovoi vopros v svete nauchnogo znaniia*, ed. V. F. Zelenin (M. and L. : Gos. izd., 1926), 191 (182–202); Dr. P. G. Bakaleinikov, *Polovoe znanie* (L., 1927), 11.

[30] A. Stratonitskii, *Voprosy byta v komsomole* (L.: Priboi, 1926), 58.

[31] Bakaleinikov, *Polovoe znanie*, 11.

[32] Dr. O. Feigin, *Chto takoe normal'naia polovaia zhizn'*. (L.: 1927), 7. For similar figures (ages 22–23 for men and 19–20 for women), see A. L. Berkovich, "Voprosy polovoi zhizni pri svete sotsial'noi gigieny," *Molodaia gvardiia*, no. 6 (1923): 250–254. See also Dr. Ia. I. Ka-

prominent venereologist lecturing in 1924 at the Moscow Polytechnic Museum, tended to throw up their hands and, unable to arrive at a norm, counseled the avoidance of sexual relations altogether: "It is impossible to establish a universal norm in this area, since differing physical particularities, as well as conditions of life and work, have enormous significance, but we can state with absolute precision that sexual abstinence for men who have not yet become sexually active is entirely unproblematic and, in any case, cannot be dangerous."[33] In 1926 in *Komsomol'skaia pravda* Professor V. Gorinevsky advised komsomol'tsy to choose the "path of battle with everything that excites and arouses sexual feeling, to commit [yourselves] to sexual abstinence decisively and irreversibly."[34]

To some extent, this manner of argumentation is evidence of lazy thinking: since distinctions are too difficult to draw, all gray areas are eliminated at one stroke. But this laziness was dictated by the terms of the discourse; the usually thoughtful health commissar, Nikolai Semashko, declared in no uncertain terms: "We have to warn our youth about corruption and sexual promiscuity. We have to ask them to abstain, for there can be no harm from abstinence, only benefit."[35]

Despite emphatic denials of monastic intentions by Lenin, Bukharin, and others, the condemnations of depravity that inevitably followed these declarations helped create a climate with strong puritanical pressures. Asceticism became a means of self-identification, an affirmation of ideological purity in an environment increasingly affected by capitalism.

The promotion of ideal models for communist youth invariably entailed the advocacy of total abstinence. Nothing short of this standard in sexual relations could be recommended to the members of communism's "next shift." In a book published shortly after his death, Vladimir Bekhterev, one of the preeminent figures in Soviet medical science, employed the prevailing

---

minskii, *Polovaia zhizn' i fizicheskaia kul'tura*, 2d ed. (Odessa: Svetoch, 1927), 28, 30: "Sexual life should begin no earlier than twenty for men and eighteen for women"; "Sexual life should not be too intensive." An exception to this restrictive discourse is an article in the Komsomol journal *Smena* recommending that "a healthy norm [for sexual intercourse] is once, twice, or three times a week." N. Sh. Melik-Pashaev, "Abort, ego posledstviia i preduprezhdenie beremennosti," *Smena*, no. 17 (1926): 11. Melik-Pashaev's article is exceptional in other ways: for instance, it is one of just a few publications in *Smena* to take a positive stance toward birth control. A letter from a komsomolka advocating birth control—and thus generating a swarm of incensed responses—explicitly took aim at the reductive nature of the discourse: "When we need only put ointment on a finger, we amputate a hand instead." Nina Vel't, "Pis'mo vtoroi komsomolki," *Smena*, no. 12 (1926): 9. Implicitly, the responses discrediting Vel't's views on sex also discredited her critique of the discourse.

[33] "Polovoi vopros," *Izvestiia*, 3 March 1925, 6.

[34] V. Gorinevskii, "Polovoi vopros," *Komsomol'skaia pravda*, 29 January 1926, 3.

[35] N. Semashko, "Polovoe vospitanie i zdorov'e," *Komsomol'skaia pravda*, 15 August 1925, 5.

negative rhetoric to support his recommendation of total abstinence for the
nation's youth:

> I will quote, as an example, a note that was handed to me by a listener at a
> public lecture on the sexual question. The note reads: "I am thirty-two years old,
> my brother is thirty-one, we enjoy complete physical health and possess signifi-
> cant intellectual work-capability and we have never had sexual relations. If we
> demand sexual abstinence from a woman before marriage, then we ought to
> demand the same from men. If you inspire yourself at a young age (fifteen to
> sixteen) with love for a particular woman, the most depraved environment will
> be powerless to play any role. I've never engaged in masturbation. Medical
> student D." Lovers of "indecencies" will say that this is petty bourgeois behavior
> or unnecessary asceticism, because there's no masturbation and no sexual rela-
> tions up through thirty-two years of age. But however that might be, this young
> man has neither seduced nor corrupted a single girl, has not been the reason for
> a single abortion, has not made any woman into a cripple, and has not forced
> any woman to sit with a child when she, like he, would rather be studying or
> active in social work.[36]

In *The Trial of Sexual Depravity*, an agitational drama for which Zalkind
provided an introduction, a parade of fallen women victimized by the "defendant" is interrupted by the appearance of a complainant's brother, Vtorov,
a student at an institution of higher learning and a Party member for several
years:

> *Defense Attorney [D]*: Witness Vtorov, you, it seems, are twenty-three years old.
> *Vtorov [V]*: Yes, twenty-three.
> *D*: Are you married?
> *V*: No, I'm not.
> *D*: Well, and how do you approach women?
> *V*: Like a comrade.
> *D*: And how do you part with them?
> *V*: Also like a comrade.
> *D*: You've had children?
> *V*: Me? . . . No, I haven't.
> *D*: You've used birth control?
> *V*: Never.
> *D*: So you are not healthy?
> *V*: I am absolutely healthy . . . I have never had a sex life.
> *D*: At twenty-three years of age?

---

[36] Akademik V. Bekhterev, *Znachenie polovogo vlecheniia v zhiznedeiatel'nosti organizma*
(M.: Narkomzdrav R.S.F.S.R., 1928), 16–17. Bekhterev was apparently not disconcerted by the
strange way in which the author of the note combined communism with the sort of long-term
chaste devotion characteristic of courtly romances and their idealistic successors.

V: At twenty-three years of age.

D: I have no further questions.

Expert [*E*]: May I pose several questions to the witness?

Court: By all means.

E: You have experienced attraction to a woman?

V: Yes.

E: What has held you back from intimacy?

V: I am a member of the Party. I need strength for the construction of a new form of life and I strive conscientiously so that my sex life does not cripple me, or a woman, or our child. I am young and won't need a woman any time soon, and I am looking for one who will attract me not for a day and not for a month, but for many years. I am looking for a woman who would be both a woman and a comrade-in-work.

E: And so far you haven't found one?

V: Sometimes it has seemed as if I have. But upon checking it's been clear that it was a mistake.

E: And how do you check?

V: I simply wait, allow the attraction to strengthen, observe her and myself, asking myself do I want a child with her.

E: And is that all that restrains you?

V: No, it's not all. I conscientiously want to begin a sex life only when a child will not frighten me.

E: Is the battle difficult?

V: It's easier in the winter. In the summer it's harder, especially at the beginning.

E: Do you suffer from insomnia?

V: No, I sleep splendidly.

E: What helps you in the battle?

V: Breaks for physical exercise. I try to avoid being alone when I have free time. Social work helps me a lot. When nature rebels, I inconspicuously avoid girls. When I am calm again I spend time with them once more.[37]

These examples show the extent to which the ascetic model dismissed as an admittedly unattainable *ideal* by mid-nineteenth-century radicals was being fervently promoted as an ideological goal for every conscientious young Soviet citizen in the 1920s. In *What Is to Be Done?* Chernyshevsky admitted that he had introduced the ascetic Rakhmetov, an ancillary character who avoids women and all other potential sources of pleasure, as a model, an exceptional standard toward which radicals should strive but which they would not be expected in practice to reach. As contemporary models attainable to his readers, Chernyshevsky furnished his audience with the imperfect

---

[37] Dr. E. B. Demidovich, *Sud nad polovoi raspushchennost'iu* (M. and L.: Doloi negramotnost', 1927), 24. The brother's name, resonant with the verb *vtorit'* ("to second"), indicates his status both as a mouthpiece for the Party and as an echo of its previously expressed views.

characters who play his novel's central roles. Now, after the Revolution, when theory was supposed to be assuming flesh, Rakhmetov was transformed into a (purportedly) *immediately* accessible model for all correctly thinking young communists.

Some voices during NEP did attack asceticism as excessively idealistic, but these, too, were soon drawn into the discursive vortex and began to espouse the same sentiments they simultaneously professed to condemn. Emel'ian Iaroslavsky, the head of the Party's Central Control Commission (the division charged with reviewing disciplinary procedures), deplored asceticism. Communists, he declared, did not have to transfer the ownership of their bicycles to their Party cells, nor did they have to live in poverty "like saints." The notion that "the poorer we live, the poorer we dress, the worse everything is, the more holy we will be " was "utterly incorrect" and contrary to the Party's goal of "making life more joyous" and of "raising the living standards of workers."[38] He decried the "priestly morality" that he discerned with increasing frequency in the resolutions of local control commissions:

> One commission resolved to exclude a woman from the Party for prostitution, and from a perusal of this resolution it was apparent that this communist's prostitution consisted in her having had sexual relations with two different men. The regional control commission reinstated this comrade in the Party, formulating the grounds for its decision in this manner: since this comrade had fought with a partisan division against Kolchak at the front and had lived constantly among men, it would be possible to *forgive* her behavior. Thus this comrade was saved only by having been in a partisan brigade, and if this had not been the case, she would have been expelled.[39]

Iaroslavsky took pains to point out that a woman's having sexual relations with two men did not constitute prostitution and that a woman should not be excluded for "incorrect sexual relations [. . .] if this did not harm the Party in any way." Even this statement provided ammunition, however, for Party commissions functioning in a world in which members were constantly encouraged to be "on guard" against pernicious influences. Was it not better to err on the side of caution? Iaroslavsky himself, two years later, would—while continuing to preach against asceticism—give the following advice to Soviet youth: "We [i.e., older, longtime Party members] spent years in prison—sometimes serving up to eight or nine years. And whether or not we so desired, we had to endure these periods of abstinence. And it is only ignorance and misunderstanding of the most fundamental hygienic truths by

---

[38] "Plenum TsKK. O partetike," *Pravda*, 9 October 1924, 3.
[39] Ibid.

the most illiterate segments of our young people that lead them to accept the idea that abstinence is harmful."[40]

The tenor of the discussion of sexual norms, or, more accurately, of what would *not* constitute acceptable behavior, should remind us of the difficulty pre-Revolutionary critics such as Novopolin and Omel'chenko had in finding a place for sexual relations in the realm between depravity and traditional bourgeois morality (or, alternatively, asceticism). Compounding this problem of establishing a sexual "middle ground" was the fact that NEP itself was a period of transition, a historical "gray" area in a culture that had difficulty accepting shades between black and white. NEP's "transitional" nature, moreover, was dual and contradictory. In the long run, NEP was part of the progression from capitalism to communism; in the short run, it was a transition *back* from impracticable, relatively pure communism to a more realistic, quasi-capitalist economy. Public discussions about sex during NEP offered the opportunity for ideological discomfort with political and economic transitions and compromises to be projected into an area where the notion of a middle ground could be resolutely resisted.

The Party's Central Control Commission emphatically rejected calls for the promulgation of rules governing sexual behavior; the facts of a given situation would have to serve local control committees as a guide to behaviors injurious to the interests of Party and class and as such "immoral" and improper.[41] This position merely fanned the flames of reductive discourse, as control commissions and journalists found depravity under every rock. Any act might be found immoral, depending on the unique circumstances in which it occurred. Rules were proposed from *outside* the central Party apparatus, but these, also, tended to stress what should *not* be done rather than promulgate acceptable norms. Many of the externally proposed moral guidelines sought to deal with the sexually charged atmosphere of NEP by reducing the causes of sexual arousal as much as possible. Dr. M. Lemberg, writing in 1925, recommended five rules for avoiding sexual stimulation:

1. Never drink alcohol.
2. Sleep on a hard bed. Upon waking stand up at once.

[40] E. Iaroslavskii, "Moral' i byt proletariata v perekhodnom periode," *Molodaia gvardiia*, no. 5 (1926): 149 (138–153).

[41] At the first plenum of the Central Control Commission, Krupskaia noted the extremely divergent views prevailing among Party members concerning the morality or immorality of particular conduct, and she asked the commission to provide directives (*ukazy*) on morality. The Secretariat and Presidium appointed a committee, which concluded that communist morality was situational: the immorality of actions had to be decided on a case-by-case basis in accordance with whether particular conduct at a particular moment was contrary to the interests of the working class, the proletarian revolution, and Party solidarity. "Plenum TsKK. O partetike," *Pravda*, 9 October 1924, 3.

3. Don't eat too much meat. Eat three hours before sleep. Urinate before going to bed.

4. Don't read erotic literature.

5. Don't lead a sedentary life.[42]

Zalkind, a more systematic and self-professed "Marxist" thinker, designed twelve "commandments," many of them overlapping and phrased in the negative:

1. Sexual life should not begin too early.

2. Sexual abstinence is essential until marriage, and marriage should occur only when full social and biological maturity has been reached (age twenty to twenty-four).

3. Sexual intercourse should only be the culmination of profound mutual affection and of attachment to the sexual object.

4. The sexual act should only be the final link in a chain of profound and complex experiences uniting lovers.

5. The sexual act should not be repeated often.

6. Sexual partners should not be changed frequently.

7. Love should be monogamous.

8. At every sexual act, the possibility that progeny will result should always be remembered.

9. Sexual selection should occur in accordance with class and Revolutionary proletarian selection. Flirtation, courtship, coquetry, and other methods of specifically sexual conquest should not enter into sexual relations.

10. There should be no jealousy.

11. There should be no sexual perversion.[43]

12. In the interests of Revolutionary expediency a class has the right to interfere in the sexual life of its members. Sexuality must be subordinated to class interests; it must never interfere with them and must serve them in all respects.[44]

Zalkind's commandments did not differ much from Omel'chenko's advice in 1908 to communist maidens of the future, although Zalkind's "medical" and "Marxist" self-assurance enabled him to present old ideas with new, "scientific" force. Like Omel'chenko, Zalkind tended to define "free love" as love that leads to intercourse infrequently. New in Zalkind's commandments was his concern not merely with intercourse but with desire and arousal as phenomena antagonistic to the interests of the working class. He coined a

[42] Dr. M. Lemberg, *Chto nuzhno znat' o polovom voprose* (L.: Priboi, 1925), 44.

[43] Zalkind never defined perversion. He did, however, insist that only 1 to 2 percent of sexual perversions were biologically determined; all other perversions, he claimed, evidenced weakness in an individual's social instincts. Zalkind's chief complaint against perversions was that they necessitated the expenditure of too much energy in the search for a partner and thus were profoundly detrimental to an individual's ability to contribute to society.

[44] Zalkind, *Polovoi vopros*, 47–59.

new formula for communist youth during NEP, "the more free trade, the less free love,"[45] and he explained:

> Free love, that is, complete trust by a society in the free romantic choice of its members, requires a state of collective development and of collective emotions from which we are still far removed—both economically and psychologically. If the contemporary human being—with his psychophysiology so utterly saturated by putrefying social conditions—were to be offered free love, in today's "free atmosphere" he would do rotten, disgusting things from which we could emancipate ourselves only by resorting for a long time to the cruelest sort of sexual dictatorship.[46]

Love had to be fettered *now*, so that it could be free (i.e., self-controlled) later. As we have seen, this call for love's bondage often translated into policies designed to reduce sexual desire—and the potential for sexual desire—to zero.

Zalkind's abhorrence of sexual desire would seem to raise some troubling questions. He claimed that purely physical sexual attraction was inconsistent with a Revolutionary and proletarian point of view. "Sexual attraction to a class enemy," he declared, "is just as much a perversion as [human] sexual attraction to a crocodile or an orangutan."[47] Yet even when directed toward an appropriate object, sexual desire had to be minimized. In an annotation to his "Ninth Commandment," Zalkind claimed that "flirtation, courtship, coquetry, and other methods of specifically sexual conquest" were bourgeois habits that introduced more arousal into the sexual act than was really necessary. This statement would seem to imply that *some* arousal was necessary. But could arousal, desire, and pleasure ever be communist or proletarian? In *I Want a Child!*, Sergei Tret'iakov "bares" the paradox at work in the reductive discourse about sex when his ideologically correct heroine, Milda, asks a young worker to help her conceive a child. When he replies, "Forgive me, Comrade, but—how should I put it?—I don't have an appetite for you," she goes behind a screen and emerges in petty bourgeois attire "with her hair curled, her face made up, and in a new, revealing dress."[48]

Zalkind's hostility to sexual arousal and his advice that young communists demonstrate their allegiance to the working class by repressing sexual arousal did have the obvious corollary seized upon by Tret'iakov: the identification of the very concept of pleasure with the bourgeoisie. In vain might Health Commissar Semashko criticize Zalkind's vulgar Marxism and assert that *both* "the working poor" and "the rich" alike derived pleasure from

---

[45] Ibid., 60.

[46] Ibid., 61.

[47] Ibid., 49.

[48] S. Tret'iakov, "Khochu rebenka," *Sovremennaia dramaturgiia*, no. 2 (1988): 227 (206–243).

sexual intercourse.[49] In Zalkind's view—and in that of other commentators whom we shall meet below—experiencing sexual desire or sexual pleasure rendered a person an honorary (i.e., "dishonorable") member of the bourgeoisie. There was a certain contradiction here, because initially Zalkind had presented pleasure as a weapon designed by capitalists to facilitate the proletariat's continued servitude. In Zalkind's writing, however, and in Soviet society at large, the narcotic and the class dispensing it became interchangeable. The bourgeoisie not only used pleasure, it *was* pleasure itself.

There was a certain historical logic to this equation. In the early twentieth century some Marxist writers had attempted to describe the contours of the typical bourgeois personality. Their focus on capitalism's reliance on egotistical forces had led them to equate the search for private pleasures with the bourgeoisie. An anonymous author, whose 1906 book *On Proletarian Ethics* was reprinted by the Soviet Central Executive Committee in 1918, claimed that the typical bourgeois was "a subjectivist, an aesthete, and a lover of pleasure; moreover, his pleasures are of a rather dubious nature."[50] While this view, at first, might seem strange and at odds with the capitalist work ethic and Marx's depiction of the capitalist's frantic attempt to amass rather than waste resources, it owed as much to Nietzsche and Weininger as to their critics on the left (in Russia, Vladimir Friche). All attacked the impotent decadence they found in turn-of-the-century bourgeois European society.[51]

Throughout NEP the equation of pleasure with the bourgeoisie continued to be a tenet of Bolshevik belief. At a meeting at the Moscow Polytechnic Museum in 1927, Viacheslav Polonsky, an influential literary critic who edited two of the leading national journals, *Novyi mir* and *Pechat' i revoliutsiia*, painted a grim but representative portrait of the typical Nepman. Essential to his depiction was his belief that the Nepman, unlike capitalist entrepreneurs or pre-Revolutionary bourgeois, knew his days were numbered and therefore saw his investment opportunities as limited. What could he do with his money?

[49] N. Semashko, "Kak ne nado pisat' o polovom voprose," *Izvestiia*, 1 January 1925, 5. Semashko's intervention against "ignorance" in the sexual debate did not take issue with the reductive discourse. Rather, the health commissar viewed Zalkind and others as according too much weight to the forces of history in their assertions about the role of class dominance in the corruption of the sex drive. Semashko's principal concern was that the reader remember that sublimation was always possible. Blaming historical circumstances for sexual depravity was not a justifiable position for young Bolsheviks; a defining tenet of Bolshevism was, after all, confidence in the power of the will to affect history.

[50] N. N., *O proletarskoi etike. (Proletarskoe tvorchestvo s tochkoi zreniia realisticheskoi filosofii)* (M.: Vserossiiskii tsentral'nyi ispolnitel'nyi komitet sovetov R.S., K. i K. Deputatov, 1918), 43.

[51] See V. M. Friche, *Torzhestvo pola i gibel' tsivilizatsii. Po povodu knigi Otto Veninger [sic!] Pol i kharakter* (M.: Sovremennye problemy, 1909).

First of all, he buys pleasure; this is the foremost and only thing for which he lives. He lives so as to grab as much pleasure as he can. This is a man who has been reborn as a pleasure machine, who can only (and wants only to) experience pleasure, a man merciless to others, who sees the rest of humanity as no more than an instrument for his pleasure.[52]

Little is to be found in such statements of detailed "Marxist" sociological analysis. The word "pleasure" slides from sentence to sentence, contaminating everything it contacts. Resting just beneath the surface is the fear that Soviet society under NEP might not be divisible into workers and bourgeois, that the villainous Nepman may be a projection of "our" own lascivious desires and of the quest for pleasure which the proletariat has been asked— in the interests of class identification—to forgo. The reluctance to admit that this division within Soviet society was *also* a division within the proletariat self lay at the bottom of much of the debate raging around Malashkin and Gumilevsky in 1926 and 1927: were komsomol'tsy really *so* corrupt, and if not how could they be portrayed as so vulnerable to corruption? If the dangerous pleasure-loving "other" of NEP was really "other," how could he be dangerous? The contortions to which A. Stratonitsky, author of *Questions of Everyday Life in the Komsomol*, resorted in an effort to resolve this question are highly instructive.

> The Nepman's street carries many temptations. Shop windows are chic, crowds rush gaily about, new attractive cars fill the streets with their roars; everything attracts attention, delights the eye, and acts on our psyches. Of course, the vast majority of our working youth responds to all this indifferently, without the least envy, anger, or dissatisfaction.
>
> Our working youth is used to working and loves peaceful, healthy labor; such things as luxury and riches—it can definitely be said—do not interest the working youth. Nevertheless there is a certain unstable element among our comrades—we see some of them even amidst our Komsomol youth—who, *somehow and absolutely by chance*, coming in contact with the Nepman's environment, are defeated by it; they begin to be attracted by the rich flashy life, and they are torn from us. There are even cases of boys and girls in our Komsomol who are corrupted by Nepmen acquaintances; luxury and gold become dearer to them than the entire workers' organization, and without noticing it they gradually break with us.[53]

The crossing of the boundary from "us" to "them" occurs inexplicably and, it would appear, through no particular fault of even "our" weakest links. The

---

[52] RGALI, fond 1328 (V. P. Polonskii), opis' 3, ed. khran. 27, 15 (Voprosy pola i braka v zhizni i literatury [Stenogram of debate held in the Moscow Polytechnic Museum on 6 March 1927]).

[53] Stratonitskii, *Voprosy byta*, 100–101.

fault is partially that of NEP's apparent ally, "chance," an especially detestable enemy for a vanguard with the mission of consciously changing history.

In reality, contacts between Komsomol youth and the bourgeoisie were probably quite limited. Students from the Sverdlov Communist University protested to Zinov'ev about the commonly expressed fear of bourgeois contamination: "Where do we run into the bourgeoisie? We live in dormitories, among other communists. Our young people have long forgotten not only their acquaintances but their family, even their working-class parents."[54] In discourse, however, the demands of class consolidation required the depiction of virtually all communists as continually in danger of being drawn over to the "other" side. Life during NEP was a series of encounters with the reborn bourgeoisie, and proletarians whose vigilance flagged were in peril of being reborn as "other."[55]

The consequences for a bourgeois who enticed a member of the working class or peasantry into the realm of pleasure were portrayed as severe. In the second "pathological" case discussed by Dr. Brukhansky, a defendant was charged with deocculating his ex-wife. The husband had been born into a peasant family but had become a member of the proletariat and joined the Party; his wife stemmed from petty bourgeois origins. The defendant claimed to have attacked her in a state of insanity: he was enraged because she had aborted a pregnancy in defiance of his wishes and had insulted his class origins. Initially acquitted by the Moscow City Criminal Court, he was ordered to stand trial a second time by the Moscow Regional Court, which declared evidence of temporary insanity to have been entirely lacking and noted with surprise that all testimony had, in fact, pointed in the other direction. On rehearing the case, the lower court again found the defendant innocent of having violated Article 149 of the Criminal Code (intentional infliction of severe bodily injury) but convicted him of violating Article 151 (infliction of bodily injury while in a state of powerful emotional agitation provoked by the victim's use of illegal force or serious insults). A conviction under the former article carried a minimum sentence of three years, while under the latter the maximum was two years' incarceration. The defendant received a term of one year in jail.

Straining to find political resonance in the most vicious criminal acts, Brukhansky professed astonishment at this result. The facts of the case, he

---

[54] Quoted in Sheila Fitzpatrick, *Education and Social Mobility in the Soviet Union, 1921–1934* (Cambridge: Cambridge University Press, 1979), 93.

[55] See, for example, the warning issued by the Presidium of the Central Control Commission in 1924 concerning the many dangers "concealed" by NEP, expecially "for those communists who come into contact with Nepmen in the course of their daily activity." "O Partetike. Proekt predlozhenii prezidiuma TsKK II Plenumu TsKK RKP(b)," in *Partiinaia etika. Diskussii 20-x godov*, ed. A. A. Guseinov, M. V. Iskrov, and R. V. Petropavlovskii (M.: Izdatel'stvo politicheskoi literatury, 1989), 160 (151–170).

claimed, warranted outright acquittal. He filled in the judicial record for his readers, explaining why the assault had been more or less justified:

> Two absolutely different people got together, the products of different social groups, people who thought in diametrically opposed ways. [The defendant] was a peasant's son, a worker hungry for knowledge, for science, with much to live for, a man who sincerely and loyally made a gift of his affection to the victim. [The victim], a daughter of the petty bourgeoisie, a product of a social group destined for extinction, had never been through life's school of work and hard knocks, was spoiled by her past, by her carefree way of life, and was unbelievably depraved, seeing in the defendant a person who could satisfy her sexual demands. [. . .] This meeting with a woman who was socially and culturally alien to him, who gave him new things in love that he had hitherto not experienced, took possession of the defendant entirely. Class contradictions, the absence of an emotional tie, his feeling of his own inferiority, all these emerged in full measure.[56]

This defendant's feeling of inferiority eventually resulted in a state "of constantly increasing emotional agitation." By the time of the assault on his wife, he "had been introduced [by her] to the culture of heightened sexual depravity."

In Brukhansky's account, the worst aspect of the victim's conduct is her initiation of the defendant into the world of refined sexual pleasure. He admits that the defendant had several sexual partners during his marriage and was not a sexual innocent; furthermore, the defendant's peasant origins were partially responsible for his "simple, primordial personality, psychologically close to that of savages or children with their simple, direct, and primitive reactions." Brukhansky views sexual relations with the bourgeoisie, however, as qualitatively different from relations with one's own class, and thus as the most important factor in the case. In Brukhansky's account, Zalkind's sex with "a crocodile" (i.e., with a class enemy) becomes sex with a being who has a totally different relation to pleasure. The lesson of Brukhansky's reflections on this brutal act is that sexual contact with a person outside his class can change a proletarian's *own* perspective on pleasure—but only to a certain degree. The working class may initially be seduced by "the culture of heightened sexual depravity" but eventually reacts with healthy violence and an act of symbolic castration.

This justification of proletarian violence is troubled by a certain paradox, because castration of the "other" must serve as an equivalence of self-castration. It was, after all, *proletarian* desire that commentators were worried about; cases such as those related by Brukhansky only "work" if one assumes that the bourgeoisie functions as the libido of the working class or, at

[56] Brukhanskii, *Materialy*, 33.

the very least, as the place to which the proletarian libido can be extrojected or exiled. (This insight, indeed, underlies Milda's concealment and erotic transformation behind the screen in Tret'iakov's play.) The idea that surgical intervention might be needed within (or against) the proletarian self lurks throughout the rhetoric of NEP desire and can be found in places other than Zalkind's vivid slash-and-steal narrative of intracorporeal warfare. In proposing to stage Tret'iakov's play, Igor Terent'ev even went so far as to appropriate for medicine the notion of the show trial from the law. His production of a drama about Soviet sex would have been a "show surgical operation" (*pokazatel'naia khirurgicheskaia operatsiia*).[57]

The most curious aspect of the discourse of castration may have been its manifestation in a *literally* surgical form. The moral almost invariably presented by the restrictive discourse was that energy expended in sexual activity could be productively channeled elsewhere. Health Commissar Semashko and a parade of professors and doctors repeatedly made the point that sexual activity wasted energy which, if allowed to collect and directed at socially productive activities, could have positive results for the nation.[58] Many short stories and poems were composed to emphasize this point,[59] and *Komsomol'skaia pravda*'s readers were informed that "sublimation is of enormous importance."[60] This was particularly true at the present time:

> The idea of sexual abstinence becomes especially desirable when new forms of governmental life are being created and when there is a great demand for social energy. At such historic moments it is necessary for the benefit of social and government service to strive for the diminution, the stilling of sexual energy in its direct form, and for the concentration of all forces. And here in our land after the October Revolution, when young Soviet Power has established itself on the ruins of the old regime, life has begun to make the highest demands on the energy essential to the development and strengthening of the new order. That is why abstinence has acquired such special value now as the key to the source of great reserves of social energy.[61]

[57] Ig. Terent'ev, "'Khochu rebenka' (Plan postanovki)," *Novyi Lef*, no. 12 (1928): 32 (32–35).

[58] Semashko, "Polovoe vospitanie i zdorov'e," 4; Dr. N. Rossiianskii, "Ob odnom ras-prostranennom iavlenii," *Komsomol'skaia pravda*, 15 August 1925, 4; Gorinevskii, "Polovoi vopros," 3.

[59] For examples, see Lev Gumilevskii, "Meshchanochka," *Komsomol'skaia pravda*, 15 August 1925, 3, and the following anonymous *chastushka*: "Не хочу бежать я к милой, её губки целовать. Дайте ручку и чернила, буду тезисы писать." (I don't want to run to my girl to kiss her little lips. Give me pen and ink, and I'll write out Party resolutions.) N. Bozhinskaia, *Prestuplenie Ivana Kuznetsova (Svobodnaia liubov')* (M.: Molodaia gvardiia, 1927), 23.

[60] Gorinevskii, "Polovoi vopros," 3.

[61] Ia. D. Golomb, *Polovoe vozderzhanie (Za i protiv). Chto dolzhen znat' kazhdyi o sovremen-nom sostoianii voprosa*, 2d ed. (Odessa: Svetoch, 1927), 30–31.

While the advocacy of sublimation was essentially a call to conscience, it was underpinned by medical evidence that surfaced regularly in discussions of sexual behavior. In the early 1920s the relatively new science of endocrinology had begun to capture the imagination of Russian doctors and, more important, of the popular (nonmedical) press. The old belief in "the sovereignty of the brain" had been displaced by new knowledge about hormones, the true "builders of the living body" (*stroiteli zhivogo tela*).[62] The knowledge that endocrinology was—albeit largely by dint of historical coincidence—a post-Revolutionary, and thus distinctly Soviet, science may account for the politically charged language that informs accounts of the glandular system's challenge to the nervous system's rule.[63] In at least one account, hormones emerge as a kind of corporeal proletariat that has finally thrown off the brain's domination.[64] Other authors used the endocrine system to explore the real meaning of the term "soul"[65] or to speculate about the feasibility of human immortality;[66] some seized upon hormonal research and hormonal manipulation as proof that God did not exist.[67]

In much of the literature on sublimation written by medical doctors, the

[62] Nik. Perna, *Stroiteli zhivogo tela. Ocherki fiziologii vnutrennei sekretsii* (Pg.: Seiatel', 1924), 7.

[63] On the history of Soviet endocrinology, see Prof. V. A. Oppel', "Endokrinologiia, kak osnova sovremennoi meditsiny," *Leningradskii meditsinskii zhurnal*, no. 3 (1926): 3–18; Prof. D. M. Rossiiskii, *Ocherk istorii razvitiia endokrinologii v Rossii* (M., 1926); N. A. Shereshevskii, "Ocherk istorii endokrinologii v SSSR," *Problemy endokrinologii*, no. 4 (1937): 452–458; B. V. Aleshin, "Gistofiziologiia endokrinnoi sistemy v sovetskom soiuze za 20 let," *Problemy endokrinologii*, no. 4 (1937): 474–498.

[64]

Hormones are chemical substances that are secreted in various parts of the body and have the significance of active agents [*aktivnye deiateli*]. And it turns out that hormones play an almost more important role in the internal order and well-being of the organism than the brain and the nervous system. The formation of hormones and their activity occur absolutely independently of the nervous system. The contrary is even true: the activity of the nervous system in many respects depends upon hormones. Hormones [. . .] are excreted in many parts of the body; with a certain justification it may be said that they are emitted by *all* parts of the body, by all of its elements, by every corner, every cell, that each cell in the body uninterruptedly manufactures substances which are excreted by that cell into the blood, which carries them throughout the entire body, where they perform their own definite action, serving as if they were the *voice* [*golos*] of that cell which thus resounds through the entire body. (Perna, *Stroiteli*, 8–9)

[65] A. V. Nemilov, "Uznaem li my kogda-nibud', chto takoe 'dusha'?" *Chelovek i priroda*, no. 4 (1924): 321–328. This article is an endocrinological manifesto directed as much against neurologists as against the devout. For another endocrinological attack on the concept of the soul, see N. N. Plavil'shchikov, "Pol i kharakter," *Smena*, no. 1 (1926): 14–15.

[66] N. K. Kol'tsov, "Vvedenie: smert', starost', omolozhenie," in *Omolozhenie*, ed. N. K. Kol'tsov (M. and Pg.: Gos. izd., 1923), 1–28.

[67] Ts. Perel'muter, *Nauka i religiia o zhizni chelovecheskogo tela* (n.p.: Bezbozhnik, 1927).

sex glands play a starring role. As positivists, the doctors were called upon to show why sublimation is effective. Invariably they stated that the sex glands manufacture products for external and internal secretion. External secretion was believed to weaken the body, especially during youth, when there was a pressing need for glandular products on "the internal market."[68] Sublimation insured that internal secretion would be maximized and biological internal resources used for building strong individuals capable of engaging in later but more productive reproduction resulting in healthier offspring. The outcome was a biological analogy to the development of socialism in a single country.

Discussion of internal secretion was often twinned with consideration of a surgical procedure presented as its functional equivalent. Around 1920 a Viennese doctor, Eugen Steinach, and Serge Voronoff, a Russian-born researcher at the Collège de France, began publishing material on operations designed to increase sex gland activity. Steinach, who earlier in his career had experimented with the use of hormones to produce "a wide range of hermaphroditism" in rats, promoted tying off the vas deferens (a procedure already in use for sterilization) to transform the testes into an organ of heightened internal secretion for the revitalization of the entire organism.[69] Voronoff pioneered the idea of grafting material from the sex glands of a young animal into an older one; he also experimented with grafts from one species of animal to another and eventually founded a clinic in Menton where he grafted sex glands from less developed primates into hundreds of human patients.[70] Steinach had published his findings in 1920 in a book entitled *Rejuvenation (Verjüngung)*.[71] This term was taken up by the Soviet press, always eager to demonstrate the covertly millennial potential of the radical positivism with which Bolshevism professed a kinship. The early and mid-1920s witnessed the publication of several collections of articles about "rejuvenation" by leading figures in the Soviet medical community as well as a flood of articles in popular science columns and journals. Most appraisals of this surgical process were highly enthusiastic, and the antireligious publishing house Bezbozhnik relied on rejuvenation experiments

[68] Golomb, *Polovoe vozderzhanie*, 24. Ejaculation and menstruation were frequently cited as examples of external secretion of the sex glands' products. The gender connotations of this parallel will be considered in subsequent chapters.

[69] Paul Kammerer, *Rejuvenation and the Prolongation of Human Efficiency: Experiences with the Steinach-Operation on Man and Animals* (New York: Boni and Liveright, 1923), 52. For a detailed description of Steinach's career and of the Steinach operation, see also Eugen Steinach and Joseph Lobel, *Sex and Life: Forty Years of Biological and Medical Experiments* (New York: Viking, 1940).

[70] Serge Voronoff, *Rejuvenation by Grafting*, trans. Fred F. Imianitoff (New York: Adelphi, 1925 [1924]); Serge Voronoff, *The Sources of Life* (Boston: Bruce Humphries, 1943 [1933]).

[71] E. Steinach, *Verjüngung durch experimentelle Neubelebung der alternden Pubertätsdrüse* (Berlin: Springer, 1920).

for its endocrinological proof of the nonexistence of God, going so far as to advise its lecturers how to answer audience questions on the procedure.[72]

In the course of its discussion of "the sexual question," the Komsomol also furnished its young readers with information on rejuvenation. Discussions of the procedure often slid effortlessly into encomia to sublimation. In one of the most extensive treatments of the subject in the Komsomol press, a certain Professor Ivan Ariamov even used rejuvenation as a jumping-off point for an endocrinological excursus in literary criticism. After describing Steinach's operation, Ariamov declared that "the development of man's creative work is directly dependent on the energetic activity of the sex glands when that activity is not accomplished by the expulsion of sexual products." He then proceeded to attribute Aleksandr Pushkin's prodigious literary output during the famous autumn of 1830 at Boldino to Pushkin's retention of his sex glands' products. Separated from his fiancée by an outbreak of cholera, Pushkin had burned with desire:

> This is what occurred as a result: "tormented by the passionate desire to see his future bride, receiving foolish, alarming letters from her, not having anyone around him with whom he might share his thoughts, virtually deprived of books, the poet devoted himself to poetic creativity with unexpected fervor.
>
> "In this period he wrote: 'The Covetous Knight,' 'Mozart and Salieri,' and 'The Stone Guest,' he nearly finished *Eugene Onegin*, and he also wrote 'The Little House in Kolomna,' 'Feast in the Time of Plague,' and many lyric poems."
>
> Thus does [the poet and critic Valery] Briusov describe the surge in Pushkin's creative work, though he does not understand its causes. For us this productive surge in Pushkin's work is now perfectly clear: his strong sexual attraction, not finding a direct outlet, was transformed into the highest of cerebral processes, into creative work.[73]

There would seem to be several logical flaws with incorporating the topic of rejuvenation into discussions of sublimation. We will reserve until later the troubling relation of gender to discussions of rejuvenation and internal secretion. For now it should suffice to make the obvious point that just as Pushkin's separation from his bride-to-be cannot be accepted as evidence that he experienced no external secretions, so the tying of the vas deferens (let alone the grafting of glandular material) in no way ensured that recipients of the rejuvenation procedure would be more likely to abstain from sexual intercourse. As Mikhail Bulgakov observed in his satirical treatment of the operation in "Heart of a Dog" (1925), just the opposite might be

---

[72] Perel'muter, *Nauka i religiia*, 37–38.

[73] Prof. I. V. Ariamov, "Znachenie sokhraneniia polovoi energii dlia molodezhi," *Komsomol'skaia pravda*, 7 February 1926, 5. Ariamov proceeded to comment upon specific lines of Pushkin's verse.

true—rejuvenated patients might engage in sexual activity with unprece-dented fervor.[74] (Steinach himself believed that tying the vas deferens on only one side would make a man more fertile).[75] In the West, rejuvenation was attacked as immoral (or, at the least, treated as titillating) on the grounds that it *promoted* sexual activity; Steinach and his associates had to protest that increased sexual potency was just a by-product of the Steinach opera-tion, not its aim.[76] At first sight, it seems astonishing that in most Soviet commentary about rejuvenation a link between rejuvenation and abstention from copulation almost always seems to be assumed. (The utter absence of a connection between rejuvenation and sexual abstinence is almost never stressed in the literature.)[77] The metaphorical attraction of images of surgical intervention, of cutting off, redirecting, and damming up, seems to have been so strong as to have conquered the basic elements of common sense. And yet

[74] M. A. Bulgakov, *Sobranie sochinenii v piati tomakh* (M.: Khudozhestvennaia literatura, 1989), 2:129–140. The relevance of rejuvenation to Bulgakov's novella—in which the testes and pituitary gland of a hooligan of lower-class origin are transplanted into a dog, who then develops rapidly into a noxious, disturbingly canine Soviet official—has been discussed by Mikhail Zolotonosov in his "Masturbanizatsiia: 'Erogennye zony' sovetskoi kul'tury 1920–1930-x godov," *Literaturnoe obozrenie*, no. 11 (1991): 93–99. Certain texts not discussed by Zolotonosov seem particularly relevant to Bulgakov's work. Anton Nemilov, a leading figure in popular science journals, wrote in one of his many treatments of the topic: "It stands to reason, that pieces of a monkey's gland, grafted into the body of a man, will not turn the latter into a baboon and will not cause the appearance of simian traits. [. . .] Just as a patient who receives an antidiphtherial serum prepared from equine blood does not begin to neigh like a horse, and a man who takes medicine prepared from canine stomach fluid does not acquire the ability to bark like a dog, so an old man, into whom is grafted a baboon's seminal glands, will receive a physiological jolt but will not in the least begin to look like a monkey." "Noveishie opyty omolazhivaniia liudei," *Chelovek i priroda*, nos. 4–5 (1925): 26–27 (25–30). Appended to Perel'muter's *Nauka i religiia* is a list of questions likely to be posed to an atheist-propagandist by an audience; several of the questions, a preamble states, actually were asked when on some unspecified date the text of the book was read in the Central House of the Peasant. Question 5 reads as follows: "Does a man with a ram's testes or thyroid begin to look like a ram?" A reassuring, negative response was provided by the author. *Nauka i religiia*, 38. In both cases we see writers unable to resist at least mentioning the embryonic scenario for a motif that Bulgakov, who was trained as a venereologist, transformed into an extremely compelling plot.

[75] Kammerer, *Rejuvenation*, 83.

[76] In terms utterly alien to those of the discourse about sex in Soviet Russia, one of Steinach's colleagues wrote, "[A]s long as there is nothing repulsive in love where young people are concerned, why should it be different with rejuvenated people as long as their appearance, their working ability, and their general acuteness of senses puts the rejuvenates in a class with people much younger than their actual years?" Ibid., 186. See also Steinach and Lobel, *Sex and Life*, 11.

[77] A notable exception is Professor Nemilov's article " 'Omolozhenie' sel'skokhoziaistven-nykh zhivotnykh," *Chelovek i priroda*, no. 1 (1925): 23–36. Nemilov's stance on rejuvenation was, however, largely negative. He favored its use for farm animals but not for human beings, since "for our Soviet Union, rich in youthful energy, there is absolutely no point in working further on the question of rejuvenating people." We shall discuss Nemilov and his work during NEP in subsequent chapters.

there is something strangely appropriate about this blindness if one accepts the proposition, tendered above, that the function of the discourse about sex was *not* to decrease sexual desire but to arouse it, for the discussion of rejuvenation procedures in Russia employed the rhetoric of castration to propel the sex glands to the forefront of popular medicine. In trying to understand the importance of sex in NEP, we should recall that every discussion of sublimation is to some extent desublimating because it foregrounds the topic of sex while professing a desire to be rid of it. The rhetoric of castration was consistently *de*sublimating; deploring the engorgement of sex, Zalkind engorged the topic all the more. Sublimation with a distinctly Russian, not Freudian, bent, sublimation of the individual into the collective, was the discourse's end. Zalkind's views on the essence of psychological treatment in a communist collective are relevant here:

Psychoneurotics should be constantly held in a living chain [*v zhivoi tsepi*] of active, healthy, forceful, and demanding social contacts in order to place [them] in a position where their disease is no longer socially profitable. By adroitly maneuvering the patient within the collective and by skillfully maneuvering the collective as a whole, we destroy the necessity for the patient to hide from society in his disease, or, more accurately, we make it impossible, absurd, and unprofitable for him to play with individualistic fictions in a game of psychoneurotic hide-and-seek.

A psychoneurosis is a network of completely treatable injuries that have damaged the organism's sense of collective being. Psychotherapy is the planned introduction, by means of collectivistic maneuvering, of the psychoneurotic patient into a system of collective being to make his social isolation and social-biological disorganization impossible.[78]

The discussion of sex during NEP should be read as occupying a central place in this process of the collective manipulation of young Soviet men and women. Talk about sex functioned as a discursive chain that might bind (or graft!) the first generation of communist youth into a tightly knit ideological community. Zalkind's imagery should not surprise us. Just as chains (to be lost) had been used by Marx as a rhetorical image for communist identity seventy years earlier, so now chains (to be gained) are depicted by Zalkind as a guarantee of a collective's productive cohesion. And yet these chains could signify something more than solidarity; they could also hint at the working class's current historical immobility and its imprisonment in a society and a world that it could not so assuredly manipulate or control. In the next chapter, we will begin to consider questions of ideological dread that in various permutations will carry us through to the end of the book.

[78] A. B. Zalkind, *Ocherki kul'tury revoliutsionnogo vremeni* (M.: Rabotnik prosveshcheniia, 1924), 64.

Chapter Four

BEHIND THE RED DOOR: AN INTRODUCTION TO NEP GOTHIC

AT THE Tenth Party Congress, Lenin laid the groundwork for the introduction of NEP in terms that warrant close examination. Arguing that the time had come to rescue the proletariat from the deplorable, declassed state of speculation and near-starvation to which the Civil War and War Communist policies had reduced it, Lenin couched the case for NEP in rhetoric that relied on a vocabulary of terror and fear:

> Each improvement in the situation of heavy industry, [as well as] the opportunity to restart several large factories, reinforces the position of the proletariat to such an extent that there is no reason to fear the petty bourgeois element, even when it is on the rise. There is no reason to fear the rise of the petty bourgeoisie and small capital. What should be feared is that the [current] conditions of extreme hunger, deprivation, and food shortages will last too long; these conditions are responsible for the utter impotence of the proletariat, for the proletariat's inability to resist the chaotic element of petty bourgeois wavering and despair. That is more terrifying.[1]

Lenin was not alone in resorting to this language. Throughout NEP, words such as "fear," "terror," and "panic" would pervade assessments of Party policy and of their long-term effect on the Soviet march toward communism. Lenin's rhetoric of fear, frequently expressed through the use of the comparative or superlative degree, was predicated on his resistance to (and anticipation of) ideological anxiety about the threat that commercial intercourse with the bourgeoisie might pose to communist legitimacy. As we shall see, the

---

[1]

Всякое улучшение положения крупного производства, возможность пустить некоторые крупные фабрики, настолько упрочивает положение пролетариата, что <u>бояться</u> стихии мелкой буржуазии, даже возрастающей, нечего. Не того надо <u>бояться</u>, что мелкая буржуазия и мелкий капитал вырастет. Надо <u>бояться</u> того, что слишком долго продолжается состояние крайнего голода, нужды, недостатка продук-тов, из которого вытекает уже полное обессиление пролетариата, невозможность для него противостоять стихии мелкобуржуазных колебаний и отчаяния. Это <u>страшнее</u>. (V. I. Lenin, "Zakliuchitel'noe slovo po dokladu o zamene rasverstki natural'nym nalogom [Desiatyi s"ezd RKP(b)]" [15 March 1921], *Polnoe sobranie sochinenii*, 5th ed., 45 vols. [M.: Gos. izd., 1958–1965], 43:83–84 [emphasis added])

various factions struggling for power within the Party were quick to accuse each other of being excessively frightened—or excessively desirous—of the interclass contacts that supposedly characterized NEP. Ideological identity was bound up with the affective categories of both pleasure and fear.

The principal fear expressed by Lenin at the end of the Civil War was that in the absence of a strong economy, the proletariat would cease to exist. He stated this point forcefully at the Tenth All-Russian Party Conference in May 1921:

> When workers lose the material, productive economic base beneath their feet, a condition of disequilibrium, uncertainty, despair, and disbelief takes possession of certain segments of them and, in conjunction with the direct provocation of our bourgeois democrats—the Social Revolutionaries and Mensheviks—, has a certain effect. [. . .]
>
> The unfortunate state of current affairs compels proletarians to resort to methods of earning income that are not proletarian, not connected with heavy industry, but are petty bourgeois, the methods of speculators. At publicly owned factories, workers are compelled to obtain manufactured goods either by theft or by private production and to exchange these goods for agricultural ones,—this is our chief economic danger, the chief danger to the very existence of the Soviet order. [. . .]
>
> During this time of transition we must be willing to incur any sacrifice necessary to save the proletariat. [. . .] We should not be loath to throw crumbs to the greedy foreign capitalists, because now, from the point of view of the building of socialism, it is advantageous to pay hundreds of millions to foreign capitalists and to receive the machines and materials necessary for the reestablishment of heavy industry and the restoration of the economic basis that will transform the proletariat into a lasting proletariat and not a proletariat accustomed to speculation.[2]

In Lenin's nightmare about what would happen in the absence of NEP, the proletariat disintegrates through no fault of its own; it is undermined by economic conditions. The importance of asceticism and purity to the Russian "progressive" tradition, however, conjured up a competing story of the proletariat's demise, and this narrative was centered on the question of ideological integrity. In this competing version, the relative wealth, comfort, and diversity of NEP threatened to seduce, fundamentally change, and thus destroy the Russian proletariat. This narrative, shadowing the Party and Komsomol in the 1920s, was a tale of ideological defloration.

I have already suggested that the bourgeois "pleasure machine" surfacing in Brukhansky's, Polonsky's, and Zalkind's comments was more an object of

---

[2] V. I. Lenin, "Doklad o prodovol'stvennom naloge [Desiataia vserossiiskaia konferentsiia RKP(b)]" (26 May 1921), *Polnoe sobranie*, 43:308–310.

ideological projection than a realistic portrait of a social type. The very phrase "pleasure *machine*" (*mashina dlia naslazhdeniia*) suggests an insidious corruption of the class that had most closely tied its fate to the factory. At a time when the bourgeoisie and the proletariat were forced to "cohabit,"[3] fears arose in the Party and Komsomol that the class enemy might not be so different from the proletarian self; accordingly, communist educators and publicists did whatever possible to insist on the enemy's otherness. As a rhetoric of self-control and discipline achieved prominence, it was important to insist that weakness within the self was *not* one's own, that it was alien and had to be rooted out. Unfortunately, the desires—long suppressed during years of struggle—that NEP might awaken in proletarian youth could not be resisted directly or in a confrontational manner. Such defiance would betoken "infantile" ideological longings and the absence of mature Leninist pragmatism. NEP had been introduced temporarily but "for a long time"; the potential proletarian victim could prevail only through a long-suffering and patient assertion of class virtue.

This dilemma—a plot of temptation endlessly repeated—gave rise to a mentality upon which we might heuristically confer the name of "Gothic"— a generic designation that might initially seem at odds with an avowedly materialistic worldview. "The Gothic" is a term that has evoked differing but related categorizations fitting certain literary works more or less well; to my knowledge it has not previously been used to describe the contours of a particular ideology or employed to investigate a distinct historical period during which its primary manifestations were not in novels (as in late-eighteenth- or early-nineteenth-century England), but in Party congress transcripts, newspaper reports, pedagogic articles, and criminal trials.

Neither linguists, literary scholars, nor historians seem to have devoted much effort to exploring the poetics of such nonliterary materials. Members of these professions with a knowledge of Russian may have felt that from an aesthetic point of view, at least, the game was simply not worth the candle. However, concepts developed in aesthetic theory are useful not only as tools for the appreciation of art. They may help us understand the workings of ideology at a particular point in time. One insight bequeathed to us by the Bakhtin Circle is the notion that consciousness is molded by language and that verbal form affects not just how we say something but even what we say and what we want to say. At various points, Bakhtin, Voloshinov, and Medvedev took different stances on the dialectical (or dialogic) relationship between the individual and the verbal, ideological environment that surrounds him, but they never departed from the idea that the verbal both em-

[3] Karl Radek, "Oktiabr'skaia revoliutsiia i ee mesto v istorii," *Novaia ekonomicheskaia politika: sbornik materialov k kursam* (Kazan': Gos. izd. Avt. Tatarskoi S. S. Respubliki, 1922), vyp. 7, 10 (3–12).

powers and limits. Our comprehension of any given situation is limited by the verbal forms available to us, one of which, Bakhtin and Medvedev tell us, is genre.[4] I will suggest that the predominant generic influence on and vehicle for NEP discourse, its ideological envelope, was Gothic. This chapter is an analytical experiment, or case study, in the relationship of genre to ideology.

According to one of its more thoughtful students, the Gothic is not only a literary genre but "a way of relating to the real, to historical and psychological facts, which will clearly contain a moment of variation as other aspects of cultural life vary, but which nonetheless has forms of continuity which we can trace through from the eighteenth century writers to the contemporary world."[5] During the past thirty years, attempts to trace these continuities have generated at least two related typologies, both sharing an indebtedness to Freud's notion of the return of the repressed. The first—elaborated by David Punter, Leslie Fiedler,[6] and Dale Peterson,[7] is a historical Gothic, literature terrified of and terribly curious about the past. In the Gothic, Peterson writes,

> Readers become witnesses to the tribulations (and the temptations) of a mind confronted by a vestige of the past that solicits or compels an unnatural extension on life. [. . .] A sudden immersion in an antiquated environment is found to awaken the most anachronistic feelings and experiences in "innocent" protagonists, who think of themselves as belonging to some later, more enlightened age. [. . .] Gothic fiction is historical romance with a vengeance; in it, contemporary characters and settings are suddenly displaced by the posthumous vitality of an ancestral presence or artifact.[8]

According to Fiedler, one can trace the rise of Gothic writing to a new consciousness of the ascendancy of the bourgeoisie and to that class's worries about its legitimacy[9]—a fear reflected in the Gothic novel's obsession with mysteries of parentage.

[4] See M. M. Bakhtin (*sic*!?) and P. N. Medvedev, *The Formal Method in Literary Scholarship*, trans. Albert J. Wehrle (Cambridge: Harvard University Press, 1978), especially 129–141; M. M. Bakhtin, "Discourse in the Novel," in his *The Dialogic Imagination*, trans. Caryl Emerson and Michael Holquist (Austin: University of Texas Press, 1981), 259–422, and "The Problem of Speech Genres" in his *Speech Genres and Other Late Essays*, trans. Vern W. McGee (Austin: University of Texas Press, 1986), 60–102. Voloshinov was far less interested in genre than were his two friends. Genre is nearly absent from his *Marxism and the Philosophy of Language*, ed. Ladislav Matejka and I. R. Titunik (Cambridge: Harvard University Press, 1973).

[5] David Punter, *The Literature of Terror: A History of Gothic Fiction* (London: Longman, 1980), 14.

[6] Leslie A. Fiedler, *Love and Death in the American Novel* (New York: Anchor, 1992), 105–161.

[7] Dale Peterson, "Russian Gothic: The Deathless Paradoxes of Bunin's *Dry Valley*," *Slavic and Eastern European Journal* 31 (1987):36–49.

[8] Ibid., 38.

[9] Fiedler, *Love and Death*, 129–131.

Closely related to this notion of the historical Gothic is that of a sexual Gothic, in which the Gothic heroine and text are haunted by repressed sexual desires. Central to this view is the prominence of repressed doubling in Gothic fiction—the self is split in order to keep sexuality and sexual plea-sure at bay.[10] Ellen Moers and Claire Kahane take this notion of a sexual Gothic one step further, interpreting Gothic fear as fear of the body and of its various physiological systems, the reproductive system chief among them.[11] Sandra Gilbert, Susan Gubar, and Eugenia DeLamotte explore the Gothic in a parallel vein, although their focus is not so much on the repres-sion of sexual desire as on the repression of women and the manner in which women are haunted by their confining sexual roles.[12]

These two approaches are not mutually exclusive, and, in the course of my discussion, I will draw on both in exploring the complex manner in which issues of class and gender shape ideological genre. Each approach illuminates the uses to which the genre has been put over the past two hun-dred years, and it is probable that no single Gothic work represents a pure instantiation of either model. Moreover, each use of a genre has potential repercussions on further applications; the character of a genre is molded by the genre's memory of its past employments and—in the case of the Gothic—of past encodings of fears.[13] Both approaches are relevant to a study of the culture of NEP, for each highlights different aspects of NEP's Gothic worldview, which, like DeLamotte's Gothic, is the creation of "a self trying to shut out something alien to self."[14]

Whatever the precise nature of the "other" that Gothic fiction obsessively desires to ward off (and, perhaps, embrace), the devices used by the genre have been remarkably durable and few. Doors play an enormous role in Gothic fiction: doors at which heroines listen, doors that either do not lock or lock from the wrong side. DeLamotte attributes the lasting presence of portal imagery in the Gothic to the genre's preoccupation with the themes of isola-

---

[10] See, inter alia, William Patrick Day, *In the Circles of Fear and Desire: A Study of Gothic Fiction* (University of Chicago Press, 1985), 26.

[11] Ellen Moers, *Literary Women* (Garden City, N.Y.: Doubleday, 1976); Claire Kahane, "Gothic Mirrors and Feminine Identity," in *The (M)other Tongue: Essays in Feminist Psycho-analytic Interpretation*, ed. Shirley Nelson Garner, Claire Kahane, and Madelon Sprengnether (Ithaca: Cornell University Press, 1985), 334–351.

[12] Sandra Gilbert and Susan Gubar, *The Madwoman in the Attic: The Woman Writer and the Nineteenth-Century Literary Imagination* (New Haven: Yale University Press, 1979); Eugenia DeLamotte, *Perils of the Night: A Feminist Study of Nineteenth Century Gothic* (New York: Oxford University Press, 1990).

[13] On genres and their "memory" see Bakhtin, "The Problem of Speech Genres," 60–102, and *Problems of Dostoevsky's Poetics*, trans. Caryl Emerson (Minneapolis: University of Minnesota Press, 1984), 157.

[14] DeLamotte, *Perils*, 13.

tion and community.[15] The endangered protagonist yearns for the society of safe, nonthreatening friends and relations and dreads contact with an evil villain who may in some respects be herself. This villain, whose castle has separated the heroine from the presexual world of her childhood and of a community uncontaminated by lust, frequently personifies not only "supernatural powers but also [. . .] social forces so vast and impersonal that they seem to have supernatural strength."[16] In early English Gothic fiction, the clergy or the aristocracy—the class enemies of the bourgeoisie—often peek out from under the villain's cloak. The terrifying power and ostensible—but perhaps illusory—alterity of these institutions is symbolized in Gothic fiction by the virtually obligatory location of the plot's action in a foreign (or foreign-seeming) locale, and by the usually foreboding titles and names of villains and castles (*The Castle of Otranto*, *The Mysteries of Udolpho*, or even *The Italian*).

The "foreign" villain—the Gothic self as other—erupts or threatens to do so in an atmosphere so dreamlike that all seems permitted. William Patrick Day writes:

> The terror that underlies the Gothic is not that some monster will emerge; such moments are, for the reader and often for the protagonists, moments of relief. The true terror lies in the possibility that the Gothic atmosphere will take over completely and that the conventional, stable division between self and Other will disappear forever. The direct representation of such a state is, of course, beyond the resources of the novelist, particularly the Gothic writer whose evidence demanded a plot, characters and action. [. . .] Fog, moonlight, twilight, and darkness, the protracted suspense and mystery of the texts are the devices by which the Gothic fantasy represents the metaphysical state of fusion of subjective and objective into identityless horror. [. . .] The common intuition that the Gothic world is a dreamscape, a land of nightmare, stems from this characteristic blurring of reality so central to its atmosphere.[17]

This oneiric quality of the Gothic text is frequently recapitulated on a smaller scale by a seemingly never-ending cycle of fainting and awakening in which the heroine finds herself trapped. When Gothic fiction ends happily, the text breaks its cycle of repetition by introducing as deus ex machina the narrative equivalent of an alarm clock: "the suffering comes to an end in much the same way that nightmares do—abruptly the dreamer wakes."[18]

Initially the notion of a NEP or communist Gothic might seem a contradiction in terms. To be sure, the Gothic novel was an extremely popular and productive model in nineteenth-century Russia, with traces found in the

[15] Ibid., 19, 29.
[16] Ibid., 16.
[17] Day, *In the Circles*, 30.
[18] DeLamotte, *Perils*, 110.

works of Pushkin, Gogol, Lermontov, and Dostoevsky.[19] Perhaps the most important work in all of Russian literature, Pushkin's *Eugene Onegin*, begins as a parodic reworking of Maturin's *Melmoth the Wanderer*.[20] Still, the heyday of classic Gothic fiction occurred well over a hundred years before the Russian Revolution, and the term "Gothic" would seem to be utterly inappropriate—both in general outlook and, equally important, in mood—when applied to the early Soviet period, a resolutely materialist age. What could be more unsuited to a communist worldview than "haunted" fiction in which the gaze flutters nervously sideways and backward rather than fixing itself on an inevitable shining future?[21]

There are strong reasons, however, for NEP's ideological discourse to have gravitated toward the model of the Gothic genre and for the influential role of that genre in shaping the views of communists. Theories about the role played in the rise of Gothic fiction by bourgeois anxieties about class legitimacy in the wake of the French Revolution find a parallel in uncertainties about the proletariat's legitimacy as a ruling class after 1917. The early, post-Revolutionary worry about legitimacy was compounded by the decimation of the working class during the Civil War and by the allegations made at the Eleventh Party Congress that the Party had become the "avant-garde of a nonexistent class."[22] Sheila Fitzpatrick has written in detail about this "Bolshevik dilemma" and the inadequacy of the Party's worldview to the prevail-

---

[19] On the influence of the Gothic novel in nineteenth-century Russian literature, see Andrew Kahn, "Semantika parodii i gibridizatsii zhanrov v 'Zapiskakh okhotnika,'" in *I.S. Turgenev: Zhizn'. Tvorchestvo. Traditsii*, ed. Zh. Zel'dkheii-Deak and A. Khollosh (Budapest: Nemzeti Tankönyvkiadó, 1994), 102–113; V. Setschkareff, "Ch. R. Maturins Roman *Melmoth, the Wanderer* und Dostoevskij," *Zeitschrift für Slavische Philologie* 21, no. 1 (1951): 99–106, Ernest J. Simmons, *English Literature and Culture in Russia (1553–1840)* (New York: Octagon Books, 1964), 152–156, 300; and Mark S. Simpson, *The Russian Gothic Novel and Its British Antecedents* (Columbus, Ohio: Slavica, 1986). Radcliffe's popularity in Russia may be measured by her authorship of more novels in Russian than in English; some of these were written by Russian imitators, but the first Russian translation of Matthew Lewis's *The Monk* was also attributed to her. A. M. Umanskii, "Radklif," *Entsiklopedicheskii slovar'*, 86 vols. (Iaroslavl': Brokgauz-Efron [Terra], 1890–1907 [1992]), 51:92.

[20] Setschkareff, "Ch. R. Maturins Roman," 100–101.

[21] Because of its frequent employment of supernatural or unexplained phenomena, the genre has not generally been exploited in the nineteenth and twentieth centuries by ideologies that claim to appeal to reason and scientific truth. Dostoevskii's employment of Gothic devices in *Crime and Punishment*, for example, is an important (and critically neglected) aspect of his much discussed ideological battle with the didactic, politically radical, non-Gothic sentimentalism of Chernyshevskii's *What Is to Be Done?* Dostoevskii's attraction to the Gothic tradition has been discussed by Leonid Grossman (*Tvorchestvo Dostoevskogo* [M.: Sovremennye problemy, 1928], 21–35), and the role of anti-Chernyshevskian polemics in *Crime and Punishment* is a commonplace, but the extent to which Dostoevskii's heightened use of the Gothic (along with his transposition of the typical victim's terror onto her murderer) in *Crime and Punishment* was itself part of the conservative author's assault on his radical rival has not been explored.

[22] *Odinnadtsatyi s"ezd RKP(b). Stenograficheskii otchet* (M.: Ts.K.R.K.P., 1922), 92.

ing situation in post–Civil War Russia: "By 1921 [. . .] the *memory* of class polarization remained strong, and the passions of revolutionary class war volatile. But the class structure itself had collapsed, the old possessing classes had disintegrated, and even the proletariat had almost vanished from the scene. The great polarization of proletariat and bourgeoisie had become a polarization of shadows and surrogates."[23]

These "shadows and surrogates" were recognized as such by many Party members who spoke at congresses and conferences throughout the 1920s. Their awareness of the phantasmatic character of the class conflict, however, was tantamount to an admission that the incarnation of the Revolution in Russia had been something of a fraud, that Marxist-Leninist theory had not assumed viable flesh. The Party was threatened by ideological breakdown; in significant respects the historical situation was similar to that which had witnessed the formation of Gothic models twelve to thirteen decades earlier. Kenneth Graham explains the rise of the Gothic in the following terms:

> Gothic enigmas assault ideological conditionings: they undermine security at many levels of existence. They create awful doubts about reason and imagination and about sanity and madness in the internal world; about the beneficence of political and religious structures and attitudes in social life; about the ambivalence of God and Satan, good and evil, at the metaphysical level of existence. Gothic narrative plays on apprehensions that a universe of disorder and transgression lurks on the borders of our worlds of order and restraint.[24]

The Gothic nature of NEP is most obvious in the relationship of early Soviet ideology to the past. It is not surprising that people who viewed themselves as utopia-bound should have targeted the concept of history for elimination. The past, when linked to the present, provides a conduit for contamination of the future; during the War Communist period, demands that the present be purged of the past frequently surfaced in central and provincial periodicals. In 1920 Andrei Platonov wrote in a peasant-oriented newspaper published by the Voronezh Party organization:

> Communism arose from capitalism and therefore has preserved many of capitalism's features and particularities. The proletariat is born of the bourgeoisie and has not yet eliminated many bourgeois manners and bourgeois ways of thinking and living. It still carries these around within it.
>
> We have to do away with this. We have to chop the past off from the future, to forget yesterday once and for all, to make the human world truly communist.[25]

[23] Sheila Fitzpatrick, "The Problem of Class Identity in NEP Society," in *Russia in the Era of NEP: Explorations in Soviet Society and Culture*, ed. Sheila Fitzpatrick, Alexander Rabinowitch, and Richard Stites (Bloomington: Indiana University Press, 1991), 15 (12–33).

[24] Kenneth Graham, "Afterword: Some Remarks on Gothic Origins," in *Gothic Fictions: Prohibition/Transgression*, ed. Kenneth Graham (New York: AMS Press, 1989), 262 (259–268).

[25] Andrei Platonov, "Vospitanie kommunista," *Krasnaia derevnia*, 30 July 1920, 2.

Platonov was not alone in his desire to amputate the past. The imagery employed during the War Communist epoch to speak about the past—particularly by Proletkul't and neo-Futurist publications—was already informed by visceral hatred of history. Poletaev and Punin attacked history as an analytical and cultural category that "gives the most superficial and conventional explanations for events in the present and in no wise facilitates creativity in the future"; they termed love for the past and for preceding generations "passéism and necrophilia."[26] "All progress is emancipation from the dead weight of culture," they claimed, rejecting "all those 'sacred' principles willed to us by history" and decrying the energy expended by society on "the maintenance of all cemeteries and on the dead of history."[27] The Proletkul't journals repeated this refrain, referring to the "vampire past," a spirit that might take possession of a Bolshevik and cause him to commit atrocious deeds.[28]

History and its tainted testament preoccupied Soviet society on more than a metaphorical level. Early Soviet jurists saw the legal concept of inheritance as the mainstay of private property and proudly pointed to the decree of 27 April 1918 eliminating inheritance rights as a measure that "struck a fatal blow to the institution of private property."[29] With this decree, explained Aleksandr Goikhbarg, one of the most visible early Soviet jurists, private property had "ceased to be something considered eternal, something passed down from generation to generation, from family to family according to the principles of individual law."[30] Goikhbarg insisted: "absolutely nothing of the institution of private inheritance has remained; this inheritance has in no respect been preserved, not in any form and not in any part. *Each and every* item of the dead man's property becomes the property of the Russian Soviet Socialist Republic."[31] Having made this emphatic statement, Goikhbarg was, nevertheless, forced to admit that since the Soviet government had not yet succeeded in establishing a satisfactory welfare state and since dependents of deceased still had to be provided for, "a certain surrogate [of inheritance] has been preserved," one assuring that a dead man's property would "support his closest, most needy, and least able-bodied relatives, as well as his spouse."[32] Goikhbarg took great pains to emphasize the differences between this surro-

---

[26] Evgenii Poletaev and Nikolai Punin, *Protiv tsivilizatsii* (Pg., 1918), 27.

[27] Ibid., 56.

[28] S. D., "Bibliografiia," *Proletarskaia kul'tura*, no. 3 (1918): 32.

[29] A. G. Goikhbarg, *Proletariat i pravo* (M.: Narodnyi komissariat iustitsii, 1919), 54. For a discussion of Goikhbarg's role in the development of early Soviet family law, see Wendy Z. Goldman, *Women, the State and Revolution: Soviet Family Policy and Social Life, 1917–1936* (Cambridge: Cambridge University Press, 1993), 51–57.

[30] Goikhbarg, *Proletariat i pravo*, 54.

[31] Ibid., 55.

[32] Ibid., 56.

gate and the real thing: creditors' claims no longer had priority over the needs of relatives, legitimate and illegitimate offspring shared equally, and, in the distribution of property, need would be more important than proximity of relation. Did these differences justify the claim that inheritance had been eliminated "entirely and without residue"?[33]

With the advent of NEP, claims that the past and its effects had been eliminated "entirely and without residue" no longer rang hollow; they disappeared entirely. Lenin, in an early speech directed at "selling NEP" to Party and populace, recognized that the term "New Economic Policy" was a misnomer.

> You cannot help noticing what a sharp reversal our Soviet government and our Party have undertaken in embarking on this economic policy that is called "new" only in regard to our previous economic policy.
>   And in essence in this policy there is more that is old than in our previous economic policy.[34]

The awareness that the "old" had arisen from the scrap heap of history pervaded discussion of many aspects of Soviet culture during the 1920s.[35] Determined to resist the past, commentators resorted to an imagery of interment, as if keeping NEP in its coffin could counter "the putrefying influence of Nepmen and petty bourgeois elements."[36] Despite bold claims made by a leading editor that Soviet citizens were "gravediggers of the old world,"[37] Rector Liadov was forced to conclude in 1925:

---

[33] Ibid.

[34] V. I. Lenin, "Novaia ekonomicheskaia politika i zadachi politprosvetov" (17 October 1921), *Polnoe sobranie,* 44:156.

[35] The identification of the private businesses that surfaced under NEP with the pre-Revolutionary bourgeoisie was not entirely accurate. More than 90 percent of NEP's businessmen employed fewer than five workers and only 26 percent had traded before 1917, although the large-scale entrepreneurs (less than 10 percent of the total) who employed more than five workers were far more likely to have engaged in private trade before 1917. Alan Ball, "Private Trade and Traders during NEP," in Fitzpatrick, Rabinowitz, and Stites, *Russia in the Era of NEP,* 92–93 (89–105). Of those engaged in private *wholesale* trade, more than half had pursued that métier before the Revolution. V. M. Selunskaia, ed. *Izmeneniia sotsial'noi struktury sovetskogo obshchestva 1921-seredina 30-x godov* (M.: Mysl', 1979), 117. Sergei Tret'iakov, a dominant voice on the constructivist journal *LEF,* provided an ideologically consistent explanation for the relative paucity of pre-Revolutionary bourgeois among the private businessmen of NEP: "the bearers of bourgeois and feudal traditions are too slow-moving and too used to living by inertia to adapt [to new, post-Revolutionary conditions], and so they despise the grubby newcomer, the Nepman [. . .], but in practical terms the Nepman learns *bon ton* from these walking corpses and he, in recompense, obviates their having to mount the scaffold of retail trade and allows them to sit in their spiders' corners and to await with prim solemnity the end of 'the holiday of the red boor.'" "LEF i NEP," *LEF,* no. 2 (1923): 76–77 (70–78).

[36] V. Dmitriev and B. Galin, *Na putiakh k novomu bytu* (M.: Novaia Moskva, 1927), 10.

[37] A. Voronskii, "Iz sovremennykh nastroenii," *Krasnaia nov',* no. 3 (1921): 244 (244–255).

We have created new forms of ritual, we have shaken the laws of the old morality, but we have not yet killed the petty bourgeois sitting within each of us.
In this respect the dead seize the living entirely [*mertvye v etom otnoshenii
khvataiut zhivykh tselikom*]. The petty bourgeois character in each of us still
exists and makes itself known in our attitude toward the family, toward each
other, in our sexual relations, and in every aspect of our personal life.[38]

The expression "the dead seize the living"—a phrase used by Marx in his
preface to the first edition of *Capital*—is found quite frequently in language
about sex during the New Economic Policy,[39] but it contained an obvious
contradiction, for, as Liadov acknowledged, the dead were not truly dead at
all ("We have not yet killed . . ."). Rather, petty bourgeois values and economics occupied a strange position on the border between this world and
"the other"; they were capable of traversing the boundary between life and
death at any moment.

"Perhaps the most prevalent theme in Gothic fiction," David Punter
writes, is "the revisiting of the sins of the fathers upon their children."[40] "The
Gothic writer knows," Dale Peterson explains, "that the buried remain, in
some sense, undead. Corpses that are marked and bear inscriptions can resurface at any time. The power of the past to command a repeat performance
despite the conscious will or rationality of a present day mentality is what
Gothic fiction is all about."[41] The centrality of the notion of "repeat performance" to the Gothic is crucial to an understanding of why the Gothic can
be both so undermining and constitutive of Marxist thought. Marxism is first
and foremost a theory about the laws of historical progression (and, in Engels's hands, of all natural processes); the disturbing phenomena of today are
part of a process that will eventually eliminate the phenomena as it proves
their historical necessity. If history is ever to repeat itself, it must be on
another plane: "the first time as tragedy, the second as farce," perhaps, as
Marx wrote in *The Eighteenth Brumaire of Louis Napoleon*, but not twice as
the same thing.[42] Marxist narrative is inherently at odds with the Gothic, but
often so resolutely at odds that the Gothic seems to have been partially

[38] M. N. Liadov, *Voprosy byta* (M.: Kommun. U-t. im. Ia. Sverdlova, 1925), 8.

[39] See, e.g., an explanation for the continued existence of sex crimes in the Soviet Union:
"Here we see how the marshy fumes of the past rise up against a background of shared progress
and cultural growth, how the dead seize the living." G. M. Segal, "K probleme polovoi prestup-
nosti," in *Pravonarusheniia v oblasti seksual'nykh otnoshenii*, ed. E. K. Krasnushkin, G. M.
Segal, and Ts. N. Fainberg (M.: Moszdravotdel, 1927), 7 (5–10). Marx used the phrase—in
French—to describe the atavistic survival of precapitalist modes of production into the late
nineteenth century. *Capital*, trans. Ben Fowkes, 3 vols. (London: Penguin, 1976), 1:91.

[40] Punter, *The Literature of Terror*, 52.

[41] Peterson, "Russian Gothic," 38.

[42] Karl Marx and Friedrich Engels, *The Karl Marx Reader*, ed. Richard C. Tucker (New York:
Norton, 1972), 436.

responsible for shaping Marxism, or, at least, to have made a strong mark. "What the bourgeoisie [. . .] produces, above all," we learn in *The Communist Manifesto*, "is its own gravediggers."[43] Marx loved to sift through the bones of the dead; his spirits soared when his ear discerned the sound of "the funereal bell that is already ringing for the Second Empire in Paris."[44] His graveyard imagery may have reflected his brash confidence in the historical inevitability that denied the bourgeoisie a future, but it may also be part of a consistent strategy to project the Gothic onto an other and thereby make it *someone else's* story. *The Eighteenth Brumaire*, a text particularly saturated with Gothic imagery, may be read on a generic level as a work that seeks desperately to turn not history but the Gothic (and the Gothic's notion of history as repetition) into farce—to transform an especially threatening worldview into a nonmenacing, trivialized, farcical attribute of one's opponent.[45] That essay, which must make sense of a historical episode of failure for the working class, ends by hurling a curse at the new, illegitimate holder of power: a rhetorical gesture that often lies at the bottom—and the beginning—of Gothic texts.[46] Seen from this perspective, Marxism presents itself

[43] Karl Marx and Friedrich Engels, *Collected Works*, 45 vols. (London: Lawrence & Wishart, 1975–1991), 6:496.

[44] K. Marks (Marx) and F. Engel's (Engels), *Izbrannye proizvedeniia v dvukh tomakh* (M.: OGIZ, 1948), 1:447.

[45] My reading of Marx is indebted to several scholars. Dominick LaCapra has pointed to the apotropaic nature of the essay's "polemical animus," which, he writes, "might be seen as a function of a concealed or even repressed fear that the proletariat itself is not the revolutionary agent Marx wishes it to be and that other groups do not hold out the transformative promise he seeks." *Rethinking Intellectual History: Texts, Contexts, Language* (Ithaca: Cornell University Press, 1983), 281, 284. (See also Fredric Jameson's more general remark about Marxism's use of the doctrine of "necessity" as a defense against according too much weight to the repeated failures of proletarian revolutions. *The Political Unconscious: Narrative as a Socially Symbolic Act* [Ithaca: Cornell University Press, 1981], 101–102.) Placing *The Eighteenth Brumaire's* horror of repetition into the context of "the poetics of *ressentiment*" that he sees haunting writers from Diderot to Dostoevskii to Céline, Michael André Bernstein remarks that Marx's famous phrase "the tradition of all the dead generations weighs like a nightmare on the brain of the living" is "surely one of the most Romantically Gothic and thus antimaterialist images of his entire oeuvre." "The Poetics of *Ressentiment*," in *Rethinking Bakhtin: Extensions and Challenges*, ed. Gary Saul Morson and Caryl Emerson (Evanston, Ill.: Northwestern University Press, 1989), 214 (197–223). In a stunning analysis of Marx's "hauntology," Jacques Derrida has recently explored the contradictory status of ghosts in Marx's oeuvre. Marx's specters include both "those that herald the best and whose event he will have greeted, those that arise from or threaten the worst, whose testimony he will have rejected. There are several times of the specter. It is a proper characteristic of the specter, if there is any, that no one can be sure if by returning it testifies to a living past or a living future. . . ." *Specters of Marx: The State of the Debt, the Work of Mourning, and the New International*, trans. Peggy Kamuf (New York: Routledge, 1994), 99. See also 106.

[46] Compare, for instance, the end of Marx's essay, "But if the imperial mantle finally falls on the shoulders of Louis Bonaparte, the iron statue of Napoleon will crash from the top of the Vendôme column," *The Marx-Engels Reader*, ed. Robert C. Tucker (New York: Norton, 1972),

as the herald of capitalism's Gothic narrative: the tale of capitalism's morally illegitimate and temporary hold on power.

Lenin's voluntaristic approach to Marxism would introduce a new refinement into Marx's gift of a Gothic plot to the bourgeoisie. A central, defining tenet of Bolshevism was the conviction that the bourgeoisie could not be relied upon to go peacefully into its grave; it had to be hurriedly helped, and proper burial might have to be dispensed with. In 1918 Lenin told a meeting of workers and deputies: "The working class is not cut off from the old bourgeois society by a Chinese wall. And when Revolution comes, it is not the same as with the death of an individual, when the deceased is carried out of the house. When the old society dies, its corpse cannot be shut up in a coffin and placed in the grave. It decomposes in our midst; the corpse rots and infects us."[47] This decomposition ought not to inhibit the building of communism; infection could be fought with proper policies, and Lenin's tone, on the whole, was no less confident than that of Marx. (Perhaps the heightened vulgarity of Lenin's language should be attributed in part to the tension introduced into Marxism by Lenin's call for the hastening of sluggish historical inevitability.) NEP's reintroduction of capitalist forms into the Russian economy, however, radically called into question the inevitability of Marxist-Leninist historical progress. NEP's "step backward" into the past gave birth to the anxious suspicion that history might function as a cycle rather than through the dialectic; if revolutions could move *counter*clockwise, all of Marx's buried and Lenin's rotting corpses might still rise to their feet. This step backward into time, moreover, might threaten to place the proletariat in the Gothic position earlier occupied by the bourgeoisie. Having "conjured up" the bourgeoisie to save the new society's economic base, the proletariat might well find itself in the place of the *Communist Manifesto*'s bourgeois "sorcerer, who is no longer able to control the powers of the nether world whom he has called up by his spells."[48]

525, with the start of Horace Walpole's *The Castle of Otranto* (Oxford: Oxford University Press, 1982), 15–16, in which the heir to the castle is crushed by a giant helmet, a catastrophe that causes the evil prince's subjects to recall the "ancient prophecy" that "the castle and lordship of Otranto should pass from the present family, whenever the real owner should be grown too large to inhabit it."

[47] V. I. Lenin, "Doklad o bor'be s golodom [Ob"edinennoe zasedanie VTsIK, Moskovskogo soveta rabochikh, krest'ianskikh i krasnoarmeiskikh deputatov i professional'nykh soiuzov]" (4 June 1918), *Polnoe sobranie*, 36:408–409.

[48] *The Marx-Engels Reader*, 340.

In his remarkable commentary to the novels of Il'f and Petrov, Iu. K. Shcheglov glosses Balaganov's discovery of an "agitational coffin" in *The Golden Calf* (1931) by referring to the frequency of funereal imagery in political demonstrations of the 1920s. Shcheglov notes that there was precedent for such "funerals" in German Marxist demonstrations of the late nineteenth century. He sees the use of funereal images as "one of the elements of public, carnivalesque and magic imagery, to which the Soviet press and mass propaganda of the 1920s so

In the discourse of NEP the "repeat performance" so central to the Gothic occurred most frequently in the theater of sex. We have already seen sexual reproduction characterized by Russian thinkers as "bad infinity"—as repetition without progress. In Berdiaev's world, this repetition had not yet acquired a Gothic taint; there was no institutionally awesome other knocking at that idealist philosopher's door. Moreover, neither Berdiaev nor Solov'ev had viewed "bad infinity"—a term they had sexualized after lifting it from Hegel[49]—as a newly acquired condition. Repetition was regressive, but it had been part of man's imperfect world since his fall from grace. As we shall see, however, during NEP the sentiments expressed by Trotsky at the conclusion of *Literature and Revolution*—"the human race has not ceased to crawl on hands and knees before god, tsar, and capital in order to bow humbly before the dark laws of heredity and blind sexual selection"—were often vented more in a tone of anxious, even horrified, defiance than with unalloyed confidence.[50] Repetition, particularly in its sexual, physiological, and reproductive hypostasis, was a repugnant and politically urgent symbol of Soviet man's recent lapse from communism to pseudocapitalism.[51]

It was not only genetic concerns (Trotsky's "dark laws of heredity and blind sexual selection") that turned reproduction into Gothic theater. Sexual passion in its hypertrophied modern form was viewed as a contaminating legacy from the capitalist past. Zalkind, whose views on this matter we have already examined, was not alone. In a 1924 article, "Sexual Education and Marxist Pedagogy," G. N. Sorokhtin advocated that Soviet educators devise a strategy to "asexualiz[e] the reality of sexual filth and pathology bequeathed to us by capitalism and strongly supported by Nepmen and by negative, as yet unliquidated phenomena of contemporary life."[52] I. Gel'man's study *The Sexual Life of Contemporary Youth*, published in 1923 with the imprimatur of the Commissariat of Health, painted the following picture of the horrors of sexual desire:

---

frequently resorted." *Romany I. Il'fa i E. Petrova, Wiener Slawistischer Almanach*, Sonderband 26, 2 vols. (1991), 2:592. In focusing on the festive, carnivalesque aspects of funereal imagery, Shcheglov ignores, however, the *anxieties* inherent in these images during NEP, when constant burial of the enemy was required because the enemy was continually resurrected.

In a separate subsection of the same commentary Shcheglov observes that this humorous vignette is also indebted in literary terms to the Gothic novel, which it parodies.

[49] Georg Wilhelm Friedrich Hegel, *Encyklopädie der philosophischen Wissenschaften im Grundrisse* (Berlin: L. Heimann, 1870), 115 (sec. 94). See also Engels's discussion of the term in his "Anti-Dühring," in Marx and Engels, *Collected Works*, 25:44.

[50] L. Trotskii, *Literatura i revoliutsiia* (M.: Politicheskaia literatura, 1991 [1923]), 196–197.

[51] For more on the symbolic, symptomatic, and gender dimensions of sex during NEP, see chapters 5 and 6, below.

[52] G. N. Sorokhtin, "Polovoe vospitanie detei v plane marksistskoi pedagogii," in *Polovoi vopros v shkole i zhizni*, ed. I. S. Simonov (L.: Brokgauz-Efron, 1925), 76 (73–94).

Man's sexual life numbers among the dirtiest and at times most horrific [*naibolee zhutkie*] pages of his existence. Born in the realm of instincts that lie deep below the level of consciousness, sexual desires explode to the surface at certain times of life, eclipsing, for more or less prolonged periods, all weaker urges and instincts and frequently overwhelming all our inhibitory and regulatory centers. And even when these roaring desires are still confined beneath the surface of conscious life, their dominion imperceptibly penetrates the sphere of consciousness and psyche and gives birth there to waves of arousal and depression, tides of creativity and apathy.[53]

Such imagery owes a debt to pre-Revolutionary discourse, most notably to Symbolism and to the metaphysics of Tiutchev. In the context of NEP, Gel'man's frightening depiction of the return of the *psychologically* repressed expanded to encompass a fear of an undead and incompletely repressed *historical* past. The anxieties produced by this union were especially prone to surface in discussions of the mental, physical, and ideological faults of the (youthful) generation that Lenin had promised would be the first to live under true communism. In the course of a discussion about Malashkin, Gumilevsky, Romanov, and "the problems of sex," Polonsky paused to comment on *Komsomol'skii byt*—a collection of essays on everyday life in the Communist Youth League. "Comrades," he told an audience at the Moscow Polytechnic Museum in 1927, "I don't remember a book from the literature of horror that might have had such an effect on me."[54]

Responses to such tales of horror often resembled a ritualized, collective exorcism of sex and of the past. In one of many agitational dramas of the mid-1920s about sex, the Party's raisonneur expounds on the evils of sexual corruption: "Comrades, we must always be conscious of where the Old World ends and where the new one begins . . . And we must stigmatize those who are still entirely in the past and who import this past into our great battle for liberation." At that moment the script calls for "a general rumble of voices" to be heard among the crowd of komsomol'tsy on stage, and just before the curtain falls all the actors are supposed to stride toward the most dissolute komsomolets, shouting: "Go away from us, Kuznetsov! Go away! Go away! Go away!"[55] This scene was repeated frequently on just a slightly more sophisticated level in the Komsomol and Party press and at countless Komsomol meetings devoted to the question of sex.

In light of my earlier remarks about the mobilizing, integrative dimension of NEP's discourse about sex, it is worth noting that the vast powers of attraction possessed by the Gothic undoubtedly played a role in the Gothic's

---

[53] I. Gel'man, *Polovaia zhizn' sovremennoi molodezhi*, 2d ed. (M. and Pg.: Gos. izd. 1923), 5.

[54] RGALI, fond 1328, opis' 3, ed. khran. 27, 12.

[55] N. Bozhinskaia, *Prestuplenie Ivana Kuznetsova (Svobodnaia liubov')* (M.: Molodaia gvardiia, 1927), 64.

prominence in discussions of sex during NEP. Edmund Burke was one of the first to write in detail about the power of terror to draw an audience; this power to attract functions provided that terror is not experienced as imminent physical danger but is mediated by art or, we might add, by discourse.[56] According to Charles Maturin, one of the High Gothic's leading practitioners, Gothic stories are "calculated to unlock every store of fancy and of feeling."[57] In their concern with psychology, the critic George Haggerty reminds us, Gothic novelists have been at the forefront of authors who sought "ways of giving imaginative worlds external and objective reality" and "of giving private experience external manifestation."[58] The power of the Gothic to invade, uncover, and display should not be overlooked in the context of the Party's preoccupation with collective mobilization and the colonization of privacy. In large measure Gothic fiction is about reader response; writing as if she had just read Pavlov or Zavadovsky, Ellen Moers argues that the Gothic utilizes fear "not to reach down into the depths of the soul and purge it with pity and terror (as we say tragedy does), but to get to the body itself, its glands, muscles, epidermis and circulatory system, quickly arousing and quickly allaying the physiological reaction to fear."[59] When *Saratovskie izvestiia*, satisfied by its success in using abortion to attract female readers, published its readers' collected letters in a small book, it placed on the cover a drawing of a terrified woman with wide, frightened eyes and disheveled hair.[60]

The crop of fiction dealing with the sexual question in 1926 and 1927 was itself criticized in "meta-Gothic" terms; the popularity of new and old works about sex was treated as representing a moment of ideologically dangerous repetition. The discussion of these works' very *appearance* on the Soviet literary scene (and of their contemporary cultural significance) utilized Gothic imagery. In a debate waged on the pages of the Leningrad dailies in June 1926, Panteleimon Romanov was accused by P. Adrianov of imitating pre-Revolutionary writers who had dealt in a bourgeois manner with the sexuality of youth.[61] Defending Romanov as a talented writer, Victor Alekseev asked why Adrianov had "felt compelled to summon such esteemed shades from a past that now seems so distant."[62] *Leningradskaia pravda* re-

---

[56] Edmund Burke, *A Philosophical Inquiry into the Origins of Our Ideas of the Sublime and the Beautiful* (London: Routledge & Kegan Paul, 1958).

[57] Charles Maturin, *The Fatal Revenge*. Cited in DeLamotte, *Perils*, 43.

[58] George E. Haggerty, *Gothic Fiction/Gothic Form* (University Park: Pennsylvania State University Press, 1989), 7.

[59] Moers, *Literary Women*, 90.

[60] S. Telegin, ed., *Abort* (Saratov: Saratovskie izvestiia, 1925).

[61] P. Adrianov, "Verbitskaia v briukakh i ee pokroviteli," *Leningradskaia pravda*, 17 June 1926, 2.

[62] Vik. Alekseev, "Guvernantka v shtanakh i ee zhertvy," *Leningradskaia krasnaia vecherniaia gazeta*, 18 June 1926, 2.

1. Cover illustration for *Abort* (Saratov: Saratovskie izvestiia, 1925).

sponded the next day that "it was not necessary to summon them. These
sepulchral shades [. . .] appear all by themselves; all that is necessary is that
the servants of NEP cleverly manage to raise just a tiny bit the coffin lid that
was put firmly into place during the October days."[63] Warning that "we are
threatened by a wave of erotic fiction of the most horrible and corrupting
[*razlagaiushchii*] sort," Viacheslav Polonsky wrote of a collection of Romanov's stories: "This book restores to our literature that nasty tone which
relishes and slobbers over sexual problems and which we associate with
Artsybashevism. We [older communists] did not battle against this slime in
our days so that it might be reborn in 1927 under the pen of a Soviet writer."[64]
A report from Tver published in *Komsomol'skaia pravda* in August 1926
revealed the following disturbing facts about youthful reading habits and
also highlighted the prevailing Gothic preoccupation with the past:

[63] L. A., "Pornografiia, pomnozhennaia na kommertsiiu," *Leningradskaia pravda*, 19 June
1926, 2.
[64] V. Polonskii, "O 'problemakh pola' i 'polovoi literature,'" *Izvestiia*, 3 April 1927, 3.

Old books published before the Revolution are now in great demand. There have even been cases when girls have come into libraries and implored:

"Give me the book that's the most battered and well-read, one where the subject is love."

There have even been requests for literature removed from the shelves—for Artsybashev and Verbitskaia, and Tarzan is snatched up at once.

Among a certain group of young people there is a great fascination with pornographic literature. Thus, for example, the director of the press section of the cell at the Vagzhanovsky Factory is avidly reading a book called *The Dead Don't Rise from Their Coffins*.

In answer to my question about what sort of book this was, he answered:

—It describes the life of a father who has sexual relations with his daughter.

It is apparent that this book gives him great satisfaction, since he is reading it for the second time.[65]

The requests for Verbitskaia and Tarzan indicate that much of this demand for pre-Revolutionary books—in Tver at least—should be attributed to the lack of interesting popular Soviet reading matter.[66] The correspondent's reaction to this list of books, however, and his focus on a "sexual" novel with a horrific title indicate how the demand to read pre-Revolutionary works was itself read with aversion, if not horror.

While the scandalous fiction of 1926 and 1927—*Dog Alley* and "The Moon from the Right Side"—may have borrowed certain themes from pre-Revolutionary literature,[67] they contained literary clichés that owed far more to the Gothic tradition. True, Artsybashev had resorted to voyeurism, "a paradigmatic Gothic motif" and essentially "the act of watching one's self,"[68] as a theme and narrative device, but his scenes of spying and eavesdropping

---

[65] Aksel'rod, "Chto chitaet molodezh'," *Komsomol'skaia pravda*, 18 August 1926, 3.

[66] The responses of workers to the "classics" of early Soviet literature indicate that many contemporary "blue-collar" readers found these works incomprehensible or boring. A twenty-year-old janitor from Briansk said of *Cement*: "It's junk. I didn't like it. It stretches on and on, and the end is nowhere in sight. Give me something more interesting." Workers were perplexed by the difficult language of Fedor Gladkov and Leonid Leonov and frustrated by the modernism of Vsevolod Ivanov. A Party member in Leningrad responded to Ivanov's "Bronepoezd No. 14–69": "It's surprising that such a book should have been published. The story has no plot and the author is semiliterate." A mail carrier from the Tver Guberniia reacted in a similar vein: "I didn't like the book, why, because this book describes an interesting thing, but the thing is not described clearly but rather as if in a fog and in addition the language is hard to make out." IMLI, fond 51, opis' 2 (Otzyvy rabochikh. Kabinet po izucheniiu chitatelia). For a discussion of Anastasiia Verbitskaia's significance in pre-Revolutionary culture, see Laura Engelstein, *The Keys to Happiness: Sex and the Search for Modernity in Fin-de-Siècle Russia* (Ithaca: Cornell University Press, 1992), 400–414.

[67] Gumilevskii transposes the final scene of *Zhenshchina stoiashchaia posredi* into the opening of his novel and borrows from Rozanov's *Liudi lunnogo sveta* the theme of handwriting as a metaphor for individuality in sexual relations.

[68] Day, *In the Circles*, 63–64.

were devoid of the fear of detection, of mise-en-abîme, and of the pronounced implication of the reader (see chapter 3) that mark voyeurism in the
sex novels of the 1920s. While the locus of seduction in *Sanin* is the great,
ghost-free, and virtually sublime outdoors, in *Dog Alley* this place is filled
by the haunted house, reincarnated as the student dormitory. As in the castles
of late-eighteenth-century fiction, the hero or heroine moves with trepidation
along a corridor with many doors, curious but terrified by what lurks behind
them. Unable to discharge his pent-up sexual passion, Gumilevsky's hero,
Khorokhorin, wanders down the hall of a women's residence:

> He walked down this long corridor, lowering his head and gritting his teeth;
> behind each door—he knew this—in each room at that very moment, perhaps,
> lying in bed, a woman was desiring a man and did not dare to summon him, just
> as he did not dare to enter. There was nothing simpler and yet nothing more
> complicated. He stopped before one of the doors and immediately staggered
> back from it as soon as he heard steps.
> "It's a nightmare, this is the nightmare of human life," he thought, and with
> insane haste he leapt out into the street.[69]

The young girl whom Khorokhorin seduces and drives mad has similarly
obsessive thoughts about sexual activity. She is terribly afraid of carnal pleasures, barely glimpsed or just out of sight, and ever so tenuously separated
by a thin wall from the young proletarian "subject":

> As a small, disobedient little girl, lying on the floor of a tight little room
> crowded with things, furniture, and children, she had peered out at night from
> under her blanket and through a chink in the wall at her mother and father—who
> were not asleep. Then she had not understood and had become angry: how could
> her mother let her father do that? But it had turned out that all her friends'
> fathers did this with their mothers. Then she had been terrified. And just re-
> cently, running through the settlement and then along the corridor of her bar-
> racks, past the yellow doors with the iron number plates, she had been unable to
> keep herself from thinking that this was being done right next door, constantly,
> invariably, with horrifying simplicity, perhaps right now, at that very minute,
> behind this door, behind this window.[70]

Gumilevsky employed other Gothic motifs as well, some of them lifted
from the classics of Russian literature that he freely copied. In borrowing
them, Gumilevsky infused them with a new, sexual significance; while Dostoevsky's *The Devils* provides *Dog Alley* with the spider as the principal
symbol of evil, in Gumilevsky's work the spider represents not just the
snares of a single villainous type (Petr Verkhovensky) but the much larger,

---

[69] Lev Gumilevskii, *Sobachii pereulok* (Riga: Gramatu draugs, 1928), 65.
[70] Ibid., 122.

Gothic enemy of universal sexuality. Khorokhorin is horrified by the power of sexual desire as he contemplates his double, Vera's other lover, the mentally ill, "fallen" komsomolets, Burov:

> In the past he had held himself erect, thinking himself superior to this sick man, but here, in one instant, as if illuminated by a blue bolt of lightning, the entire evening [of sexual frustration and desire] flashed before him, and he was terrified: for himself, for Burov, and for all those like them entangled in the snares of that enormous, white, and satiated sexual spider which covets not blood but the best thing in a person—his brain.[71]

The Gothic nature of this sexual spider is foreshadowed in Khorokhorin's first meeting with the nymphomaniacal Vera, a medical student who, shrouded in her fur coat, approaches him in a tram at the novel's opening. Khorokhorin is certain that he has seen this woman before and suddenly remembers: "he recognized her face, now covered with the ash of electric light, an evening face hidden in a pile of fur; [then] it had been a smooth pink little face with fastidiously protruding lips bent over the amorphous breast of a prepared corpse in the anatomical theater."[72] If Gothic fiction, as several critics have noticed, tends to produce texts rich in architectural or geological representations of the female genitalia,[73] this scene effectively manages to transpose Vera's sexual organs from the lower half of her body to the upper and to associate them with one of the most obviously Gothic scenes in the novel: the contact of the living with the flesh of the dead. It also provides an example of how the positivist impulse so dear to the Marxist tradition can be corrupted by the literature of horror and disgust.

In Soviet literature Gumilevsky's Gothic focus on boundaries and, in particular, on doors as images that function as distressingly unreliable partitions between the self and the self's more repulsive desires was not an isolated phenomenon. More interesting, however, is the appearance of Gothic imagery in political and pedagogic discourse. In early explanations of NEP's character and goals by Party leaders, Bolshevism frantically tries to maintain its ideological chastity as it cowers in a house in which it has been required to remove all latches from windows and locks from doors. Kuibyshev spoke of a "forced halt in our progressive movement toward communism, [a moment] when old forms of social interaction are pressing forward from all sides and through all chinks and straining to strengthen themselves."[74] In

---

[71] Ibid., 80.

[72] Ibid., 14–15.

[73] See, inter alia, Cynthia Griffin Wolff, "The Radcliffean Gothic Model: A Form for Feminine Sexuality," in *The Female Gothic*, ed. Juliann E. Fleenor (Montreal: Eden Press, 1983), 207–223.

[74] V. Kuibyshev, "Novaia ekonomicheskaia politika i zadachi zhenotdelov," *Kommunistka*, nos. 16–17 (1921): 10 (10–11).

1921, Lenin provided one of the clearest depictions of proletarian power as heroine in history's haunted house:

> Here is what our current battle comes down to: who will win, who will bene-
> fit—the capitalist, whom we are admitting through the door or even through
> several doors (and through many doors that we do not know about and that open
> without our knowledge and against us [и во много таких дверей, которых
> мы не знаем и которые открываются помимо нас и против нас], or the
> proletarian power of the government?[75]

The Gothic resonance of the passage above sets the tone for many scenes in writing during and about NEP that try to answer the same question, often in a sexual key and informed by a spirit similar to that motivating Zalkind's observation that "sexuality is [. . .] an extremely subtle diplomat, who cleverly crawls through the narrowest of slits."[76]

Trapped in her castle, the Gothic heroine often recalls her childhood, a Garden of Eden inhabited before her agonizingly slow, perhaps still reversible, fall. Soviet society of the NEP era also had its Golden Age—the period of War Communism. As we have already seen, this idealization of pre-NEP years was in no sense unproblematic; as we shall see in chapter 7, some pragmatic communists deemed the survival of this idealization just as dangerous as the survival of capitalism's "relics." Many social commentators, however, particularly when writing about youth and sexuality, tended to remember this era with great fondness—as a time unburdened by questions of sexuality and a period of maximum sublimation. Most of the NEP surveys of sexual attitudes included a question about how the Revolution and Civil War had affected the sex drives of youth. I. Gel'man's 1923 study of 1,615 Moscow University students found that the Revolution had weakened the sex drive of 53 percent of the male respondents and 31.5 percent of the women. (A contrary effect was noted by only 13.4 percent of the men and 9.5 percent of the women, with the remainder [33.6 percent and 59 percent, respectively] observing no change.) Gel'man presented this statistic as evidence of how "large social movements with their corresponding tensions make use of all types of energy that accumulate in the organism. [. . .] Sexual energy is transformed into social energy."[77] Studies conducted in other cities reached similar conclusions about the Revolution's effect on sex drive.[78] While none

---

[75] Lenin, "Novaia ekonomicheskaia politika," 44:160.

[76] Zalkind, *Polovoi vopros v usloviiakh sovetskoi obshchestvennosti* (L.: Gos. izd., 1926), 47.

[77] Gel'man, *Polovaia zhizn'*, 82.

[78] A study conducted in the same year at the Sverdlov Communist University in Moscow reported that among men sexual desire had been weakened by the Revolution in 43.4 percent of the cases and strengthened in 8.14 percent. The Revolution had had a debilitating effect on the sexual desire of 22.8 percent of the women and in only 6.4 percent had it intensified sexual desire. "Anketa o polovoi zhizni studentov kom. un-ta," *Zapiski kommunisticheskogo univer-*

of the surveys provided a statistically significant representation of the Soviet population as a whole, and while students confronted with questions about the Revolution's sexual "coefficient" knew what was expected of them, the question's inclusion in all questionnaires and its triumphant interpretation certainly indicated a desire on the part of the researchers that these statistics be universally true.

Zalkind provided a "scientific" explanation for the data. Moreover, in doing so he warned that for the proletariat NEP was a far from healthy time:

> In periods of acute revolutionary tensions, in an epoch of increasing and widespread class warfare, the proletariat finds it easier to sublimate—to organize socially—its sexual life. The demands of class and practical concerns [*real'nost'*] are simply too strong; they require that the proletarian devote himself [to them] entirely, undividedly, and for a long time. No extra energy is left over for parasitic activity: all energy goes toward solidarity, toward class hatred, daring action, and a feeling of one's own dignity, toward a search for new military devices and means. In such periods a man as a whole becomes richer, he experiences no emotional hunger, and sexuality loses its thievish rights. However, when class war gives way to class workdays [*klassovye budni*], we observe a return to old ways. Once more there is generalized emotional hunger and irresponsible, frivolous sexual satiation.[79]

Such statements might have given rise to the inference that class warfare would even be *preferable* to the daily grind of NEP. The author of a sexual survey in Yakutsk, aware that his analysis of data might be so interpreted, hastened to add, "I in no way wish to suggest that in order to prevent premature sexual activity we need such calamities as Civil War." All that was required, wrote N. V. Gushchin, was better sublimation.[80] Still, the image of War Communism as a Golden Age persisted in social discourse and frequently served as a foil to the negative phenomena of NEP. In the literature of NEP, recollections of War Communism often intervene in a text to check the threat of sexual desire. Indeed, the safest member of the proletariat was one who had been so affected by the Golden Age that he could no longer be aroused. Lev Sosnovsky, who often penned reports from the judicial front in the Party and Komsomol press, wrote an article in 1926 about a valuable

---

siteta imeni Sverdlova 1 (1923): 380, 401 (370–409). A Rostov-on-the-Don survey in 1926 produced similar figures (weakening of sex drive in 40.7 percent of the men and 14.8 percent of the women, intensification of desire in 16.8 percent of the men and in none of the women). Dr. A. K. Platovskii, *Polovaia zhizn' sovremennogo studenchestva* (Rostov-on the-Don: Sovet sotsial'noi pomoshchi pri tuberkuleznykh i venericheskom dispanserakh, 1920), 29.

[79] A. B. Zalkind, *Polovoi fetishizm. K peresmotru polovogo voprosa* (M.: Vserossiiskii proletkul't, 1925), 36.

[80] N. V. Gushchin, *Rezul'taty polovogo obsledovaniia molodezhi g. Iakutska* (Iakutsk: Narkomproszdrav IaASSR, 1925), 45.

Party official who had been framed in a paternity suit by enemies resentful of his effective work on the Party's behalf. The case against this model citizen was dropped and the komsomolka who brought the accusation punished when the defendant produced a doctor's certificate proving that he had been left impotent by an injury sustained in the Civil War.[81]

In a 1923 article, Sergei Tret'iakov described the political and cultural condition of NEP as follows: "The Revolution has leaped from the barricades and the tribunes of mass meetings to the ledgers of offices and factory administrators, to the auditoriums of workers' preparatory schools and workshop schools. A *war of endurance* is being waged, and victory will belong to the side with the stronger nerves."[82] Such a characterization of NEP as a period of anxious waiting is essential to an understanding of the era's Gothic bent. One principal factor differentiating Gothic writing from the adventure novel or military tale is the former's renunciation of a focus on activity. The Gothic heroine is compelled, by force or her own virtuous respect for authority, to wait, to minimize external resistance, and at the same time to protect a core of chastity, the defense of which requires perpetual, nervous vigilance. Providing his readers with a preview of the text to come, Maturin writes near the start of *Melmoth the Wanderer*,

> A storm without doors is, after all, better than a storm within; without we have something to struggle with, within we have only to suffer; and the severest storm, by exciting the energy of its victim, gives at once a stimulus to action, and a solace to pride, which those must want who sit shuddering between rocking walls, and almost driven to wish they had only to suffer, not to fear.[83]

If the first post-Revolutionary years constituted an ideological "storm without doors," NEP represented a withdrawal to an enclosed but still endangered corner.

The representation of NEP as dangerous because relatively peaceful runs throughout political and cultural commentary on the period. One of the most remarkable manifestations occurs in *Revolution and Youth*, Zalkind's study of the effect of NEP on students at the Sverdlov Communist University (where he lectured) and at other Party-run institutions of higher learning. According to Zalkind, 40 to 50 percent of the communist students suffered from nervous disorders. At least one-quarter of these, he added, suffered from some type of psychoneurosis:

> The majority of [these] comrades fell seriously ill during the pause in the fighting, that is, after 1921. Previous flare-ups of illness (during the period of

---

[81] L. Sosnovskii, "Alimenty," *Komsomol'skaia pravda*, 24 October 1926, 2.

[82] Tret'iakov, "LEF i NEP," 71.

[83] Charles Maturin, *Melmoth the Wanderer* (Oxford: Oxford University Press, 1989 [1820]), 63.

fighting) were usually quickly liquidated as soon as the political situation demanded these ill people's attention. These psychoneurotics are composed chiefly of people who have come out of the petty bourgeoisie and the intelligentsia; they also include a comparatively large percentage of women.

A significantly large number of these psychoneurotic communist students were driven to nervous fits by NEP—and not only because they found NEP ideologically unacceptable (although for some that is how it was), but because [NEP brought] an overly sharp transition from an atmosphere of pitched battle to gray, prosaic everyday life.[84]

Zalkind provides three case studies of psychoneurotic communist students. They are worth examining at length because they distinctly express the features Zalkind and many of his contemporaries disseminated as representative of the age:

1. Comrade S., twenty-two years old, from a petty bourgeois background, a member of the Komsomol since 1918 and a student at a workers' preparatory school, suffers from insomnia, poor work capacity, great irritability, unsociability, elevated heartbeat, and unfounded fears. [He complains of] constant heaviness in his head, considers himself unsuitable for everything, is disappointed in his Party comrades and in the revolutionary character of contemporary life, but not in the idea of the Revolution itself. Medical examination has found a series of objective disturbances of the nervous system: heightened muscular reflexes, heightened vascular activity, etc. In the past Comrade S. served at the front for two and a half years, during which time he was exposed to serious risks, was entrusted with a position of responsibility (as his division's commissar) and felt completely well. Since that time—"NEP has got me down,"—"there's no longer anywhere to go," "nothing but boredom and anger"—"saintly people, leaving the battles of the Revolution, have begun to rot in the prose of normal workday life [*v proze budnei*]." (These are his words exactly—Comrade S. is not without literary talent.)

We have here a typical case of a clinical psychoneurosis, which the old neurology would certainly have tried to treat with medicine, electricity, and other items from the Latin kitchen, although, since the roots of this disease are exclusively social (false social orientation), the treatment should be social [. . .] reeducation in accordance with the principles of the Party [*partiinoe vospitanie*].

2. The second case is not less, but probably more, characteristic; Comrade P., twenty-four years of age, from a petty bourgeois family, a member of the Party since 1918, suffers from hysterical hallucinations, cries out military commands during his fits,—suffers from headaches, a total inability to perform mental work, and insomnia. He spent the war years at the front, fought against bandits,

---

[84] A. B. Zalkind, *Revoliutsiia i molodezh'* (M.: Kommunisticheskii universitet, 1924 or 1925 [both dates are listed on the cover pages]), 37.

Ukrainian counterrevolutionaries, Makhno. When the enemy took power he went underground and once, all alone in hiding, observed a savage pogrom by bandits that left an indelible impression on him and filled him with tremendous, inexhaustible hatred for the White Guard. He served in emergency revolutionary tribunals, often exposed himself to mortal danger, always seethed with energy, and displayed agility, fearlessness, and mercilessness to enemies, yet felt very tender toward children, whom he always tried to save—regardless of the danger that threatened him.

During the transition to peacetime, he served as the head of a division of the Cheka pursuing the last political and criminal bandits remaining in his region. From 1922 on he has been left "without anything to do"; he must switch to "peaceful" work. This "doesn't suit" him. He keeps trying to show that real peace has not yet come, that the enemy has dug in deeper, that the enemy has sunk deep roots, that it is early to celebrate peace. Still, he has no more military commissions and, given quiet, administrative work, he gradually falls ill. Triumphant Nepmen, fat and made-up,—shop displays, blatant economic criminality,—all this drives him into a frenzy, deprives him of rest, of mental agility, and causes him physical pain. [. . .]

An objective psychophysiological examination has determined that all of Comrade P.'s mental processes are intact, that his moral foundation is strong, but that over the past year and a half he has developed a propensity for frequent, so-called narrowing of thought (for hysterical somnambulism), when it is as if Comrade P. moves into another world *where he acts upon his desires*, desires so alien to the contemporary, peaceful reality: he is once again in battle, he issues commands, races after the enemy, *serves the Revolution in his own way*. [. . .]

3. With the third case the outlook is not good. F. is twenty-six years old, from the intelligentsia, in the Party since 1919. [She suffers from] acute nervous excitability—she shakes, trembles, becomes excited at the least noise. She suffers from severe neuralgic pains that doctors have determined to be psychosomatic, from constant melancholy, gross distractibility [*grubaia otvlekaemost'*], from elevated heartbeat and disturbed sleep; her analytical capability is not affected and she energetically takes care of her appearance despite her depressed mood.

It turns out that she went into the Revolution "solely for the sake of romantic feelings": brightly, loftily, heroically. She was a junior political commissar; in battles at the front she had to experience quite a lot. Retreating with her division, she was captured by a group of White Cossacks and raped. After that there was a sharp change: despair from which she never recovered;—a feeling of emptiness inside her and around her, a gradual break with everything surrounding her and the appearance of the nervous symptoms described above. The institution of higher learning, in which she enrolled for distraction, did not provide her with any solution; she did not devote herself to her studies. By the time of our only medical consultation with F., she had already been expelled from the Party as a useless element and was about to leave for home.

Characteristic of this case is a burden that F. did not have the strength to bear—namely, the fact of rape. The author has had occasion to meet with at least ten Party comrades who were raped during the bloody struggle with the enemy, and only F. and one other reacted to rape as *an irremediable misfortune* (by the way, F. did not contract venereal disease nor did she become pregnant as a result of the rape). The remaining comrades are, in general, completely normal sexually, are endowed with healthy femininity, and reacted to rape *in a revolutionary manner* [*po revoliutsionnomu*], understanding that bloody conflict is accompanied by all kinds of cruel experiences and that one has to be capable of bearing everything; they did not experience any sort of ideological crisis afterward. This is the best sort of proof that *with the correct, firm social and class orientation* sexuality alone, even the most burdensome, does not create psychoneurosis and plays only a secondary role, *an ancillary one in relation to the influence of social factors.*[85]

In none of the cases was the student involved from a proletarian background, and yet—if it was true that half of the students suffered from NEP-related neuroses—Zalkind surely could have provided a proletarian example. Why were *these* three cases presented as representative? One could conclude that working-class youth did not become so dramatically, so grippingly ill—but it might also be that Zalkind thought a story about a proletarian communist student whom NEP had made mentally ill was to some extent taboo or, at least, not the sort of tale that needed telling. In any case, it is fascinating to observe how Zalkind is troubled by the relationship between ideological and psychological normality. He calls the diseases of these three students "an irrational reaction to NEP," but in the first two cases (the treatable ones, he later says), his explanation is *too* rational and makes their conditions an understandable, indeed, almost logical response to the current ideological situation. Zalkind's book is striking in its frenzied campaign to ideologize trauma and consider it a result of inactivity rather than of violence. Moreover, for Zalkind ideological trauma is treatable and strangely healthy because it is motivated by healthy, revolutionary desires. In its explication of these cases *Revolution and Youth* points toward questions that the author's loyalty to Party authority does not permit him to utter: How "unfounded" are the nervous fears that Zalkind seeks to allay by maneuvering these individuals within the collective? Are the conditions of these young communists pathological, or is NEP itself a form of pathology?

This last question hovers around NEP discourse and leaves its mark on many of the era's texts, including *Cement*. The general yearning for an earlier, purer, and presexual time is expressed forcefully in Gladkov's novel. The author does not present Polia Mekhova as a flawless character; she is a weak idealist who cannot accept the ideological compromises demanded by

---

[85] Ibid., 41–45.

the Party in its battle with the intractable facts of real life. Nevertheless, Gladkov offers her to the reader as a pathological "type," and the scenes in which she appears provide us with a fine example of how the Gothic surfaced during the 1920s in the least traditional settings. (What genre would seem more uncongenial to the Gothic than the production novel?) More than any other character in *Cement*, Polia calls attention to divisions within the proletarian personality and to the need for struggle against personal feelings and desires. "We must," she exclaims, "bring about a revolution within ourselves. Within ourselves we must wage the most merciless civil war. There is nothing more obstinate and lasting than our habits, feelings, and prejudices." A rabid opponent of NEP, she is accused of "infantile leftism," an apt Leninist term for a communist who would resist ideological adolescence by retreating to the War Communist Golden Age. The Gothic import of her character becomes apparent, however, only in the chapter in which she is raped by Bad'in. Entitled "Nightmare," it commences with a description of Polia walking the streets of NEP:

> She looked not to the side but only downward—at her own legs and at those of others. She could not lift her head to look firmly at the shop windows, through the open doors, at the people who looked different from the way they had before. She didn't look, but she saw that women were no longer the same this spring as they had been not so long ago. Elegance was in full bloom: hats with bouquets, transparent cambric, fashionable French high heels. [. . .] In the coffeehouses, through the open doors, in the twilight that was turning gray from the smoke of tobacco, phantoms crowded and moved chaotically through the distant rumble of voices, the crash of plates, and the sound of rattling dice; and from who knows where, from the depths of this tobacco hole came the barely perceptible sounds of a string orchestra.
>
> Where did this all come from? And why had it come so rapidly, so impudently, so luxuriantly? Why had it all passed her—Polia—by and settled so painfully, so confusingly, and with such melancholy in her thoughts?
>
> It was this way: As if she suddenly found herself in a strange land, lost and bereft of something precious and irretrievable, without which she could not live. And also: shame, disgrace, and unfounded fear. She was afraid lest a worker or some wretch eaten away by hunger, with putrefying eyes, should approach her and ask point-blank:
>
> "So this is what it's all come to? This is what you wanted?"[86]

The exotic foreign landscape, vital to Gothic fiction, has become the strange country of NEP, a world populated by phantoms and starving monsters who should, according to everything Polia believes, have existed only in the cap-

[86] Fedor Gladkov, "Tsement," *Krasnaia nov'*, no. 5 (1925): 99 (no. 1, 66–110; no. 2, 73–109; no. 3, 47–81; no. 4, 57–87; no. 5, 75–111; no. 6, 39–74).

italist past. Moreover, the scene may be read as a disturbing echo of one of Marx's more elaborately narrativized and vivid images from *The Eighteenth Brumaire*. In his bitter indictment of the sham revolution of 1848–1851 in France, Marx describes the plight of the French after the advent of Napoleon III as follows:

> An entire people, which had imagined that by a revolution it had increased its power of action, suddenly finds itself set back into a dead epoch and, in order that no doubt as to the relapse may be possible, the old data again arise, the old chronology, the old names, the old edicts, which have long become a subject of antiquarian erudition, and the old henchmen, who had long seemed dead and decayed. The nation appears to itself like that mad Englishman in Bedlam, who fancies that he lives in the times of the ancient Pharaohs and daily bemoans the hard labour that he must perform in the Ethiopian mines as a gold digger, immured in this subterranean prison, a dimly burning lamp fastened to his head, the overseer of the slaves behind him with a long whip, and at the exits a confused mass of barbarian mercenaries, who understand neither the forced labourers in the mines nor one another, since they have no common speech.[87]

Marx's scene is certainly indebted to Gothic captivity novels such as Maturin's *Melmoth*, and Gladkov may have taken his cue from similar sources. There is probably no direct influence of Marx's passage on Gladkov's text, but in its use of the Gothic, *Cement* was reflecting many of the Marxist anxieties about repetition that I have discussed above. To be sure, Gladkov was following the Marxist model of making the Gothic someone else's story—the Gothic narrative in *Cement* is part of a plot that splits Polia off from healthy communists. Nevertheless, her commitment to the Revolution's original goals indicates at least the potential for her predicament to serve as a representation of the plight of all communists.

In the unrecognizable land that, during War Communism, used to be hers, Polia is plagued by terrible dreams:

> She had nightmares, and for hours on end she was tormented by insomnia. In these nocturnal hours she heard what she heard by day—she heard it clearly—importunate and torturing—distant and alluring—a string orchestra was playing, dice clattered, and under her windows on the street, dim voices plaintively cried:
> —Help us. . . . Brothers . . . Misfortune!
> She leapt from the bed, shuffled to the window on her bare feet, and, with beating heart and a pounding ache in her head, she stared out into the night. Silent, empty gloom; no one was there. She listened carefully and then returned to the stuffiness of her bed. She fell asleep. Again she was awakened by strange, fantastic jolts. And again—a distant fiddle, the clatter of dice, laugh-

---

[87] *The Marx-Engels Reader*, 438.

ter, and heartrending entreaties making themselves heard over the crying of
infants.[88]

The ideological status of Polia's character leads the reader to contextualize
this scene as evidence that she is losing her grip on reality. Frightened by
NEP, Polia has succumbed to a Gothic panic. How might she have protected
herself? Zalkind, it will be recalled, proposed "communist education" as a
curative measure, and the Sverdlov Communist University, according to its
rector, existed to prevent young communists from falling into epistemological and affective error. Class interests, Liadov said, rarely failed comrades
during the Civil War, but "when it becomes necessary to resolve Party questions in the terrifyingly confused relations [*strashno zaputannye otnosheniia*]
that prevail now, during NEP, class instinct alone is not enough; it has become necessary to receive a distinctly revolutionary Marxist upbringing, to
learn to understand all aspects of life dialectically."[89] Unfortunately, thinking
dialectically entailed an interpretive reading of daily events with the help of
a corrective lens that was both epistemological *and* imaginative.

From Marx's point of view, imagination was not necessarily a bad thing.
Favorably comparing the French and English Revolutions to the pseudo-
Revolution of 1848 in Paris, Marx noted that in the former "the awakening
of the dead [. . .] served the purpose of glorifying the new struggles, not of
parodying the old; of magnifying the given tasks in imagination, not of taking flight from their solution in reality; of finding once more the spirit of
revolution, not of making its ghost walk again."[90] But imagination can often
lead to delusion when its function of "magnification" is turned onto objects
that generate fear.

Polia, it would seem, misinterprets reality. She sees in NEP dangers that
should not frighten her as they do. Nevertheless, her delusions are in one
respect consistent with Marxist optics, for Marxists were supposed to see
more than the static, present object that could not be transcended by the
untrained eye. Rebuking Feuerbach in *The German Ideology*, Marx claimed
that the philosopher did not see things correctly: "in Manchester, for instance, Feuerbach sees only factories and machines, where a hundred years
ago only spinning wheels and weaving looms were to be seen, or in the
campagna di Roma he finds only pasture lands and swamps, where in the
time of Augustus he would have found nothing but the vineyards and villas
of Roman capitalists."[91] Feuerbach's problem was that he did not see the past

---

[88] Gladkov, "Tsement," no. 5, 100.
[89] M. N. Liadov, "O zadachakh i perspektivakh kommunisticheskogo universiteta imeni Ia. M.
Sverdlova," *Chem dolzhen byt' kommuniversitet?* (M.: Kommunisticheskii universitet, 1924), 7
(3–12).
[90] *The Marx-Engels Reader*, 438.
[91] Marx and Engels, *Collected Works*, 5:40.

in the present, but that, perversely, is just what Polia does. We have already
seen Tret'iakov encouraging communists to "remember" that during NEP—
all appearances to the contrary—they were not in their gardens but at the
front lines. Tret'iakov certainly did not speak with the Party's authority, but
he and his fellow theoreticians writing for *LEF* knew their Marx,[92] and his
exhortation was in many respects a dramatization of the imaginative imperative in Marxist epistemology. Paradoxically, that second "patient" of Zalkind's, the one who always thought he was at the front, did not require a
"communist education"; his problem was that he—like Polia—already had
one. Essentially, Zalkind and Liadov were calling not so much for education
as for the inculcation of *trust*; the Party's official line had to be relied upon
to lead young communists out of NEP's dark and tangled maze. This demand for ideological trust was itself fertile soil for Gothic narrative, since
the genre has historically been built upon stories of the illegitimate exercise
of power and of trust betrayed.

Let us return once more to the "Nightmare" of *Cement*. The Gothic fog in
Polia's bedroom thickens on the night of her rape:

> She could not sleep.
>
> The songs of the working masses, swirling crowds, red faces, red banners, the
> Red Guard and its fiery hail of bayonets, Comrade Lenin on Red Square. From
> afar it was clear how [Lenin's] teeth flashed, how he thrust out his chin and his
> hand with its parted fingers, beckoning. [. . .] How long ago it was! . . . It was
> like a dream, like images of early childhood. [. . .]
>
> There was a quiet knock at a door; it wasn't clear at whose.
>
> —Well, who is it?
>
> Bad'in's voice, and from his voice it was clear he was smiling.
>
> —Little Polia, are you asleep? Open the door and step out for a minute.
> There's some work to be done.
>
> —I can't, Bad'in. Tomorrow.
>
> —That's impossible, little Polia. Get up and come out here.
>
> His voice rasped and then became clear. The cylinder clicked and the door
> opened. Dim light moved out into the emptiness of the corridor. How? How
> could it have happened that this night she had forgotten to lock her door? In a
> flash she saw that Bad'in looked very strange. Half-white, half-black.
>
> —Well, it's better this way. You are too slow on the uptake.
>
> He shut the door and turned the key. The walls vanished again in the gloom,
> and the gloom became bottomless. And together with the gloom, making the
> gloom thicker, he came—himself gloom. He walked toward her in all his un-
> bearably weighty vastness. He who was inevitable had come.

---

[92] See, for example, Boris Arvatov's reading of *The Eighteenth Brumaire* in his "Marks o
khudozhestvennoi restavratsii," *LEF*, no. 3 (1923): 76–96.

And for some incomprehensible reason, through hands extended in horror, she asked with a choking whisper:

—What do you need, Bad'in? . . . What do you need?

And she had no time to drop her hands; he fell on the bed with terrifying weight and pressed her to the pillow. [. . .] She was choked by his stale heavy body, from his sweat and from the intoxicating smell of alcohol. She did not resist; crushed by the darkness she was not able to resist. Why, when it was all inevitable and irreversible? . . .

She did not know when Bad'in had left. The bottomless darkness swirled in sparks and moaned. Somewhere a large crowd howled and thunder resounded with an immense crash. [. . .] Had Bad'in been there or not? Perhaps it was just the usual nightmare. After all, nightmares are always real as life. Isn't that why they are so terrifying? [. . .]

She lay motionless, all naked and exhausted. Her shirt had been crushed into a wet ball above her breasts and stank with sweat and some sort of noxious unknown smell. And for a long time she could not feel her body. It was as if she had just a head and no body. Everywhere there was emptiness and infinity: a black abyss. [. . .] It was so good and peaceful, there was nothing, and time did not exist.

Steps—those of Sergei [her neighbor]—shuffled to her door and stopped. Why had Sergei come to her door? Polia heard those steps, her heart trembled, and her body suddenly filled with blood and spasms.[93]

I have quoted from this chapter at length because it captures in such condensed form the terrors and desires shaping Soviet ideology in the 1920s. The ideological assault on communism and Bad'in's sexual assault on Polia are explicitly paired as nightmarish, frightening, and shameful. Rape—or, at least, the threat of rape—is a quintessential moment in the Gothic; the collapse of borders between the self and an other, an event potentially present in any act of sexual intercourse, is bound up in rape with the themes of crime, humiliation, unwanted penetration, and the defeat of one's will, an especially horrifying event for members of the Bolshevik political vanguard.[94] In Gladkov's equivalency of sexual and ideological violation, the body from which Polia seeks to detach herself after the rape serves as a counterpart for the political and ideological realities of the 1920s, from which, try as it might wish, the communist subject could not float away. The scene of Polia's rape is prefaced with a memory of a happy time that the author explicitly links to "childhood." Where a Gothic heroine in a moment of terror sadly recalls a deceased father and protector, Polia remembers Lenin

---

[93] Gladkov, "Tsement," no. 5, 101–102.

[94] On rape in the Gothic, see Punter, *The Literature of Terror*, 416. On the importance of boundaries and their transgression in the Gothic, see Eve Kosofsky Sedgwick, *The Coherence of Gothic Conventions* (New York: Arno Press, 1980), 13–14, and DeLamotte, *Perils*, 13.

and the age of War Communism. The significance of Polia's rape is compounded by the identity of her rapist. Bad'in, the local Party representative and thus one of Lenin's heirs, betrays the trust of and abuses an all too steadfast, indeed, "infantile" believer in the Revolutionary cause.

"Time did not exist," Polia fantasizes in an effort to deny the fact of the rape. On a broader scale this utopian wish to be free of the body and time may be seen as *the* fantasy of the New Economic Policy, for ideological purity was being defiled not only by the bourgeoisie but also by history itself. The student or worker dormitory was a substitute for the more threatening castle of cyclical or nonprogressive *time*, for a temporal edifice of endless repetition. Repetition during NEP, an era characterized even by those who justified it as "a transitional period in a transitional period,"[95] threatened to plunge Soviet communism into a *mise-en-abîme* of ideological failure. Utopian chronology—in which "then" is separated from "now" by a chasm that cannot be recrossed—is inherently non-Gothic. DeLamotte writes of Gothic time:

> The same events seem to recur again and again, trapping the protagonist in a single instant of time yet simultaneously evoking the nightmare of eternity. Through repetition, Gothic romance translates into symbolic form what [Frank] Kermode in *The Sense of an Ending* terms *chronos*: "purely successive, disorganized" time. [. . .] Suspense—the state of being intolerably in transition with no sense of what or where the end may be—is the subject and technique of Gothicism.[96]

When informed that the chasm of time has been bridged, that the gates to the City must be left unlocked and its citizens left bereft of a defense from encroaching armies of the past, the utopian mentality reacts by creating Gothic discourse that mirrors its predicament.

The tying together of class and sexual fears in a Gothic package had a thematic as well as historical justification. We have already seen that pre-Revolutionary Russian culture juxtaposed communal to egotistical desire. The longing for social intercourse with many others stood in stark contrast to the pursuit of sexual intercourse with a single other. The Gothic genre fits this dichotomy well, for the menaced heroine perceives that her fate teeters between two types of community—on one hand, presexual (or virtually asexual) relationships with her family, faithful servants, and a rather boring, "safe" suitor; on the other, a passionate, predominantly sexual relationship with a dark and lone pursuer. Discourse about Nepmen frequently highlighted the isolation of these enemies. Polonsky defined the Nepman as "an

---

[95] G. Zinov'ev (paraphrasing Lenin), *Filosofiia epokhi* (M. and L.: Moskovskii rabochii, 1925), 4.

[96] DeLamotte, *Perils*, 95–96.

opportunistic type, an acquirer of things, most often a predator and a speculator. That's why he is so despicable. That's why in the majority of cases he
is a loner. Nepmen do not exist as a social group and they never can. Under
current conditions they cannot organize. They exist as [. . .] a whole series
of individuals feeding in one way or another on the economic organism."[97]

In literature of the mid-1920s communists who associate too intimately
with Nepmen, or with a single member of the opposite sex, find themselves
tainted by this separateness and isolated from their former communities—as
if just a moment's temptation or arousal could suffice to conjure up foreign
land, castle, and moat. After his meeting with Vera, *Dog Alley*'s Khorokhorin is unable to participate in the activities of his Komsomol club: "He
looked at everyone, listened carefully, and then he understood clearly that
[Vera's] bare knees, the flower-patterned hood [of her robe], and her warm
little hand had cut him off from these people. His personal life, which only
he could understand, had grown like a snowball rolling down a hill."[98] The
sole defense against being "cut off" in this way was to respond with the
prescribed psychological (counter)castration with which we are already familiar, to sublimate the self into the collective and to sacrifice one's personal
life to the Party. Expelled from the Party, Sergei in *Cement* realizes that
"personal life" is a "remnant of the accursed past. It was something he had
received from his father, from his youth, and from the romanticism of the
intelligentsia. All this had to be destroyed at its roots."[99] Only by completely
eradicating individual desire at its source could one be sure of one's place
within the community, certain never to be "alone," face to face with a single,
hostile and powerful "other," with a class enemy or with one's own material
and sexual desires. The Gothic model provided Soviet ideology under NEP
with a well-tested model for the expression of anxieties about being together
and being alone.

[97] RGALI, fond 1328, opis' 3, ed. khran. 27, 4.
[98] Gumilevskii, *Sobachii pereulok*, 41.
[99] Gladkov, "Tsement," no. 6, 64.

Chapter Five

NEP AS FEMALE COMPLAINT (I):
THE TRAGEDY OF WOMAN

IF sexual desires and fears are central to the creation of Gothic discourse, the place of women in Gothic narration suggests that sexuality in the Gothic is fundamentally and, perhaps, insidiously feminized. Gothic fiction is frequently narrated from what is, at least ostensibly, a woman's point of view and tells itself by focusing on the predicament of a trapped, imaginative heroine with limited knowledge and limitless fears. This linkage of the Gothic with "the feminine" has been read in two ways—the writing and reading of Gothic fiction may support *or* threaten to destabilize established social hierarchies. Feminist critics who take either position tend to see sexuality as "the" central issue in Gothic fiction; for them, the genre's importance lies in its reinforcement or subversion of established patterns of sexual behavior.[1] But what if, as early Soviet and some later Western commentators have argued, sex is—at certain periods and in certain cultures—largely or partially a metaphor for other insecurities: economic, class, and, above all, utopian?[2]

In determining the place of sex in NEP ideology, we must focus attention on an issue that hitherto we have more or less ignored: that of gender and, in particular, of female gender. We must approach this topic with care and pay particular attention to the manner in which gender combines with other

[1] Compare Juliann E. Fleenor's introduction, Joanna Russ, "Somebody's Trying to Kill Me and I Think It's My Husband," Kay J. Mussell, "'But Why Do They Read Those Things?': The Female Audience and the Gothic Novel," all in *The Female Gothic*, ed. Fleenor (Montreal: Eden Press, 1983), 3–30, 31–56, and 57–68; Eugenia C. DeLamotte, *Perils of the Night: A Feminist Study of Nineteenth-Century Gothic* (Oxford: Oxford University Press, 1990), 185–189; and Maggie Kilgour, *The Rise of the Gothic Novel* (London: Routledge, 1995), 9–10. In a recent study, Kari J. Winter states the case for a subversive reading: "The main task of the Gothic heroine is to uncover and name the horrors that fill her world." *Subjects of Slavery, Agents of Change: Women and Power in Gothic Novels and Slave Narratives, 1790–1865* (Athens: University of Georgia Press, 1992), 12. Arguably, this has been the interpretive task of the Gothic's scholars rather than the goal of Gothic characters or authors.

[2] In their reading of (bourgeois) interest in sex as expressive of other, nonsexual anxieties, some early Soviet critics, including Valentin Voloshinov, in some respects anticipated the conclusions of recent, more sophisticated scholarship that has been informed by a very different methodology. Compare Voloshinov, *Freudianism: A Critical Sketch* (Bloomington: Indiana University Press, 1987 [1927]), with Thomas Laqueur, *Making Sex: Body and Gender from the Greeks to Freud* (Cambridge: Harvard University Press, 1990).

sources of potential contamination. We need not decide at the outset whether the underlying anxiety is sexual masquerading as political or political masquerading as sexual, nor ought our enterprise be the reductive work of framing an indictment against early Soviet ideology on the grounds of its misogyny. Our task is to draw together poetics and politics in analyzing the particular meaning of "woman" for NEP.

In his speech identifying Nepmen as "pleasure machines," Viacheslav Polonsky named woman as a principal object of degenerate, latter-day capitalist lust:

> A man who has money wants to have everything, and in the assortment of products that he consumes, woman represents a product far from the least in value.[3]

While Polonsky's perspective evinced sympathy for women as victims, it also permitted the identification of women with Nepmen through its contaminating insistence on an intrinsic association between them. Capitalism—a patriarchal institution—had turned women into instruments of pleasure, but now these instruments were *identified* with the agents of their corruption. According to Liadov's survey of the history of human sexual behavior, the birth of private property had led men to acquire women as they would livestock, the chief source of wealth at that unspecified time. The results he considered catastrophic:

> And man began to create the qualities that he needed in his woman-slave. In the stuffy atmosphere of the harem, eternally [*vechno*] artificially stimulated by spicy food, erotic songs, dances, and tales, and by the artificial cultivation of certain parts of her organism, free and harmoniously developed woman was transformed into a passionate animal who thought only about how to satisfy her master's lust. It was precisely there, in the harem, that all of contemporary woman's purely female qualities—so sharply different from masculine traits— were cultivated.[4]

Liadov's reference to the "purely female" illustrates how the commentators who frequently "defended" women from masculine lust during NEP may not have been viewing the beneficiaries of their protection purely as victims. Masculine lasciviousness is depicted by Liadov as awakening in women depraved femininity that is nevertheless femininity in its essential, unalloyed form. In his story of the interplay of property, class, and gender over the course of history, pure femininity is purely "artificial."

Liadov's use of the word "eternally" is also interesting, for how eternal were these "artificially stimulated" female qualities? Along with others, he

---

[3] RGALI, fond 1328 (V. P. Polonskii), opis' 3, ed. khran. 27 (Voprosy pola i braka v zhizni i literatury [Stenogram of debate held in the Moscow Polytechnic Museum on 6 March 1927]), 5.
[4] M. N. Liadov, *Voprosy byta* (M.: Kommun. u-t. im. Ia. Sverdlova, 1925), 31.

argued that "the eternal feminine" was not a biological given and could be purged by intense cultural work, much of which should be carried out among unenlightened men. In a book on everyday life in the Komsomol, A. Stratonitsky agreed that *men* had turned women into animals and criticized contemporary men for seeing women as objects, for pursuing them with "devouring" hungry looks and praising their beauty. "It is no wonder," he explained, "that a young girl gets to thinking and starts spending a lot of time on her appearance. The woman in her awakes prematurely; sensual curiosity and purely feminine interests appear at an early age. And it is in this way that the city prepares infinite cadres of prostitutes, coquettes, and depraved women."[5] Woman was man's tragic but nonetheless dangerous creation: a victim who had become a monster. Her monstrosity, though, was her essence. Man's fault, at least in Stratonitsky's version of the story, was in uncovering it too soon.

Komsomol pundits took frequent aim at the accoutrements of monstrosity. Jewelry and feminine clothes were signs of ideological contamination and sources of temptation for proletarian Adams still striving desperately to retain a foothold in Eden. On the pages of *Komsomol'skaia pravda* Dr. I. Kallistov expressed the problem in a scientific vein: "Contemporary female fashions are conditioned reflexes for the arousal of enflamed emotion. That is why it is essential to battle for the expulsion of 'Parisian fashions' from our lives and for the creation of hygienic, simple, and comfortable clothing."[6]

For several centuries Russian culture had been intermittently waging a battle with foreign—frequently French—fashion in clothing, behavior, and language. During the NEP era negative foreign influences, distinctly feminized (recall that dismembered corpse's "manicure" and "pedicure" and, above all, sex), occupied a place in the Gothic ideological milieu, where in feminine guise they performed a function equivalent to the ancestral portraits ever-present in Gothic fiction's haunted foreign castles. Even P. Ionov's declaration on the pages of *Pravda* in 1926, "women's underwear [*damskie pantalony*] has come to occupy an unnaturally large place in our literature,"[7] a call to eliminate female clothing (and intimate clothing at that) from the literary language, used two words with evident French roots to target the sartorial trappings of femininity. But once these trappings were divested, one wonders what new visions their removal would reveal, especially if the "purely feminine" was itself unalterably foreign. The problem with "women's underwear" seems to have been that there was nothing beneath it; removing it would entail eliminating the body that it signified rather than covered.

Already we have seen Weininger, Fedorov, and Berdiaev equate woman

[5] A. Stratonitskii, *Voprosy byta v komsomole* (L.: Priboi, 1926), 44.

[6] Dr. I. Kallistov, "Polovoi vopros i fizkul'tura," *Komsomol'skaia pravda*, 29 July 1925, 3.

[7] P. Ionov, "Bez cheremukhi," *Pravda*, 4 December 1926, 5.

with the principle of pleasure. The statements by Liadov and Stratonitsky quoted above *appear* to represent some movement away from these pre-Revolutionary views; these Soviet commentators were at least aware that masculine desire had been in some—historial—sense projected onto women. Their historicization of the pre-Revolutionary philosophical paradigm might, therefore, be taken as a step away from that paradigm's essentialistic misogyny. With equal justification, however, one might say that Soviet commentators were importing these pre-Revolutionary misogynistic views into the new ideological discourse, rehabilitating them and "biologizing" history under the pretense of historicizing biology. Questions of class and property brought out the worst, "purely female" side of woman, but, conversely, this process of feminization was helpful to Soviet communists in highlighting the horrors of property and class.

It is instructive to examine how Liadov's book transformed the standard pre-Revolutionary Marxist line on the gender consequences of capitalism. The authoritative source on the issue was August Bebel, cofounder and leader of the German Social Democratic Party, whose influential 1883 book, *Woman and Socialism*, had been translated into Russian in the 1890s by the young Liadov himself.[8] According to Bebel, in limiting the scope for female activity in society, capitalist economic oppression had "led to a number of traits of characters peculiar to women, that are more fully developed from generation to generation. Men seem to find satisfaction in ridiculing these traits, but they forget that they themselves are to blame for them." In Bebel's view, these traits included "talkativeness and scandal-mongering; the inclination to discuss the most insignificant things at the greatest length; the exaggerated interest in outward display; the love of dress and coquetry; envy and jealousy toward the members of her sex, and the tendency of being dishonest and hypocritical." Bebel added that these traits had "developed under the pressure of social conditions and [. . .] been further developed by heredity, example and education."[9]

When updating Bebel for his lectures at the Communist University, Liadov grafted Bebel's moderately Lamarckian condemnation of the fate of gender under capitalism onto the pre-Revolutionary Russian philosophical, misogynistic discourse. Moreover, he ignored important aspects of Bebel's book. Bebel had attacked Catholicism for identifying woman with "the flesh" and using that identification as a justification for woman's enslavement. Unlike Liadov, whose view of women would be more "Catholic" than "socialist" in Bebel's terms, Bebel generally had a positive view of sexu-

---

[8] S. V. Deviatov, *M. N. Liadov: Zabytaia biografiia* (M.: Vsesoiuznyi zaochnyi politekhnicheskii institut, 1992), 26.

[9] August Bebel, *Woman and Socialism*, trans. Meta L. Stern (New York: Socialist Literature, 1910), 145.

ality's place in human life: "The sexual impulse is perennial in man. It is his strongest impulse, and must be satisfied if his health is not to suffer. As a rule this impulse is strongest with healthy, normally developed human beings, just like a hearty appetite and good digestion are proofs of a healthy stomach and are essential to a healthy body."[10] Bebel accepted completely "the necessity of satisfying the human desire for love" and claimed that woman was "oppressed as a sex being" because her options in the choice of a partner were severely limited. Women were more likely to commit suicide between the ages of fifteen and thirty, he wrote, due to their "ungratified sexual impulse, love-sorrow, secret pregnancy or the deceit of men."[11]

In his revision of Bebel's views, Liadov was no doubt influenced by the collectivist tendencies that were already present in pre-Revolutionary Russia and came in the 1920s to dominate ideological discourse as the Party sought to mobilize Soviet youth. Another factor at work may have been Liadov's lifelong concern with the importance of history; his major claim to fame was as the Party's first historian. In 1906 he had written the first history of the Social Democratic Party—a work republished several times in the 1920s[12]— and had lectured on Party history at the Party schools on Capri and in Bologna before teaching that subject in the 1920s in Moscow as rector of the Communist University. His series of lectures on "questions of everyday life," with their hostility toward female physiology and "pure" femininity, should be read as driven, in part, by the uneasy coexistence of his Marxist view of history as inexorable progress with his current anxieties about NEP as repetition. Liadov's forward-striving desire lashes out in frustration against the stout-walled prison of everyday life (*byt*), in which every day brings another round of the same routine.

Characterized by Berdiaev before the Revolution as basically a bourgeois category of human experience,[13] after the Revolution "*byt*" was attacked from all sides and slated for renovation by otherwise highly disparate voices in early Soviet culture. Kazimir Malevich considered the entire category of *byt* bourgeois,[14] and Vladimir Maiakovsky was later to attribute his self-inflicted death to *byt*'s shoals,[15] but one should not be blind to the concept's gendered connotation; throughout the 1920s society's hostility toward this ontological category revolved around the equation "*byt* = woman." This

---

[10] Ibid., 497

[11] Ibid., 101–102.

[12] M. N. Liadov, *Istoriia Rossiiskoi sotsial-demokraticheskoi partii* (SPb.: 1906). According to Deviatov, the book was republished three times under the title *Kak nachala skladyvat'sia RKP(b). M. N. Liadov: Zabytaia biografiia*, 110.

[13] See chapter 1, above.

[14] Aleksandar Flaker, "Byt," *Russian Literature* 19 (1986): 4–5 (1–13).

[15] Vladimir Maiakovskii, *The Bedbug and Selected Poetry* (Cleveland: World Publishing Co., 1960), 236.

association was implicit in the manner in which Soviet society divided the world. In 1924 and 1925 *Knizhnaia letopis'*, the catalog that listed all new Soviet monographs (and a wonderful, underutilized point of entry into the early Soviet worldview) created the single category of "*Byt*. The Condition of Women. Folklore." (Occasionally, "Children's Diseases" was included in the listing.) Trotsky, who, like Liadov, wrote a book entitled *Questions of Everyday Life* (*Voprosy byta*), noted a dangerous tendency to juxtapose the concepts of *byt* and Revolution and urged Soviet citizens not to scorn the "small deeds" essential for the construction of a prosperous country's economic base.[16] Nevertheless, it was Trotsky who, in the same year, attacked Anna Akhmatova and other women poets, charging that their world was *too* narrow, limited to the inside of an apartment and watched over by a "gynecological god": "a friend of the house fulfilling from time to time the duties of a medical specialist in female ailments."[17] Trotsky's equation of the narrow world of the home with femininity and female sexual physiology would be replayed over and over during NEP in the opposition between War Communism (as retrospectively reconceived) and NEP. If War Communism had signed itself phallically—with bayonets, huge towers, powerful locomotives, and earthshaking explosives—then NEP was apt to be represented "vaginally" in the self-descriptive portraits to which its discourse gave birth. The Revolution, Pil'niak wrote in his NEP novel, *Machines and Wolves*, was a period when "women's muffs disappeared in Russia because women grew masculine,"[18] when "children were not born to workers,"[19] and when a man could "know the secret of a machine's birth."[20] Now the muffs had reappeared, women's sexuality was again mysterious, indirect, and all-encompassing, and capitalists were penetrating through "open doors" (Lenin) and all sorts of "chinks" (Kuibyshev). The female reproductive system became an obsession for critics of NEP; normal physiological functioning became a sign that something was societally wrong.

Liadov's hostility to NEP—and its representation in his gendered retelling of history—may be attributable to a long-standing antipathy toward compromise and a deep affinity for the culture of War Communism. In 1909 Liadov had been briefly allied with Aleksandr Bogdanov and the other "ultimatists," who broke with Lenin over his pragmatic willingness to engage in tactical compromise after the failed first revolution.[21] Liadov does not seem to have

[16] Lev Trotskii, *Voprosy byta* (M.: Krasnaia nov', 1923), 9.

[17] Lev Trotskii, *Literatura i revoliutsiia*. (M.: Krasnaia nov', 1923), 30.

[18] Boris Pil'niak, *Mashiny i volki* (L.: Gos. izd., 1925), 19.

[19] Ibid., 93.

[20] Ibid., 74.

[21] The Party schools at Capri and Bologna, where Liadov taught, were associated with the "Ultimatist" movement. Nikolai Semashko, the health commissar during NEP, had taught at the rival, Leninist school at Longjumeau. His attack on Liadov in *Izvestiia*, to which I have already

been associated with the Proletkul't, but his brief, pre-Revolutionary moment of political "deviance," arising from his desire for ideological consistency, may account for the hostility of his lectures toward the conventional characteristics of NEP.[22] In any case, the association of "*byt*" and woman in an image of femininity that represented the undead past was characteristic not only of Liadov but widespread throughout NEP. As Bolsheviks struggled to create a "new *byt*" in place of the "absolutely rotten," "extremely conservative," "inimical," and "hateful" *byt* that "we have inherited from the accursed past,"[23] as they struggled to save woman from her ideological backwardness, they continued to use both "*byt*" and "woman" as useful skeletons in history's closet. The appearance of woman in ideological discourse frequently served to remind Bolsheviks of the flaws in the Revolution's incarnation and of the necessity of patiently preserving ideological virtue. Lenin's comment to Klara Zetkin, uttered in the context of a call for more attention to woman's domestic plight, serves as an instructive example of woman's ideological role in NEP's historical narrative:

> The domestic life of woman entails her daily sacrifice of herself in thousands of trifling matters. The old law of the husband's reign continues to live on in the old form. His wife objectively and covertly revenges herself on him for this; woman's backwardness—her lack of any understanding for her husband's revolutionary ideas—weakens his vitality and his determination to fight. These are the tiny worms that, unnoticed, slowly eat away and gnaw.[24]

The passage above is striking in its simultaneous defense and abhorrence of women. Here Lenin comes close to echoing one of Tolstoi's less hostile remarks about women in "The Kreutzer Sonata": the great Russian writer argued that because women have been humiliated and deprived of equal rights, "they take revenge on us by acting on our sensuality and by catching

---

referred in the introduction, may in part have been a settling of old scores. For a discussion of the schools, see Jutta Scherrer, "Les Écoles du Parti de Capri et de Bologne: La formation de l'intelligentsia du parti," *Cahiers du monde russe et soviétique* 19 (1978): 259–284.

[22] Liadov was predisposed to some of the utopian ideation that characterized Bogdanov's programmatic, neo-Fedorovian writing. In an article reflecting on his educational mission, Liadov wrote that the study of the social sciences at the Communist University should be presented as an investigation "of how from absolute, slavish submission to the forces of nature, mankind has gradually progressed to the subjugation of nature for the benefit of man." "We must explain," he continued, "how every step in this direction carries mankind from the kingdom of unconditional, blind necessity into the kingdom of conscientious creativity." M. Liadov, "O zadachakh komuniversiteta imeni Ia. M. Sverdlova," *Metodika prepodavaniia obshchestvennykh nauk v komvuzakh, sovpartshkolakh i shkolakh politgramoty* (L.: 1925), 73 (63–78).

[23] N. A. Semashko, *Novyi byt i polovoi vopros* (M. and L.: Gos. izd., 1926), 4–7.

[24] Klara Tsetkin, "Iz zapisnoi knizhki," in *Vospominaniia o V.I. Lenine*, ed. M. P. Mchedlov, M. Ia. Pankratov, A. M. Sovokin, and N. V. Tropkin, 5 vols. (M.: Politicheskaia literatura, 1984), 5:53 (38–61).

us in their nets."[25] Lenin, however, is more concerned with ideological than with sexual seduction; for him it is woman's potential to infect man with her backwardness and to make him, like herself, a creature of the past that makes woman both an object of disgust and an essential part of the rhetoric of ideological consolidation.

The tie between everyday life and the perpetuation of history's "old law" was especially prominent in discussions of "sexual *byt*," the place of sex in everyday life. According to Dr. L. M. Vasilevsky, one of the most active participants in the popular "debate" about sex: "In no area does the inheritance of the past speak more strongly than in the area of sexual *byt*: here in truth 'the dead seize the living.' To the hideous stratification wrought by the centuries are united the fragility, instability, and vagueness that are always characteristic of transitional epochs."[26] The commissar of health, Nikolai Semashko, returned to this question of the survival of the past in a widely disseminated speech entitled "The New *Byt* and the Sexual Question": "*Byt* constitutes a part of ideology[. . . .] Revolutionary economic changes are made frequently, but revolution in the sphere of ideology comes late. Let us recall our situation today: we have still not wrought an ideological revolution."[27]

Woman served as a constant reminder of this ideological lateness, of the inability of Bolshevik man to free himself of time. The link between attraction to women and enmeshment in the past figured in many of the era's texts, but perhaps nowhere was it accorded clearer iconic formulation than in Grigory Kozintsev's and Leonid Trauberg's 1926 film *The Devil's Wheel*. The movie relates the plight of Vania, a sailor from the *Aurora* who, delayed by a young woman named Valia in an amusement park, cannot return to his ship and becomes embroiled with a gang of criminals. In the scene explaining the hero's failure to arrive on time for his ship's departure, Vania is grasped tightly by Valia and trapped by centripetal force as they spin around on one of the park's attractions, a gigantic horizontal "Devil's" wheel that turns into a huge clock. An intertitle states, "Time flies, and Vania is unable to stop it." This utopian nightmare of imprisonment in temporality has its reprise later in the film, when the couple find themselves forced to serve as lookouts for thieves plundering a clock-repair factory: they cling to each other in the street beneath a giant clock, as their embraces function to distract the attention of a passerby from what is happening inside the building. In both scenes, time and woman are linked as signifiers of the trapped hero's inabil-

---

[25] L. N. Tolstoi, *Povesti i rasskazy v dvukh tomakh* (M.: Khudozhestvennaia literatura, 1978), 2:145.

[26] L. M. Vasilevskii, "Polovoe vospitanie i polovoe prosveshchenie," *Leningradskii meditsinskii zhurnal*, no. 2 (1926): 87 (87–94).

[27] N. A. Semashko, "Novy i byt i polovoi vopros," *Sud idet*, no. 7 (1926): 399 (399–414).

2. *The Devil's Wheel*, Grigorii Kozintsev and Leonid Trauberg, Leningradkino, 1926.

ity to reunite with an ideal (and all-male) community.[28] This linkage is reinforced at several other points in the film. A clock, for instance, shows the
time to be 9:30, and several frames later a woman tightrope-walker's legs
mimic the position of the clock's hands. Throughout the movie repetition
and physical revolution (the hands of the clock, the whirl of criminals dancing, the up-and-down motion of Vania and Valia as they become acquainted
on a roller coaster (in Russian, "American hills") serve as negative figures.
Vania's enjoyment of his relationship with Valia is fleeting; several close-ups
reinforce the extent of her pleasure and his gloom. Eventually, Vania leaves
the thieves and spends the night sleeping in front of the former Winter Palace, where this deserter from the *Aurora* sorrowfully recalls "another October night." Time, repetition, and woman have thwarted the Revolution by
transforming apocalypse into an object of nostalgia.

Not surprisingly, woman's prominence in reproduction played an important role in the Gothic discourse binding sex and woman to the past. Al-

[28] *Chertovo koleso*, dir. Grigorii Kozintsev and Leonid Trauberg, Leningradkino, 1926. Valia's
connection to the flesh and to the past is demonstrated by a scene in which her father, a butcher
(i.e., a member of the petty bourgeoisie) punches Vania, who falls into a slab of meat.

though there was a natalist trend in the Soviet press,[29] calls of encouragement for the creation of new citizens coexisted with a savagely misogynistic critique of maternity. Criticism of blind, unthinking, and animalistic motherhood had been prevalent in the early twentieth century; to varying degrees Fedorov, Berdiaev, and Solov'ev had founded their utopian philosophies on the elimination of mothers. The imagery of the Russian Futurists had been distinctly hostile to procreation, seeing in reproduction and young children the mere repetition of the past rather than a leap into the future.[30] As we have already seen, the Proletkul't also declared war on maternity. During NEP, antimaternal imagery migrated from poetry and philosophy into popular science and lectures given to future communist cadres. Fear of the past now generated scholarly and, often, what amounted to epidemiological attacks on the past's carriers—women. In his book on everyday life, Liadov insisted that parents isolate themselves from their progeny for the children's good.[31] Since fathers were apparently more willing than mothers to follow this suggested course of action, Liadov reserved the brunt of his attack for the latter. We require teachers to have degrees, he argued, but we forget that mothers are utterly ill-equipped to deal with a child's psychology and to eliminate the negative effects of the past:

> A child is born physically and morally healthy. But in raising it we instill in it our hereditary diseases, our hereditary character traits. At the moment of birth a mother often rewards her child with the gonorrhea that its father transmitted to her. Nervousness, tuberculosis, shrewishness, all these are imbibed with a mother's milk.[32]

[29] In attacks against sexual depravity, in physiological handbooks for young girls, and in pamphlets against abortion, maternity (at a mature, biologically suitable age) was often portrayed as woman's ultimate goal. The principal importance of such language may, however, have been its deployment as part of an argument against engaging in (premature) sexual relations. At any rate, the drastic cutbacks in public health facilities during NEP and the inability of the Soviet state to care for many abandoned and orphaned children in the country made the implementation of an effective natalist policy problematic. In a recent study, Susan Gross Solomon finds a marked absence of natalist arguments in abortion debates in the Soviet Union as compared to discussions about that topic elsewhere in Europe. "The Demographic Argument in Soviet Debates over the Legalization of Abortion in the 1920s," *Cahiers du Monde russe et soviétique* 33 (1992): 59–82.

[30] It is also possible, as Aleksandr Zholkovskii suggests, that misogyny may have been the *primary* motivation behind at least Maiakovskii's metaphoric abuse of women and of objects and functions associated with them. See his "O genii i zlodeistve, o babe i vserossiiskom masshtabe (Progulki po Maiakovskomu)," in A. K. Zholkovskii and Iu. K. Shcheglov, *Mir avtora i struktura teksta* (Tenafly, N.J.: Hermitage, 1986), 255–278.

[31] Liadov, *Voprosy byta*, 25.

[32] Ibid., 27. Here, too, a comparison with Bebel is instructive. Bebel had made a similar remark, that women, unlike members of all other "professions," were not specially educated for the task. *Woman and Socialism*, 150–152. Bebel's solution, however, was simply more education. Liadov's modest proposal was a departure from Bebel, as was the literal and sexual turn that he gave the matter in his brochure.

Unlike the pre-Revolutionary utopian philosophers, Liadov was not deni-grating reproduction itself, but, like them, he was attacking the "honored" position long occupied by the mother in Russian culture and trying to de-prive mothers of a central role in the molding of future generations.

A similar focus on woman's role as a carrier of the past was characteristic of the work of Anton Vital'evich Nemilov, an important figure whose career and place in the early Soviet discourse about sex merit more than passing attention. Born in 1879 into the family of a civil servant, Nemilov enrolled in 1897 at Saint Petersburg University, where he became involved in radical politics and from which he was expelled for a brief time. Initially he studied mathematics and physics, but soon he shifted his attention to anatomy and histology; in his second year of study he began publishing scholarly papers on animal physiology. By 1910 he was a professor of anatomy and histology at the Stebutovsky (later Saint Petersburg) Agricultural Institute, on the fac-ulty of which he remained until 1930. In 1913 he began to teach histology at Saint Petersburg University, attaining the rank of professor five years later. He soon became the director of a number of laboratories and departments at the Institute of Animal Husbandry as well as at his alma mater. Although his early research was on the nervous system, by 1921 his work was devoted almost entirely to glandular function, and he made important contributions to the study of the testes, seminal vesicles, and ovaries.[33]

In addition to numerous articles in scholarly journals, Nemilov was also the author of a series of medical textbooks.[34] He held important administra-tive posts, including the position of vice-rector for scholarly affairs at the University of Saint Petersburg from 1925 to 1929. For our purposes Nemilov is most interesting as a major force in Soviet popular science. With other leading lights in Soviet science he actively collaborated on the "popular, scientific, and historical" journal *Priroda* (Nature) and in 1925 became one of four editors of the popular-science journal *Chelovek i priroda* (Man and nature). A statement from the editors of the latter periodical presumably reflected Nemilov's view about the ideological importance of popular sci-ence:

> The editors' principal and fundamental goal is to make the journal an organ for
> the provision of knowledge about the natural sciences to a wide circle of work-
> ers. Entering the final struggle with capitalism, a worker should arm himself
> with all the data of the exact sciences[. . . .] As it teaches a materialistic world-

[33] Prof. Z. S. Katsnel'son, "Anton Vital'evich Nemilov (k 35-letiiu nauchnoi, pedagogicheskoi i obshchestvennoi deiatel'nosti)," *Priroda*, no. 8 (1936): 132–136. On Nemilov's scholarly con-tributions, see B. V. Aleshin, "Gistofiziologiia endokrinnoi sistemy v sovetskom soiuze za 20 let," *Problemy endokrinologii*, no. 4 (1937): 487, 490 (479–498).

[34] See, inter alia, *Kurs prakticheskoi gistologii. Posobie dlia prakticheskikh zaniatii po mikroskopicheskoi anatomii* (M. and Pg.: 1923); *Obshchii kurs mikroskopicheskoi anatomii cheloveka i zhivotnykh* (M. and L.: Gos. izd., 1925); *Obshchii kurs endokrinologii* (L. and M.: Gos. izd., 1932); *Endokrinologiia* (M. and L.: Sel'khozlit, 1938).

view to the masses, the journal will shed light on all questions of contemporary social life that concern the biological nature of man.[35]

In keeping with this credo, Nemilov published several popular science books throughout the 1920s.[36] By far the most important was *The Biological Tragedy of Woman*, which went through five editions in the second half of the decade.[37] The later editions expanded to include letters from readers, most of them female; the afterwords to these later editions were designed to assume the role of a public forum on sex and the female body.

Portraying himself in *The Biological Tragedy of Woman* as a realist who recognized the inevitability of sexual difference, Nemilov depicted woman as a prisoner of her own body, the victim of hormonal functioning that robbed her of her will. He viewed woman as the victim of an evolutionary paradox: mankind's greatest accomplishments, those which distinguished man from animal, were the result of the proportionately larger role played in the human body by hormones. In men, hormones produced greater mental creativity; in women, unfortunately, they led to emotional and physical instability tantamount to constant biological torture. The key to woman's tragic lot lay in her extraordinary gonads. "In the small and frail body of a woman," Nemilov told his readers, "nature has placed enormous ovaries— the size of a hippopotamus's—with hypertrophied incretory functioning."[38] Not only the ovaries but the female sex organs in general symbolized the tragic, powerful role played by sexuality in human evolution: "A purely 'human' feature of the female sexual apparatus is the marked development of the organs of lust [*organy sladostrastiia*], something we see neither in humanoid apes nor in other animals lower on the evolutionary ladder."[39]

Nemilov relied on Western European sources for much of his information. In support of his argument that the huge size (proportional to body weight) of the human vagina and uterus made women especially vulnerable to "sexual dictatorship," Nemilov cited Hans Friedenthal's 1912 work *Sonderformen der menschlichen Liebesbildung*. Nemilov's view that woman was a creature reducible to her reproductive organs was not unique; this opinion was shared by medical men throughout Europe and the United States in the

---

[35] *Chelovek i priroda*, no. 1 (1925), inner front cover.

[36] See, inter alia, *Kak ustroen chelovecheskii kostiak?* (Pg.: Gos. izd., 1921); *Vnutrennie dvigateli chelovecheskogo tela (Gormony)*, 3d ed. (M. and Pg.: Gos. izd., 1923); *Krov'. Populiarnyi ocherk* (L.: Obrazovanie, 1924); *Zhizn' i smert'. Obshchedostupnyi ocherk* (L.: Gos. izd., 1924); *Kak poiavilas' na zemle zhizn'?* (L.: Obrazovanie, 1924); *Son i snovidenie. Populiarnyi ocherk* (L.: Obrazovanie, 1925).

[37] All editions were published by Seiatel' in Leningrad. The dates are 1925 (4,000 copies), 1925 (6,000 copies), 1927 (7,150 copies), 1929 (6,200 copies), 1930 (6,200 copies).

[38] A. V. Nemilov, *Biologicheskaia tragediia zhenshchiny*, 2d ed. (L.: Seiatel', 1925), 64.

[39] Ibid., 62.

late nineteenth and early twentieth centuries.[40] To some extent, Nemilov's work may have been a by-product of his aggressive promotion of endocrinology over neurology, a field in which sex differences are not so absolutely relevant.[41] In the ideological context of NEP, however, Nemilov's formulation and dissemination of his views on woman's hormonal burden made a substantial contribution to the equation of woman with the flawed, "disorganized" body bequeathed to Soviet Russia by ancestors whose influence the Bolsheviks could not negate, a body in which utopian aspirations for universal transformation were repeatedly sabotaged by the resistance of pre-Revolutionary, recalcitrant nature. This point became particularly clear when Nemilov spoke of woman's function in human reproduction:

> A woman plays the role of a biological incubator in whom new life comes into being. For all the suffering she incurs as she brings a child into the world, a woman is not even granted the joy of creation that crowns the creative pains of artists and inventors. For no woman can influence the meeting of gametes—she does not even suspect that it is taking place. No woman knows to whom she will give birth—a second Newton or an absolute idiot. [. . .] The tragedy of a woman's biological calling lies in the fact that unconsciously [or against her will—*nevol'no*] and completely, so to speak, "in the dark" she joins chains of hereditary particles and thus fatally stretches threads from the past to the future.[42]

In the book's conclusion, Nemilov stressed the particularly Gothic nature of these "chains" "in the dark":

> Each sexual act is first of all an extremely crucial process, since its consequences for all life may be enormous. Here, as we have seen, two chains of hereditary units that stretch from the distant past to the fog-shrouded future join

[40] See G. J. Barker-Benfield, *The Horrors of the Half-Known Life: Male Attitudes toward Women and Sexuality in Nineteenth-Century America* (Evanston: Harper & Row, 1976), 91–97; Laqueur, *Making Sex*, 216; Louise Lander, *Images of Bleeding: Menstruation as Ideology* (New York: Orlando Press, 1988), 45–48; Carroll Smith-Rosenberg and Charles Rosenberg, "The Female Animal: Medical and Biological Views of Woman and Her Role in Nineteenth Century America," *Journal of American History* 40 (1973): 335 (332–356).

[41] Nemilov's endocrinological partisanship is perhaps most on display in a 1925 article entitled "The Truly Human in the Nature of Man," in which he attributes the course of human evolution to glandular development:

Man is the most "hormonal" of all living things, and in the battle for a place under the sun hormones are a more powerful weapon than strong muscles, claws, horns, teeth, and quills. Not one other animal has such perfected "organs of management" as has man. Thanks to the extreme "sensitivity" and, if one can so put it, plasticity of hormones, man has become what he is, a social creature, a being capable of transforming surrounding objects into instruments of production, into the means of extending his power over the surrounding world. ("Istinno-chelovecheskoe v prirode cheloveka," *Chelovek i priroda*, no. 2 [1925]: 16–17 [13–18].)

[42] A. V. Nemilov, *Biologicheskaia tragediia zhenshchiny*, 3d ed. (L.: Seiatel', 1927), 102–103.

together; that which has been forgotten, which seemed forever overcome [*izzhitoe*], can, thanks to the sexual act, come alive once more and throb with life to the sorrow of those around it, who, rather than producing something socially useful, must work to support the life of this unnecessary member of the collective. And this unnecessary thing, which unexpectedly appears from oblivion, contains in itself, or, more accurately, in its sex glands, all the potential not to expire but to repeat itself so many times in future generations that in fifty years its harmful hereditary substance may be distributed among more people than now inhabit the globe.[43]

Participating in sexual reproduction, woman turned herself into the arena of the future's penetration by the past.

The thrust of Nemilov's book, and of an earlier monograph, *Life and Death: A Popular Survey*, was to warn the Soviet public against utopian ideation. If his message in the first book was that immortality is impractical[44]—a more conservative and controversial statement in 1925 than it would be today[45]—the second book contended that sexual equality would never be possible:

> Even in communist society, when not only in word but in deed woman will have equal rights with man, her comrade, when there will be public cafeterias, and when the public upbringing of children will have been organized, the "biological tragedy" will remain.[46]

This position was a dramatic revision of Bebel's analysis of woman's plight in capitalist society. Bebel had insisted that woman's tragedy was social; her oppression would end when society was radically restructured by fundamental changes in the relationships of production. When Bebel devoted a few pages to woman's physiological suffering, he was concerned with sexually transmitted diseases brought by men to the marriage bed.[47] Nemilov's portrait of woman as an inevitable, perpetual victim of her own immutable physiology introduced an important change into the rapport between "woman and socialism." Responding to critics, such as Vladimir Bekhterev, who insisted on the social nature of woman's tragedy,[48] Nemilov conceded that there were both social and biological sides to the woman question. Neverthe-

---

[43] Ibid., 153–154.

[44] A. V. Nemilov, *Zhizn' i smert'. Obshchedostupnyi ocherk* (L.: Gos. izd., 1925), 77.

[45] Unlike many of his colleagues, Nemilov was always extremely cautious about "rejuvenation" experiments, doubting that they would be of use to a vigorous nation like the Soviet Union. He did, however, express enthusiasm for their use in prolonging the lives of animals. See his "'Omolozhenie' sel'skokhoziaistvennykh zhivotnykh," *Chelovek i priroda*, no. 1 (1925): 23–36.

[46] Nemilov, *Biologicheskaia tragediia*, 2d ed., 39.

[47] Bebel, *Woman and Socialism*, 150–152.

[48] V. M. Bekhterev, "Nedootsenka sotsial'noi roli zhenshchiny," *Vestnik znaniia*, no. 11 (1925): 771–774.

less, he refused to apologize for devoting so little time to the former. "These days, social literacy has spread more widely than biological literacy," he explained, adding, "I have purposely stressed the biological side and brought it into sharp relief, because the facts that I have adduced here are, so to speak, the ABCs of sexual enlightenment, which ought to be known by everyone who would approach the woman and sexual questions 'as a Marxist.' "[49] Yet in his narration of history as a process subject to repetition and chance, Nemilov was introducing a seriously destabilizing and frightening element into the Marxist scheme of human progress. What could be more threatening to a Bolshevik than picturing the story of humanity as an eternal game of repetition and chance, as "a spinning roulette wheel" (Nemilov's version of Kozintsev's and Trauberg's "Devil's Wheel") that one "has no chance at all to influence."[50]

Nemilov confided to his readers that communists had not spoken of "biological inequality" prior to the Revolution lest their remarks play into the hands of "dark forces":

[But] now that social and juridical sexual equality has been achieved, now that there is already no returning to past ways of life, there is no longer any need to hush up well-known things, and we can speak candidly and sincerely. We must acknowledge that biological inequality exists between the sexes and that it is much more profound and more serious than it seems to people unacquainted with the natural sciences.[51]

By voicing such sentiments in an era preoccupied with the possibility of a return of the historical repressed, Nemilov's book took its place in a discourse that already associated women and female sexuality with the past and with the terrible "other" who held and withheld the key to a return to the Golden Age. In its struggle to free itself from the castle of real time, Soviet ideology under NEP tended to attack savagely—at least on the level of discourse—all of its presumptive jailers. One of these jailers, Nemilov was saying, was female biology.

Nemilov devoted a great deal of space to his portrait of history's biological captive, depicting an Everywoman brutally and unceasingly tortured by her own reproductive system. Pregnancy, in particular, was a cruel process in which "nature establishes its dictatorship over a woman's body," forcing her to direct all her strength toward the preservation of an embryo or fetus and "mercilessly demanding absolute self-sacrifice from all the mother's organs."[52] Here the womb serves as a locus for fears of parasitism, with the fetus

---

[49] Nemilov, *Biologicheskaia tragediia*, 3d ed., 145.
[50] Ibid., 103.
[51] Ibid., 48.
[52] Ibid., 44.

vampirizing the mother who, in turn, limits the utopian aspirations of society. Nemilov's description of parturition follows:

> Childbirth is often called a physiological process, but for anyone who has the slightest conception of this act it is clear that such a term is entirely inappropriate. If we must talk about physiological [i.e., normal] parturition (for there also exists pathological parturition), then all the same it would be more correct to use another expression and call it a "physiological catastrophe." If breathing, the circulation of blood, and digestion are "processes," then it is inappropriate to apply this word to the expulsion of the human fetus from the mother's body, an act after which the entire surface of the uterus constitutes one large wound.[53]

The view of birth as a virtually pathological act was not unique to Nemilov nor even to Russian doctors,[54] but its contextualization in *The Biological Tragedy* endowed it with particular horror. While Nemilov's account may have been especially emotional in its rhetorical outbursts, more important was his assertion that these awful facts had survived the Revolution and would have to be accommodated in a necessarily less than perfect world.

In addition to describing at length the various physiological agonies inflicted on a "normal" woman of childbearing age, Nemilov addressed the presumed relief of menopause. Unfortunately, here, too, there was no escape from the castle, and once again Nemilov resorted to his beloved imagery of temporal fetters:

> In the worst cases life after menopause is an unmitigated chain of suffering, the causes of which may be traced to various moments in a woman's earlier sexual life. Even in the best cases it is a sad fading of physical and spiritual vitality and a prolonged approach to death. [. . .] In men this condition [i.e., the loss of reproductive potency] goes entirely unnoticed in the overwhelming majority of cases, but in a woman it is precisely menopause that marks the start of the infirmities of old age and is a terrifying herald of death.[55]

To prove his claims about reproduction and menopause, Nemilov affixed letters from female readers in subsequent editions of his book. "I myself lived through only one pregnancy," one reader testified in the second edition,

[53] Ibid., 44–45.

[54] See P. G. Bondarev's statement that although pregnancy is a natural physiological function, "pregnancy and labor stand on the border between physiology and pathology, which is why they are so liable to succumb to various deviations." *Vliianie iskusstvennogo vykidysha na zhenshchinu. (Abort i vnutrenniaia sekretsiia matki.)* (Simferopol', 1925), 3. The frequency of Dr. G. B. Getsov's repetition of the phrase "pregnancy is not a disease" in his brochure for expectant mothers is a revealing measure of the prevalence of this equation of pregnancy with pathology. *Pamiatka beremennoi zhenshchiny i kormiashchei materi. Na poluchenie posobii po materinstvu,* 7th ed. (Kiev: Kievskaia okruzhnaia strakhovaia kassa, 1925), 3. (For American parallels, see Barker-Benfield, *The Horrors of the Half-Known Life,* 103–104.)

[55] Nemilov, *Biologicheskaia tragediia,* 3d ed., 46.

"but it was an absolute horror [*sploshnoi uzhas*]."[56] In his afterword to the book's third edition, in which he referred to maternity as "woman's Golgotha,"[57] Nemilov included the following excerpt from a reader's letter: "A woman suffers bloody tortures! What injustice! You are absolutely right that maternity's joys are not equal to its sufferings, and its sufferings are not only physical. The best time of a woman's life must be spent in disease and hideousness; liberation comes only during the period of our withering. Love is poetry, but maternity is prose. Our sex's tragedy, which, unfortunately, many women do not understand, is horrible."[58] Nemilov was in agreement with these sentiments. He himself concurred with Hypocrates that "a woman's entire life is one long, uninterrupted disease."[59]

The letters were not all written in the same vein. Several readers objected to Nemilov's terrifying reading of life's "prose." One student wrote: "It would seem from your little book that a woman finds peace only in death. Well, let's say you are right: in that case all women ought long ago to have done away with themselves, but in the majority of cases this does not occur."[60]

Nemilov was sensitive to the agony and pointlessness of a life without joy. In his book on life and death, he explained that immortality, while scientifically feasible, was impractical since an "immortal" human being would essentially be a prisoner of science:

> It is unlikely that anyone would agree to become immortal since he would have to live behind seven seals and under a glass bubble without all the things that make life beautiful. But it is possible that some sort of living creature will be forced for the greater glory of science to live for an indefinitely long time and that for man's edification the care of this eternal life will be passed down from one generation to the next as the eternal flame was in bygone times.[61]

The quality of life was more important than its quantity, Nemilov patiently explained to his eschatologically minded readers, and therefore science should strive to extend enjoyable life rather than to conquer death altogether. Reading his books seriatim, however, one wonders how women—with their lives of "constant" disease and torture—fit into Nemilov's humanistic worldview. How might it be possible to end a woman's agony? A powerful image in Nemilov's book on life and death may provide a key:

> The famous French researcher [Charles-Édouard] Brown-Séquard showed how difficult it is to pinpoint the precise moment separating life from death. In an interesting, albeit rather cruel, experiment, he decapitated a dog that had lived

[56] Ibid., 140.
[57] Ibid.
[58] Ibid., 141.
[59] Ibid., 94.
[60] Ibid., 142.
[61] Nemilov, *Zhizn' i smert'*, 77.

for a long time in his laboratory. The head was then injected with fresh warm canine blood through its large, pulsing carotid arteries. It immediately came alive, began to open its mouth, shake its ears, and even turned its eyes toward a person who was loudly calling its name. The writer of these lines once had occasion himself to observe a woman cut in half by a train. Since the train had powerfully crushed down the edges of the cut, a relatively large amount of blood remained in the upper half of the body and continued to nourish it. Thus the upper half of the body continued to live for about another quarter of an hour. The unfortunate woman continued breathing, she winked, and her face was contorted by convulsions, while the lower half of her body, which had been cast [otbroshena] several meters away and from which much blood had escaped immediately after the accident, had long ago grown stiff and did not show the slightest signs of life.[62]

The switch in this passage into autobiographical narrative and the inclusion of this powerful image, unparalleled as a vivid example in Nemilov's popularizing books, frame the scene above as an important and traumatic moment in Nemilov's scientific popular narrative. Does not this woman, parted from her "discarded" lower half[63] represent—however perversely—woman emancipated from the organs that hold her prisoner? This horrific vision, or, one could say, this horrific real-life experiment, distorts and represents, as in a dream, the wish that may have motivated the writing—and some of the reading—of *The Biological Tragedy of Woman* and which was repeatedly pronounced utopian by its author. Bodily and historical limitations could be overcome by the elimination of the female body; communism could be attained as a society without women. Granted "her" wish to be deprived of her body ("it was as if she had just a head and no body"), would Gladkov's Polia Mekhova, too, really have been capable of surviving?

Nemilov's desire to discard the female body was expressed, if at all, in repressed form; outwardly, he was arguing for understanding and tolerance of the terrible facts of woman's life. In NEP discourse we often see more direct attacks on woman and her body. One of these is prominent in *October*,

---

[62] Ibid., 43–44. Brown-Séquard (1817–1894) was professor of experimental physiology at the Collège de France and a pioneering figure in both endocrinology and rejuvenation. Brown-Séquard caused a minor sensation when in 1889 he injected himself with an extract prepared from the sex glands of guinea pigs and dogs. See N. M. Knipovich, "Broun-Sekar," *Entsikopedicheskii slovar'*, 86 vols. (Iaroslavl': Brokgauz-Efron [Terra], 1890–1907 [1990]), 8:740, and N. K. Kol'tsov, "Vvedenie: smert', starost', omolozhenie," in *Omolozhenie. Sbornik statei*, ed. Kol'tsov (M. and Pg.: Gos. izd., 1923), 20 (1–28). As late as 1927, Soviet newspapers contained advertisements for a potency-enhancing product marketed as "Séquard's liquid." Iu. K. Shcheglov, *Romany I. Il'fa i E. Petrova. Wiener Slawistischer Almanach. Sonderband 26*, 2 vols., 1:273.

[63] The verb "*otbrosit'*" means to "cast away" in various senses, including to "reject" or "discard."

Sergei Eisenstein's tenth-anniversary present to the Soviet state. Eisenstein devotes special attention to the last defenders of the Winter Palace: a female battalion. These defenders of the Old Regime receive more individual attention than the Bolshevik troops who overcome them; it is as if Eisenstein's concern lies more in smashing this female resistance than in heroicizing the soldiers of the new order. In Eisenstein's hands the historically accurate fact of the women's battalion's presence becomes the vehicle for a caricature of femininity; ideologically repulsive women soldiers enjoy undressing, applying makeup, and lying on top of one another.[64] A brassiere hangs from one of their rifles, metonymically becoming a symbol—if not a weapon—of reaction. When a representative of this battalion receives the Bolsheviks' ultimatum, her bust is accorded prominent attention. Finally, when the palace has been successfully stormed and the last women soldiers routed in the tsarina's bedchamber, the sailors, discovering the tsarina's toilet, look, smirk, and laugh. (Meanwhile, old women are trying to steal bottles of wine from the tsar's cellars.)[65]

Eisenstein's savage attack on femininity is only slightly idiosyncratic. As Judith Mayne argues in her groundbreaking study of gender in early Soviet cinema, "Eisenstein's vision of the sexual contours of the Revolution offers a representation 'in amazingly bold relief' [. . .] of a dynamic that emerges in many Soviet films of the period."[66] It is essential to realize that these "sexual contours" were bound up with retrospective yearning for the first few post-Revolutionary years, with fears of the newly risen, pre-Revolutionary dead,

[64] For a contemporary account of the defeat and fate of the female battalion, see V. A. Amfiteatrov-Kadashev, "Iz dnevnika 1917 goda," *Literaturnaia gazeta*, 20 July 1994, 6.

[65] *Oktiabr'*, dir. Sergei Eisenstein, Sovkino, 1928. This scene is in no sense Gothic. Eisenstein's revolutionary exuberance for his medium overcame all backward-looking nervous glances at the past. The scene may, however, have been conceived as a parody of one of the most famous Gothic moments in ideological literature: Edmund Burke's depiction of the flight of Marie Antoinette from her bedchamber moments before the arrival of "a band of cruel ruffians and assassins" who, reeking with blood, "rushed into the chamber of the queen and pierced with a hundred strokes of bayonets and poniards the bed, from which this persecuted woman had but just enough time to fly almost naked, and, through ways unknown to the murderers, had escaped to seek refuge at the feet of a king and husband not secure of his own life for a moment." *Reflections on the Revolution in France* (Indianapolis: Bobbs-Merrill, 1955), 82. Eisenstein transports this moment from the French to the Russian Revolution (right down to the destruction of the empress's bedspread), but he shows us this moment from the revolutionaries' perspective, thus transforming ideological terror into triumphantly ebullient ideological farce.

[66] Judith Mayne, *Kino and the Woman Question: Feminism and Soviet Silent Film* (Columbus: Ohio State University Press, 1989), 56. Mayne adds: "In *October*, female autonomy is portrayed as perverse and unnatural. Yet, at the same time, virtually all versions of female identity with any kind of active component are portrayed as perverse and unnatural. In other words, it is not clear where the line is drawn between perversity and normality as far as women are concerned" (57). For an opinion that Eisenstein's films should *not* be treated as "typical" in their use of gender, see Denise J. Youngblood's review of Mayne's book in *Russian History* 17 (1990): 123–125.

and with NEP ideology's consequent loathing (virtually a self-loathing) for the era that gave it its name.

Repeatedly, ideological concerns during NEP required the representation of some kind of female human sacrifice. In December 1925, *Komsomol'skaia pravda* printed the following summary of the film *The Road to Happiness*:

> A girl falls in love with Sharonov, a Red Army soldier, who impregnates her. The soldier is demobilized and returns home to his wife. Nastia learns of this wife's existence and, seeing the hopelessness of her fate, hangs herself. She is saved. In a short time she gives birth in a [government] maternity ward. At the very same time, Sharonov's wife is running to a midwife, who feeds her roots and casts spells. As a result, the wife dies in childbirth. Sharonov marries Nastia. All's well that ends well.[67]

Ends well . . . for whom? Was the death of the Old Woman a necessary correlate of the instruction of the New Woman? Is the most important aspect of this happy ending the wife's death or Sharonov's new marriage? *Komsomol'skaia pravda* emphasizes that this is a story about differences between the Old (Bad) Woman and the New (Good) Woman. Only the latter may breed, and her reproduction must be fed by the destruction of her opposite number and, perhaps, by her own attempt at self-destruction—an attempt the depiction of which may be more important than its eventual outcome. The film's plot summary reveals the pernicious way in which the campaign for female enlightenment could be paired with a veiled wish for the elimination of woman, much the way Weininger's and Berdiaev's concepts of androgyny concealed a wish to be rid of femininity beneath their statements about the desirability of sexual integration. Did the road to happiness have to be littered with female corpses?

Iakov Protozanov's 1924 film *Aelita* answered in the affirmative.[68] Based on Aleksei Tolstoi's 1922 novel of the same name, the film chronicled a proletarian revolution on Mars.[69] A fundamental difference exists, however, between *Aelita* in print and on the screen; the movie, shot two years after the novel's publication, is essentially a film about NEP that projects contemporary ideological anxieties onto the Red Planet.

The film contains an important character altogether lacking in the book, a

---

[67] Boris B——ich, untitled review of *Doroga k schast'iu*, *Komsomol'skaia pravda*, 12 December 1925, 4. The health commissar called the film, which was directed by S. Kozlovskii, "a model for popular-education filmmaking." N. Semashko, "'Doroga k schast'iu,'" *Izvestiia*, 11 December 1925, 7.

[68] *Aelita*, dir. Iakov Protozanov, Mezhrabprom-Russ, 1924. For a discussion of Protozanov's career, see Denise Youngblood, *Movies for the Masses: Popular Cinema and Soviet Society in the 1920s* (Cambridge: Cambridge University Press, 1992), 105–121.

[69] Aleksei Tolstoi, "Aelita," *Krasnaia nov'*, no. 6 (1922): 104–149; no. 1 (1923): 52–91; no. 2 (1923): 36–57.

corrupt speculator, Victor Erlikh, who fondly recalls "the old days" before the Revolution and secures a position as a Soviet bureaucrat, which he turns to his financial advantage. He lodges in the house of the hero, an engineer named Los, and attempts to seduce Los's wife, taking her to a secret "high society" ball attended by Nepmen. Although his wife remains faithful, Los suspects her of adultery. Upon his return from a long, work-related trip, Los stands in the vestibule of his house and watches shadows that appear to be those of his wife and Erlikh kissing in an open door on the second floor. The door closes, obliterating the shadows, and a few moments later Los's wife descends the stairs. Los shoots at her, she falls, and he flees to a train station where he imagines a voyage to Mars.

The prolonged fanciful preparations for this voyage (in the novel occurring in "reality" rather than in the hero's mind) require that Los disguise himself as Spiridonov, his former assistant who, disillusioned with NEP and women, has left the USSR because "the past turned out to be stronger than I." During the preparations and the flight to Mars, Los fancies that he is being observed by Aelita, a Martian princess. The imagined scenes on Mars revolve around Aelita's attempts to break free of her despotic king, who keeps her confined to her room. When he arrives on the Red Planet, Los and Aelita fall in love, partly because he keeps seeing his "dead" wife in her place. Los and his Red Army assistant, Gusev, organize a proletarian uprising, which Aelita supports in order to grab supreme power for herself. When she orders her soldiers to fire on the Martian proletariat, Los pushes her off a high architectural ledge and she disappears from the film.

In the movie Mars serves as a double for the Earth, a screen onto which the Soviet Revolution seeks to duplicate itself. But Mars also serves as a cinema within the cinema, an arena for the resolution of earthly anxieties. The Martian scenery—virtually all of it interiors—in which Aelita, Los, and the Martian working class are trapped, would seem to present a curious setting for NEP Gothic. Yet the extraterrestrial locale manages to mirror— albeit at times with distortion—the "real" action on Earth, where sex and foreign penetration (of either Jewish or German origin: Erlikh is a foreign name) produce disturbing anxieties and lead to terrible acts. Most important, in his Martian daydream, Los repeats the act for which he has been compelled to flee—the murder of his wife. His statement to his wife when he finds her alive ("I was out of my mind. I'm so happy I missed") demands to be questioned by the viewer, particularly if she suspects that "every dream is the fulfillment of a wish."[70] The initially comical episode in which Los's

[70] Sigmund Freud, *The Interpretation of Dreams* (New York: Avon, 1965 [1900]), 155. At least one other critic has drawn attention to the double-murder theme in *Aelita*. L. Pliushsch reads Los's destruction of Aelita and his wife as an important part of both spouses' rebirth as new Soviet citizens. *La victoire sur le soleil: Russe 1905–1935*, documentation accompanying an exhibition and film program at the Cinémathèque de Toulouse, 1984. In the most comprehen-

assistant, a Red Army soldier, arrives at the spaceship dressed as a woman (his wife has hidden his clothes) may be read as an ominous sign that Mars will resemble Earth; no matter how hard the Soviet man tries to escape from women and the past, the message of this film may be that neither can be left behind.

The need for female sacrifice affected even a film that professed to be concerned with liberating women from domestic imprisonment. Avram Room's *Bed and Sofa* tells the story of a housewife, Liudmila, who lives with her domineering husband, Kolia, in a single room. When Volodia, Kolia's old Civil War buddy, arrives in Moscow, he is forced by the housing crisis to seek shelter in the couple's room and on their couch. Volodia's sensitive attention to Liudmila and his interest in exposing her to the modern innovations of Soviet power (radio, the cinema, aviation) win her affection. (It is through fortune-telling, however, that he gets Liudmila into bed; her attraction to Volodia may be ideologically correct, but her "fall" is not.) Volodia soon displaces Kolia in the bed, and Kolia moves to the couch. Once he has won Liudmila, Volodia proves as much a male tyrant as was Kolia, and Liudmila, finding herself pregnant with a child of uncertain paternity, leaves them both. She removes her picture from the frame hanging on the wall and at the movie's end is shown on the train carrying her away from Moscow.

Room's film has been criticized for promoting maternity as a substitute for real independence.[71] Viktor Shklovsky, the film's scenarist, admitted that one of the movie's mistakes was to make its female protagonist "idle": "We didn't know where to put the woman and so we simply sent her out of town."[72] Expelling woman from the City, however, is far from a neutral action in the pro-industrial Soviet context, and the argument can be made that the movie is yet another story of female elimination. Women can be

---

sive analysis of the film to date, Ian Christie notes that "in terms of allegory, there is a distinct echo of Maiakovsky's *Mystery Bouffe*, which ends with representatives of the unclean class killing Queen Chaos and declaring 'the door into the future is open.'" Ian Christie, "Down to Earth: *Aelita* relocated," in *Inside the Film Factory: New Approaches to Russian and Soviet Cinema*, ed. Richard Taylor and Ian Christie (London: Routledge, 1991), 99 (80–102). Inasmuch as Maiakovsky's work is part of the War Communist ethos, Protozanov's film's echo of it (and the movie's resonance with many other contemporary works) should be read as a piece of War Communist nostalgia. Aelita's death, far from being a step on the road to rebirth, may be the film's culminating moment; along with the attempted murder of Los's wife, it may be the closest Protozanov and his scriptwriters (Aleksei Faiko and Fedor Otsep) would allow themselves to come to a representation of gynocidal desire on earth. In the film, Aelita is reborn not as a new Soviet woman but as the advertisement for tires that has provided the "day residue" for Los's dream. This association of women with a capitalist genre (product promotion) further serves to link woman with the cohabiting enemy.

[71] Mayne, *Kino and the Woman Question*, 123–129.

[72] Viktor Shklovskii, *Za 60 let: raboty o kino* (M.: Iskusstvo, 1985), 138.

liberated in the Soviet metropolis only by their expulsion from it; the film promotes the notion that the only good woman is a woman who is no longer here. Employing Eve Kosofsky Sedgwick's concept of "homosocial" desire, Judith Mayne argues that Kolia and Volodia "might be the real couple" in the movie, but she does not place that valuable insight into historical context.[73] The marriage of these two comrades from the front represents a War Communist union in opposition to the bourgeois, heterosexual relationship of each with Liudmila. The men never overcome their immersion in bourgeois culture; at the film's conclusion they are about to engage in the cozy petty bourgeois pastime of tea. Even in this degraded, travestied state, War Communist nostalgia manages to expel woman from society's center at the very moment when she is sprung from her domestic trap.[74]

The blank frame in Liudmila's room proclaims that woman's tragedy during NEP was not only biological or social but also representational. The nature of this tragedy was not that there was no room for woman but that woman's place had to be *shown* in the process of being cleared or emptied, even at moments when woman seemed most capable of escaping her bourgeois "frame."[75] NEP discourse repeatedly used woman and her negation as a figure onto which to cathect ideological anxieties; the depiction of woman's elimination became a ritual rhetorical gesture in the literature about sex. It is certainly not coincidental that of the three psychoneurotic students whose cases were singled out by Zalkind for special attention, only the woman was pronounced beyond all help. Of such hopeless cases Zalkind wrote:

> It is necessary to avail ourselves of the help of Party doctors and control commissions to filter out from among psychoneurotics those (like our third case) whose false orientation is in actuality caused by their *incurable* ideological fragility. The Party should give up on them; they are independent agents [literally, cutoff slices, *otrezannye lomti*] and their presence in the ranks of the Party's youth can only be harmful, since with their emotionality and heightened excitability, a trait liable to find flagrant expression in ideological crises, they only

[73] Mayne, *Kino and the Woman Question*, 120.

[74] Within a few years, Liudmila's departure from Moscow would have been an ideologically exemplary action . . . provided she were leaving to take part in one of the First Five Year Plan's massive construction projects.

The degradation and coddling of vibrant masculinity is a prominent but virtually ignored aspect of the film. Rather than view the film as about what happens to Liudmila, one could interpret it as a story about Volodia's transformation when he is forced to exist in proximity with woman and domestic bliss. Masculinity in the film seems to have been rendered inoperative or immobile. This theme receives striking manifestation in the scene in which Kolia reclines next to the petrified genitals of one of the horses on the Bolshoi's roof. NEP, like the Medusa, turns man to lazy, contemptible bourgeois stone.

[75] The conclusion of *The Devil's Wheel* is also curious in its tacit dismissal of Valia from the narrative. In the film's happy ending Vania returns to his mates on the *Aurora*, while Valia simply disappears.

provoke unnecessary ferment and tensions and sometimes infect others with their falsely directed passions.[76]

Here, filtered through Zalkind's favored metaphor of amputation, woman's removal from the body politic enables that body to survive and thrive. Woman thus serves Zalkind as the castrated organ of man, the removal of which restores the natural balance of biological forces favorable to collective, class-conscious activity. Zalkind does not specify that these severed, independent agents/slices *must* be women, but the female sex of the only such slice encountered in his book fosters that impression. Elsewhere, Zalkind has no problem identifying pernicious, capitalism-induced "excitability" (*vozbuzhdaemost'*) as a female trait: "The sexual isolation of woman, her constant failure to be satisfied, her sexual hunger, and her erotic sensuality heighten her general excitability, endowing this characteristic with constant—although indistinct—sexual features (acute femininity, unconscious and conscious coquettishness), all of which becomes a profoundly irritating lure for man."[77]

The gender of communism's dispensable "severed slice" *was* clearly specified by one of the era's most frequently represented historical myths: the legend of the seventeenth-century rebel Sten'ka Razin. Tens of plays, poems, and stories were based on Razin's life during the first post-Revolutionary decade. Early Soviet writers saw in Razin a forerunner of the Revolution,[78] and a certain Professor N. N. Firsov published a book in 1920 entitled *Razinism as a Sociological and Psychological Phenomenon of Popular Life* in which he claimed that "by virtue of the enormous sweep of his limitless, audacious, and unparalleled will, Razin embodied the popular ideal of the physical and spiritual power of a 'free' [*vol'nyi*] man."[79] Firsov's book had originally been written and delivered as a lecture in 1905, and Razin had been hailed as a revolutionary by Russian leftists since at least the 1870s, but now a particular episode in Razin's life—his hurling his lover, a captured princess, into the Volga—was accorded special attention. As early as 1918, Punin and Poletaev singled out this episode as the moment when "the Great Russian" first "understood that the beauty of [individualistic] civilization [as contrasted with communal "culture"] impedes free creativity and represents an unnecessary and enfeebling refinement of life."[80] Several years later, at

[76] A. B. Zalkind, *Revoliutsiia i molodezh'* (M.: Kommunisticheskii universitet, 1924 or 1925), 47–48. The introduction to this volume was written by Liadov.

[77] A. B. Zalkind, *Polovoi fetishizm. K peresmotru polovogo voprosa* (M.: Vserossiiskii proletkul't, 1925), 37–38.

[78] See, inter alia, Iu. Iur'in, *Spoloshnyi zyk (Sten'ka Razin)* (Pb.: Gos. izd., 1920); Al. Altaev and A. Feliche, *Ataman Stepan Razin* (Pb.: Gos. izd., 1920).

[79] N. N. Firsov, *Razinovshchina, kak sotsiologicheskoe i psikhologicheskoe iavlenie narodnoi zhizni* (M.: Russkii bibliograficheskii institut, 1920).

[80] Evgenii Poletaev and Nikolai Punin, *Protiv tsivilizatsii* (Pg., 1918), 136.

the height of NEP debate on sex, Gumilevsky seized upon the episode as a model for Revolutionary youth. In *Dog Alley*, Zoia, a "positive" heroine who overcomes the evil "heredity" of her petty bourgeois roots, exclaims to a dissolute komsomolka as they argue about "proper" sexual behavior:

> "Wait! Recently I saw women on the riverbank loading wood and singing. They were singing that song about the Persian princess—you know it, we all know it, it's a wonderful song,"—she hurried, seeking a lost thought and then she blurted out:
>
> "That's it! That's exactly it! The renunciation of carnal joy for the sake of the principle of responsibility! For the sake of the struggle! 'To the devil with the princess,' the cohort [*druzhina*] is muttering: 'the *ataman* has become a woman [*baba*], and there's still battle ahead.' You remember, you remember, last year's questionnaire at the university, then the report and conclusions drawn from it, that during the Revolution, during the Civil War sexual emotions were fewer and dulled." She had to catch her breath. [. . .] Sexual ecstasy, sexual feeling may, it turns out, yield to revolutionary ecstasy.[81]

In Zoia's speech we find another example of the "materialization" of old myths that was so common during the 1920s, the application of pre-Revolutionary ideas and metaphors to post-Revolutionary everyday life. The never subtle Gumilevsky, fearing his readers might miss the significance of this scene, repeats it. Later in the novel, Zoia closes her eyes, hears the song, and sees "the waves of the Volga devouring the Persian princess, and it seemed so simple to her to renounce the joys of the flesh for the sake of the principle of obligation and struggle."[82]

Simple for whom? Gumilevsky's heroine appears to identify with Razin, never with the princess, but Razin's song, when listened to with gender-attentive ears, suggests that the only way to commit oneself to battle—to sublimate sexuality—is to eliminate woman, an act of "popular will" that will facilitate the return of those (retrospectively) untroubled days of War

---

[81] Lev Gumilevskii, *Sobachii pereulok* (Riga: Gramatu draugs, 1928), 51. The popular song to which Gumilevskii's heroine refers (and which also featured prominently in Artsybashev's *Sanin*) was set to the words of Dmitrii Sadovnikov's 1883 poem "Iz-za ostrova na strezhen'" during the 1890s. V. G. Bazanov, B. L. Bessonov, and A. M. Bikhter, *Poety-Demokraty 1870–1880x godov* (L.: Sovetskii pisatel', 1968), 555.

[82] Gumilevskii, *Sobachii pereulok*, 117. Gumilevskii was evidently quite attached to this scene. In a 1925 story he made use of it as well, once more without reference to the importance of the sex of its heroes. The story's "good" komsomolka explains to her "bad" counterpart: "Just yesterday on the pier I heard some blind men singing that old song about Sten'ka Razin! A Volga song, a good song! And just look, what do we have there? Renunciation of the desires of the flesh for the sake of the idea of responsibility! The grumbling of the *druzhina* brought him to his senses and he threw off the princess! Sexual ecstasy is transformed into energy for the purpose of an exploit." Lev Gumilevskii, "Meshchanochka," *Komsomol'skaia pravda*, 15 August 1925, 3.

Communism and "revolutionary ecstasy." NEP's stories about sex frequently purport to be about the difference between Good and Bad Women, and yet if we analyze it, the difference between women in these works is always superficial and rarely the central difference that is repeatedly dramatized throughout the decade. That central difference is between marked and unmarked gender, between the Old Woman and the New Soviet Being, a being whom we might be tempted to classify as androgynous or male, except that this new being remains haunted by a femininity that can never be purged. One of the constantly formative features of this being-always-in-the-process-of-becoming is its rejection of female gender. Woman, in other words, is ideological lost wax in the casting of the new Soviet citizen, and so henceforth it might be best to speak about this entity as the new Soviet non-Woman.

In this context we should turn, finally, to a short story published by Andrei Platonov in 1927. "Ivan Zhokh" is essentially a two-part work. The first tells how, in the late eighteenth century, a pretender named Ivan Zhokh leads a group of Old Believers in a rebellion against the empress and, failing, takes them into Siberia to find refuge. In the second part, a group of communist partisans stumbles upon the home of Zhokh's descendants, "Eternal-City-on-the-faraway-River," and learns about its past. As the partisans near the city Zhokh built, they are in a desperate state, chased by Kolchak and "losing their last courage" (*muzhestvo*, literally virility). This loss is appropriate, for in the eternal city, resplendent with Greek architecture, there are no women and few noncastrated men. Castration, however, is not the founding act of sexual violence upon which the Old Believers have built their timeless walls. A native of Eternal-City-on-the-faraway-River gives the partisans a lesson in what might be called "ahistory":

> Zhokh pretended to be Tsar Petr Fedorovich just like Emel'ian Pugachev. But Teshcha [one of his followers] strangled Zhokh because Zhokh had gotten himself a wife from the Urals, where he had once lived and fought against Catherine the Great. This same Teshcha took pity on Zhokh's woman, for she was already with child. Later, she conceived a son by Teshcha as well. No sooner had she given birth to his son, Georgy, than Teshcha cut out her uterus with a bread knife, and she died.[83]

Platonov's insistence on a lethal hysterectomy as the foundational utopian myth serves as a remarkable insight into the sexual implications of Russian "totalitarian" thought. By the mid-1920s, Platonov had abandoned many of the radical, Proletkul't-inspired positions that he had advocated at the start of the decade. He was now composing stories that narrativized and carried through to their logical conclusion many of the philosophical and discursive tendencies that surrounded him. "Ivan Zhokh" is set in the Civil War era and

---

[83] Platonov, *Epifanskie shliuzy* (M.: Molodaia gvardiia, 1927), 105.

is ostensibly about noncommunists (religious sectarians). But while the story should be read as directed primarily against the utopian philosophers (Solov'ev, Berdiaev, Fedorov, and, to some extent, Weininger) who had influenced Platonov during his youth,[84] we should not forget that this was a story written during NEP about the War Communist era. Platonov's remarkable literalization and politicization of pre-Revolutionary metaphors was composed within an ideological atmosphere colored by Civil War nostalgia and anxiety about the impurities of NEP. Compared to many of his contemporaries, Platonov was far more conscious and critical of the pernicious dimensions of the representational uses of gender in Russia, but his story, in conjunction with the other examples from the 1920s that we have just surveyed, indicates the extent to which pre-Revolutionary ideas and figures survived and were ideologically recontextualized in the Soviet Russia of NEP. In our next chapter we shall see how woman's representational tragedy plays itself out in the work of a very different figure: the staunchest defender of women among the Bolsheviks, Aleksandra Kollontai.

[84] On Platonov and Fedorov, see Elena Tolstaia-Segal, "Ideologicheskie konteksty Platonova," *Russian Literature* 9 (1981): 231–280, and Ayleen Teskey, *Platonov and Fyodorov: The Influence of Christian Philosophy on a Soviet Writer* (Aversham: Avebury, 1982). Platonov discusses Weininger in an early article, "Dusha mira" (1920), reprinted in Andrei Platonov, *Vozvrashchenie* (M.: Molodaia gvardiia, 1989), 21–31. Another writer recalls that Platonov was intensely interested in Weininger and in later years spoke about him "so tenderly and sympathetically, as if the young, misguided Weininger were crying in the next room." Iury Nagibin, "Eshche o Platonove," in *Andrei Platonov: Vospominaniia sovremennikov. Materialy k biografii,* ed. N. V. Kornienko and E. D. Shubina (M.: Sovremennyi pisatel', 1994), 75.

Chapter Six

NEP AS FEMALE COMPLAINT (II):
REVOLUTIONARY ANOREXIA

NEAR THE END of Aleksandra Kollontai's 1923 novella, "Vasilisa Malygina," the eponymous heroine (Vasia, for short) feels compelled to consult a gynecologist. Vasia's periods have stopped, and after a brief, "slightly terrifying" (135) examination the physician arrives at the obvious diagnosis: Vasia is pregnant. Although the child's paternity is not technically in doubt, the scene functions as a twentieth-century materialist's version of the Annunciation, for Vasia has abandoned her NEP-contaminated lover several pages earlier, and to her it seems "as if [Vladimir] were not the father" (136). Vasia begins to dream with delight about how she and her girlfriends will raise the child collectively in a nurturing situation ideal for the formation of a young communist.[1]

At this moment attentive readers of the novella may feel inclined to object. Are we not observing a case of narrative malpractice? The theme of "blood" has played a dominant role so far in the work, with each appearance of the word marking a moment of heightened tension in the plot and indicating the heroine's ideological or sexual repugnance at observed events. Vladimir's alluring mistresses all are healthy women with large, blood-red (*krovavye*) lips, and the proof of his infidelity—one of the work's most dramatic moments—occurs when Vasia arrives for a visit and the couple retires for the night:

---

[1] The novella was originally published in Moscow in 1923 in a collection titled *Liubov' pchel trudovykh* (*The Love of Worker Bees*). All page citations of "Vasilisa Malygina" in my text are to *Svobodnaia liubov'* (Riga: Stock, 1925), a Latvian edition that reprinted the original 1923 text but changed the title—apparently without Kollontai's permission—to "Svobodnaia liubov'" (Free love) to make the book more enticing on the capitalist market. "Vasilisa Malygina" has been translated into English twice, by an anonymous translator as *Red Love* (New York: Seven Arts, 1927) and by Cathy Porter in the collection *Love of Worker Bees* (Chicago: Academy Press, 1978). (In her bibliography of Kollontai's work [in Alexandra Kollontai, *Selected Writings* (London: Alison & Busby, 1977), 322], Alix Holt cites another edition of "Vasilisa Malygina" published in London in 1932 under the title *Free Love*. I have not seen the British edition but suspect that it is a reissue of the 1927 American translation.) Both translations take liberties in attempts to make Kollontai's simple, didactic style more appealing to the Western reader. All translations provided here are mine; I have endeavored to make them as literal as possible.

Vasia began to make the bed and pulled back the blanket. What was that! Her
temples pounded. Her legs shook . . . A woman's bloody bandage . . . On the
sheet there was a bloody stain. (29)

Might Vasia's doctor have confused cause and effect, and might pregnancy
be important primarily as a deus ex machina through which distasteful physiological functioning is brought to a halt? While the gynecologist's diagnosis
would be appropriate in the case of a "real" woman, Vasia is, after all, a
character who has never enjoyed flesh-and-blood existence. Diagnosis in a
text represents less the detection of a medical fact than the manifestation of
authorial (and, perhaps, cultural) repugnance or desire. Can the attentive
reader arrive at another, more textually appropriate, diagnosis, a diagnosis,
furthermore, that speaks to the text's place in Kollontai's oeuvre and the
ideology of NEP?

"Vasilisa Malygina" is essentially a story about what happens to communists during the New Economic Policy. It is a tale of corruption and resistance to corruption, the chief stages for which are the dining-room table and
the bedroom. The pairing of these two arenas should not surprise readers of
the epoch's ideological texts. During NEP, excess in eating and excess in
sexual behavior were two of the traits used to distinguish the bourgeois from
his or her hardworking proletarian counterpart. Sexual consumption and gastronomic consumption were routinely lumped together as signs of social corruption, the oil necessary to the proper functioning of NEP's "pleasure
machine." Books attacked monks and nuns and the "sexual depravity and
corruption so characteristic of the sated [*sytaia*] and idle life in monasteries."[2]
Morality tales written for Komsomol consumption portrayed young women
postcoitus as having "lackluster eyes, hastily arranged hair, and a sated
[*sytoe*], dull expression" on their faces.[3] Aron Zalkind explained that "rich,
secure segments of society, possessing an excess of energy for which they
have no outlet ('fat drives people wild' [*s zhiru besiatsia*]), develop a monstrous sexual sensuality toward which they direct the overwhelming portion
of their parasitic interests."[4] Films routinely depicted Nepmen and Nepwo-
men gorging themselves on rich, sweet foods, and it was normal for a camera to slide from male double chin to ample female breasts or bared thigh.[5]

[2] A. Zorich, untitled review of *Moshchi*, by Iosif Kalinnikov, *Pravda*, 9 April 1926, 5.

[3] Lev Gumilevskii, "Meshchanochka," *Komsomol'skaia pravda*, 15 August 1925, 3.

[4] A. B. Zalkind, *Polovoi vopros v usloviiakh sovetskoi obshchestvennosti* (L.: Gos. izd, 1926),
8.

[5] See, inter alia, Iakov Protozanov's 1924 *Aelita* and Fridrikh Ermler's 1928 *House in the
Snow Drifts* (*Dom v sugrobakh*). In the former, the villain, Viktor Erlikh, enriches himself by
stealing sugar from the Soviet state. In the latter, a well-fed woman speculator hides contraband
under her skirt; she is "delivered" of her treasure, however, by the Cheka. In Oleg Frelikh's
1927 film *The Prostitute* (*Prostitutka*), the opening scenes of debauchery (with titles—by Viktor

Protecting one's ideological purity during NEP entailed not only controlling sexual urges but also refraining from overeating and, in general, from surrounding oneself with opulence. However, just as the dictate to sublimate sexual desires quickly developed into the recommendation that young communists abstain entirely from sexual intercourse (and from all noncollective physical pleasures), so vigilance against gastronomic indulgence and rich living was transformed by reductive logic into a dictate to survive on the minimum quantity of food, sleep, and shelter necessary to sustain human existence. In the puritanical discourse of the 1920s, sexual excess could be equated with the consumption not only of rich foods but of as little as a small piece of bread.[6]

The spartan current in Soviet society of the 1920s was strongly influenced by events in the first year of NEP. The Tenth Party Congress, which in its replacement of grain requisition by taxation effectively inaugurated NEP, spent much of its time coping with rebellious Party factions, among them the so-called Workers' Opposition. Chief among this group's complaints—which were shared by many intellectuals and workers outside the Party—was that the Party leadership had lost touch with its members and, as a consequence, the Party as a whole had become susceptible to penetration by "foreign" elements. The leaders of the Workers' Opposition demanded that Party leaders regularly abandon the lofty comfortable existence of bureaucrats and immerse themselves in the impoverished conditions that defined the everyday lives of real workers.[7] Lenin, in a speech at the congress, acknowledged that while he disagreed with the organizational methods of the Workers' Opposition and with many of its "Menshevik" platforms, he found merit in its attack on the Party's recent and ongoing incorporation of unsuitable members.[8] Following his lead, the congress called for a thorough purge of the Party's membership, an action that became a source of pride in the months to come. "No other party in the world has purged its ranks," one Party journalist declared; "Every party tries to gather as many members and votes as it can. Only our Communist Party tries to achieve the qualitative

---

Shklovskii—such as "The Spirit of Commerce") make the link between lust and gluttony particularly apparent.

[6] Gumilevskii, "Meshchanochka," 3.

[7] For a detailed description of the Workers' Opposition's demands, see Beatrice Farnsworth, *Aleksandra Kollontai: Socialism, Feminism, and the Bolshevik Revolution* (Stanford: Stanford University Press, 1980), 212–283; Larry E. Holmes, *For the Revolution Redeemed: The Workers' Opposition in the Bolshevik Party 1919–1921*, The Carl Beck Papers in Russian and East European Studies, no. 802 (Pittsburgh: University of Pittsburgh Center for Russian and East European Studies, 1990); M. S. Zorkii, *Rabochaia oppozitsiia. Materialy i dokumenty* (M. and L.: Gos. izd., 1926).

[8] V. I. Lenin, "Zakliuchitel'noe slovo po dokladu o edinstve partii i anarkho-sindikalistskom uklone [Desiatyi s"ezd RKP(b)]" (16 March 1921), *Polnoe sobranie sochinenii*, 45 vols. (M.: Politicheskaia literatura, 1958–1965), 43:110.

improvement of its membership."[9] The congress, in addition, commissioned the Central Committee to wage a "decisive battle against the misuse of office and material advantages by Party members" and endorsed "the policy of eliminating differences in the material circumstances of Party members."[10] While the congress did not address the question of material advantages of Party members over the population as a whole, as the purge unfolded, between August and October of 1921, this second question became acutely important in light of the horrible famine raging in the Volga region.

The purge and the famine were the two leading headlines through much of the summer and into the late autumn. It was inevitable that the two topics would be linked. The pages of the provincial press provide a fascinating example of the resulting tensions within the Party during NEP's first summer. On 18 July, Georgy Pletnev, coeditor of the recently launched *Ogni*, the organ of the Voronezh Council of Party Journalists, attacked an author who under the pseudonym of "Communist" had written an article that had demanded better conditions for Party workers:

> Such a Communist is not worth a plugged kopeck. Starve with everybody else, walk about in rags like everybody else, and feel the pain of others' deprivation—that is how a communist should be. That's the only communism that can be recognized as such; those are the only real communists. A communist should be first in line to participate in the foul, oppressively difficult present; only later will he be rewarded with a shining future.[11]

Several days later, responding with a counterattack in the Party's *Voronezhskaia kommuna*, "Communist" proclaimed: "The Party is the brain and head of the entire socialist organism. If the brain and heart grow weak, so will the entire organism." "Communist" defended additional rations for Party workers, who, he asserted, were fulfilling the same function now that soldiers had performed during the Civil War. Most important, "Communist" endeavored to show what would happen if Pletnev's "counterrevolutionary" advice were followed:

> If we have to go down the road of "real communism," then we have to follow it all the way—we should not be satisfied by making ourselves as poor as the most deprived; we should yield to them the lion's share even of the pitiful crumbs that they receive and we should make ourselves poorer and hungrier

---

[9] Nik. Olegov, "Chistka kommunistov-bol'shevikov," *Nasha gazeta* (Voronezh), 4 October 1921, 2. The purge resulted in the expulsion of 20 percent of the Party's membership; another 3 percent left voluntarily. Membership fell from 658,839 to 499,484. Iu. P. Sharapov, *Iz istorii ideologicheskoi bor'by pri perekhode k NEPu* (M.: Nauka, 1990), 32–33.

[10] *Desiatyi s"ezd RKP(b). Stenograficheskii otchet*, 3d ed. (M.: 1963), 567.

[11] G. Pletnev, "O kommuniste," *Ogni*, no. 3 (18 July 1921): 3.

than the poorest of our poor brothers. This is what the logic of your concept of communism demands.[12]

"Communist" was particularly concerned with the religious connotations of Pletnev's position. If the Party were to heed Pletnev, "Communist" wrote, its members would be "transformed from militant revolutionaries with rifles and hammers into Gospel-toting Tolstoians concerned with refraining from sin rather than with annihilating the bourgeoisie." By not eating, the Party would ensure that it would itself be "eaten alive" by a bourgeoisie exuberant over this turn in communist policy. Attacking Pletnev's "counterrevolutionary" obsession with the present, "Communist" urged in the (collectively Nietzschean) language of the Proletkul't that the Party's members needed all their energy if in the midst of "the tremendous storms that are shaking all humanity" they were to continue their struggle to become "true creators, makers of the Man-God."[13]

Ten days later in a letter published in *Voronezhskaia kommuna* Pletnev complained cryptically that he was unable to respond fully to "Communist" "for reasons beyond my control," and called for a public debate with his adversary on "the burning issue" of "asceticism and communism." "Let the masses have their say about the improvement of communists' living standards," he urged; "under today's conditions only a scoundrel is well-off and fills up his stomach." In closing, he wrote, "the Party must share the pain of the poorest peasants and workers; it should not detach itself from the masses."[14]

Andrei Platonov, then a prolific young local journalist at the start of his literary career, sided with Pletnev in an impassioned article entitled "Communist! Prove you're a communist!" that called upon all Party members to donate "everything necessary" to their starving brothers: "A comrade who doesn't meet this responsibility should be ashamed of himself and have a bad conscience."[15]

The debate in the Voronezh press was not explicitly about NEP. The question of economic well-being, however, was inextricably linked to the wisdom of the Party's new policy. Writing several days later in a special "Party Issue" of *Pravda*, Evgeny Preobrazhensky attacked communists who were still confused about the propriety of the Party's current course. If in March such ideological doubts had been "natural or forgivable," they were impermissible now, when it was "necessary to awake in the masses of the Party an appetite [*probudit' appetit*] for management, for deficit-free, profitable man-

---

[12] Kommunist, "Asketizm ili kommunizm," *Voronezhskaia kommuna*, 11 August 1921, 3.

[13] Ibid.

[14] "Pis'ma chitatelei," *Voronezhskaia kommuna*, 21 August 1921, 4. The relegation of Pletnev's comments to the letters page and the tenor of his remarks suggests that he himself may have been purged from the Party.

[15] Firsov (Andrei Platonov), "Kommunist! Pokazhi, chto ty kommunist," *Voronezhskaia kommuna*, 10 August 1921, 1.

agement of the socialist economy."[16] Preobrazhensky himself was soon voicing doubts about the inequitable distribution of wealth that NEP had produced in the countryside, where economic "appetite" fast became an identifying attribute of the kulak, but the language of his initial, authoritative promotion of the policy indicates the extent to which food served in 1921 as an ideological figure. The promotion of NEP as an appetite stimulant at a time of great famine struck some communists as virtually obscene; Pletnev and Platonov plainly saw collective, empathic hunger as more in keeping with their view of the communist ideal.[17]

The Party's Central Control Commission, instituted shortly before the Tenth Party Congress, did not use language as impassioned as Platonov's, but it too viewed as essential to the proper conduct of a communist the rejection of all indulgences associated with NEP. Successfully arguing in 1922 for the permanent retention of the Central Control Commission and its local appendages within the Party's organizational structure, Aron Sol'ts, one of its prominent members, declared that under NEP the behavior of communists would be held to more rigorous standards of discipline than had hitherto been the case:

> In the past, a communist could preserve himself as a communist [*sokhranit' sebia v kachestve kommunista*] simply by carrying out decrees and following the path laid down by the Party, but now, under the new economic conditions, that is simply not enough. A communist must know that we do not allow ourselves to take advantage of the concessions we are making to the petty bourgeoisie and peasantry. We may have decided to permit commerce, but this does not mean that a communist can trade. We may have offered petty bourgeois elements the opportunity to enrich themselves because our own efforts will not suffice to get production going again, but this doesn't mean that communists may enrich themselves. The [Central] Control Commission has already seen many cases of [communists enriching themselves]. [. . .] A permanent organ must exist to fight corruption arising in this direction.[18]

It was NEP and its temptations, Sol'ts argued, that required the Party to monitor ethical behavior. "Now discipline is many times more essential than earlier," he warned.[19]

---

[16] Evgenii Preobrazhenskii, "Bol'she vnimaniia partii," *Pravda*, 17 August 1921, 1. In this article Preobrazhenskii used the term "appetite" twice to refer to profitable economic conduct.

[17] The circumstances behind his departure are not yet clear, but within a couple of months, Platonov was no longer a member of the Party. E. D. Shubina, "Sozertsatel' i deiatel' (1899–1926)," in Shubina and N. Kornienko, *Andrei Platonov. Vospominaniia sovremennikov. Materialy k biografii* (M.: Sovremennyi pisatel', 1994), 139–140 (138–154).

[18] *Odinnadtsatyi s"ezd rossiiskoi kommunisticheskoi partii (bol'shevikov). Stenograficheskii otchet* (M.: Ts.K.R.K.P., 1922), 150–151.

[19] Ibid., 152.

Asceticism has a rich tradition in Russian cultural history, and we should not be surprised to find it in a Revolutionary incarnation.[20] In the context of NEP, however, this latest hypostasis played a part in a unique, historical constellation of cultural and ideological factors, and close "listening" to the utterances it produced can shed interesting light on the fantasies and fears of early Soviet society. The question of Revolutionary asceticism, under the star of which NEP was born, would continue to plague the Party long after the horrors of the Volga famine had receded into the past. Throughout the next half-dozen years communists would be repeatedly cautioned against excessive asceticism (and, implicitly, against a communist monasticism that would uncomfortably associate the Party with the Church) at the same time as the campaign against dissolute behavior made asceticism a more likely reaction. And nourishment, like sexuality, would continue to play a role in this debate, in part because, at least during the early years of NEP, many Soviet citizens *did* hunger, even in areas not struck by famine.[21] Under these circumstances, the body became an appropriate canvas for the painting of ideological portraits, its shape and functions serving as indicia of a commitment to either proletarian solidarity or the depraved pursuit of pleasure. A double chin, fat belly, and large bust symbolized the Nepman (or *nepmansha*) and, shortly after, the kulak. Poor eating and weight loss functioned as signs of the preceding, War Communist period, but paradoxically were often *positive* signs, indicative of unwavering attachment to an increasingly distant collectivist ideal. Oral as well as genital asceticism functioned as behavioral identity cards for the ideologically committed builders of communist society.

Where women were concerned, secondary sex characteristics—or the relative lack thereof—were extremely useful in ideological portraiture. Skinny women were stylish throughout Europe and in the United States for most of the decade; for example, the flapper cut her hair short and concealed her bosom under loose clothing. Under NEP the thin female body was not only fashionable; it was invested with ideological purity, while its antipode—the

---

[20] The debate about the material welfare of the Party had a precedent as far back as the battle in the fifteenth century over the propriety of the Orthodox Church's ownership of property. See A. Arkhangel'skii, "Nil Sorskii," *Entsiklopedicheskii slovar'*, 86 vols. (Iaroslavl: Brokgauz-Efron [Terra], 1890–1907 [1990]), 21:150–152.

[21] A 1922 study reported that throughout Russia average body weight had fallen by 20 to 30 percent over the past few years. The author of this study, one of the leading figures in Soviet biology, attributed much of the national weight loss to psychological factors:

Doctors have noticed that in the last few Revolutionary years their patients frequently complained of excessive defecation. This can be explained partially by the change in the quality of food—when one survives on a largely vegetable diet the amount of nondigestible material is much greater. But it is also highly likely that a significant portion of that which might have been mastered by the human intestine remained undigested as a result of poor work by a digestive system upset by nervous disequilibrium. (N. K. Kol'tsov, *Prichiny sovremennogo iskhudaniia* [Pb.: Vremia, 1922], 46)

woman who could not be confused with a man—was not simply "old-fashioned" but the Enemy.

Nastia, the heroine of Leonid Leonov's *The Badgers* (1924), serves as an early example of the ideal female type under NEP. Leonov, a fellow traveler whose work in the 1920s sought to capture aesthetically the ideological anxieties of the age, informs his reader several times that Nastia resembles a boy and has a flat chest, a detail that in its repetition virtually becomes a poetic epithet. Eventually, Nastia's small bosom is important to the plot; she is able to disguise herself as a boy in order to join a band of latter-day Razins in their forest lair. "In the door stood a stately lad of about twenty-two, with Nastia's looks, as if he were her younger brother. The usual dull color of her skin hid the femininity of her face. Semen's wide shirt, adroitly tied with a bridle strap, masked her female appearance."[22] Other women in the novel are neither so fortunate nor so protean. When watching Katia, the novel's incarnation of female sexuality, undress, Nastia fearfully compares her own thin body with the more ample figure of her contemporary, "as if she foresaw in [Katia's body] a threat to herself."[23]

Of the various parts and functions of the female body, however, the uterus and its potential accessibility to penetration appear to have aroused the most anxiety. The foundational gesture (hysterectomy) in Platonov's "Ivan Zhokh" is an exceptionally clear case of this anxiety's intensity and of the representational lengths to which speakers would go in resolving it, but we find other instances of uneasiness in a variety of texts. Dr. A. B. Gofmekler, author of the hygiene brochure *What a Woman Should Know about Herself*, considered that a woman should know the following: "[The inner reproductive organs] resemble a bat, if you extend its wings to the sides. The mouse [i.e., the center of the bat] would be the uterus, and the ligaments or lateral folds would be the bat's wings."[24] Such impressionistic, repugnant, and non-Revolutionary metaphors do not appear ever to have been deployed to explain male physiology. Dr. Ia. D. Golomb, whose *Sexual Life: Normal and Abnormal* described the uterus as a "squashed pear" and the fallopian tubes as "tentacles," employed an image much more consonant with the Revolution's usual iconography when speaking of male anatomy: "The male sexual organs are a complex apparatus that may be compared with a railroad line equipped in its principal sector with a productive center. This is called the 'testicle.'"[25] The incorporation of male physiology into ideologically positive images and the resigning of female physiology to ideologically discordant, or even disgusting, representations had important parallels when gender en-

[22] Leonid Leonov, *Barsuki* (M. and L.: Gos. izd., 1927 [1924]), 234.

[23] Ibid., 87

[24] A. B. Gofmekler, *Chto dolzhna znat' o sebe zhenshchina* (M.: Gos. izd., 1925), 7.

[25] Dr. Ia. D. Golomb, *Polovaia zhizn': normal'naia i nenormal'naia* (Odessa: Chernomorskii meditsinsko-sanitarnyi otdel, 1926), 4, 6–7.

tered into discussions of sublimation. Could specifically female sexual functioning be sublimated? If so, how would one demonstrate that such sublimation was occurring? Conversely, what kind of evidence could serve as proof
of noncompliance?

It is in this context that we ought to approach the ideological function of
menstruation. During the NEP era, menstruation—or, more precisely, its absence—came to serve as a reminder of a precapitalist, protocommunist
Golden Age. Already we have seen Liadov treating nonseasonal desire as a
by-product of private property. According to him, the natural sexual rhythm
of human beings had been disrupted by capitalism, and he considered current
female physiology to be this disruption's most prominent sign. Liadov held
up the animal kingdom, in which female animals are sexually available only
once a year, as an example of "natural" sexual behavior; he implied that
precisely this allegedly natural situation would prevail again in communist
society, by which time contemporary woman's hypertrophied sexuality
would atrophy. Zalkind went further, dwelling in detail on the modus by
which capitalism and the market had led man—or, more precisely, woman—
to lose his (or her) biological link to nature.[26] As we have seen, the health
commissar Nikolai Semashko observed that menstruation antedated capitalism, and proposed that the propagation of faulty science be replaced by
education about internal secretion and the value of sublimation.[27]

Liadov and Zalkind did not invent their theory of culturally induced sexual availability out of whole cloth. Most likely the idea was derived from the
Finnish anthropologist Edward Westermarck, whose belief that "the pairing
of our earliest human or half-human ancestors [. . .] was restricted to a certain season of the year"[28] was cited by Engels in *The Origin of the Family,
Private Property and the State.*[29] Although Westermarck did not directly refer to menstruation in his discussion of seasonal mating, the notion that
primitive women did not menstruate but went into heat annually was certainly implicit in his equation of early human beings with "lower" animal
species.[30] Without citing him as the origin of their "wide range of historical

[26] Zalkind, *Polovoi vopros*, 23–28.

[27] N. Semashko, "Kak ne nado pisat' o polovom voprose," *Izvestiia*, 1 January 1925, 5. Cited
in my introduction, above.

[28] Edward Westermarck, *The History of Human Marriage*, 5th ed., 3 vols. (London: Macmillan, 1925), 1:81. Originally published in 1891.

[29] Frederick Engels, *The Origin of the Family, Private Property and the State*, trans. Alick
West (New York: International Publishers, 1970), 115.

[30] Westermarck's views on seasonal mating were adopted by several figures in late-nineteenth-century Europe, including the English feminist Elizabeth Wolstenholme Elly, who attributed menstruation to centuries of "masculine abuse" and sought to free women from "bodily
subjection." See Sheila Jeffreys, *The Spinster and Her Enemies: Feminism and Sexuality 1880–
1930* (London: Pandora, 1985), 32–34; Thomas Laqueur, *Making Sex: Body and Gender from
the Greeks to Freud* (Cambridge: Harvard University Press, 1990), 152, 216.

sources," Liadov and Zalkind built on Westermarck's conclusion that "the more man has abandoned natural life out of doors, the more luxury has increased and his habits have got refined, the greater is the variability to which his sexual life has become subject, and the smaller has been the influence exerted upon it by the changes of the seasons."[31] They transformed this hypothesis by projecting it into the arena of class warfare. Young cadres under Liadov's tutelage at the Sverdlov Communist University learned that year-round sexual desire was the product not only of the progress of civilization but of the growth of capitalism and the market. They could find additional confirmation for the pathological nature of menstruation by referring to Nemilov's dramatic treatment of menarche as *the* moment of stark transition from a woman's "happy childhood" to her regular, tragic subservience to the dictatorship of sex.[32]

While Nemilov's approach to menstruation is more medical and "scientific" than "Marxist" (Zalkind) or "historical" (Liadov), history on one occasion does enter into his account; he mentions that, in 1919 and 1920, women across Russia became amenorrheic from lack of proper nourishment.[33] This detail of menstruation's cessation during difficult or turbulent times was pervasive in sexual education pamphlets of the period,[34] and commentators seeking to influence the sexual conduct of Soviet youth during NEP seized upon this fact as *positive* experimental data. In *What Is Essential to Know about the Sexual Question*, ten thousand copies of which were published in 1925, Dr. M. Lemberg wrote:

---

[31] Westermarck, *The History of Human Marriage*, 1:101.

[32] A. V. Nemilov, *Biologicheskaia tragediia zhenshchiny*, 2d ed. (L.: Seiatel', 1925), 73. Nemilov did not insist on the historical abnormality of menstruation. Rather, he contended that since menstruation had always been present, it, like all other components of woman's "biological tragedy," barred the way to genuine sexual equality. His description of woman's monthly torture as a "wave" that sweeps through her body and overcomes her will does not seem to have differed significantly from Western models. See Louise Lander, *Images of Bleeding: Menstruation as Ideology* (New York: Orlando Press, 1988), 40–41. Nor do Nemilov's views on menstruation as habitual disequilibrium diverge widely from the pre-Revolutionary viewpoint of P. I. Kovalevskii, a professor at Kazan University and an expert in forensic psychiatry. P. I. Kovalevskii, "Menstrual'noe sostoianie i menstrual'nye psikhozy," *Arkhiv psikhiatrii, nevrologii i sudebnoi psikhopatologii* 23, no. 1 (1894): 73–79. (For the place of Kovalevskii's views in the context of pre-Revolutionary beliefs about female sexual deviance, see Laura Engelstein, *The Keys to Happiness: Sex and the Search for Modernity in Fin-de-Siècle Russia* (Ithaca: Cornell University Press, 1992), 128–167.) The only significant difference on this point between Nemilov and Kovalevskii is that the latter maintains an ever imperiled distinction between "normal" and "abnormal" menstruation, while the former considers all menstruation pathological. What links Nemilov's account to those of Zalkind and Liadov is that all three view female physiology as being at odds with the realization of Revolutionary ideals.

[33] Nemilov, *Biologicheskaia tragediia*, 2d ed., 82.

[34] See, for example, Dr. M. A. Shestakova, *Chto dolzhna znat' o svoem zdorov'e kazhdaia zhenshchina* (M. and L.: Kooperativnoe izdatel'stvo, 1925), 11.

When we look soberly at the matter, it becomes clear that sexual abstinence, especially during youth, cannot be harmful. On the contrary, it is extremely beneficial for the growing and developing organism and strengthens the nervous system.

However strong the sexual instinct, in healthy people it surfaces only when all other essential bodily requirements have been met—food, water, and warmth.

The massive proof of this can be seen during periods of hunger. During extended periods of malnourishment sexual attraction weakens and is even temporarily extinguished in men. In some women menstruation (the monthly flow of blood connected with the maturation of female reproductive cells) ceases.

Energy that enters the youthful organism in the form of food and drink usually is expended in its entirety in the satisfaction of the intense demands of growth. Where there is sufficient physical work no excess remains.[35]

Was Lemberg implying that harboring excess energy was *more* dangerous than having too little? On which side was it better to err? Was he hinting that menstruation—which he analogized to male sexual excitement—might be sublimated just like sexual arousal?

In the 1920s, writers of various degrees of sophistication consistently linked menstruation and ejaculation as analogous functions, both of which entailed the "external" secretion of hormonal products.[36] Internal secretion by the sex glands led to the construction of a healthy body, while external emissions, especially if "excessive," were thought to weaken the body. Interestingly, in discussions about limiting external secretions, texts that hitherto had been dealing with male and female endocrinology abruptly shifted their focus to the excreting male body, and so semen, rather than blood, was viewed as evidence of hormonal disequilibrium. Measures to limit (or repress) menstruation were never mentioned, and so the process of female "external hormonal secretion" remained an implicitly dangerous problem lurking unsolved beyond the page.[37] In passages such as Lemberg's, however, War Communist amenorrhea emerges as an example of the way menstruation might be "solved" in a Revolutionary milieu, and we should read his attention to the absence of menstruation during the Civil War as analogous to Liadov's and Zalkind's nostalgia for a golden precapitalist age when women bled only once a year. In a culture where near-starvation and poor health could function as measures of ideological chastity, a plus rather than a minus might well be placed in front of amenorrhea. How, for instance, did

[35] Dr. M. Lemberg, *Chto neobkhodimo znat' o polovom voprose* (L.: Priboi, 1925), 42.

[36] Golomb, *Polovaia zhizn'*, 7; V. Bekhterev, *Znachenie polovogo vlecheniia v zhiznedeiatel'nosti organizma* (M.: Narkomzdrav R.S.F.S.R., 1928), 14–15.

[37] See, for example, Ia. I. Kaminskii, *Polovaia zhizn' i fizicheskaia kul'tura* (Odessa: Svetoch, 1927), 12–15, and Bekhterev, *Znachenie polovogo vlecheniia*, 14–18.

readers of sexual surveys respond when informed that owing to poor living conditions menarche occurred much later in prolctarian and peasant girls than in their petty bourgeois contemporaries?[38] Interclass comparisons were a common feature in such statistical enterprises undertaken with regard to masturbation, venereal disease, and frequenting of prostitutes—in each case to the bourgeoisie's detriment and the proletariat's advantage.[39] Soviet commentators on the sexual question criticized the early age at which Soviet youth engaged in sexual relations.[40] Once menstruation had been associated with sexual desire and pathology, was delayed menarche understood as class-conscious and beneficial? Late-nineteenth-century European and American doctors commonly equated early menarche and frequent menstrual flow with excessive desire.[41] Were these elements, too, being projected into the context of class conflict and being drawn into the overall pattern of emerging Soviet asceticism?

This constellation of questions about the ideological significance of female physiology, along with the idealization during NEP of a proletarian body from which all fat has been purged, raise the question of whether we might usefully speak of "Revolutionary anorexia" as a "disease" affecting Soviet society during NEP. Such an approach, however tentative, would take seriously the metaphor of the collective body propounded so insistently during the War Communist era and recalled so nostalgically by many writers, educators, and Party workers during NEP. Moreover, this socioclinical approach would be in keeping with Soviet models of sociopsychological health utilized during the NEP era. We have already seen Brukhansky grope for symptomatic meaning in "popular" events like violent crimes and domestic disputes; writers in the Komsomol press also were adept at using metaphors of illness and health in their analyses of social problems. According to Mikhail Reisner, one of the more thoughtful early Soviet critics of psychoanalysis, the problem with Freud's equation of various neuroses with social institutions was that the author of *Totem and Taboo* failed in his social diagnoses to take seriously his own analogies between individual and collective neuroses. If we agree with Freud, Reisner explained:

---

[38] S. Ia. Golosovker, *K voprosu o polovom byte sovremennoi zhenshchiny Kazani* (Kazan': Kazan'skii meditsinskii zhurnal, 1925), 8.

[39] "Anketa o polovoi zhizni studentov Kom. Un-ta," *Zapiski kommunisticheskogo universiteta imeni Sverdlova* 1 (1923): 370 (370–409); Golosovker, *K voprosu o polovom byte*, 11; N. V. Gushchin, *Rezul'taty polovogo obsledovaniia molodezhi g. Iakutska* (Iakutsk: Narkomproszdrav, 1925), 44.

[40] V. Gorinevskii, "Polovoi vopros," *Komsomol'skaia pravda*, 29 January 1926, 3; N. Semashko, "Polovoe vospitanie i zdorov'e," *Komsomol'skaia pravda* 15 August 1925, 4; A. B. Zalkind, *Polovoi fetishizm. K peresmotru polovogo voprosa* (M.: Vserossiiskii proletkul't, 1925), 30.

[41] Lander, *Images of Bleeding*, 20–21.

We can diagnose a personality—but never a society—as sick and subject it to treatment. From this follows the completely logical conclusion that an individual who in the grip of sexual ideation vents repressed desires by creating various symptoms is a neurotic. But a society acting in the same way is a healthy society, one that saves repressed energy through sublimation. And if as a result of this sublimation we obtain results completely analogous to a neurosis, then [according to Freud] they do not count. Here society seeks refuge in and appeals to a new, higher authority—history itself.[42]

This distinction between individual and social mental disease, Reisner argued, had no justification. The marriage of Marxism and Freudianism, he urged, would be a branch of sociological medicine that diagnosed and treated social neuroses.

Is there a fundamental difference between individual and social symptoms that would render a psychoanalytic diagnosis of social neurosis untenable? Although initially it might seem strange to use terms such as repression, hysteria, the uncanny, and anorexia in speaking about a discrete historical epoch, the reader should remember that even in their application to the individual mind and body these terms are interpretive tools or models used by the analyst to help her decode somatic and verbal language. They may be equally useful or limited in interpretations of *cultural* responses, including readings of ideology. Of course, the distinctness of the individual body makes its symptoms more concrete and recognizable. An individual symptom, however, must still be "read," integrated into a particular discourse. As P. Hamburg writes, "The symptom is a sign, and like all signs carries a complex register of symbolic meanings." "A form of communication," "an act of mental architecture that both embodies and mitigates suffering," the creation of a symptom

> permits the preservation of a measure of integrity instead of a free-fall into chaos. [. . .] The symptom arises in response to an impasse (developmental, psychological, biological) that threatens to disrupt the self. The symptom manifests the ongoing pain of that impasse, while significantly containing its psychological consequences.[43]

We may study a historical period through the analysis of its discursive—or figurative—symptoms, which is precisely what I have been doing in previous chapters. When drawn into a systemic whole, the bizarre image, the

[42] M. A. Reisner, "Freidizm i burzhuaznaia ideologiia," introduction to V. Fittel's *Freid: ego lichnost' uchenie i shkola* (L.: Gos. izd., 1925), 31. For an overview of early Soviet views on Freud, see Aleksandr Etkind, *Eros nevozmozhnogo: istoriia psikhoanaliza v Rossii* (SPb.: Meduza, 1993); Martin A. Miller, "Freudian Theory under Bolshevik Rule: The Theoretical Controversy during the 1920s," *Slavic Review* 44 (1985): 625–646.

[43] P. Hamburg, "Bulimia: The Construction of a Symptom," *Journal of the American Academy of Psychoanalysis* 17 (1989): 134 (131–139).

unspoken and often illogical assumption underlying an argument, and the unveiling of a new scientific hypothesis all help us chart ideological anxieties and desires as much as the investigation of psychosomatic paralyses, stutters, and mysterious pains provides a key to understanding an individual's repressed wishes and fears. The ideological or cultural diagnostician must proceed with care, for her enterprise depends mightily on the degree to which a discourse centers on questions of internal cohesion. In a context where the demand for collective unity is high, however, reading discourse symptomatically can help historians grasp the relationship between utterances and piece together a collective text that issues forth—as "an act of communication and self-preservation"—from the collective body.[44] In the remarks to come I will, in effect, be picking up the trail of many Soviet writers of the period and actualizing, even narrativizing, a corporal metaphor. What follows is an analytical experiment in personification, a trope that was, as we have seen, a dominant rhetorical figure for the ideology of the age. The "incarnation" of communist theory in Soviet Russia relied on implicit notions about the necessity of giving ideology a collective body. I intend to trace the particular contours of that body as it was repeatedly figured in the ideology of NEP. Anorexia will be less a diagnosis than a scholar's analytical tool.

How does anorexia apply to and help us understand the discourse of NEP? The psychoanalytic and psychodynamic theories surrounding anorexia are diverse; original hypotheses associating the condition with "the symbolization of pregnancy fantasies involving the gastro-intestinal tract"[45] have long been abandoned, and the disorder "has been reinterpreted along the lines of each new development in psychoanalytic thought, so that to trace the history of its explanatory literature is almost to follow the historical course of psychoanalysis itself."[46] In general, however, while views on the condition's etiology vary greatly, contemporary psychoanalytic and psychodynamic studies of the problem tend to agree that although anorexia primarily manifests itself as an eating disorder, it also is—primarily—a mental condition motivated by hatred and fear of the body, a "disease" that seeks to demonstrate its mastery over that body by *willing* the body into virtual oblivion. Trying to devise a "multi-dimensional" definition of anorexia, Paul E. Garfinkel and David M. Garner find at the disease's core "concern about con-

---

[44] For a discussion of "symptomatic" textual analysis, see Jane Gallop's *Around 1981* (New York: Routledge, 1992), 2–10.

[45] John V. Waller, M. Ralph Kaufman, and Felix Deutsch, "Anorexia Nervosa: A Psychosomatic Entity," in *Evolution of Psychosomatic Concepts. Anorexia Nervosa: A Paradigm*, ed. M. Ralph Kaufman and Marcel Heiman (New York: International Universities Press, 1964 [1940]), 260 (245–273).

[46] Jules R. Bemporad and David B. Herzog, introduction to *Journal of the American Academy of Psychoanalysis* 17 (1989): 1 (1–3).

trol" over the body and the consequences of submitting to natural development. The adolescent starving herself to the point where she resembles "a walking skeleton,"[47] "characteristic female body curves disappear,"[48] and menstruation ceases is declaring war on her physical, sexual self and on "aspects traditionally binding the female to the material earth."[49] Anorexia is not a form of symbolic suicide or attempted suicide, Garfinkel and Garner emphasize, but "a statement about autonomy."[50] "Anorexics," they say, "have a sense of anhedonia [lack of pleasure] with a desire to remove the physical and live only through their mental beings."[51] The denial of pleasure, in conjunction with hostility toward physiology and, above all, with the violent rejection of sexual desire, is part of the anorexic's strategy to regain control over a real world slipping through her grasp. It is, to use the language of the Soviet 1920s, a desperate form of corporal "sublimation."[52]

[47] Hilde Bruch, *The Golden Cage: The Enigma of Anorexia Nervosa* (Cambridge: Harvard University Press, 1978), 2.

[48] Paul E. Garfinkel and David M. Garner, *Anorexia Nervosa: A Multidimensional Perspective* (New York: Brunner/Mazel, 1982), 14.

[49] Angelyn Spignesi, *Starving Women: A Psychology of Anorexia Nervosa* (Dallas: Spring Publications, 1983), 5.

[50] Garfinkel and Garner, *Anorexia Nervosa*, 10.

[51] Ibid.

[52] Although initially anorexia seems an analytical model far removed from that of Gothic literature, there is considerable overlap between these two models from two distinctly different fields. Freud's own clinical narratives have been compared to Gothic writing (see, in particular, Michelle A. Massé's reading of Freud's "Dora" in *In the Name of Love: Women, Masochism, and the Gothic* (Ithaca: Cornell University Press, 1992), 16–18) and may represent a unique positivist offspring of the genre. Where anorexia is concerned, clinical first impressions of anorexics by the doctors who treat and write about them nearly always have Gothic overtones. Patients are invariably "cadaverous females" (Spignesi, *Starving Women*, 10) with "hair like that of a corpse, dry and lustreless" (Garfinkel and Garner, *Anorexia Nervosa*, 14). Bruch provides the following description of a patient before treatment:

> When she came for consultation she looked like a walking skeleton[. . . .] Most striking was the face—hollow like that of a shriveled up old woman with a wasting disease, sunken eyes, a sharply pointed nose on which the juncture between bone and cartilage was visible. When she spoke or smiled—and she was quite cheerful—one could see every movement of the muscles around her mouth and eyes, like an animated anatomical representation of the skull. (*The Golden Cage*, 2)

Spignesi, in her analysis of the condition, writes that the anorexic "evokes memories of shades, ghosts and hags and carries up to us the world of shade, specifically the shade of the female" (*Starving Women*, 10). John A. Sours calls anorexics "caricatures of Modigliani sculptures with their gothic, ethereal verticality." "Their facial muscles," he adds, "stand out in relief, creating an eerie image, like a skull on display in an anatomy laboratory." *Starving to Death in a Sea of Objects: The Anorexia Nervosa Syndrome* (New York: Jason Aronson, 1980), 4. In present-day Western societies one can read anorexia as a horrific Gothic projection of the ideal woman; Susie Orbach's comments that the anorexic "is a caricature of the message beamed at all

Anorexia most often surfaces in adolescence, a stage when the attractions of a secure childhood are still strong and stand in stark opposition to the complicated, insecure world of adulthood lying ahead. A patient of Hilda Bruch's—an analyst who sees the anorexic's hatred of the female body and rejection of sexuality as motivated by a fear of failure and of "ordinariness"—concludes that "anorexia nervosa isn't an attempt to make yourself suffer; it's an attempt, from a postlapsarian vantage point, to recapture Eden."[53] A. H. Crisp, one of the more prolific writers on the topic, reaches a similar conclusion, writing that in the anorexic's body "mature biological sexuality is eliminated from the system [and] childhood is biologically reestablished."[54] R. A. Geist sees the condition as a form of "disintegration anxiety," as a "desperate attempt to preserve a sense of an integrated, purer self which seems to be breaking up in the context of an apparently changing environment."[55]

To summarize, anorexia is a condition that may occur when illusions of security and self-worth founder on the shoals of the daunting realities of adult life in the real world. As a patient of Bruch's succinctly states, "When you are so unhappy and you don't know how to accomplish anything, then to have control over your body becomes a supreme accomplishment. You make out of your body your very own kingdom where you are the tyrant, the absolute dictator."[56] Frustrated by feeling powerless in adult society, the adolescent can do things to and with her own body. It becomes a convenient arena for the acting out and self-deceptive "mastering" of real-world failures and fears.

During NEP what motivated the turn against the body, the abrupt about-face from an imagery of corporal strength and harmony to one of bodily corruption and danger? The analogy with anorexia would suggest that as the dream of Worldwide Revolution faded, as a totally noncapitalist economy appeared increasingly unrealistic, as self-assurance yielded to disillusion-

---

women" and that her condition is "a parodoxical embodiment of stereotyped femininity and its very opposite" sound quite similar to analyses of the Gothic by recent feminist critics. Susie Orbach, "Visibility/Invisibility: Social Considerations in Anorexia Nervosa—A Feminist Perspective," in *Theory and Treatment of Anorexia Nervosa and Bulimia: Biomedical, Sociocultural, and Psychological Perspectives*, ed. Steven Wiley Emmett (New York: Brunner/Mazel, 1985), 137 (127–138). Both critical studies of the Gothic and clinical studies of anorexia center on issues of corporal boundaries, self-control, purity, and preservation of a childhood utopia.

[53] Bruch, *The Golden Cage*, 71.

[54] A. H. Crisp, "Diagnosis and Outcome of Anorexia Nervosa: The St. George's View," *Proceedings of the Royal Society of Medicine* 70 (1977): 465 (464–470).

[55] R. A. Geist, "Self Psychological Reflections on the Origins of Eating Disorders," *Journal of the American Academy of Psychoanalysis* 17 (1989): 13 (5–27).

[56] Bruch, *The Golden Cage*, 62.

ment, the collective body that had seen itself expanding indefinitely to include

> everything that can move
> and everything that cannot move
> and everything that barely moves[57]

turned inward and initiated an ascetic purge of its basic functions. The targets of the collective corporal purge were much like those of the individual anorexic. Excess fat became all fat; promiscuity became any sexual behavior; excessive pleasure become any pleasure—all in the name of exerting "inwardly" control that could no longer be exercised domestically or abroad. The body was the staging ground for an assault against national, political, and economic ordinariness and against the temporal cycles of unexceptional, everyday life (*byt*). Menstruation, depicted in patriarchal, Western societies since at least the nineteenth century as useless, nonproductive, repetitive action,[58] provided a convenient forum for channeling cultural, political, and economic anxieties. In other words, menstruation was the latest incarnation of "bad infinity." Prior to the Revolution, with the notable exception of the work of Fedorov, science had not penetrated the discourse of utopian philosophy. Now, in a culture that worshiped materialism and science, the nitty-gritty of female sexual physiology was fair game for the latest speculation about pitfalls on the road to an ideal state of communal being.

In the analogy between the psychologies of the anorexic and NEP, individual adolescence—the "transitional time" (*perekhodnoe vremia*)[59] of individual physiology when insecurities of sexual adult life arise and childish fantasies are tested against the unsympathetic real world—corresponds to the "transitional time" (*perekhodnoe vremia*)[60] of communist society in the 1920s; the anorexic's nostalgia for childhood had its counterpart in yearning for the simpler time of War Communism.

There is, however, a fundamental difference between anorexia in an individual woman and that of Soviet ideology under NEP. The individual anorexic who sees her body as "a despicable threat and not an object of pleasure or beauty"[61] and who "reveals a gross mistrust of the body to carry out automatic regulatory processes without conscious control"[62] suffers from

---

[57] V. V. Maiakovskii, "150,000,000" (1921), *Sochineniia v trekh tomakh* (M.: Khudozhestvennaia literatura, 1965), 3:99.

[58] See Emily Martin's excellent study of the metaphors of menstruation in her *The Woman in the Body: A Cultural Analysis of Reproduction* (Boston: Beacon Press, 1987), 27–53.

[59] Lemberg, *Chto neobkhodimo znat'*, 37.

[60] "O partetike. Proekt predlozhenii Prezidiuma TsKK II Plenumu TsKK RKP(b)," in *Partiinaia etika. Diskussii 20-kh godov*, ed. A. A. Guseinov, M. V. Iskrov, and R. V. Petropavlovskii (M.: Politicheskaia literatura, 1989), 161 (151–170).

[61] Sours, *Starving to Death*, 226.

[62] Garfinkel and Garner, *Anorexia Nervosa*, 149.

what M. Selvini Palazzoli calls "intrapersonal paranoia."[63] For the anorexic, hatred of the female body is self-hatred. For the would-be collective body of NEP, hatred of the female body was hatred of that part of the self which had been made "other." Gynocidal figures in NEP discourse reduced half the population to objects of a purging frenzy while leaving the bodies of the other half "untouched." Female physiology and female sexuality symbolized the disorganized corrupted body and the biological scars left by capitalism; although one can find instances—such as the castration of her husband by Anastasia E.—where an author's depiction of the desexing of the *male* body responds to social fears and desires, in fiction and in pedagogic and medical literature woman bears the brunt of the assault against the flesh.[64]

The campaign against the body and its female incarnation was not waged by men only. Rather, the campaign was an *ideological* assault rooted in the "language" of NEP.[65] Women, too, participated in the purging of the feminine, and a startling example is provided by the articles and fiction of the "feminist" Aleksandra Kollontai.

The daughter of a military officer, Kollontai was born in Saint Petersburg in 1872 and spent many of her adult years in Europe as a Marxist propagandist and scholar of the "woman question." Returning to Russia in 1917, she played an active role in the founding of the Soviet state. In October 1917, Kollontai was a member of the Central Committee that authorized the Party's seizure of power, and after the Revolution she became the nation's first commissar of public welfare and later director of the Party's Women's Division. From 1923 until the end of the Second World War, she served as a Soviet diplomat and ambassador in Norway, Mexico, and Sweden.

Recent historical studies have portrayed Kollontai as a "Bolshevik feminist," a crusader for women's rights and sexual freedom in a class-conscious society.[66] This view does not conflict with the opinions of her detractors in

[63] Cited in Sours, *Starving to Death*, 213.

[64] Anorexia, too, does not "attack" only women. Male sufferers are, however, much rarer. See Bruch, *The Golden Cage*, viii.

[65] It is worth noting that this discursive campaign had a corollary in economic life. Writing in *Kommunistka* in 1921, I. Lerner complained that in the transition to the new, semicapitalist economy women were being purged wholesale, that they were the first "inefficiency" attacked in the drive for greater productivity. "The simple, clear measures now required by our new economic life, along the rails of which we are moving with such difficulty, have nothing in common and can have nothing in common with the [current] outrage of wholesale, unfounded removal of women [from the workforce], which, needless to say, no one will allow to grow into a 'system.'" "Zhenskii trud i novaia ekonomicheskaia politika," *Kommunistka*, nos. 16–17 (1921): 15 (12–16). In fact, the discursive system of NEP did operate upon the principle of "removing" women, or, at least, upon negating femininity in its rawest, most dangerous forms—those physiological processes and bodily parts upon which the anxieties of economic and social contamination were most easily projected.

[66] See, inter alia, Barbara Evans Clements, *Bolshevik Feminist: The Life of Aleksandra Kollontai* (Bloomington: Indiana University Press, 1979); and Iring Fetscher, afterword to Alex-

the early 1920s. She was attacked by critics of various ideological persuasions for encouraging libertinism in Soviet youth.[67] But how radical was Kollontai in the early 1920s? Did her writings manage to challenge the prevailing discourse outlined above or did they constitute just another of its many hypostases?

Perhaps the most controversial of Kollontai's contributions to the debate on sexuality during NEP was her article "Make Way for Winged Eros" in *Molodaia gvardiia* in 1923. On the surface, Kollontai appeared to renounce the concept of monogamy for other, less traditional forms of sexual relationships, thus answering the question Engels had left—despite his evident preference for monogamy—unresolved. As we have already seen, Kollontai called for love to be played on "many strings," so that it would bind the collective together more tightly. However, had Kollontai had her way, the Soviet sexual orchestra would have performed in muted tones. She phrased the entire question of communist sexuality in a manner wholly in keeping with the reductive, puritanical discourse: "How can sexual relations be structured so that as they increase the general sum of happiness they do *not* contradict the interests of the collective?"[68] Moreover, in the tradition of the pre-Revolutionary definition of "free love" she hinted that the greater Eros's wings, the less often sexual relations would occur: "The boldest fantasy is powerless to grasp [Eros's future] form. But one thing is clear: the more strongly the new mankind will be welded together by lasting ties of solidarity, and the greater its spiritual-emotional union in all aspects of life, comradeship, and society, the less room will remain for love in the contemporary sense of the word."[69] While exulting in the triumph of "Winged Eros," Kollontai spoke of sexual activity in terms that compressed its legitimate sphere. Her language—"the boldest fantasy is powerless [or impotent] to grasp its form" (*samaia smelaia fantaziia bessil'na okhvatit' ego oblik*)— hints at a gulf between an imagined ideal future and a realm of the flesh that the perfect society will lack the "potency" to grasp. The literal implications of Kollontai's observation, "the morality of the working class, insofar as it has already crystallized, distinctly discards the *external form* [*otbrasyvaet vneshniuiu formu*] assumed by love relations between the sexes,"[70] suggest a discomfort with the *shape* of sex and with the physical contours of inter-

---

andra Kollontai, *The Autobiography of a Sexually Emancipated Communist Woman* (New York: Herder and Herder, 1971), 110 (105–135).

[67] See, inter alia, B. Arvatov, "Grazhd. Akhmatova i tov. Kollontai," *Molodaia gvardiia*, nos. 4–5 (1923): 147–151; Finogen Budnev, "Polovaia revoliutsiia," *Na postu*, no. 1 (1924): 243–249.

[68] A. Kollontai, "Dorogu krylatomu erosu," *Molodaia gvardiia*, no. 3 (1923): 118 (111–121) (emphasis added).

[69] Ibid., 123.

[70] Ibid., 122.

course. Kollontai dreams of a time when the outer shell—or body—of sexuality will be shed, leaving us only with love's content: the disembodied joy of angels equipped with ropes that bind rather than arrows that pierce.

Kollontai's fiction is a particularly useful source for the study of the ideological significance of sex during NEP.[71] Her gender-related posts in the Soviet government and her publicistic and scholarly writings on the moral and economic oppression of women have led biographers and critics to read her fiction as simply the literary expression of her desire for female autonomy and have led them to avert their gaze from disturbing elements that do not support this interpretation.[72] Kollontai's fiction tends to inspire optimistic readings from her biographers because her longer imaginative writings *end* with a woman's release from the chains of male dominance. These liberations, however, occur only in the final pages of narratives dominated by themes of terror and imprisonment. The stories often revolve around repetitive episodes of shock, horror, and paralysis of the will. To prefer moral to fable, to read her fiction as undiluted tales of liberation, reveals more about contemporary Western than about early Soviet ideology.

"Vasilisa Malygina" is the story of a committed young communist who in the early 1920s leaves her housing commune to visit her lover, now a factory director, in the provinces. NEP is in full swing, and Vasilisa discovers that her lover, to whom she was so close during the first post-Revolutionary years, has become a different person in the changed, neocapitalist climate. Vladimir (Volodia, for short), known to his comrades as "the American" for his pre-Revolutionary travels in the United States, installs Vasilisa in a mansion, and as the days pass, Vasilisa, deprived of contact with the working class, becomes a virtual prisoner of Volodia's new, bourgeois home and lifestyle. Gradually, as she explores the mansion's closets and drawers and talks

---

[71] In 1922 and 1923 Kollontai published five short stories and two novellas, the longest of which is "Vasilisa Malygina." Kollontai's oeuvre also includes the stories "The Love of Three Generations" and "Sisters," which were originally published along with "Vasilisa Malygina" in *The Love of Worker Bees (1) Liubov' pchel trudovykh* (M., 1923). The year 1923 also witnessed the appearance of a novella, "A Great Love," and two stories, "Thirty-Two Pages" and "An Overheard Conversation," which were all originally published by Kollontai under her maiden name, A. Domontovich, in *Zhenshchina na perelome (Psikhologicheskie etiudy)* (M. and Pg.: Gos. izd., 1923). Another short story, "Soon (in Forty-Eight Years)," was published separately in an extremely small edition (two hundred copies) in Omsk. A. Kolontai (*sic!*), *Skoro (Cherez 48 let)* (Miniatiurnaia biblioteka, 1922).

[72] Three lengthy biographies of Kollontai have been published: Clements, *Bolshevik Feminist*; Cathy Porter, *Alexandra Kollontai: A Biography* (London: Virago, 1980); and Farnsworth, *Aleksandra Kollontai*. None treats her fiction at length, and none raises the issue of the body's representation. Cathy Porter's introduction to an English collection of Kollontai's stories analyzes the fiction in greater detail but similarly ignores the status of the body (see Kollontai, *Love of Worker Bees*, 7–20). Birgitta Ingemanson provides a more sophisticated reading of Kollontai's fiction ("The Political Function of Domestic Objects in the Fiction of Aleksandra Kollontai," *Slavic Review* 48 [1989]: 71–82), but here, too, the body is missing.

with local communists and workers, Vasilisa makes unsettling discoveries about her lover's ideological betrayal of the Revolution and his sexual betrayal of her. Finally, after ignoring many disturbing hints, she is confronted with undeniable proof that Volodia has taken a mistress. At the story's conclusion, Vasilisa leaves her lover and returns home to help workers in a textile factory and to raise in a collective crèche the "communist" child she is carrying.

While usually treated as a story of a woman's liberation, "Vasilisa Malygina" has also been criticized for providing a rather facile solution (maternity) to a woman's domestic and social problems.[73] On closer inspection, the novella proves to contain a frenzied struggle against the female body in which female physiology and capitalism are paired as enemies of the communist state. The work's first paragraph, introducing Kollontai's heroine—who is called by the usually masculine nickname of Vasia—already brims with physiological anxieties and with the desire to eliminate the body that produces them:

> Vasilisa is a worker, a knitter. She is twenty-eight. Thin, emaciated [*khudosochnaia*], pale, a typical "child of the city." She has had typhus, and her hair is short and curly; from afar she looks like a boy, flat-chested in a shirt with a collar at the side and with a worn leather sash. She isn't pretty; only the eyes are attractive [literally, "good"—*tol'ko glaza khoroshie*]: black, affectionate, attentive, and thoughtful. You look into them and your heart is warmed. Such eyes can't pass by another person's grief. (3)[74]

Throughout the novella Kollontai dwells on Vasia's body, telling her reader how poorly Vasia fits into feminine clothing, how little she eats, how she refuses the extra rations to which she is entitled as a Party member. When Vasia leaves the city to visit her lover in the countryside, she finds that he has a young errand boy, also named Vasia, working for him, and although the lad makes few appearances, this "coincidental" doubling serves to em-

---

[73] See Judith Mayne, *Kino and the Woman Question: Feminism and Soviet Silent Film* (Columbus: Ohio State University Press, 1989), 128. In a collection of articles published in 1913 Kollontai herself remarked that maternity in literature usually functions as merely a "surrogate for happiness," a "last refuge" for a woman who has failed at love. A. Kollontai, *Novaia moral' i rabochii klass* (M.: Vserossiiskii tsentral'nyi ispolnitel'nyi komitet sovetov R., K. n K. deputatov, 1919).

[74] This passage is essentially an updated version of a clichéd description of a sincere, but not pretty, young girl, an earlier variant of which is found in Tolstoi's *Boyhood* (*Otrochestvo*): "Liubochka is not tall and, as a result of rickets, her legs are still bent and she has an unattractive torso. The only good thing in her whole figure are her eyes, and those eyes are truly beautiful: large, black, and with such an indefinably pleasant expression of importance and innocence that they cannot help attracting attention." Lev Nikolaevich Tolstoi, *Detstvo. Otrochestvo. Iunost'* (M.: Nauka, 1978), 122–123. In Tolstoi's version, this portrait describes a character of secondary importance and is incidental to his plot, while in Kollontai's novella the description is both literally and figuratively the text's point of departure.

phasize the similarities between Vasia's form and the male body. When Vasia recovers from a bout with typhus and notices that her hair is gone, she exclaims to Vladimir with a start:

> "My braid isn't here any more! Did they cut it off?"
>
> "Don't worry! You are a real boy now. You're my Vasiuk [*Vasiuk i est'*]."
>
> Vasia smiled. She felt well. So well, the way one can feel only in childhood. (33)

This is an odd moment, because the braid has already acquired significance as a sexual symbol; Vasia first attracts Volodia's attention when her hair falls from under her cap as she becomes "heated" (*zagoriachilas'*) while addressing a political meeting: "it was with that braid that she had 'bewitched' Vladimir" (*kosoiu-to i "privorozhila" k sebe Vladimira*)(15). Its removal is a metaphor for female castration: Vasia is deprived of her one "feminine" attribute capable of evoking male sexual response.

The reference to Vasia's childhood suggests a return to an earlier state of "presexual" development. In her lectures at Sverdlov Communist University, where she, like Liadov, taught, Kollontai professed belief in a corresponding state of *social* development, an era of prehistoric communism, when man roamed the earth in small groups, there was no private property, and "the physical attributes of women, her nimbleness and strength, differed little from those of men": "Many distinctive female features—the developed bosom, the thin waist, the large rounded form of the body, and the weakness of the muscles—developed only later, over generations, as women were transformed primarily into [breeding] "females" [*samki*] with their principal role that of producer of the species."[75] Vasia has this precapitalist body, and her

---

[75] Kollontai, *Polozhenie zhenshchiny v evoliutsii khoziaistva. (Lektsii chitannye v Universitete imeni Ia. M. Sverdlova)* (M.: Gos. izd., 1922), 5.

There is a striking parallel between Kollontai's story of the female body's (d)evolution and Aleksandr Bogdanov's utopian representation of the female form in *Red Star*, his 1908 novel about communism on Mars. When Bogdanov's hero, Lenni, visits a museum on the Red Planet, he is impressed by the similarities between sculptures of male and female bodies: "I noticed that male and female forms were more alike than among the majority of races on earth[. . . .] This was truer, however, of the statues from the recent [communist] epoch[. . . .] In statues of the capitalist period sexual differences were more strongly expressed. It is obvious that woman's domestic slavery and man's feverish battle for survival distorted the body in two divergent directions." A. Bogdanov, *Krasnaia zvezda. Inzhener Menni* (Hamburg: Helmut Buske, 1979), 93. Nevertheless, a fundamental difference separates Bogdanov's and Kollontai's treatment of this theme. In Bogdanov's novel, where pleasure and sex are viewed positively, and where the ideal personality is Nietzschean, the relative absence of sexual difference is experienced by the hero as intensely erotic. Lenni is made uneasy by his strange feelings toward two characters who, he later discovers, are actually Martian women. One of the novel's emotional climaxes comes when Lenni learns the truth about one of these figures, his doctor:

> Explain to me, why am I so strongly attracted to you? Why am I so unusually glad to see you?
>
> Most probably, I think, because I have treated you[r illness], and you unconsciously

return to childhood is a symbolic return to a pure, primordial communist time. In "Vasilisa Malygina," where corporeality is so resolutely feminine, this precapitalist body is equated with the absence of a body. When, early in the story, Volodia is arrested and the lovers are separated, Vasia feels immediately invigorated: "Her fatigue was forgotten. It was as if Vasilisa no longer had a body" (*Ustalost' zabyta. Tochno i tela net bol'she u Vasilisy*) (31). One of Volodia's faults is that he attempts to give Vasia a(n adult woman's) body, and her breasts and hips become noticeable only when she has a dress made from the expensive fabric he has bought for her. Having a woman's body becomes tantamount to dressing oneself as an ally of the bourgeoisie. The female body virtually does not exist until draped with the diaphanous desire for property and incarnated simultaneously by physical desire and ideological disgust.[76]

"Vasilisa Malygina" and its chief character are obsessed with purity, both ideological and sexual. The action takes place primarily in the provincial town to which Vladimir summons Vasia, and most of the dramatic tension revolves around her discovering the extent of his ideological and sexual infidelities. The word "pure" (*chistyi/chistaia*) surfaces repeatedly, as Vasia questions both her lover's and her own ideological and sexual correctness. The pursuit of purity is compulsive and endless; the disquieting message of most of the novella is that one can never be clean. Vasia's old comrade, Mikhailo Pavlovich, who is Vladimir's antagonist and the head of the local purge commission, tells her: "I'm purging the Party. [. . .] I purge and I

---

project onto me your joy at recovery. And perhaps . . . there is another reason . . . that I am . . . a woman.

Lightning flashed in front of my eyes, everything grew dark, and my heart seemed to stop beating . . . In a second I madly pressed Netti in my embrace and kissed her hands, her face, her large, deep eyes, green-blue, like the sky of her planet. (120)

The scene is interesting because it underscores the difficulties experienced by Russian "progressives" in dealing with sexual attraction. What ultimately sends Lenni into Netti's arms is a simple denotative word, not the erotic connotation of a physical difference in Netti's form. This scene seems to hold out the hope that one might minimize ideological contamination by making sexual attraction dependent on pure denotation. The moment also suggests the potential for repressed homoeroticism in the work of Bogdanov and his male Proletkul't comrades. The essence of the Proletkul't's male communist's wish is that a sexual object not be connotatively "other," that the minimum denotative difference necessary for sex be kept within a field of connotative sameness.

[76] Volodia makes Vasia see her own body. His insistence on the materialization of her flesh is one of the early signs that his priorities are incorrect. When he buys boots for her, she tries them on and "it was as if she were seeing her legs for the first time"(35). At his "mansion" Volodia immediately takes Vasia into the bedroom and turns her toward a large mirror in the armoire: "You see, how convenient it is, you can see all of yourself in this mirror when you dress. Inside there are shelves. For your ladies' underwear, little hats, and other bits of clothes" (*Dlia bel'-ishka tam damskogo, shliapok, da triapok*) (45).

purge, but there's still a lot of filth" (*Partiiu chishchu. [. . .] Chishchu, chishchu, a vse nechisti mnogo*) (65).

Kollontai tells her reader that the two lovers have been intimate since soon after the Revolution, and she dwells on Vasia's nostalgia for October 1917 and the years preceding NEP, when the air was heavy with the purity of ideological commitment (and when lovers spent most of their time apart!). In contrast, the atmosphere of NEP is thick in the novella with Gothic overtones that set off the bright Golden Age of the Revolution and Civil War. Volodia tells Vasia upon her arrival at his house that she will be a "lady of the manor" (*pomeshchitsei budesh'*) (44), and it is in this aristocratic setting, with its grandfather clock, paintings in gilded frames, and stuffed hunting trophies, that Vasia makes her chilling discoveries. She "wanders its rooms," overcome by "melancholy" (56). "She herself did not know what was wrong, but all was so unusual, so strange. And she herself was such a stranger, unneeded by anyone" (56). "Something was torturing Vasia, gnawing at her. She couldn't say what, exactly, but her soul was uneasy" (56). "As if in a dream" (58), Vasia tries to understand what has happened to Vladimir and to her old, ideologically pure world, but she seems intentionally blind to Volodia's affairs. The days drag on, "melancholy and long"; the evenings are spent "in the dark apartment" waiting for Volodia to return (108). Vasia is repeatedly depicted lying sleepless in bed—or waking suddenly to see her lover primping for his next meeting with Nepmen or with his mistress. In effect, Vasia's confinement in the mansion reproduces in Soviet context the basic contours of the Gothic chronotope, and her gradual discovery of "the American"'s treachery (the national epithet may be indebted to Radcliffe's "Italian") follows closely the epistemological guidelines of Gothic narrative.[77] The image of the bloody menstrual bandage re-

---

[77] Other fiction by Kollontai from this period—including stories situated abroad before the Revolution—are also replete with Gothic motifs. In "Thirty-Two Pages" a young woman runs in terror across a vacant lot near a factory, pursued by phantoms that turn out to be her abusive lover, who concludes from her frightened, disheveled appearance that she has been assaulted or raped in this industrial wilderness. In "A Great Love," the heroine waits for her lover for days on end in a German hotel, which, with its long, deserted corridors, resembles a haunted house full of "melancholy and fear." In this story we find a confluence of motifs that establishes an affinity between Kollontai's critique of female dependence and Liadov's portrait of the harem as the source of today's sexual horrors:

> Her stay in [the town of] G. had become a sort of "voluntary captivity" [*dobrovol'noe zatvornichestvo*]. Earlier, when they had only just become intimate, Natasha had been amused by this "play captivity" and its slyly arranged meetings with Semen Semenovich. She called [him] "pasha" and herself a harem "odalisque." She enjoyed the sudden shift from anxious, busy reality [. . .] to total anonymity—she lost her name for days on end—, as well as the absolute seclusion from life and people. [. . .] But now, in G., the role of harem odalisque oppressed and irritated her. (Domontovich, *Zhenshchina na perelome*, 12)

In this context, it is worth recalling that Kollontai, like Liadov and Bogdanov, taught history at

turns repeatedly to haunt Vasia at important moments—much as the veil haunts Emily in Radcliffe's *Mysteries of Udolpho* or as the red room returns in *Jane Eyre*. At one point, the novella seems about to blurt out its generic secret. Kollontai's heroine "walks back and forth through the dark and empty rooms":

> She felt chilled. She huddled up and hid her hands in her sleeves. She walked up and down the dark empty rooms. It seemed to Vasia that in this strange, unkind house, some sort of unexpected grief would befall her. . . . Disaster was lying in wait.
>
> A premonition?
>
> Did communists really believe in premonitions? But, then, what was all this? Whence this melancholy, unnamed, inescapable, uncalled? (56)

Paradoxically, the eruption of capitalism and infidelity as supernatural elements is a "natural" occurrence in the post-Revolutionary universe in which they are not supposed to exist . . . "natural," that is, if we take the word to mean an event fully in keeping with the ideology of the period. Buried by the Revolution, capitalism and sexual promiscuity can resurface only when the worldview of War Communism has begun to collapse. Refusing to accept phenomena of the new reality, the War Communist acolyte sees them as phantoms.

NEP is not only terrifying in Kollontai's novella, it is also repulsive, like an insect that has crawled onto the stage of Soviet culture. Kollontai's positive characters cannot stomach NEP: "NEP gets stuck in my throat" (*NEP poperek gorla*), Mikhailo Pavlovich says (64). Volodia's life is "disgusting" (*postylaia*), as is the fate of the "House Commune" founded by Vasia during War Communism and now unable to meet NEP's requirement of economic self-sufficiency:

> It was as if people had "desecrated" [*opoganili*] her beloved child. It was like in childhood, when her brother Kol'ka would show her a candy. When she would reach out for it Kol'ka would laugh slyly and say, "And now I'll go and desecrate your candy," and he would spit on it. "Now, Vasilisa, take your candy. Delicious!"—but Vasilisa, offended and in tears, would turn away. (7)

This early heterosexual intrafamilial experience—an act of oral desecration symbolizing a preliminary loss of innocence and leading to the temporary rejection of food—is restaged throughout the novella in new, historical and ideological, contexts colored by adult sexuality. Revulsion is occasioned by

---

the "Ultimatist" Party school in Bologna in the winter of 1910–1911. Jutta Scherrer, "Les Écoles du Parti de Capri et de Bologne: La formation de l'intelligentsia du parti," *Cahiers du monde russe et soviétique* 19 (1978): 263 (259–284). The Party's implementation of NEP may have recalled to Kollontai and Liadov an earlier distasteful episode in Leninist pragmatism, when Lenin had supported Bolshevik participation in the pre-Revolutionary Russian Duma.

the bodies of Volodia's mistresses. Where Vasia is "only eyes," these women are big busted with large, bloodred lips. The motif of blood (*krov'*) suffuses the novella, often appearing at moments of great dramatic tension. Vasia suffers from anemia (*malokrovie*) (6, 41)—this condition prevents her from becoming pregnant—and her face looks as if it "does not have a drop of blood" (*ni krovinki v litse*) (4). Vasia has joined the Bolsheviks, we learn on the work's first page, because she was horrified by the slaughter of the First World War, "a bloody affair" (*krovavoe delo*). When she goes to visit Volodia at the front—in a flashback at the start of the novella—she finds him in the company of another woman, a nurse with "swollen lips and large breasts" (30). When it comes time for bed, Vasia finds the menstrual bandage, the shocking appearance of which ("What was that! Her temples pounded. Her legs shook") (29) was quoted at the start of this chapter.[78]

The images of thick lips and the menstrual bandage return whenever Vasia is forced to question how far Volodia has departed from communist ideology. Vasia consistently tries to separate ideological and sexual purity in her mind, but the issues persist in merging uncomfortably. The novella's epistemological climax occurs when Vasia discovers the existence of Volodia's mistress. Consumed by jealousy, curiosity, and doubt, Vasia decides to lie in wait with another woman and catches a glimpse of her rival, Nina Konstantinovna, in the public gardens:

> So there she was! A white dress, flimsy, covering her whole body with soft folds. The outline of her breasts was visible under the dress. On her long hands she wore sand-yellow gloves; a hat of similar color was pulled over her eyes . . . Vasia could not see her face. The only thing visible were her lips—bright as if smeared with blood.
> —What lips she has, they're bloody!
> —"That's from makeup," [Vasia's companion] Mariia Semenovna said. "And you should see her eyes. It's as if they have been smeared with soot. I'd like to take a cloth and wipe all that filth from her face. If I were smeared, yes and painted, too, you'd also think me a beauty." (113–114)

The detested "other woman"—the bourgeoise with whom Kollontai so emphatically resists identifying her heroine—is here reduced to facial symbols of female genitalia—bloody and repulsive lips. Resisting Mariia Semenovna's implication that any woman might look like this, Vasia stays as far away as possible from these rapacious signs of femininity.[79] The word used

---

[78] To compound the sense of disgust underlying the scene, Kollontai later describes Vasia's hallucinations when, during a subsequent illness, Vasia lies delirious in the same bed and imagines that she is being overrun by mice. She wakes and discovers Volodia bending down above her (32–33).

[79] Susan Ryan has suggested to me that in light of Vladimir's epithet—"the American"—and his sojourn in an English-speaking world, it may not be inappropriate to view the name of

for filth—*nechist'*—with secondary connotations of "evil spirits," "vermin," syphilis, and, above all, defilement[80]—recalls not only the purging of the Party ("I purge and I purge, but there's still a lot of filth") but also Vasia's disgust at the desecration of her housing commune. Nina Konstantinovna implicitly reasserts the identification between oral and genital functioning in the novella when she insists that Vasia's attitude toward sex is akin to "fasting" (118).

In the midst of her nightmare, Vasia dreams of salvation in the form of the Gothic's usual narrative miracle: "It seemed to her that she was just on the verge of waking, that she would find herself 'home' in the House Commune. She remembered the Housing Committee, her comrades. [. . .] Life had been hard then, but joyous" (58). Vasia's eventual renunciation of Volodia—and the subsequent (and consequent) cessation of her menses—are a recovery of lost ideological innocence amidst the dissolution of NEP. Vladimir (reborn capitalism) and the repugnant functions of the adult female body are purged from the narrative simultaneously in a post-NEP recovery of an ostensibly sublated, but more plausibly prelapsarian and pre-NEP world. Significantly, Vasia's pregnant body is never seen; the reader leaves Vasia before she begins to "show." Not pregnancy per se but the first few months of pregnancy prove to be woman's ideal—that is, least visibly female—physiological time.

In essence, Kollontai's heroine has faithfully followed the policy mandated by the Party during NEP: she has cohabited with the agents of capital and has mated with someone who has transferred his loyalties to the "dead" class. Strengthened (and fertilized) by her experience, she abandons capitalism and merrily begins a new, postcapitalist life. Still, the proportionately large number of pages spent on the disturbing aspects of intercourse with the enemy leads one to suspect that the novella's ending has been grafted onto the body of the text as precipitously as the hurried endings of its Gothic predecessors, in which all troubling elements are explained away in a few dense, unconvincing paragraphs. Has Vasia profited from capitalism without being tainted by it? Within the novella's Gothic paradigm, can the female body be celebrated after functioning—albeit in the interests of class struggle—as a sign of ideological contamination? Commenting derisively on Kollontai's fiction and on the title of the collection (*The Love of Worker*

Kollontai's heroine as a verbal and iconic representation of the terrifying object and foreign "home" from which Vasia tries so hard to escape: *Va*(silisa Maly)*gina*. Kollontai knew English well; during trips to England and the United States she frequently used English when addressing large public meetings. For her letters during her trip to the United States, see A. M. Kollontai, *Revoliutsiia—velikaia miatezhnitsa. Izbrannye pis'ma 1901–1952* (M.: Sovetskaia rossiia, 1989), 126–136.

[80] Vladimir Dal', *Tolkovyi slovar' zhivago velikoruskago iazyka*, 4 vols. (SPb. and M.: M. O. Vol'f, 1881), 2:543.

Bees) in which "Vasilisa Malygina" initially appeared, the writer of a sexual education manual remarked that "the author has made a mistake even in the title of her book. 'Worker' bees are sexless and, consequently, never experience desire."[81] Worker bees are, in fact, sexually undeveloped *females*, a scientific fact of which Kollontai was probably unaware but which renders Kollontai's metaphoric title all the more revealing and accurate.[82] The reader of "Vasilisa Malygina" may well suspect that the book's happy ending was premised on a symbolic and figurative insemination too artificial to produce healthy offspring in real life.

In light of her renown as a defender of women and of "free love," it is surprising to find in Kollontai's novella such relentless repugnance toward female physiology. In her pre-Revolutionary writing, disgust at physicality does not appear to play any role. In a 1913 essay, "The New Woman,"

---

[81] Lemberg, *Chto neobkhodimo znat'*, 39.

[82] The use of the worker bee metaphor to describe women seems to go back in Russia at least to an article published in 1891 by Il'ia Mechnikov, the zoologist and microbiologist who would later receive the Nobel Prize for his pioneering work in immunology. Writing in a popular journal in the midst of much controversy over "The Kreutzer Sonata," Mechnikov speculated that eventually a division of labor would occur among women that would anticipate future anatomical distinctions among them. A few would engage in reproduction; the majority would be employed in other socially useful work. French wasps had evolved to this condition: "big females" laid eggs, while "little females" performed social functions such as guarding the young against enemies and intruders. Bees, he noted, had evolved further, so that the working females were anatomically different from the queens. "Zakon zhizni: po povodu nekotorykh proizvedenii gr. L. Tolstogo," *Vestnik Evropy*, no. 9 (1891): 249–252 (228–260). A quarter of a century later, A. N. Rakhmanov, one of the foremost Soviet gynecologists and chair of the first Soviet panel formed to study birth control, speculated on the future evolution of half of the species:

> It may be assumed that the human female organism will complete its evolutionary course and that new, asexual women will be created, like worker bees. They will not experience sexual feelings, nor will they suffer from sexuality's oppression, but will acquire the ability to resist work-related fatigue and to go without sleep (bees neither tire nor sleep).
>
> The remarkable change that is occurring in woman's sexual instinct—which at times we find incomprehensible and thus pathological—appears to hint that this evolution is occurring. (A. N. Rakhmanov, "Problema ogranicheniia zachatii i obshchii obzor protivozachatochnykh sredstv," in *Protivozachatochnye sredstva i ikh primenenie*, ed. E. I. Kvater [M.: Okhrana materinstva i mladenchestva, 1926], 11 [7–13])

Kollontai *may* owe her title to Mechnikov, but she provides a rather nightmarish version of relations between these two types of females who in her account are not yet sufficiently distinguished from each other to prevent the development of a striking autorevulsion of one type in the presence of the (not yet sufficiently) other.

There is at least one use of the apian metaphor in early-twentieth-century England. In *The Truth about Women*, published in London in 1913, C. Gasquoigne-Hartley attacked women who did not want to procreate, comparing them to "worker bees" who had a lethal sting but were infertile. (Discussed in Jeffreys, *The Spinster and Her Enemies*, 142.)

Kollontai welcomes women's recognition and acceptance of their physical drives and desires. It is worthwhile, however, to pay attention to the language employed. The essay is a search through recent literary works for astute and prophetic reflections of the new, heroic type of woman who was just beginning to appear in real life:

> For the woman of the past the supreme sorrow was betrayal by or loss of her beloved; for the contemporary heroine it is the loss of *herself*, the rejection of her own ego in favor of her lover, for the sake of preserving romantic happiness. The new woman does not rebel so much against external chains: she protests against "romantic captivity" itself; she fears the fetters that love, given our crippled psychology today, places on lovers . . .[83]

On one hand, Kollontai here calls for the rejection of the type of captivity narrative so essential to Gothic writing. On the other, by repeatedly using the language of "fetters" and "chains," she projects the theme of captivity inward, so that the Gothic predicament, which so many of today's critics see as the external projection of inner anxieties, explicitly becomes a conflict within the self. "Contemporary heroines," Kollontai writes at the conclusion of the essay, "must fight a war on two fronts: with the outside world and with the tendencies of their female ancestors that lie deep within them."[84] Arguably, in "Vasilisa Malygina" this conflict of a woman with her own interior becomes literalized, the female body and its insides functioning as hostile representatives of the not so deeply buried past.

To fully understand the development and significance of Kollontai's anti-corporal Gothic, we must trace the ideological evolution of her figures and explore the effect of genre on her attempts to communicate a political message, for it is through the lens of genre that we can most clearly understand how "The New Woman" succumbed to Revolutionary anorexia. Kollontai's ideological anorexia, like that of NEP, has its roots in a central, traumatic event: the challenge to the Party of the Workers' Opposition. In 1923, when the novella was written, Kollontai was serving as Soviet ambassador to Norway, a posting in large measure intended to remove her as a central player in Party affairs. Two years earlier, she had emerged as a principal spokesperson for the Workers' Opposition and had been entrusted with giving written formulation to the faction's demands.

Published on the eve of the Tenth Party Congress in March 1921, Kollontai's *The Workers' Opposition* has attracted the attention of both her biographers and Party historians, but it has been read almost exclusively for the *content* of its demands and not for the way those demands are narrated and

---

[83] A. Kollontai, *Novaia moral' i rabochii klass*, 26.
[84] Ibid., 35.

expressed. With benefit of hindsight and in light of Kollontai's later fiction, however, *The Workers' Opposition* is fascinating as a *proto*-Gothic text. Kollontai professes to tell the story of the Party's "deviation from that part of the class line to which we so passionately adhered [. . .] during the first part of the Revolution." "How did this all come about," Kollontai asks, "how did it happen that our stalwart Party, forged in the battle of the Revolution, allowed herself to be led astray from the straight class path and began to travel along the trails of that detested opportunism which she has always branded as so disgraceful?"[85] "Party" (*partiia*) is a feminine noun in Russian, and Kollontai's brochure tells the story of "her" "corruption." Kollontai's term for this process, *razlozhenie*, a word signifying both moral and physical decay, appears throughout the brochure and charts the Party's fall from Revolutionary grace. The Workers' Opposition emerges as the sole political force that has maintained its proletarian purity in the face of the bourgeois specialists, the "immigrants from the past," who have "snuck into our Red Army, bringing with them their odor of the past."[86] The new bureaucrats have built up a bureaucratic system "inherited from the past" and filled it with elements "foreign" to the working class, with "strangers from another world" (*prishel'tsy iz drugogo mira*).[87] Speaking of these elements, Kollontai cannot contain her disgust; indeed, disgust so suffuses her brochure that she represents it as experienced by both sides of the ideological conflict: "It is precisely this stratum, broadly diffused throughout Soviet institutions, this stratum of the petty bourgeoisie with its hostility toward communism, its dedication to the stagnant mores of the past, with its revulsion at and fear of revolutionary acts, that is corrupting our Soviet institutions, bringing with it a spirit absolutely alien to the working class."[88]

In this climate of mutual repugnance, the leaders of the Workers' Opposition, who "understand, or rather sense with their healthy class instinct," that "the working class is playing an increasingly small role in the Soviet republic," have taken refuge in the most appropriate shelter:

> The first thing that they have done was to join with the lower classes, to go into their class organ—the trade unions—the organ that during the past three years has least of all been subject to the corrupting influence of infiltrating [or interbreeding], alien, nonproletarian interests, of the interests of the peasantry and of the bourgeois elements that have cuddled up to the Soviet system, of interests that are deforming our Soviet institutions and leading our policy astray from a distinct, class-conscious course into the swamp of opportunism.

[85] A. M. Kollontai, *Rabochaia oppozitsiia* (M., 1921).
[86] Ibid., 12–13.
[87] Ibid., 26, 28.
[88] Ibid., 11–12.

And so the Workers' Opposition is, first of all, composed of proletarians connected with the workbench and the mine shaft; it is the flesh of the flesh of the working class.[89]

We should not overlook Kollontai's reference to working-class corporeality. Repeatedly, she returns to the idea of incarnation: it is the working class's task to "incarnate the Party's program in life"; "to the working class in Russia has fallen the lot of incarnating communism, of building new, communist economic forms."[90] These references to the flesh and to the menace posed to the working class by various ideological ghosts do not yet provide the necessary material for a full-bodied Gothic narrative. At this point they are simply highly charged moments of metaphorical intensity embedded in a policy-oriented brochure; only retrospectively can they be assigned to a *proto*-Gothic plot. After the failure of the Workers' Opposition and the removal of its members during the summer of 1921 from influential positions in the Party and the more powerful unions, these images of the flesh would themselves be "incarnated" in fictional narrative, and Kollontai's beloved class "organ," in which she had been so quick to take cover, would become a source of revulsion. The comforting spatial metaphor of an inner and "lower"(-class) place to which a communist could always come home gives way in "Vasilisa Malygina" to disturbing physiological images of a defiled, leaking internal space no longer secure against penetration.

Kollontai's ideological revulsion would increase during the following years. The Workers' Opposition did not absolutely oppose NEP in principle, but its members were disturbed by the ideological taint surrounding its enthusiastic implementation.[91] At the Third International Congress of the Comintern in the summer of 1921, Kollontai criticized NEP forcefully, and in early February 1922, she handed to the Comintern's Expanded Plenum a "declaration" signed by twenty-two Party members. This protest against the Party leadership, which Bolshevik leaders such as Bukharin and Trotsky treated as evidence of an extremely troubling breach of discipline within the Party, relied heavily on the imagery of danger and corruption so prominent in Kollontai's brochure.[92] Later that year, at the Eleventh Party Congress, members of the Workers' Opposition were harshly censured for their declaration; a resolution, adopted by the congress, threatened Kollontai with expulsion if she continued to manifest an "anti-Party attitude."[93]

In the last speech she would make as an important Party personage, shortly before she was dismissed as director of the Women's Division and

[89] Ibid., 4–5.
[90] Ibid., 10.
[91] Zorkii, *Rabochaia oppozitsiia*, 55–56.
[92] See ibid., 59, for the text of the declaration.
[93] *Odinnadtsatyi s"ezd*, 533.

dispatched to Norway, Kollontai defended in the following terms her decision to submit the "Declaration of Twenty-Two" to the Comintern:

> The Comintern is that institution in which we feel great trust and to which we have turned precisely because we have seen that something is not right in our Party [*v nashei partii tvoritsia chto-to ne ladnoe*]. I would say that right now a morbid, onerous process is occurring in our Party. Red blood corpuscles are leaving us. [*Ot nas ukhodiat krasnye krovianye shariki.*] What then, will remain of our Party, if all of her red blood corpuscles—the working class—leave her? Naturally, she will then become lymphatic, sluggish, hypoactive, uncreative. It is the fear generated by this picture, by this process, that has forced us to turn to the Comintern with our Declaration. [. . .] These days the working class does not feel "at home" in our Party; if the working class felt that workers would find a comprehensive response to their needs in the Party and an opportunity to fight with the dark phenomena that surround us, workers would throng to the Party, but instead the masses are standing on the sidelines, and workers are leaving the Party.[94]

This vivid picture—a metaphorical hemorrhage occurring in a place that used to be but is no longer "home," in the midst of a battle with "the dark phenomena that surround us"—should be read as an important moment in the development of Kollontai's Gothic narrative of ideological revulsion. In 1922, on the verge of absolute political defeat, she was already using striking physiological metaphors as part of a rhetorical strategy aimed at shocking the Party into recuperative action.

In some respects, it seems logical that when Kollontai began to write fiction, the Gothic suggested itself as a narrative arena in which her polemical metaphors of ideological disgust and disquiet could develop. Since her speeches had revolved around a rhetoric of alarm, it was not surprising that her fiction would as well. It was also likely that Kollontai would write in a genre with a tradition of women as central figures. Yet for all their reliance on what with hindsight I have termed a proto-Gothic register, Kollontai's political speeches do not rely on issues of gender or sexuality. The hemorrhaging organ might be located anywhere in the body and might belong to either sex.

Kollontai's turn toward sex had much to do with political restrictions of the day. In the Russia of NEP, political revulsion was becoming unmentionable, while the taboo on sex was weakening in accordance with the dictates of a self-consciously materialistic age. In this environment, talk about sex became a metaphor—and symptom—for thoughts about something else: politics and ideology. In this light, Kollontai's case offers interesting support for Eugenia DeLamotte's contention that the Gothic's power springs from a

---

[94] Ibid., 177.

tense opposition between terror and the demands of a rigid code of decorum.[95] According to DeLamotte, the genre frequently tells the story of a woman's quest to preserve her individual, different voice while making her peace with the misogynistic social conventions that would reduce her to silence. In "Vasilisa Malygina" this fundamental act of silencing that renders self-assertion taboo is not represented directly within the text but has occurred *before* the text's writing. Whether Kollontai consciously chose her genre, all of these factors influenced the production of a Gothic text.

For all its appropriateness, a fundamental paradox underlies Kollontai's generic refuge: her effort to resist a resurgent bourgeoisie by means of class-conscious fiction was itself "possessed" *in its very form* by a type of narrative that, at least in its origin and historical development, is quintessentially bourgeois and has frequently been beset with (occasionally self-directed) misogyny. Kollontai's attempt to cloak her political message in the Gothic presents a stark example of how genre, like the clothes Volodia would have Vasia wear, shapes content as well as form.

Kollontai's use of and possession by the Gothic raises an important theoretical issue. Much recent work has been informed by a critical desire to "*demetaphorize*" the Gothic by illuminating the ostensibly unspeakable anxieties the Gothic encodes in repressive, metaphorical discourse. Recent Gothic criticism has been steeped in an analytical yearning for simile and for the transformation of opaque figures into legible metaphors. Cognizant of this desire that the Gothic produces in its critics, one might define the Gothic with reference not only to its obvious motifs (imprisonment, repetitive action, obscurity) but also to the manner of its interpretation and to the surfacing of an anxious critical need to dispel semantic obscurity by mooring metaphors to their referents. (Here we should recall Edmund Burke's inclusion of obscurity as a category of the sublime;[96] not only does the Gothic deploy obscurity [the darkened chamber, the crypt's gloom] thematically to produce terror in its readers, it also utilizes obscurity semantically to make itself a sublime object of interpretive desire for contemporary critics.)

If there is a lesson to be learned from the variety of metaphorized fears found to be central to the Gothic over the past few decades, it may be that we should approach the Gothic at least in part from a functional point of view. Instead of specifying the particular object or fear that the Gothic represents, we ought to focus on the Gothic's primary importance as signifier. While many recent readings of the Gothic have attempted to present a totalizing, synchronic explanation for the genre's social and psychological uses

---

[95] Eugenia DeLamotte, *Perils of the Night: A Feminist Study of Nineteenth Century Gothic* (New York: Oxford University Press, 1990), 178–181.

[96] Edmund Burke, *A Philosophical Inquiry into the Origin of Our Ideas of the Sublime and Beautiful* (London: Routledge and Kegan Paul, 1958), 58–64.

and roles, it is worthwhile bearing in mind that the Gothic may be useful as a metaphorical vehicle for different encoded fears at different times.[97] No newly encoded fear, however, manages to preserve its difference intact. Prior encodings survive and continue to influence the development of the genre long after the fears that motivated them have dissipated. As Bakhtin understood so well, genres have concrete traditions and each new contribution to a genre influences that genre's unfolding and forces itself upon the creative world of its successors.[98] Each new appropriation of the genre is not only enriched but also *limited* and/or *distorted* by prior users. This limitation still functions when "[artistic] inheritance proceeds not from father to eldest son but from uncle to nephew";[99] even distant (or ideologically hostile) relatives are not spared by the indirect path of inheritance from recalling their "benefactors." In this sense, every genre is Gothic—at least in Dale Peterson's virtually historiographic use of the word[100]—and so the Gothic itself is doubly haunted, for it not only encodes particular fears but serves as a parable about possessed communication. To slip again into Russian Formalist terms—the Gothic "lays bare" the nature of genre: the Gothic may be "about" the very activity of expressing oneself in a conventional code.[101]

The generic dilemma of Kollontai's novella illustrates the treacherous status of genre for texts that ally themselves with the promulgation or defense of a revolutionary ideal. In scattered comments made by Marx and Lenin one can already sense an awareness of the danger posed by genre to the communist narrative of history. For Marx, the proletarian Revolution will

---

[97] Eve Kosofsky Sedgwick's study of the Gothic provides an exceptional and strikingly polyphonic reading of the genre. Sedgwick employs several models of metaphorical interpretation—all the while foregrounding her own simultaneous seduction by and resistence to the interpretive urge. As a result "metaphor" in her analysis is not annihilated by an inexorable desire for transparency; rather, it retains an opacity that allows it to serve Segwick as an independently interesting actor in the functioning of the genre. Eve Kosofsky Sedgwick, *The Coherence of Gothic Conventions* (New York: Methuen, 1986).

[98] Bakhtin's conceptualization of genre is spelled out most fully in his essay "The Problem of Speech Genres" in his *Speech Genres and Other Late Essays*, trans. Vern W. McGee (Austin: University of Texas Press, 1986), 60–102. My reading of Kollontai's encounter with genre has also been influenced by the comments on genre made by Bakhtin in the revised, second edition of his study of Dostoevsky: *Problems of Dostoevsky's Poetics*, trans. Caryl Emerson (Minneapolis: University of Minnesota Press, 1984), 157.

[99] Viktor Shklovskii, *Za 60 let: Raboty o kino* (M.: Iskusstvo, 1985), 14. The quotation is from an article first published in 1919.

[100] Dale Peterson, "Russian Gothic: The Deathless Paradoxes of Bunin's *Dry Valley*," *Slavic and Eastern European Journal* 31 (1987): 38 (36–49). See chapter 5, above.

[101] To the extent that all expression occurs in a conventional code, that "the speaker is [never] the Biblical Adam" (Bakhtin, "Speech Genres," 93), the Gothic has implications beyond literary expression and is founded upon an important existential truth for all users of language.

come only after the repetition of forms has been purged.[102] One can read Lenin as urging that genre will be defeated by a massive consolidation; there will be no such thing as a distinct generic worldview because all genres will be united in the cognitive, axiological vision of the all-encompassing Bolshevik eye.[103] Avant-garde Soviet theoreticians proposed their own solution to the genre problem: a world in which "we live our own lives, and we do not submit to anyone's fiction"[104] and where "the facts of Revolutionary reality" would not be "paralyzed by translation into the language of aesthetic illusion."[105] In this context, Kollontai's use of the Gothic to write about the dangers of the reborn bourgeoisie is both inevitably self-defeating *and* appropriate, because it highlights what Marxism has always "known" about verbal form.

Such literary and philosophical considerations were doubtless far from Kollontai's mind when she wrote "Vasilisa Malygina." She did not realize that as a politically engaged writer she, like her "New Woman," had to fight a battle on two fronts—not only with the political and economic conditions of the present day but also with the legacies that had shaped the genre in which she was expressing her views. Where genre is concerned, "the dead [*always*] seize the living," and that is what makes genre such an instructive prism for examining NEP.

To the extent that in its genre Kollontai's novella reproduces the ideological predicament of NEP, "Vasilisa Malygina" is the consummate example of NEP's literary incarnation, and one can read its ambivalent (or hostile) attitude toward femininity as a sign of an internally directed ideological suspicion that occasionally borders on self-hatred. What renders the book particularly interesting is that the misogynistic history and emotional intensity of the Gothic destabilize the direction and nature of Kollontai's signifying process; in Kollontai's arena of symbolic expression, signifier and signified ter-

---

[102]

The social revolution of the nineteenth century cannot draw its poetry from the past, but only from the future. It cannot begin with itself, before it has stripped off all superstition in regard to the past. Earlier revolutions required world-historical recollections in order to drug themselves concerning their own content. In order to arrive at its content, the revolution of the nineteenth century must let the dead bury their dead. There the phrase went beyond the content; here the content goes beyond the phrase. *(The Marx-Engels Reader,* ed. Robert C. Tucker [New York: Norton, 1972], 439)

[103] "Marxism has not conquered for itself its universal historical significance as the ideology of the Revolutionary proletariat by discarding the axiological achievements of the bourgeois era but, on the contrary, by mastering and reworking everything that had value in the more than two-thousand-year development of human thought and culture." Lenin, "O proletarskoi kul'ture" (8 October 1920, first published in 1926), *Polnoe sobranie sochinenii,* 41:337.

[104] Dziga Vertov, *Kino-Eye,* trans. Kevin O'Brien (Berkeley and Los Angeles: University of California Press, 1984), 71.

[105] Sergei Tret'iakov, "LEF i NEP," *LEF,* no. 2 (1923): 74 (70–78).

rorize each other. In effect, in its deployment of physiological metaphors first utilized in political speeches, Kollontai's novella transforms figure into fiction. Strangely, however, it is in moving from the "real world" of political conventions to novelistic fiction that Kollontai endows her horror with a far greater degree of physicality, as images acquire the representational flesh of fictional characters who seem more palpable than political metaphors. The result is a strange rapport between signifier and signified in which the status of each is disturbed and to some extent deformed by the female body. (To cite only one of the most striking examples of this process, in "Vasilisa Malygina" the adjective "red" falls victim to representational desecration; from a valuable proletarian sign it is transformed into a marker of female physiology and disgusting bourgeois flesh.) Even when she is aware of the ideological constraints under which Kollontai was working, today's reader may be disturbed by the manner in which woman in Kollontai's prose vacillates between serving as a sign of ideological anxiety and representing anxiety's cause. Kollontai's transition from author of political manifestos to a writer of novellas and short stories should by itself have provided her with a measure of ideological cover. In making this move, however, Kollontai exposed herself to the danger that her metaphors, loosened from their referents, would acquire new connotative power as they were realigned in a distinct generic tradition. In the Gothic Kollontai simultaneously found both refuge and nightmare.

One other generic factor is relevant to the etiology of Vasilisa Malygina's ideological "condition." Many pre-NEP (and pre-Revolutionary) articles by Kollontai as well as her collection *The New Morality and the Working Class* (1919) manifest that programmatic civic sentimentality which was the trademark of "progressive" Russian writers like Aleksandr Radishchev, Nikolai Chernyshevsky, and Nikolai Nekrasov. After the Revolution, Kollontai's sentimentality was treated with derision and revulsion by members loyal to the central Party bureaucracy.[106] Such a reaction is not surprising—tears, purity of spirit, and a great capacity for relatively passive suffering were not ideal qualities for materialist members of a revolutionary vanguard bent on exterminating its enemies. Sentimentality may have been appropriate as a tool for arousing popular indignation in bygone tsarist days but was inherently non-

---

[106] See, for example, Bukharin's speech at the Tenth Party Congress, where in the course of an attack on the Workers' Opposition he quoted derisively from Kollontai's 1921 article "The Cross of Maternity" and called it "disgusting, sentimental Catholic trash." *Stenograficheskii otchet desiatogo s"ezda Rossiiskoi kommunisticheskoi partii, 8–10 marta, 1921*, 103. Bukharin himself was not above sentimental behavior. When informing Bolsheviks in Petrograd about the heavy casualties sustained by their ultimately victorious comrades in Moscow, Bukharin was reported to have thrown himself in tears "on the breast of a bearded worker." His sobbing quickly infected those around him; soon many were in tears. Cited in Stephen F. Cohen, *Bukharin and the Bolshevik Revolution* (Oxford: Oxford University Press, 1980), 59.

Bolshevik now, when the proletariat had proved itself capable of seizing power; as a generic worldview sentimentalism closely approximated the pacifist, petty-bourgeois, or Menshevik perspective Lenin so often reviled. Lenin used the Workers' Opposition's virtuous sentimentality as a weapon against the group, deriding its adherents' "impermissible" and "childish" response to NEP: "bursting into tears."[107] Members of the Workers' Opposition themselves cautioned against sentimentality. In a letter subsequently cited by the Party as incriminating evidence, a member of the Opposition argued for more reliance on Realpolitik.

> [At the recent meeting of the metalworkers' union] the Central Committee began cynically and openly to knock our base out from under us, and our people in the audience reacted with tearful entreaties [*sleznitsami*]. Tearful entreaties show the extent to which our comrades are honest, sincere, and infinitely dedicated to the Party, the Revolution, and the unions, but they also reveal a failure on the part of our comrades to understand basic politics. A sincere, honest person always comes up the loser against someone who knows politics. [. . .] Answer impudence with impudence, respond to attacks by organizing and attacking right back, just avoid introducing sentimental things into politics. . . .[108]

Kollontai's political declarations in support of the Workers' Opposition strike a balance between expressions of compassion and anxiety; the former are drawn from a traditional, sentimental storehouse, while the latter owe much to Gothic tradition. In Kollontai's *fiction*, however, the Gothic becomes dominant as the purity of her earlier vision of communism is contaminated by repugnance at the Party's new course. The transition from the "sweet" outlook of pre-Gothic sentimentalism to the more troubled, queasy Gothic worldview is forcefully captured early in "Vasilisa Malygina" in the scene where Vasia compares NEP's "desecration" of her housing commune to her brother's spitting on her candy.

Kollontai's evolution from sentimentalism to Gothic closely parallels the historical (d)evolution of Gothic fiction. For all its subsequent versatility as a vehicle for the expression of diverse anxieties, Gothic fiction, at least in Leslie Fiedler's well-argued paradigm, was historically a form of sentimentalism transformed by the new anxieties of the first decades following the French Revolution.[109] In many Gothic novels, ontogeny recapitulates phylogeny: in *The Mysteries of Udolpho*, for example, the serenely sentimental

---

[107] "Seeing that we are retreating, some have even—impermissibly and childishly—burst into tears [*rasplakalis'*][. . . .] Out of the best communist feelings and communist aspirations, some comrades have even cried because good Russian communists—just imagine it!—are retreating." *Odinnadtsatyi s"ezd*, 19–20.

[108] Zorkii, *Rabochaia oppozitsiia*, 55–56.

[109] Leslie Fiedler, *Love and Death in the American Novel* (New York: Anchor, 1992), 106–119.

countryside of southern France's valleys gives way to the Gothic terror of the Apennines and the Pyrenees, and quotations of Thomson's pastoral verse yield to lurid selections from a rediscovered and recontextualized, protoromantic Shakespeare. We can observe this process most clearly by noting how, in the Gothic, the graveyard is transformed from a location of contemplation to a frightening metaphor for the potential of the past to surge forth at any moment. "Vasilisa Malygina" follows this pattern: the (in actual fact, brutal) days of the Civil War, now sentimentalized as an ideologically halcyon age, yield to the horrors of NEP. At one point, Vasia intercepts a letter to Volodia from his mistress, Nina Konstantinovna, and when she sits down in the public garden to read it, "Vasilisa Malygina" captures in condensed fashion the terrifying transition from epistolary sentimentalism to Gothic horror:

My dear bright Volia [a diminutive for Volodia]! My lord, my beloved master! Once again I haven't heard a word from you. It's been three days, and not a line. Can you really have forgotten, have fallen out of love with your own capricious little Nina? Your little Egyptian monkey? I won't believe it! I won't! . . . And all the same, I'm frightened. You are with her, and I'm alone. [. . .]

Volia, Volia! My beloved, my madly beloved, won't this [his relationship with Vasia] ever end? Won't you save your own little Nina? Aren't you sorry for her? Won't you protect her?

I'm crying, Volia . . . Don't you have pity for your "little monkey"? My silky hands want to wind themselves around you. My breasts—"that cup of languor"—are yearning for your caress.

Volia! I can't suffer any more! I can't live apart. Why have you sent me to Moscow? For what?

But let this be the last time. When you move to a new region, find me a little house outside the city. So that nobody knows that I'm there . . . "A secret little house," where you will come to me when darkness falls. [. . .]

Nikanor Platonovich tells me that in the new part of town you are to be given a splendid mansion . . . With a dining room in the Gothic style. But there's no light in the dining room. I've already had my eye here on a wonderful chandelier, a bit expensive, but really artistic. I'm sure you'll like it. [. . .]

Yours from my little legs to my hot little lips, your (and only your) "sweet little girl," Nina.

P.S. Guess what? I'm so happy—I've found in Moscow that powder *L'Origan Coty*. (118–119)

This letter, replete with diminutives and clichés appropriate to the eighteenth century's cult of feeling, horrifically appropriates the sentimental language of Kollontai's own early work, distorting communist sentimentality into repellent corruption. Nina, with her "hot little lips" and her devotion to organs of pleasure and *L'Origan Coty* (a product doubly obnoxious because it bears the name of the anticommunist perfume magnate who by this time was editor of the conservative *Le Figaro*) rather than to the organs of the Revolution, provides a terrifying representation of what can happen to women who are unable to escape their enslavement to the lords of NEP and to foreign capital. Nina circulates from one man to another, reproducing in her sexual behavior the activity of capitalist lucre. In the world of NEP this kind of financial circulation has replaced the retentive circulation of healthy communism; blood no longer nourishes the body but is dispersed outside it. The metaphoric "blood" earlier spied on Nina's lips is not only the product of a symbolically genitalized face, it also represents the red corpuscles sucked from the proletariat by the vampire of bourgeois sexuality. Not surprisingly, when Vasia reads Nina's letter and is afforded a glimpse of NEP's woman, "everything within her trembles" (118). The Gothic has erupted within the sentimental—within Nina's letter (the architectural move from "little house" to mansion with "Gothic dining room"), within "Vasilisa Malygina," and within Kollontai's ideological worldview. The garden in which she has been reading is metaphorically transformed into a graveyard: she feels as if she has just attended "the burial of her dead happiness" (120).

"*Her* dead happiness." The most troubling aspect of Kollontai's Gothic may be its success in transforming its heroine into a ghost. Kollontai can resist the flesh only by draining Vasia of blood. This bleeding Vasia white (a process that must be depicted as an end result, because the sight of blood leaving her would tie her too closely to the flesh's presence) would seem to be in contradiction with Kollontai's praise of the Workers' Opposition as "the flesh of the flesh of the working class." Ostensibly, Kollontai's novella resists the wrong sort of incarnation. Its ending (Vasia's abandonment of Volodia and the announcement of her pregnancy) is most simply (and superficially) read as expressing a desire for incarnation of the correct, immaculate kind. And yet, one can read Vasia's ghostly appearance and the story's termination before the birth of her child as an acknowledgment that the cycle of repetition has not been broken, that Volodia's seed has led to the child, and that no incarnation can ever be pure. The novella's repetitive representations of disgust may be born of the revolutionary's fear of being trapped in an endless cycle of revulsion occasioned by the taint that inevitably attaches to victorious communism's physical shape or even its verbal form.

Finally, although Kollontai and the Workers' Opposition were defeated at the Tenth and Eleventh Party Congresses, their Gothic discourse (as well as their call for a purge of the Party) found a home in Bolshevik ideology. The Workers' Opposition made "fear" and "panic" the disturbing pedal notes of the Tenth and Eleventh Congresses; many of the speeches revolved around the question of whether "panic" already existed in the rank and file or was being sown there by the Opposition.[110] Ideological correctness quickly came

---

[110] See, for example, the series of speeches made at the Eleventh Congress by Aleksandr

to be measured in terms of knowing what to fear and what not to fear.[111] Bukharin initially fought communist Gothic discourse; like communist sentimentality, communist fears struck him as inappropriate to a Bolshevik's voluntaristic worldview. At the Comintern's Third International Congress in the summer of 1921, he rejected the protest Kollontai had delivered to the delegates only minutes earlier: "Comrade Kollontai says (and this is the most noteworthy thing in all her interesting notions) that we are threatened by great danger. Her brilliant formula proclaims: 'I am seized by the strongest anxiety.' What follows from this? With the strongest anxiety you can't do great deeds."[112] In the years to come, "the strongest anxiety" *would* become a marked rhetorical feature in much cultural discourse, and, as we have seen, even Lenin's speeches would display traces of the Gothic imagery that came to dominate discussions of NEP.

Most remarkable of all is that Kollontai, who had been a leading figure in

---

Shliapnikov, a leader of the Workers' Opposition, Lenin, and Iurii Larin, one of the leading figures in shaping the Soviet economy. Shliapnikov repeatedly pressed the panic button in his indictment of Party policy:

When Party divisions lose their connection, when they don't know what's going on, when they don't know where to go, then there's panic. And in the Party we have panic now, because the Party as an entity, as a living organism, isn't participating in political life. [. . .] In connection with the New Economic Policy we see a reassessment of values and a search for a new base, a new point of support outside of the proletariat. It is this that provokes alarm and makes us uneasy to the highest degree.

Lenin responded with an attack on fear: "The most dangerous thing during a retreat is panic." Larin, always quotable, accused the Opposition of "panicism" (*panikerstvo*). *Odinnadtsatyi s"ezd*, 91–98.

The significance of "panic" in sexological discourse during NEP was recently the subject of a fascinating paper by Frances Bernstein, "Panika, polovoi vopros i problema muzhskoi seksual'nosti v konsul'tatsii po polovoi gigiene," Conference on Russian Everyday Life 1921– 1941: The Formation of Soviet Subjectivity, University of Economics and Finances, Saint Petersburg, 16 August 1994.

[111] See, for example, Lenin's speech to the Tenth All-Russian Conference of the Party in May 1921:

[Our task] is to give some freedom to capitalism that grows on the basis of small property ownership and small trade; we should not fear it, for it is in no wise terrifying for us.

In light of the general economic and political situation prevailing today, when the proletariat has in its hands all the sources of heavy industry and when there can be no talk of any denationalization, we have nothing to fear from [capitalism]. And, when we suffer mostly from an utter lack of products, from utter impoverishment, it is ludicrous to fear that capitalism existing on the basis of small-scale commercial agriculture poses a threat. To fear this means that one completely fails to take into account the balance of power in our economy[. . . .] (Lenin, "Doklad o prodovol'stvennom naloge" [26 May 1921], *Polnoe sobranie sochinenii*, 43:313–314)

[112] *Tretii vsemirnyi kongress kommunisticheskogo internatsionala. Stenograficheskii otchet* (Pb.: Gosudarstvennoe izdatel'stvo, 1922), 380.

the creation of NEP's Gothic discourse, became a prominent *object* of disgust for her Party adversaries. Her political views, her articles for the Komsomol, and finally her fiction were reviled in one article after another. Much of the criticism of Kollontai and her writing was heavily gendered. In the transcript of the Third International Congress of the Comintern, the attacks on Kollontai by Bukharin and Trotsky, as well as hostile comments shouted by Radek from his place in the audience, amount to a verbal gang assault; Kollontai's erstwhile comrades on the Central Committee alternately represent her as a frightened woman and a ludicrous "Valkyrie."[113] Critics claimed that Kollontai dealt in female pathology rather than with the problems of normal women; Zalkind charged that Kollontai had "forgotten" to tell her readers that one of her heroines was "of the clitoral type [to which belong] the majority of prostitutes" and which is distinguished by "a peculiar external irritability of the sexual organs."[114]

Reading such charges and situating Kollontai within the discursive disgust swirling around her, the contemporary critic may feel inclined to return to the feminist theories of the Gothic presented in chapter 4: Gothic discourse, even when its primary concern is with politics or class, may well seek a female object within the collective body upon which to direct its anxious revulsion. While the defeat of the Workers' Opposition may have been a foregone conclusion given the balance of power in the Party, one should not overlook the manner in which the "sentimental" views of the Workers' Opposition were publicly attacked by being identified with Kollontai—and feminized. Early Soviet Gothic, in fact, may be the product of a dialectics of disgust, in which particular ideological or class fears interact with the terror of the female body endemic in many patriarchal societies. In any case, today, as we read the savage attacks made throughout the 1920s on Kollontai, we are apt to pity her and, resisting the misogynistic forces in our own culture,

---

[113] Ibid., 368–380.

[114] Zalkind, *Polovoi vopros*, 53. The exaggerated characterization of Kollontai as a proponent of sexual promiscuity has been adopted uncritically in some recent scholarship. Roger Pethybridge does not cite a source in support of his claim that Kollontai "said that making love was of no more consequence than taking a sip of water." *The Social Prelude to Stalinism* (London: Macmillan, 1974), 51. This simile, which would not have been characteristic of Kollontai, probably predates the Revolution and may well be of non-Russian origin. Kollontai did say, as had Bebel, that "the sexual act must not be seen as something shameful and sinful but as something which is as natural as the other needs of [a] healthy organism, such as hunger and thirst." Alexandra Kollontai, *Selected Writings*, 229. This remark, which is followed by Kollontai's assertion (repeated in "Make Way for Winged Eros") that the greater an individual's intellectual and emotional development "the less place will there be in his or her relationship for the bare physiological side of love," is far from comparing intercourse to a "sip" or a "glass" of water, words that tar Kollontai with a carefree attitude toward intercourse that she never possessed.

may tend to empathize.[115] We should not, however, ignore the paradoxical role played by Kollontai in early Soviet ideology. Kollontai played a leading part in shaping the rhetorical contours of the NEP era she so reviled. Having made this contribution, she was relentlessly pursued by her own figures. In her post-Revolutionary writing, Kollontai stumbled into a trap implicit in her choice of genre; as a public figure she was subsequently pursued through the long corridors of a generic castle she had helped to construct and which she continued discursively to haunt. Revolutions may well consume their children; in this case revolutionary discourse devoured one of its aunts first.

[115] In a review of the three Kollontai biographies Simon Karlinsky is especially critical of their tendency to ignore Kollontai's complicity in the deeds of the Party and state that she served for so long. "The Menshevik, Bolshevik, Stalinist Feminist," *New York Times Book Review*, 4 January 1981, 3, 12, 14.

Chapter Seven

THE CASE OF CHUBAROV ALLEY: COLLECTIVE RAPE
AND UTOPIAN DESIRE

The "Facts" of the Case

On 11 September 1926, Soviet newspapers carried details of a horrible crime. A gang of drunken Leningrad youths returning from a funeral had abducted a young woman subsequently identified as "Liubov' [the name means "Love" in Russian] B.," taken her to a vacant lot near Chubarov Alley, and raped her for several hours. Gang rapes had been reported previously, receiving sparse and dry coverage in the Komsomol and Party press, with a paragraph or two summarizing the occurrence and containing the sentence pronounced to emphasize that the affair was a closed book, incapable of posing additional harm.[1] Such reports worked against the creation of sustained narrative interest and were rarely accorded a sequel. The rape in Chubarov Alley was reported in startlingly explicit detail by the Komsomol papers. The most lurid colors were employed to describe the area in the Ligovka district where the crime had occurred, and the conversations between the victim and her "forty" assailants were related word for word. Moreover, extensive press coverage continued for several days and became a serialized, ongoing narrative. Reports of the assault in *Smena*, the daily organ of the Leningrad Komsomol, and in the Moscow-based *Komsomol'skaia pravda*, were in some respects indistinguishable from episodes of a nineteenth-century roman-feuilleton. The generic difference between the descriptions of the Chubarov case and the materials that readers of the Komsomol and Party newspapers usually consumed was so startling as to demand immediate attention:

> The San-Galli Garden.
> In truth, it's not a garden. It's a dirty lot with a dozen broken trees and paths overgrown with grass and littered with beer bottles, cans, rags, and feces. It stretches out along Ligovka[2] and opens onto Predtechenskaia Street. Or rather, it doesn't open onto Predtechenskaia but has been forced to open onto it by a local gang that has ripped boards out of the fence every two or three meters, so that

[1] See "Novye zhertvy khuliganskogo nasiliia," *Komsomol'skaia pravda*, 21 September 1926, 2, for bulletins on other cases contemporary to the Chubarov affair.

[2] Ligovskii prospekt, a street notorious for its lawlessness since at least the start of the twentieth century.

you can crawl out of it onto Predtechenskaia. Predtechenskaia, a street where in broad daylight old and young alike play feverish games of *"ochko," "orlianka,"* and *"pristenochka."*[3] Where there is a bar on every corner. Where at night "the ring of the tambourine and the moans of the guitar" [*gde bubna zvon, gitary stony*] can be heard along the dark, unlit street. Where the gang roams. And in the crumbling houses the gang has set up its lairs. There it plans its "dry and wet" deeds.[4]

And it is here, amidst all this filth and drunkenness, so little washed by the Revolution, that the Kooperator factory is located. The factory's workers live in damp, unenticing houses along Predtechenskaia Street near the factory.

And it was here, several days ago, that an act of brutality occurred the likes of which old Peter[5] cannot remember [*zverstvo kotorogo ne pomnit Staryi Piter*].

Brutality, which claimed as its victim a twenty-one-year-old peasant girl, Citizen B., who had come to Leningrad to study at a Rabfak[6] and who lived with her brother, a medical student.

On Saturday, 21 August, at ten in the evening, she set out to see her girlfriend on Tambov Street. She walked along Ligovka. The street was noisy. Tens of drunks wandered aimlessly, and the air was thick with curses. Not paying attention to any of this, the girl went on her way.

Now came Chubarov Alley, and she turned into it to reach Predtechenskaia. She never made it there. She was stopped and surrounded by boisterous [*zalikhvatskie*] local youths, of whom not a few were workers at the Kooperator. The youths were in a fine mood. Earlier in the day they had buried a comrade and had been imbibing heavily [*krepko zalozhili*] to commemorate his death. When they had carried their friend to the Volkovo Cemetery, they had already been fairly drunk, and they had put away a few more [*eshche dobavili*] while at the cemetery. And now these fellows stopped Citizen B. They threw a dirty rag over her eyes:

—Shut up,—the gang [*bratva*], nineteen to twenty-five years old, warned.

They didn't give her a chance to say much. They grabbed her arms and dragged her along Predtechenskaia into the San-Galli Garden. They pushed her through a hole in the fence, into the garden. In the garden the beasts took the

---

[3] Colloquial names for forms of gambling roughly equivalent to "blackjack," "pitch-and-toss," and, possibly, a game of dice played against a wall.

[4] Thieves' slang for crimes the commission of which will (wet) or will not (dry) require the shedding of blood.

[5] Saint Petersburg.

[6] Rabfaki—workers' faculties—were schools established in 1919 to ensure "the preparation of workers and peasants for higher education in the shortest period of time." For more on the ideological and institutional significance of the Rabfaki, see Christopher Read, *Culture and Power in Revolutionary Russia: The Intelligentsia and the Transition from Tsarism to Communism* (London: Macmillan Press, 1990), 220–229, and Sheila Fitzpatrick, *Education and Social Mobility in the Soviet Union 1921–1934* (Cambridge: Cambridge University Press, 1979), 49–62.

blindfold off her eyes. The girl saw that something was amiss [*Devushka uvidela chto-to ne ladnoe*]. A large crowd had surrounded her. Their eyes were burning. They were cursing. They were laughing. Someone was singing songs.

—Unbutton it,—rasped a voice, and they began to take off her coat.

Citizen B. thought they were robbers, and she offered them her coat, if only they would let her go.

—What? Let you go?—The beasts roared.

—Lie down . . . It'll be better that way!—and with a blow they knocked her legs out from under her.

She fell. She lost consciousness, but the beasts did not lose theirs. One after another they satisfied their raging passions.

Someone grumbled:

—We'll be heard. And so that they wouldn't be heard,[7] they dragged her to another place. The girl regained consciousness for a moment. She felt pain in her body. Her tongue stuck to the roof of her mouth; she was not able to say a word.

—She's not breathing, the bitch! shouted the beasts waiting their turn.

—She better not have croaked [*ne zagnulas' by*],—one of the beasts said,— We have to bring her back to life [*nado ozhit'*].

And the brutal reanimation [*zverskoe ozhivlenie*] began. They beat her in the side, they beat her in the face, they pulled her hair and dragged her about the garden, they dragged her for a long time. Finally, they succeeded in making her gasp.

—She's spoken,—the beasts' voices cheered up, and once more they continued their disgusting work. One after another they raped the girl. Those who enjoyed themselves too long were dragged off.

Among the youths appeared Citizen K., no longer young, a forty-nine-year-old worker at the Kooperator.

—Don't butt in, old man, you don't have it anymore, but you're still hanging out with the girls [*u tebia ne to-e, a ty tozhe s devchenkami vozish'sia*],—the beasts laughed at the old man and didn't want to give him a turn at the victim.

—Just have a look now—whether I've got it or not,—and the forty-nine-year-old K. savagely began to do what twenty youngsters had already done before him.

Rare are scenes [*redki byvaiut takie kartiny*] such as the one that occurred in the San-Galli Garden, and not only nineteen-year-olds came to this show [*i na etu kartinu prishli ne tol'ko 19-letnie molodtsy*], children came as well. They watched from the bushes.

The beasts knew what they were doing. Fearing that their victim might later identify them, they took off her underwear and covered her face with it.

When no fewer than twenty people had finished their business and they had

---

[7] "Хлопает. И чтобы не хлопало . . ." The Russian here is obscure.

pulled the suffering and exhausted girl to the exit to Predtechenskaia, from somewhere or other came a group of ten more, and the girl was raped again. . . . This violent savagery continued for a long time . . .

At the exit from the garden, they grouped around their victim. Someone asked:

Has everyone done it? [*A vse imeli delo-to?*]

Everyone,—the voices responded.

At the exit from the garden they threatened the victim and with their fists extracted a promise from her that she wouldn't tell anyone what had happened.

Barely able to move, Citizen B. made her way home and there, along with the janitor, informed a policeman on duty. The police immediately carried out a raid and arrested five people. Two admitted participating in the rape.[8]

As the papers repeated the details with only slight variations in the days that followed, the amount of space given over to coverage was astounding. On 12 September *Smena* devoted two full pages to the event, which became known as "The San-Galli Affair" and "The Case of the Forty Hooligans." Equally remarkable was the suddenness with which the papers were filled with indignant popular reaction. On 12 September *Smena* published twenty-seven declarations from various collectives, each purporting to have been signed by tens or even hundreds of citizens. Outrage was not merely local: Moscow's *Komsomol'skaia pravda* carried reports nearly as detailed as *Smena*'s and provided additional evidence of popular rage. Perhaps most unusual were the demands for punishment. *Komsomol'skaia pravda*'s account was entitled "Shoot the Villains!" and many of the petitions similarly demanded the "supreme measure of punishment."[9] Rape, however, was not a capital offense, and the punishment for other gang rapes, as reported in the press, was rarely more than five years in jail.[10] Nevertheless, the deputy

[8] Vl. Khediashev, "Liudi—zveri," *Smena*, 11 September 1926, 3.

[9] The following example is typical:

We women workers at the Zinov'ev paper factory are indignant about the conduct of this band of scoundrels, about their bestial abuse of this girl.

Such acts must not be repeated in Lenin's city.

We demand swift and extremely severe punishment for the participants in this case, up to and including the supreme measure of punishment. (*Smena*, 12 September 1926, 3)

[10] According to Article 169 of the R.S.F.S.R. Criminal Code, the punishment attendant upon a conviction for rape was supposed to be at least three years, five if the victim killed herself thereafter. B. S. Bruk, ed., *Chubarovshchina. Po materialam sudebnogo protsessa* (M. and L.: Gos. izd., 1927), 60. (By way of comparison, the minimum sentence for murder was eight years.) Article 28, however, provided that in *any* case a judge could impose a lesser penalty than the one authorized by the code if he specified the reasons for leniency. *Ugolovnyi kodeks R.S.F.S.R.* (Pg.: Petrogubispolkom, 1922), 14–15. According to one report, between 1924 and 1926 the average sentence for rape in the R.S.F.S.R. was less than two and a half years; 12

prosecutor of the Leningrad Guberniia (region) insisted that *this* event was different and could be classified in no way other than as "sexual banditry." He added:

> We are treating this crime as an act of villainous sexual corruption, as violence compounded by threats. This crime is not only a rape. And so, the Prosecutor's Office has considered the matter of the *crime's reclassification.*[11]

Article 10 of the Russian Federation's Criminal Code provided that in cases where a crime was not specifically covered by an article in the code, a court could punish the offender by applying the article dealing with the "most similar" act.[12] Applying this doctrine of analogy, the prosecutor decided that the crime most like gang rape was not rape but banditry, a capital offense covered by Article 76 and defined as "organization of and participation in bands (armed gangs) and in attacks, robberies, and raids on Soviet institutions and private citizens organized by outlaw bands, including the stopping of trains and the destruction of railway lines regardless of whether these actions are accompanied by murder or robbery."[13]

In the following fortnight the Soviet press and, in particular, the Komsomol organs continued to highlight the crime. Sketches were published of the alleged ringleader, Pavel Kochergin, and of some of the other defendants, and, more sensational still, the victim herself was interviewed—a procedure that was condemned by several Komsomol journalists themselves.[14] Information was provided on the defendants' backgrounds and on the factory in which they worked. Finally, Emel'ian Iaroslavsky, then a secretary of the Party's Central Control Commission and the editor of several Party publica-

---

percent of all convictions for rape resulted in a suspended sentence. B. S. Man'kovskii, "Sovremennaia polovaia prestupnost'," in *Pravonarusheniia v oblasti seksual'nykh otnoshenii,* ed. E. K. Krasnushkin, G. M. Segal, and Ts. M. Fainberg (M.: Moszdravotdel, 1927), 99–101 (77–107).

[11] "Delo Ligovskikh khuliganov," *Smena,* 12 September 1926, 3.

[12] *Ugolovnyi kodeks R.S.F.S.R.* (1922), 9.

[13] *Chubarovshchina,* 54. At the trial, the prosecution defended this application of the analogy doctrine by producing a set of instructions issued by the Commissariat of Justice on 20 October, two months *after* the alleged commission of the crime. The instructions, stating that Article 76 should be applied to gang rape, had no legislative effect and therefore could not be viewed as a *new* legal interpretation, the prosecution argued. Since a set of instructions could legally disseminate only already existing law, the prosecutors continued, a law corresponding to it had to exist! In other words, there were grounds in the code for applying Article 76 because the (presumably infallible) Commissariat of Justice said there were; this was not a case where a new law (or a new interpretation of a law) was being accorded retroactive force. *Chubarovshchina,* 61.

[14] "Delo v Sadu 'San-Galli,'" *Smena,* 15 September 1926, 3. Criticism of the interview was particularly fierce in *Komsomol'skaia pravda*'s report on a conference dealing with hooliganism. "Kak vesti bor'bu s khuliganstvom," 23 September 1926, 3.

3. The Chubarov defendants in the dock. Courtesy of the Saint Petersburg Militia Museum.

tions as well as a frequent commentator in the Soviet press on morality and the problems of youth, intervened to protest the lurid reports:

> Are we illuminating these facts as we should? I personally think that extremely detailed reports of how a rape occurred and the daily savoring of these details in the press cause far more harm than good. For we must not forget that such descriptions attract the attention not only of many adults but also of numerous adolescents. They affect the imagination in the most horrible manner, they arouse unhealthy curiosity, they must work in the most destructive way on the vulnerable psyche of those of a transitional age. Who needs them, these details? Why do we have them? In order to arouse the indignation of public opinion? [. . .] Is not the very fact of a girl's violation by forty men sufficient to evoke revulsion? Do we need also to describe the details of this act for several days? This isn't necessary. It's harmful.[15]

Immediately coverage was curtailed, but five weeks later, as the prosecution prepared for trial, articles on the case sprouted once more, particularly since a correspondent for *Smena* and *Komsomol'skaia pravda* was to serve as the "social prosecutor" during the judicial process. The trial finally began on 16 December in the Leningrad Guberniia's Criminal Court and continued for ten days, during which the Leningrad papers received more than fifty-four thousand signatures demanding the strictest of punishments.[16] On the eve of the verdict *Komsomol'skaia pravda* declared, "This case's great significance lies in its having posed the question point-blank: who will lead our

[15] Em. Iaroslavskii, "Protiv khuliganstva," *Smena*, 25 September 1926, 2.
[16] "Chubarovskie khuligany pered sudom," *Komsomol'skaia pravda*, 24 December 1926, 2.

4. The San-Galli Garden: the scene of the crime (police photo). Courtesy of the Saint Petersburg Militia Museum.

youth, Pavel Kochergin and his comrades or the Soviet public and the Komsomol?"[17] The following day, twenty-two of the twenty-six defendants were convicted of rape, banditry, and/or perjury. Finding that their crime constituted a "threat to the foundations of Soviet law and order," the court sentenced seven defendants to death, three to ten-year terms, three to eight years, and the rest to lesser sentences.[18] On appeal some sentences were commuted, but five of the defendants were put to death on 26 January 1927.[19]

What accounts for the prominence accorded to the Chubarov affair? Why did this particular event become the focus of so much journalistic commotion, and why was this gang rape accorded such prosecutorial attention that defendants were executed who would ordinarily have received only several years in jail?[20] Was it, as the "social prosecutor" at the trial suggested, really

[17] "Chubarovskie khuligany pered sudom. Nakanune prigovora," *Komsomol'skaia pravda*, 28 December 1926, 1.

[18] "Prigovor po delu chubarovskikh nasil'nikov," *Smena*, 29 December 1926, 4.

[19] "Priveden v ispolnenie," *Komsomol'skaia pravda*, 28 January 1927, 2. Slight discrepancies concerning the exact number of defendants and the precise sentences exist among the various reports of the trial. Cf. *Chubarovshchina*, 92.

[20] See "Zveri," *Smena*, 6 November 1926, 4, and "Sud. Podmoskovnye 'chubarovtsy,'" *Komsomol'skaia pravda*, 28 December 1926, 4, for cases of gang rape contemporary to the Chubarov trial where sentences did not exceed five years.

In 1927, Professor A. A. Zhizhilenko, a Soviet jurist and the editor of the Publications Division of the Leningrad Criminal Court, criticized the application of Article 76 to gang rapes. Not

"an attack on the worker-family, on the life of a working region, on Soviet law and order, on the emancipated woman, and on the foundations of Soviet society?"[21] If the publicity surrounding the case was part of an organized campaign—and the amassing of thousands of signatures within a day of the first report (published over three weeks after the assault) certainly indicates that it was—to whom was it useful, and why was it successful in generating so many expressions of horror? Most important, how did the crime mesh with the social discourse surrounding it? To understand the meaning of Chubarov Alley, we must first examine in detail the context in which it occurred.

THE CORRUPTION OF THE INNOCENT

By the time the Chubarov story "broke," the Soviet press had been conducting a crusade against hooliganism for several months. The crusade had intensified early in the summer with the unleashing of attacks on the allegedly corrupting influence of the recently deceased poet Sergei Esenin and had featured regular reports of unlawful acts by youths.[22] Individual cases, such as that of Koren'kov (see chapter 2), were highlighted, although none received attention remotely resembling that of the crime in Chubarov Alley. On 17 September, in the midst of the first wave of detailed reports on the Leningrad rape, *Izvestiia* devoted four columns to the problem of hooliganism, and two days later it published a new poem by Vladimir Maiakovsky,

---

mentioning the Chubarov case by name, he observed that the application of Article 76 required the presence of a band and not a "mob which has assembled by chance," that the band had to be armed, and that it had to act with definite goals. None of these elements was usually present in a gang rape, he said, concluding, "without a doubt rape and banditry are not similar crimes." L. G. Orshanskii and A. A. Zhizhilenko, eds., *Khuliganstvo i prestuplenie* (L. and M.: Rabochii sud, 1927), 128 (121–130). Elsewhere Zhizhilenko was quoted as arguing that Article 76 could be applied to a gang rape only if the rape occurred in the midst of mass disturbances and was perpetrated by men participating in the mass disturbances. M. Pershin, "Polovye prestupleniia," *Rabochii sud*, no. 9 (1927): 769 (768–776).

Interestingly, the revised R.S.F.S.R. Criminal Code, which went into effect late in 1926 but was not applied retroactively to the Chubarov case, included a new provision specifically covering gang rapes. The maximum penalty authorized was eight years. *Ugolovnyi kodeks R.S.F.S.R. red. 1926 goda* (M.: N. K. Iu. R.S.F.S.R., 1925), 40. This revision insured—even before the sentences were pronounced—that the Chubarov case would have unique value as a symbol but no value as precedent.

[21] *Chubarovshchina*, 8.

[22] Esenin killed himself in Leningrad on 27 December 1925. The initial reaction from the Komsomol press was neutral. *Komsomol'skaia pravda*, in a short obituary on 1 January, praised Esenin as a contemporary elegist. Only in early summer 1926 did the Party attack Esenin as a symbol of the lack of ideological fortitude in Soviet youth. For a detailed analysis of the ideological and aesthetic repercussions of Esenin's (and others') suicides both within the Soviet Union and among Russian emigrés, see Anne Nesbet, "Suicide as Literary Fact in the 1920s," *Slavic Review* 50 (1991): 827–835.

"The Hooligan," in which the poet reacted to the Chubarov affair.[23] The same day, *Komsomol'skaia pravda* devoted half of its issue to the battle against hooliganism, declaring in its front-page editorial, "Hooligans—whether they intend it or not—are genuine enemies of the building of socialism."[24] Hooliganism and sexual "depravity" were commonly treated as part of the same scourge: the corruption of the nation's youth. Lev Sosnovsky, the founder of several important Bolshevik publications and a regular contributor to *Pravda* who had become extremely active in the campaign against hooliganism, quickly tied the Leningrad gang rape to other phenomena he had already excoriated. At the core of the hooligan's worldview, Sosnovsky wrote, was an individual's refusal to acknowledge the subjectivity of an other. The hooligan treated his fellow citizens, and particularly women, merely as the objects of his desires, and this, the columnist asserted, was exactly how Esenin had regarded women:

> "Yes! The Earth has a bitter truth
> I saw it with my childhood's eye!
> The dogs take their turns
> Licking the bitch gushing juice."

I cite these lines with squeamishness. Do they really have a place in the poetry of our days? Petersburg's forty hooligans could hardly invent a better "truth of the Earth" in their defense.[25]

The campaign against hooliganism had at least two aims, the most obvious being the control of crime. The Komsomol press did not publish national crime figures, but it did carry some alarming reports quantifying the incidence of hooliganism. In the Ivanovo-Voznesensk Guberniia (region), prosecution against hooliganism increased by 117 percent in 1925 and by September 1926 was already up 166 percent over all of the preceding year.[26] According to the deputy commissar of justice, the number of cases of hooliganism handled by administrative organs had doubled over the past two years.[27] Much of this crime wave may reflect increases in prosecution or changes in classification rather than alterations in extralinguistic reality. As defined in the Criminal Code, hooliganism was an extremely vague term: "mischievous acts committed with obvious disrespect for society."[28] Pursuant

[23] Vladimir Maiakovskii, "Khuligan," *Izvestiia*, 19 September 1926, 3.

[24] *Komsomol'skaia pravda*, 19 September 1926, 1.

[25] L. Sosnovskii, "Razvenchaite khuliganov," *Komsomol'skaia pravda*, 19 September 1926, 2. The poem quoted was "Poi zhe, poi! Na prokliatoi gitare," originally published in Berlin in 1923. For the text of the entire poem, see Sergei Esenin, *Sobranie stikhotvorenii*, 4 vols. (M. and L.: Gos. izd., 1926), 1:194–196.

[26] "V pokhod na khuliganstvo," *Komsomol'skaia pravda*, 26 September 1926, 2.

[27] Orshanskii and Zhizhilenko, *Khuliganstvo i prestuplenie*, 15.

[28] The relevant text of the Criminal Code is cited and discussed by the health commissar,

to a Central Executive Committee resolution, instructions were issued in June 1926 that called on judicial and investigative employees to "make their maximum effort" to "deal rapidly with the remains of the ulcer of hooliganism";[29] this exhortation may have encouraged arrests that earlier would not have been made.[30] Speaking at the Fifteenth Party Conference in November 1926, Politburo member Mikhail Tomsky charged that the problem of hooliganism had been grossly exaggerated, and he amused his fellow delegates with stories of how some local authorities had misapplied the statute to "playing music in private houses after 10 P.M.," "shooting slingshots," "approaching swimmers of the opposite sex," and "throwing stones and other objects at passing animals."[31] It may be that hooliganism was not so distressingly common a phenomenon in everyday life as the reports of prosecutors and journalists would suggest. For readers of the daily press, however, the flood of published reports on hooliganism made hooliganism a "reality" and an insistent part of the literary and journalistic sign system that reflected and formed ideological consciousness.

The second, and in many respects far more notable, aspect of the campaign against hooliganism was its role in the Party's battle for increased prominence in the lives of the young. To a significant extent the source of the campaign against hooliganism may have been not an increase in youth crime but the Party's desire for greater control over youth. In other words, an apparently ancillary consequence of the campaign may have been hooliganism's primary "source" and hooliganism itself may have been a chiefly discursive phenomenon. Of course, those writing and reading about hooliganism justified their activity by finding sources other than an originary desire

---

Nikolai Semashko, in his "K psikhologii khuliganstva," *Izvestiia*, 17 September 1926, 3. See also A. Estrin, *Ugolovnoe pravo R.S.F.S.R.* (M.: Iuridicheskoe izdatel'stvo narkomiusta, 1923), 91.

Although hooliganism had been a concern before the Revolution, the czarist criminal codes— unlike the Soviet ones—had never treated it as a distinct offense. On the difficulty of defining hooliganism in the pre-Revolutionary years, see Joan Neuberger, *Hooliganism: Crime, Culture, and Power in St. Petersburg, 1900–1913* (Berkeley and Los Angeles: University of California Press, 1993), 13, 18–35.

[29] See, e.g., Chief Judge Nakhimson's instructions to judges and prosecutors in the Leningrad Guberniia. Orshanskii and Zhizhilenko, *Khuliganstvo i prestuplenie*, 172.

[30] In Leningrad the jump in arrests for hooliganism in the third quarter of 1926 was remarkable. In the first quarter of that year 152 people charged with hooliganism passed through the holding cells of the Leningrad People's Court. The figures for the second, third, and fourth quarters were 652, 2043, and 1093. Alleged hooligans accounted for 13.4, 36.1, *59.7*, and 49.1 percent of all criminals passing through the cells. V. Z., "K bor'be s khuliganstvom v Leningrade," *Rabochii sud*, no. 3 (1927): 221 (221–222). See also Peter H. Solomon's account of the changes in the administrative and judicial disciplining of hooliganism during the 1920s, "Criminalization and Decriminalization in Soviet Criminal Policy, 1917–1941," *Law and Society Review* 16 (1981–1982): 16–17 (9–43).

[31] Orshanskii and Zhizhilenko, *Khuliganstvo i prestuplenie*, 3–5.

for control. For them, hooliganism came from outside; it was the product of influences external to the would-be utopia, either because these influences came from beyond the country's geographical boundaries or because they came from the past. The problem of hooliganism was one of geographical and historical transmission. If the links to the impure bourgeois environment that surrounded Soviet youth on every physical and temporal side except the future could be dissolved, hooliganism and sexual depravity—the argument went—would disappear, giving way to a highly developed class consciousness.

In the Party and Komsomol press, the sources of hooliganism and of its frequent companion, sexual depravity, were usually traced to two disparate mentalities attributed to corresponding periods of Soviet history: War Communism and NEP. In the former period, according to columnists looking backward, all behavioral niceties had been thrust aside: "At that time—in the smoke and crash of the Civil War's battles, we had no time to be concerned with our level of culture."[32] The pre-NEP era was retrospectively characterized by writers such as Pil'niak as a time of apocalyptic, elemental forces, a period when established, repressive codes of behavior gave way to liberated instinct. Other writers retrospectively valued War Communism for a different reason, viewing the years before NEP as a wonderful time of absolute consciousness and of unbesmirched ideological purity. According to the official, Party-approved viewpoint of the mid-1920s, however, the mentality of War Communism also had entailed an unnatural and premature mode of thought in its utopian aspirations.[33] Now that the transitional epoch had begun, the crude habits of War Communism needed to be cast off: "For new times, new songs" (Novye vremena, novye pesni).[34] Hooligans were portrayed as Revolutionaries who were having difficulty adjusting to the absence of war; their excess energy was being channeled in the wrong directions.[35]

Certainly, neither the Party nor the Komsomol intended that ideological purity be the price paid for better manners. Bourgeois ways of life, resuscitated along with the reintroduction of elements of a capitalist economy, were tempting Soviet youth, dragging the former "heroes" of the Civil War into an abyss of uncontrolled moneygrubbing, gambling, and fornication. According to G. Bergman, who launched the campaign against Esenin, "the least resistant of our young people are poorly withstanding the test of NEP, of this ordeal that is far more difficult than the fire of war. Deprivation, inequality, our disorganized way of life, the influence of bourgeois and semibourgeois

---

[32] "Protiv raspushchennosti," Komsomol'skaia pravda, 6 November 1925, 1.

[33] "Doklad tov. Bukharina po programmnomu voprosu," Pravda, 1 July 1924, 3.

[34] "Protiv raspushchennosti," 1.

[35] Ia. Bugaiskii, "Khuliganstvo," Molodaia gvardiia, no. 12 (1926): 132–142.

elements,—all these often sully and crush the young, untempered soul."[36] As Taras Kostrov, the editor of *Komsomol'skaia pravda*, admitted in April 1926, Soviet youth had to fight a "battle on two fronts." He warned against the dangers posed both by those who were attacking petty-bourgeois behavioral codes, waving the red flag of "*meshchanstvo*" (petty-bourgeois behavior) for the purpose of justifying their own "*khamstvo*" (boorishness), *and* by those who were reintroducing petty-bourgeois values.[37] Essentially, the problem was that young people liked the transitional epoch either too little or too much. Rejection of its necessary economic "contradictions" could lead to ideologically antisocial behavior, to a coarse proletarian naturalism (an acting out of the proletarian id), or to suicidal despair (revolutionary melancholy and depression). In contrast to youths of the above dispositions, who, depending on their behavior, were classified as "uncultured" or "pessimistic," there were those who threw themselves wholeheartedly into NEP, drinking and gambling, ready to exploit and be exploited. Often the line between rejection and acceptance of NEP was blurred, as portraits of youthful depravity combined elements of War Communism's crudeness with self-destructive despair and acquisitive egotism.[38]

The presence of the very word "hooliganism" in the Party press was redolent of the odious, "shameful" period of reaction that had followed the suppression of the first Russian Revolution and also witnessed the popularity of Artsybashev and other purveyors of "the sex question." Joan Neuberger has recently examined the importance of hooliganism as a cultural phenomenon at the start of the century, and, in many respects, the language of the Chubarov account may owe something to the language of pre-Revolutionary reports.[39] According to Neuberger, however, rape was rarely associated with hooliganism prior to the Revolution;[40] a contribution of the Chubarov affair to Russian culture may have been the imbrication of hooliganism and sex. The massive scale of the coordination of the campaign against hooliganism was something entirely new, as were the severe sentences handed down to the Chubarov rapists. The most important difference between pre-Revolutionary and NEP reporting on hooliganism, though, was ideological. As Neuberger details at great length, hooligans before the Revolution were por-

---

[36] G. Bergman, "Esenin—znamia upadochnykh nastroenii," *Komsomol'skaia pravda*, 15 June 1926, 2.

[37] T. Kostrov, "O kul'ture, meshchanstve i vospitanii molodezhi," *Komsomol'skaia pravda*, 1 April 1926, 1.

[38] Leonid Leonov's *The Thief*, originally published in 1927, provides a fine example of this blurring, bringing together in NEP's dens of iniquity the heroes of yesterday and the would-be profiteers of today. *Vor*, 3 vols. (Riga: Literatura, 1928).

[39] See, in particular, the headlines cited by Neuberger involving "brutality" (*zverskoe, zverstvo*). *Hooliganism*, 222.

[40] Ibid., 232–233.

trayed as "other"; they belonged to a class different from those to which the readers and publishers of popular journals belonged. After the Revolution hooligans were represented as members of "our" class fallen victim to the past. In the Chubarov case this identification generated profound—and, as compared to the pre-Revolutionary period, profoundly different—ideological anxieties.

Pervading the descriptions of hooliganism was a rhetoric of infection and corruption.[41] An imagery of pus, filth, and epidemic raged in the Soviet press, coloring all descriptions of problems of youth. It is not surprising that attacks should have focused on venereal disease. (In 1919 Lenin himself had compared the conquest of capitalism to the conquest of syphilis; the former, he said, was more difficult.)[42] In the mid-1920s, as anxieties about ideological infection grew more intense, the language employed to discuss syphilis became especially striking: "every hour, every minute, hundreds, thousands, millions of syphilitics do their terrible work, sowing contagion around themselves."[43] The 17 September 1926 issue of *Izvestiia*, which launched the most intense phase of the antihooliganism campaign, contained a cartoon captioned "The Hooligan Bacillus." The drawing showed a "hooligan," further identified as a "shameful disease" (*durnaia bolezn'*—the same term used for sexually transmitted infections) on a microscopic slide; in his left hand he held an extremely phallic knife.

How does one battle a disease? In his attack on Esenin's pernicious influence among young, "untempered" Soviet men and women, Bergman employed the rhetoric of infection as he argued for greater attention to the realm of "personal life":

> The chief task at hand is healing our youth. No one has ever seen the small-pox microbe. But we have learned to vaccinate—and now man laughs at the microbe.
>
> A revolutionary, communist, Marxist "vaccine" is especially necessary among our student youth. [. . .] All the more necessary is thoughtful work among these young people. We should not brush Esenin aside and so forth but should try to understand his appeal. We should not abandon the weakest to fight alone with life and with death but surround them with comradely attention. [. . .] Then it will not be difficult to dispose of all that is rotten.[44]

Out of this desire for disease control was born the war on "personal life" discussed in chapter 2. This inoculatory policy would require that the forces of control enter Esenin's territory—the intimate life of the young—and sub-

[41] See, inter alia, Anat. Gorelov, "Luna s pravoi storony," *Smena*, no. 7 (9 January 1927): 3.
[42] V. I. Lenin, "Velikii pochin" (July 1919), *Polnoe sobranie sochinenii*, 5th ed., 45 vols. (M.: Politicheskaia literatura, 1956–1965), 39:20.
[43] "Sud nad sifilitikom," *Pravda*, 11 July 1924, 7.
[44] Bergman, "Esenin—znamia upadochnykh nastroenii," 2.

due (or sublate) it from within. The seemingly perverse dynamic by which the campaign against "personal life" operated—arousing desire in order ultimately to appropriate it—followed all the rules of proper epidemiological procedure. The Komsomol had been insufficiently concerned with the intimate and the personal; now these spheres threatened to stand in the way of increased governmental control and had to be subverted from within.

THE CORRUPTION OF THE EXPERIENCED

The rhetoric of contagion and disease was not confined to discussions of youth. Questions of purity plagued the Party throughout the mid-1920s, and the battles for power within it were fought along a discursive axis preoccupied with corruption. While an obsession with the preservation of ideological (in this case "truly Leninist") chastity would be natural in the self-proclaimed transitional phase of any movement with utopian leanings, it was all the more to be expected given the specific characteristics of NEP, for NEP was itself a type of vaccination on an unprecedented economic and ideological scale. A limited amount of capitalism had been reintroduced into the Soviet economy, the argument went, so that communism could master its tools and use them for anticapitalist ends. Attacking Grigory Sokol'nikov, the finance commissar and a Zinov'ev supporter, at the Fourteenth Party Congress in December 1925, Stalin spelled out the dynamics of NEP in a formulation that smacked of inoculatory tactics:

> The problem is that Comrade Sokol'nikov does not understand the dual nature of NEP, the dual nature of its system of commerce. [. . .] He does not understand the dialectic of development within the framework of a transitional period, when the methods and weapons of the bourgeoisie are used by socialist elements to overcome and liquidate capitalist elements. It's not at all that commerce and the monetary system are methods of "a capitalist economy." The fact is that the socialist elements of our economy are mastering the methods and weapons of the bourgeoisie in order to overcome capitalist elements, using these methods and weapons for the construction of our economy's socialist foundation.[45]

Those who made use of this inoculatory logic strove to protect its formulation from others' charges (and from their own fears) of ideological taint. Even in a medical context there are obviously profound logical and psychological resistances to the notion of vaccination; it can be illogical and terrifying to introduce agents of disease into the body (personal or politic) for the sake of remaining well.

The battle between the Moscow-dominated Party leadership and the

---

[45] Quoted in V. K., "O NEPe, goskapitalizme i stroitel'stve sotsializma," *Komsomol'skaia pravda*, 10 January 1926. Sokol'nikov was removed from his post as finance commissar shortly after the congress.

Leningrad opposition, which erupted publicly at the Fourteenth Congress in December 1925 and continued through 1926, revolved around discomfort with NEP. All the combatants professed loyalty to the New Economic Policy and accused their opponents of being loyal in the wrong way. Zinov'ev and Kamenev rebuked Bukharin and, to a lesser degree, Stalin for "idealizing" NEP. Focusing on the impurities NEP had introduced, Zinov'ev admitted the necessity for these impurities but insisted that they not be confused with inherent characteristics of socialism.

> To take the bull by the horns, I think it is essential, first of all, to respond to those who are now trying to portray the matter as if we didn't have any kind of state capitalism and, indeed, almost no capitalism of any kind. I believe that what we have here is an attempt by several comrades to declare here and now that NEP is socialism. [Audience responds with laughter and noise.] Such a point of view, such a position amounts to idealization of NEP, idealization of capitalism. [Voice in the hall: "Who thinks that?"] It is incontestable that NEP is the road to socialism, but it seems to me equally incontestable that NEP is not socialism.[46]

Each side accused the other of favoring ideological retreat. On the eve of the Fourteenth Congress, *Pravda*, anticipating this debate, took special pains to indicate that no retreat was occurring:

> In his time Lenin called NEP a retreat. And now, in NEP's fifth year, several comrades stubbornly see in NEP only this side, not noticing that, introducing NEP, we retreated in order *to take a running start and leap forward*. Now we are completing this leap forward. Stubborn repetition of words about retreat at a time when we have passed to the offensive and are conquering step by step cannot be called by any other name but disbelief in the socialist ways of our development.[47]

At the congress, this line of thinking was espoused by Stalin and Bukharin, whose supporters accused the Leningrad faction of "pessimism" and "lack of faith." Zinov'ev and Kamenev were charged by Stalin's followers with being too partial toward War Communism; the Leningrad faction, in turn, accused Stalin and Bukharin of being too soft on those who had enriched themselves during NEP—the Nepman and the kulak. Discussion grew particularly heated when Zinov'ev's supporters charged their Moscow adversaries with pandering to the kulaks under the pretense of trying to win over the "middle peasant" (*seredniak*). When this allegation was itself cited as evidence of a deviation from the Party line, members of the Leningrad faction retorted that if theirs was a deviation it was a "proletarian" one.

---

[46] "Sodoklad tov. Zinov'eva," *Komsomol'skaia pravda*, 22 December 1925, 3.
[47] "Privet XIV partiinomu s"ezdu," *Komsomol'skaia pravda*, 18 December 1925, 1.

Bukharin had tried to establish a "Seredniak-Bolshevism," they claimed, but no such animal could exist; there was only "proletarian Bolshevism."[48] Although Zinov'ev denied that he wanted to go "back" to War Communism,[49] his faction was unable to resist being tarred with the War Communist label, in part because its members argued that there was less danger from War Communism than from the idealization of NEP.[50] The Party was not menaced from below (misguided, pessimistic workers and poor peasants), the Zinov'ev-controlled *Leningradskaia pravda* contended, but by elements at the top of the economic ladder.[51]

While Zinov'ev and Kamenev concentrated on impurities as they attempted to demonstrate the flawed, naive, and overly optimistic mentality of their opponents, and while their rhetoric was centered on the potential for *loss of control*, Stalin spoke of impurities only within the context of their constant *supervision*. The general secretary assured his listeners that impurities were being constantly and firmly managed. Here the discourse of inoculatory dialectics was especially useful. Capitalism had been reintroduced to the Soviet economy so that that economy would ultimately be more resistant to capitalism. Repeatedly Stalin returned to the question of control, taking issue with those whose language was not sufficiently obsessed with the issue or whose definitions expressed the slightest fear that in NEP the capitalist microbe would infect instead of immunize:

> The question of NEP. I have in mind Comrade Krupskaia and her speech on NEP. She said: "NEP is in essence capitalism that we permit to exist under certain well-known conditions, capitalism, which the proletarian state holds on a chain." That we hold capitalism on a chain and will hold it there for so long as it exists, that's a fact, that's true. But that NEP is capitalism,—that's nonsense, utter nonsense. NEP is a special policy of our proletarian state, predicated on conflict between socialist and capitalist elements, on an expanding role played by socialist elements to the detriment of capitalist elements, on the victory of socialist elements over capitalist elements, on the destruction of class divisions, and on the construction of the foundation on which the socialist economy will be built. Anyone who does not understand this transitional, dual nature of NEP deviates from Leninism. Does the opposition agree with Comrade Krupskaia that NEP is capitalism, or not? I think that there is not one member of this congress who could be found to agree with Comrade Krupskaia's formulation. Comrade Krupskaia (may she forgive me) has uttered absolute nonsense about NEP.[52]

[48] I. Bardin, "Gde glavnaia opasnost'," originally published in *Leningradskaia pravda* on 18 December 1925, and reproduced in part in *Novaia oppozitsiia* (L.: Priboi, 1926), 65.

[49] "Zakliuchitel'noe slovo tov. Zinov'eva," *Komsomol'skaia pravda*, 30 December 1925, 2.

[50] See, e.g., "Rech' L.B. Kameneva," *Komsomol'skaia pravda*, 24 December 1925, 1.

[51] Bardin, "Gde glavnaia opasnost'," 64.

[52] "Zakliuchitel'noe slovo tov. Stalina," *Komsomol'skaia pravda*, 30 December 1925, 2. The

Although Kamenev and Zinov'ev were decisively defeated at the congress, their faction, now dislodged from control of the Leningrad press organs, continued to struggle with Stalin through 1926. At the Fifteenth All-Union Party Conference in November 1926, the divisive issue was whether socialism could win an "ultimate" victory within one country. In a sense, this was a nonissue. No one, not Stalin, Bukharin, Zinov'ev, Kamenev, nor Trotsky, the new ally of the recently defeated opposition leaders, claimed that socialism could be "completely" built in one land. All were acutely disturbed by the question of capitalism's penetration of their society and shared the belief that if the capitalist nations were not "converted," the construction of socialism within the Soviet Union could not be assured. Their differences, once again, lay in how they framed their thoughts about the demon that possessed them all. Should the focus be on what was happening outside the USSR or on the events occurring within, with the dangers from without or with "the internal strengths and internal resources" (Bukharin)[53]— which, when properly marshaled and augmented, could help the Soviet economy catch up with the West? Stalin argued that "on the basis of the internal strengths of our Revolution" the "victory of socialism" within the Soviet Union could be achieved. He distinguished this victory from "the *ultimate* victory" of socialism within the USSR, which he defined as "the creation of an absolute guarantee against intervention and attempts to restore capitalism, a guarantee predicated on the socialist revolution's victory in at least several lands."[54] In actuality, the policy differences between the two sides were minimal. The real issue was which personalities and factions would control the Party and its power. The ideological obsession with purity generated the language in which the struggle for power was acted out and which insured that factional strife erupted precisely around the issue of corruption of the Revolution. The Fourteenth Congress and the Fifteenth Conference were two sides of the same utopian coin, the counterfeit of which was so universally feared. At the first gathering attention focused more on corruption from within, at the second on corruption from without.

IDEOLOGICAL RESONANCE

Throughout 1925 much of the struggle between the Leningrad and Moscow Party factions took place within the Komsomol. According to Komsomol First Secretary Nikolai Chaplin, the organization's highest ranking official, in

---

section of the speech from which the quotation is taken is entitled "NEP, no ne kapitalizm" (NEP, but not capitalism).

[53] "XV Vsesoiuznaia Konferentsiia," *Komsomol'skaia pravda*, 9 November 1926, 1.

[54] "XV Vsesoiuznaia konferentsiia VKP(b). O vnutripartiinom polozhenii i oppozitsionnom bloke v VKP(b)," *Komsomol'skaia pravda*, 6 November 1926, 1.

early 1925 Zinov'ev and Kamenev had begun using the Bureau of the Komsomol's Central Committee, where they controlled a majority, to criticize the
reluctance of the Party's Central Committee to expel Trotsky from the Politburo. Their followers had further aggravated the hostility between the two
sides by unexpectedly introducing a measure at a Komsomol plenum to expand the Komsomol's ruling bureau, with the aim of further packing it with
the opposition's supporters. Chaplin wrote to the Party's Central Committee,
asking to be relieved of his duties since work had become impossible. On 12
February the Party issued the Komsomol a warning:

> The Central Committee of the Russian Communist Party warns the Bureau of
> the Central Committee of the Komsomol that if there are any more steps
> taken—by whatever side—in furtherance of factional policies that threaten the
> unity of the Central Committee and the Komsomol as a whole, the Central Com-
> mittee of the Party will be forced to take measures guaranteeing the preservation
> of unity.[55]

Claiming that it was being persecuted, the Leningrad Komsomol soon sent
out announcements of an upcoming conference to seventeen other regional
Komsomol groups, snubbing the Moscow branch of the organization. Fierce
debates ensued within the organization's bureau, where a motion to condemn
the Leningrad organization failed. Again, the minority appealed to the
Party's Central Committee, which appointed an investigatory commission
that subsequently ordered the removal of four bureau members. An extraordinary plenum of the Komsomol's Central Committee met in March, heard
reports from Bukharin and Andreev, elected a new, Moscow-leaning bureau,
and condemned, in an unpublished resolution, the old bureau and the Leningrad Regional Komsomol.

The Leningrad Komsomol's tactics were similar to those of the Leningrad
Party leadership. It portrayed itself as having remained true to Leninist principles, while the Party and particularly the Moscow Komsomol had fallen
victim to the proponents of what *Smena* called a "new NEP."[56] It also argued
that the Party was catering too much to wealthy peasants and was, in general, tilting away from its identification with the proletariat. Chaplin and his

---

[55] "Komsomol i oppozitsiia. Doklad tov. Chaplina na plenume MK RLKSM ot 7ogo ianvaria
1926 goda," *Komsomol'skaia pravda*, 15 January 1926, 3. My account of the struggle in the
Komsomol summarizes information disclosed in Chaplin's speech and in an editorial published
three days earlier: "Komsomol za edinstvo lenintsev," *Komsomol'skaia pravda*, 12 January
1926, 1. For a brief, later Soviet discussion that does not appreciably diverge from Chaplin's,
see V. Sulemov, *Soiuz molodykh bortsov* (M.: Molodaia gvardiia, 1971), 199–200. See also
N. B. Lebina, *Rabochaia molodezh' Leningrada: Trud i sotsial'nyi oblik, 1921–1925 gody* (L.:
Nauka, 1982), 87–90.

[56] "Vnutripartiinoe polozhenie," *Smena*, 22 December 1925, 1.

allies in the Party were incensed by remarks in Leningrad Komsomol and Party publications which implied that the Komsomol was more Leninist than the Komintern and more Bolshevik than the Party.[57]

Events reached a head in the weeks preceding the Fourteenth Congress. After the Party's October Central Committee Plenum, the Leningrad Komsomol amassed all speeches in which Bukharin had used the unfortunate phrase "enrich yourselves" (in speaking about the Party's policy toward the peasantry). Annotated with remarks such as "Here Bukharin rejects Lenin" and packaged in a "blue folder" marked "secret," the speeches and articles of Bukharin and others in the Moscow faction were sent to Komsomol officials sympathetic to Zinov'ev. Chaplin, who considered this act tantamount to "corruption of the youth," had the Leningrad faction harshly criticized on the eve of the congress. In *Smena* the Leningrad Party organization protested that it was being attacked by proponents of an anti-Leninist deviation and charged that the signal for the attack had been given at the recent Moscow Regional Party Conference.[58] Recapitulating in early 1926 the factional battles of the past year and, ironically, tapping into the "squandered energy" analogy so often used at the time in discussions of sex, *Komsomol'skaia pravda* editorialized: "It may well be that no previous oppositional movement within the Party wasted so much energy as this one in seeking to turn the maturing generation of Leninists against our Party."[59]

Not only the larger cultural concerns but also the internecine Komsomol struggle created the context for the furor over the rape in Chubarov Alley. Given recent Party conflicts, it was no coincidence that the event chosen to exemplify the terrible corruption of Soviet youth and, in particular, of members of the Komsomol occurred in Leningrad. Saint Petersburg has a rich history in Russian cultural mythology as a source of corruption, and reports on the Chubarov case were to draw on this myth repeatedly. The recent fight with the Leningrad Party organization provided an additional, post-Revolutionary subtext, for it could be argued that the organization whose members had participated in the rape had been shaped by the opposition. At an "extraordinary" conference of the Leningrad Party organization called in early 1926 to rebuild local structures without Zinov'ev's loyalists, Bukharin urged that special attention be paid to the local Komsomol, because its young, easily influenced members might have been led by Zinov'ev's brand of Leninism to reject everything that had occurred in the USSR since the collapse of

---

[57] See "Komsomol i oppozitsiia," *Komsomol'skaia pravda*, 15 January 1926, 3. The anonymous author of this article was particularly incensed by the assertion of *Iunyi proletarii*, the journal of the Leningrad Komsomol, that "Wherever we look, we see that the Komsomol is the most Bolshevik-inclined organization."

[58] "Vnutripartiinoe polozhenie," 1.

[59] "Komsomol za edinstvo Lenintsev," *Komsomol'skaia pravda*, 12 January 1926, 1.

War Communism.[60] Iaroslavsky seized upon the locale of the crime in an effort to explain how it could have happened:

> *Komsomol'skaia pravda* has taken notice of the extraordinary number of acts of hooliganism that have occurred recently among members of the Komsomol. It seems to me that this fact is connected with the growth of the Komsomol, with a growth that has been far from constantly regulated. In particular, the Komsomol grew so quickly in Leningrad in 1925 that there could be no question of serious communist education among the youthful mass newly admitted to the organization. And there can be no doubt that given such unrestrained massive growth those who were admitted were insufficiently checked.[61]

Disgust at the crime became disgust at the legacy of the opposition and its War Communist leanings. Moreover, *Smena*, which led the campaign against the Chubarovtsy and "*chubarovshchina*" ("chubarovitis" or "chubarovism"), had been the flagship of Zinov'ev's Leningrad Komsomol. Its control had changed hands on 12 January 1926, after a new leadership had been installed in the Leningrad Party organization.[62] *Smena*'s participation in the trial (through its "social prosecutor") served as a symbol of the repudiation of the opposition by its former organs. The paper's new editor, David Khanin, even anticipated the Chubarov event with an article entitled "Bolshevik Education of Youth and the Opposition," which was published in the September 1926 issue of *Molodaia gvardiia* alongside "The Moon from the Right Side" and accused the opposition of seeking to infect Soviet youth with "a lack of discipline."[63]

It was also significant that the victim of the attack was a peasant who had moved to Leningrad to study. Her identity not only recalled the antipeasant bias of Zinov'ev's "proletarian deviation" but also maximized the event's power as a symbol of corruption. Commentators were quick to point out that the seedy Chubarov Alleys of the former capital were the wretched counterpart of Nevsky Prospect—long a symbol of foreign, artificial values:

[60] *Novaia oppozitsiia*, 299. From the time of its founding Saint Petersburg—as a representative of Western and perhaps "unnatural" influence—has always been "other" in Russian culture. The persistence of this status during NEP and, perhaps, its intensification (see Katerina Clark, "The 'Quiet Revolution' in Soviet Intellectual Life," in *Russia in the Era of NEP*, ed. Sheila Fitzpatrick, Alexander Rabinowitch, and Richard Stites [Bloomington: Indiana University Press, 1991], 229 [210–230]) was certainly not impeded by the entrenchment in Leningrad of the Zinov'ev-led opposition.

[61] Iaroslavskii, "Protiv khuliganstva," 2.

[62] For accounts of the rout of Zinov'ev's followers in the Leningrad Party organization, see Z. M. Ivanova and E. A. Remizova, eds., *Ocherki istorii leningradskoi organizatsii* (L.: Lenizdat, 1969), 155–156; and Iu. V. Voskresenskii, "K istorii razgroma Zinov'evskoi novoi oppozitsii," *Voprosy istorii KPSS*, no. 5 (1967): 62–71.

[63] D. Khanin, "Bol'shevistskoe vospitanie molodezhi i oppozitsiia," *Molodaia gvardiia*, no. 9 (1926): 97 (94–102).

What is *chubarovshchina*? *Chubarovshchina* is unhealthy, rotten confusion, the cursed inheritance of the capitalist regime that, flowing from prostituted Nevsky Prospect, has penetrated into our midst and overwhelmed unsteadfast workers as yet untempered in their class mentality. . . .[64]

Chubarov Alley is a kind of branch of Nevsky Prospect, that formerly fashionable and utterly prostituted bourgeois street which has now collected along itself all the filth from the Nepmen of the metropolis.[65]

A formulation was thus found that reconciled Petersburg's traditional image as a source of contamination with its honored position as the Cradle of the Revolution. The city was made to symbolize the proletarian virtues of the Revolution as well as the bourgeois forces threatening them. Ironically, this formulation preserved, through a simple reversal, a topos of the pre-Revolutionary press discourse on hooliganism, in which the power of hooliganism to disrupt social order had been measured by the phenomenon's appearance on Nevsky—the topographical center of bourgeois and petty-bourgeois values.[66]

Liubov' B. was not the only victim of the Chubarov affair. Part of the reason the campaign against the Chubarovtsy had such resonance was that for all its careful orchestration it seems to have both expressed and provoked an unprecedented degree of horror in the bearers and formulators of Soviet ideology. Much of this horror was caused by the identity of the perpetrators, half of whom may have been members of the Komsomol[67] and who included one of the founders of the Kooperator factory's Komsomol cell (the first Komsomol cell in all of Leningrad's Volodarsky region)[68] and at least one candidate for membership in the Party. Iaroslavsky wailed, "*How could it happen, that among forty rapists there were five members of the Komsomol?* [other reports set the number of komsomol'tsy much higher]."[69] It was not so much the presence of komsomol'tsy among the rapists that was so painful as the fact that all of the rapists were members of the proletariat. *Komso-*

---

[64] "Protiv chubarovshchiny," *Komsomol'skaia pravda*, 28 December 1926, 1.

[65] I. Bobryshev, "Pereulki i tupiki," *Komsomol'skaia pravda*, 1 March 1927, 3.

[66] Neuberger, *Hooliganism*, 31–34, 80–82.

[67] "'Geroi' Chubarova pereulka," *Komsomol'skaia pravda*, 29 September 1926, 2.

[68] Untitled editorial, *Smena*, 12 September 1926, 1.

[69] Iaroslavskii, "Protiv khuliganstva," 2. Demographic and sociological information was collected on the Chubarovtsy while they were in jail but was not published in the Komsomol press. According to a report published in a collection of semischolarly articles in 1927, of twenty-five defendants questioned, eight were members of the Komsomol, two were candidates for Party membership, and six were former members of either the Party or Komsomol (i.e., 64 percent were or had been associated with Party organizations). Perhaps more distressing was that twenty-two were skilled workers; the defendants generally earned good salaries and had not been driven to crime by financial need. Only six had prior criminal records. *Khuliganstvo i prestuplenie*, 153–169.

mol'skaia pravda exclaimed: "After all, the Chubarov crime was committed beneath the very walls of the factory; it was committed by young workers, with the participation of members of the Komsomol. All this requires that we undertake a decisive and stubborn battle with *chubarovshchina*."[70]

The penetration of this awful crime into the proletariat's youth, up to "the very walls" of a factory in the Cradle of the Revolution, prompted a terrible identification—not with the object of the criminal act but with its perpetrators. Anatoly Gorelov confessed: "The burden of the past that the accused received as their inheritance is not their personal grief alone. [. . .] The voice of their infected blood cries out in us."[71] *Smena* argued that the rapists had to be held accountable for their acts. Hooliganism was a natural result of capitalism, but under the dictatorship of the proletariat, where the worker was privileged and not isolated from cultural achievement, it ceased to be a natural phenomenon and became an individual aberration.[72] There were those who disagreed—proletarian origin was commonly seen as a mitigating circumstance during criminal sentencing—and the vigor with which *Komsomol'skaia pravda* and *Smena* argued against clemency may indicate that their crusade against the Chubarovtsy was meeting unexpectedly strong resistance which was not often permitted to surface among the many avowals of support for the prosecution that poured out on the newspapers' pages in petitions from collectives.[73] On 17 September Mikhail Pershin, the lead prosecutor on the case, spoke out in *Smena* against draconian punishments and argued that hooliganism should be combated through social work and the study of "*byt*":

> Is it really not clear to us that behind lathes and at the workbenches of metalworkers, in trucks and even in Komsomol clubs, there is no shortage of men, workers born and bred, *who have not yet committed but are potentially capable* of committing rape and many other such things? And does our cultural and professional experience and our work in the Komsomol not tell us of cases where hooliganism has been sharply reduced and where even the most seemingly hopeless people have been "put on the path of the righteous," thanks to an attitude toward cultural work that is neither vapid nor sentimental but *founded on genuine knowledge and "investigation" of the facts of proletarian life?*[74]

---

[70] "Protiv chubarovshchiny," 1.

[71] Anat. Gorelov, "Surovyi prigovor," *Smena*, 15 September 1926, 3.

[72] "Ligovskoe bytie i khuliganskoe 'soznanie,'" *Smena*, 18 September 1926, 1.

[73] An article and a letter in *Smena* indicate that workers at the Kooperator factory were indignant at the Chubarov campaign and astounded by calls for the death penalty. "Ne rano li shum?" *Smena*, 16 September 1926, 3.

[74] "'V zashchitu' nasil'nikov," *Smena*, 17 September 1926, 3. This line of argument, refashioned to meet the needs of the 1920s, may have been cribbed from Dostoevskii. See his 1873 article on the Nechaev affair, "Odna iz sovremennykh fal'shei," in his *Polnoe sobranie sochinenii v tridtsati tomakh* (M.: Nauka, 1972–1988), 21:125–136.

The "San-Galli Affair" can be read as a proletarian tragedy, a horrific orgy in which the halo of a repulsive, diseased martyrdom spread to aggressors and victim alike.

The social contagion represented by the Chubarov crime was reflected by the obsession with the physical details of sexual disease in the newspaper reports. The first detailed account of the rape in *Komsomol'skaia pravda* concluded, "An initial medical examination established that Citizen B. had been a virgin prior to the rape, and a second determined that the hooligans not only raped a virgin but infected her with venereal disease."[75] The Komsomol papers repeatedly returned to the evidence of venereal disease, sometimes adding new details. On 25 September *Komsomol'skaia pravda*'s "own correspondent" on the scene reported, as if in a news flash:

THE CASE OF THE FORTY HOOLIGANS

Leningrad, the 24th. (Our corr.)

A second medical examination of the Rabfak student B., raped by forty hooligans, has determined that *the victim is infected with gonorrhea.*

Medical specialists went to the hooligans' place of incarceration and examined eleven of them. *Several of them have long been ill with venereal diseases; others were infected during the rape by their own comrades.*[76]

This preoccupation fit quite well with the prevailing portrait of venereal disease in the papers: an infection spreading rapidly and out of control. In *Smena* a report even stated that the simultaneous outbreak of venereal disease among the defendants was one of the most "weighty" pieces of evidence against them.[77] That the simultaneous presence of the disease in an early form was not merely circumstantial proof hints at the degree of fear of the condition, as if infection was almost as horrendous a crime as the rape itself.

Often there is in the horrific an element of the uncanny, where the spectator or victim—paralyzed before an image of terror—sees in the event before him a distorted reflection of his own desire. What, after all, was the gang rape in Chubarov Alley and the infection of Liubov' if not a collective act? Had not the Komsomol been directing its members to bridge the gap between the individual and the collective, to end the situation in which a worker's "narrowly personal life lies beyond the threshold of our collectives?" In this crime committed beneath the walls of the Kooperator factory, work and leisure, individual and collective had merged. In vain Iaroslavsky tried to ward off the appalling notion that the rape in Chubarov Alley was in any sense a communist act:

[75] "Rasstreliat' merzavtsev!" *Komsomol'skaia pravda*, 14 September 1926, 2.

[76] "Delo soroka khuliganov," *Komsomol'skaia pravda*, 25 September 1926, 2.

[77] "Vesskie uliki," *Smena*, 14 September 1926, 3.

We must have *collective responsibility* [emphasis added] for one another; there must be a much *tighter connection and cohesion* among members than exists today. We must work so that every komsomolets, wherever he may be, remembers that he is first of all a komsomolets, that he is a member of the Leninist Communist Youth League. It's perfectly clear that the lads who turned up among these forty rapists had no such thought, no such consciousness. In fact, they were not komsomol'tsy, they were not Leninists, and nothing about them was communist or Leninist.[78]

The very words chosen to describe the Chubarovtsy at their trial mirrored and mocked his imperative: "it's an extremely cohesive group"; "it brought with it into the courtroom the cruel Chubarov code of collective respon- sibility."[79] The collective rape was the literal, down-to-earth fulfillment of the policy for which Iaroslavsky was still calling in the crime's wake:

Each Komsomol cell must shake itself into action upon hearing about such facts and begin to think long and hard about *who is in its ranks, about how the members of the Komsomol conduct themselves. Questions of private life [. . .] cease to be private in the life of the Komsomol. They become collective facts; a cell must know how each of its members lives [iacheika dolzhna znat', kak zhivet kazhdyi ee chlen].*[80]

On one hand, Iaroslavsky's article is a typical expression of the utopian desire for the elimination of potentially disruptive differences, of rifts be- tween individual members and the collective. But on a coarse, physiological level, his words acquire another sense, for the Chubarov affair was indeed a collective action of "members" (in Russian "*chlen*" has the same sexual connotation as "member" in English), and the Komsomol's interest in and horror at the Chubarov workers' sexual activity were, in fact, an attempt to learn and control "how each of its members lives" (*kak zhivet kazhdyi ee chlen*). Moreover, in the reports of venereal transmission, with their vivid evocation of disease leaping from one proletarian's genitalia to another's, a homoerotic fascination is apparent, for in these accounts the rapists virtually

---

[78] Iaroslavskii, "Protiv khuliganstva," 2.

[79] N. Mikheev, "Chubarovskoe delo," *Smena*, 19 December 1926, 4. Even the initial reports of the rape seem to parody official discourse: "When thirty hooligan-beasts had finished raping the girl, about ten more human beasts came to relieve them [*na smenu im prishlo*] and they, too, took turns raping the girl." "Rasstreliat' merzavtsev!" 2. Komsomol'tsy were often called a "change of the guard" (*smena*) (i.e., an eventual replacement for the Old Bolsheviks), but here the notion is horribly distorted. The rapists' questions and answers to one other—"Has every- one done it?" "Everyone"—make the rape sound like a conspiratorial, pre-Revolutionary terror- ist act. At the trial, this simultaneously horrific and parodic dimension of the tale was further highlighted. Pavel Kochergin defended himself by claiming that the victim was a prostitute. Instead of paying her, he said, he had handed her "a coupon for a subscription to *Smena*," which she had mistaken for money in the dark. *Chubarovshchina*, 38.

[80] Iaroslavskii, "Protiv khuliganstva," 2.

engage in collective intercourse—not only with the victim but also with each other, through the vehicle of a passive, symbolic object named Love. Here one can also read a distorted reflection of utopian desires; the homosexual tinge to the reports, never explicitly discussed but undoubtedly accounting for much of the horror, mirrored (again, through distortion) a current in early Soviet thought. Influenced by misogynistic thinkers like Nikolai Fedorov, some early extremists such as Andrei Platonov had envisioned communism exclusively as a society of men,[81] and we have seen (in chapter 5) how plots in NEP stories and films repeatedly—almost ritualistically—depicted the elimination of woman as a necessary step in the long or short march to communism. In the mid-1920s the Komsomol press continually battled with the relics of this utopian sexual chauvinism (and with the general societal contempt for women from which it had sprung), bemoaning the belittling of women and their absence among the leaders of Komsomol cells.[82] In the society of Chubarov Alley, women are virtually eliminated—the only one who remains has just a single function: to facilitate the intercourse of men with men.

The very name of the factory at which the rapists worked—Kooperator—compounded the uncanniness of the event's hideous parody of ideological desire. Cooperative enterprises had been a keystone of NEP. In 1923 Lenin had declared, "It's precisely thanks to NEP that cooperation has attained a uniquely vital importance."[83] Cooperatives were regarded as a kind of antiviral agent capable of competing with private enterprise and eventually eradicating it, a corrective introduced to ensure that the inoculatory process proceeded according to plan: "It's impossible to take control of trade, or of industry, all at once. Extreme flexibility is called for if we want to replace a private, capitalistic trade apparatus with a governmental one, and cooperation is the institution that can facilitate the transformation of private trade into state trade."[84] Equally important, cooperatives were intended to facilitate one of the fundamental goals of NEP, the union of the proletariat and peasantry: "The New Economic Policy, the course upon which Vladimir Il'ich set sail after the victory of the Red Army over the Intervention, signifies nothing if not the union of the revolutionary proletariat with the peasantry, and cooperation has an essential role in the befriending of workers with

[81] A. Platonov, "Budushchii oktiabr'," *Voronezhskaia kommuna*, 9 November 1920, 1.

[82] On 6 January 1927, *Komsomol'skaia pravda* published an open letter from women in the Komsomol attacking their male colleagues for regarding women as lesser beings and for preventing them from engaging in serious Komsomol work. "Otkrytoe pis'mo devushek-komsomolok," 1.

[83] Lenin,"O kooperatsii" (26 and 27 May 1923), *Polnoe sobranie sochinenii*, 45:369.

[84] "Mezhdunarodnyi den' kooperatsii. Torzhestvennoe zasedanie v Bol'shom teatre," *Pravda*, 6 July 1924, 5. The quoted passage is from a speech by Mikhail Kalinin, then the chairman of the Central Executive Committee.

peasants."[85] The act of organization that occurred in the garden adjacent to the "Kooperator" factory was an appalling realization of the "*smychka*" (the joining of workers and peasants) which the New Economic Policy was intended to achieve.[86] From their hiding places in the bushes, watching the rape of a peasant by workers, the local children were observing the primal scene of NEP.

It is worth noting that the majority of the rapists were returning from a comrade's funeral and that *Smena*'s initial narrative of the rape proceeded directly from the Volkovo Cemetery to Chubarov Alley. In this context, the Chubarov case can be read as another NEP ghost story, one perhaps more chilling than the others we have examined because it purportedly had a real flesh-and-blood victim. Certainly, the language with which the Chubarov trial was conducted abounded with Gothic elements. The prosecutor called the case "the most nightmarish of crimes" (*koshmarneishee prestuplenie*), and the word "nightmare" surfaces several times in the abbreviated and heavily edited published judicial record.[87] In the initial accounts of the rape, portal imagery had played a major part, with the *Smena* correspondent, in particular, focusing on the many apertures through which the gang crawled from San-Galli to the street. The description of the rape in *Smena* had a cinematic, dreamlike quality that probably owed more to the oneiric narration of Gothic fiction than to the pre-Revolutionary films of Evgeny Bauer with their rather decadent penchant for graveyard depictions and overtones of necrophilia.[88] In the account more and more rapists materialize out of the night, and, as in a Gothic novel, the heroine repeatedly loses and regains consciousness. On the verge of death, she is brought back to life (*nado*

---

[85] Ibid. The article is quoting Leonid Krasin, the commissar of foreign trade.

[86] This was especially so since the raped woman had arrived in Leningrad to study in a Rabfak. The attendance of peasants at these institutions was trumpeted as proof that peasants were "tying their fates" to the Revolution. A. Kollontai, *Polozhenie zhenshchiny v evoliutsii khoziaistva. (Lektsii chitannye v Universitete imeni Ia. M. Sverdlova)* (M.: Gos. izd., 1922), 197. It was not mentioned in the press that Liubov' B. was the daughter of a middle-peasant (*seredniak*). This detail, which appears in a 1927 volume containing edited versions of the attorneys' speeches to the court, might have made the victim an ideologically less sympathetic victim. *Chubarovshchina*, 34.

[87] *Chubarovshchina*, 11, 56, 67, 86. The collection does not contain the defendants' testimony.

[88] The putrefaction of Chubarov Alley as limned in the Komsomol press was particularly cinematic. ("The San Galli Garden. In truth, it's not a garden. It's a dirty lot with a dozen broken trees and paths overgrown with grass and littered with beer bottles, cans, rags, and feces. . . .") Compare, for example, the landscape of the San-Galli Garden with that portrayed in Kozintsev and Trauberg's film *The Devil's Wheel*: "On the outskirts of town there are old houses that threaten to collapse," the titles tell us, and immediately we find ourselves in a world of criminal gangs and urban decay. The cinematic quality of the Chubarov nightmare is captured by the description of the rape—at least in the initial *Smena* report—as a kind of "picture" and spectacle of communal importance (*i na etu kartinu prishli ne tol'ko 19-letnie molodtsy*).

ozhivit') when the "Forty Hooligans" wish to continue their assault. More-over, the story of the rape was narrated in large part from the terrified vic-tim's point of view; the rapists occasionally are only voices, as if the reader were hearing them with Liubov' B. The foreignness of the name of the rape's locale, the San-Galli Garden, became a shorthand name for the entire event, lending further Gothic resonance to the scene. The bits of hooligan's jargon tossed into the accounts—"*ochko*" and "*orlianka*" (two card games) and "*sukhie i mokrye dela*" ("dry and wet deeds")—added more than a little of the exotic spice so characteristic of the language of NEP. Like Gladkov's Polia, Citizen B. found herself walking through a strange land that was no longer her own.

The accounts of the Chubarov affair published in the press disturbed judi-cial officials. Senior Assistant Prosecutor Pershin complained in November 1926 that the press had undermined the judicial investigation and had erro-neously implicated innocent people in the crime. The press was not reflect-ing the "jurisprudential meaning" of criminal prosecutions: it was neither showing "how [or] why a particular article of the Criminal Code was applied to a particular action" nor "imparting to the reading masses knowledge about a particular article of the law."[89] Pershin's comments and his opposition to overly severe punishments in the case indicate that his view of the prosecu-tion's purpose was not shared by the papers that gave the rape so much space. Pershin appears to have been motivated by more traditional considera-tions of justice and popular education, while for the Party and Komsomol press the case had more to do with ideological mobilization and political consolidation.[90]

At a public "dispute" on crime reporting in March 1927, several of Per-shin's colleagues added their voices to his criticism of the press for not fostering jurisprudential literacy in its readers. The word "genre" was never spoken, but speaker after speaker complained that crime reports owed too much to pre-Revolutionary feuilletons and novels and failed utterly to teach readers about Soviet jurisprudence.[91] However, several speakers were willing

[89] Mikh. Pershin, "Kachestvo sudebnogo otcheta i khroniki," *Rabochii sud*, no. 21 (1926): 1281 (1279–1282).

[90] In early 1927, Pershin published an article in which, without referring to the Chubarov case, he outlined the typical features of gang rape in urban and rural settings and argued that in neither case did the crime "have anything in common with crimes against the governmental order or with the defiance of governmental authority or of the militia." "Polovye prestupleniia. Po deistvuiushchemu sovetskomu pravu," *Rabochii sud*, no. 9 (1927): 771 (768–776).

[91] "Sudebnye otchety i publika," *Rabochii sud*, no. 10 (1927): 871–880. The meeting was concerned with court reporting in general, but the Chubarov case probably brought the issue to a head. Although the extensive coverage given to the Chubarov case was exceptional in all sectors of the print media, it apparently marked less of a generic departure for the non-Party and non-Komsomol press than it did for *Smena* and *Komsomol'skaia pravda*. (See, for example, Mikhail Zolotonosov's account of the coverage of the prosecution of several defendants accused

to acknowledge that the problem was not the fault of the press alone. The chief Leningrad prosecutor admitted that crime reports could not do "without embellishments" (*bez vsiakikh prikras*): "If our papers begin to print more positive, more thorough, but more boring articles, nobody will read them. Thus the whole question lies in the exposition."[92] The chairman of the Court of the Leningrad Guberniia, which hosted the event, was in favor of improving the quality of crime reporting but not necessarily of changing its form. "A good feuilleton," he said, "is the best form of propaganda."[93] Newspapers had long known that the feuilleton, and especially the serialized feuilleton, was an excellent help in selling papers, and the king of them all, Eugène Sue's *Les Mystères de Paris* (first published in the Parisian *Le Journal des Débats*), had had enormous success in Russia. Sue's urban Gothic had undergone profound changes—most notably in the hands of Dostoevsky—but in many respects the reports on the Chubarov affair represented a return to the lurid features of the original. In one of his few forays into literary criticism, Karl Marx had subjected Sue's feuilleton to a withering attack and had unmasked the conservative class allegiances beneath its supposed progressivism.[94] In the comments of Soviet judicial officials one senses an uneasiness about whether this bourgeois, tainted genre could be mastered and—like features of a capitalist economy—ultimately put to productive use in the service of Soviet communism.[95]

The very notion of crime—and of a system of criminal justice—was itself somewhat Gothic in the Soviet 1920s. Lenin's *State and Revolution* had

---

of organizing "dens of depravity" in Saint Petersburg in late 1924 and early 1925. Unlike the Chubarov prosecution, this earlier case was presented as an indictment of the intelligentsia, and, in particular, of members of the intelligentsia unsympathetic to the October Revolution. Accordingly, it produced almost no ideological introspection. It did not result in sentences in excess of five years. "ZK: Zagadki kriminal'no-ideologicheskogo konteksta i kul'turnyi smysl," *Russian Studies* 1, no. 1 [1994]: 93–116, and 1, no. 2 [1995]: 112–157.)

At the "dispute," Prof. L. G. Orshanskii, the director of the Scientific Section of the Leningrad Court's Office of Criminology, complained that there was too much of "the adventure novel" in contemporary crime reports. "Even the most superficial attempt," he said, "can find the parents and grandparents of today's crime reports; one need not go far back through the centuries—just one hundred years." Orshanskii was not a literary scholar, and while outlaw novels—with their focus on brigands—doubtless played a role in some crime reporting, the Chubarov reports, with their emphasis on the terrible plight of the victim and their refusal to lionize the perpetrators as defenders of any sort of popular interest, owed much more to the hundred-year-old Gothic tradition.

[92] "Sudebnye otchety," 876.

[93] Ibid., 878.

[94] Karl Marx and Friedrich Engels, *The Holy Family, or Critique of Critical Criticism*, in their *Collected Works*, 45 vols. (London: Lawrence & Wishart, 1975), 4:55–77, 162–209. The critique of Sue was authored by Marx alone.

[95] In this context, see Neuberger's discussion of the "sketch" (*ocherk*) in pre-Revolutionary crime reporting. *Hooliganism*, 235–236, 243–248.

predicted that while "excesses" (criminal acts) would probably occur in any community, in a communist society no particular apparatus would be necessary for dealing with them. The armed collective would enforce the law on its own with "simplicity and ease," a task that would be made easier because poverty had always been the "root cause" of criminal behavior: "With the elimination of this chief cause, excesses will inevitably begin to die out."[96] Originally, the Soviet republics had attempted to dispense justice without criminal codes. On 12 December 1919 the R.S.F.S.R. had adopted a very short list of "Guiding Principles of Criminal Law" in which the elements of particular crimes were not spelled out. The only definition of crime had been the rather tautological phrase "a violation of the social order that criminal law protects"; courts had been directed simply to protect the community with whatever measures of social defense they deemed fit.[97] The deputy justice commissar, like Lenin, had boasted that no bourgeois criminal codes were necessary in the land of the Soviets: "without particular rules, without codes, the armed nation has coped with and will continue to cope with its oppressors."[98] Only under NEP had a criminal code been adopted; it was, in a sense, a symptom of the period. As one interpreter of the 1922 code explained, the code was necessary because the hold of the past on the present was still strong:

> The final destruction of all remnants of the past [*perezhitki proshlogo*] and of all exploitation will sooner or later render the application of compulsion by one man to another—and, indeed, any sort of government at all—unnecessary. In real and perfect communist society, people will cease to understand the words "crime," "punishment," and "court." But the R.S.F.S.R. is not yet free of all the foul acts of its former leaders, nor of the ignorance of people who cannot part with their filth, or with the sins of their previous life of servitude.[99]

"Crime is our legacy from the [old] order we have overthrown," a publication of the Commissariat of Justice explained in 1923.[100] The criminal codes were generally presented as a more realistic approach to a difficult and lasting problem, but, like the legal codes that the "Children of the Sun" write

---

[96] Cited in A. A. Gertsenzon, "Nekotorye voprosy postroeniia sovetskoi kriminologii," in *Prestupnik i prestupnost'*, ed. E. K. Krasnushkin, G. M. Segal, and I. M. Feinberg, 2 vols. (M.: Moszdravotdel, 1927), 2:136 (135–151).

[97] *Rukovodiashchie nachala po ugolovnomu pravu R.S.F.S.R.* (M., 1919), 3.

[98] Ibid., 1.

[99] Estrin, *Ugolovnoe pravo*, 4. For more on the debate about the survival of law under NEP and communism, see Wendy Z. Goldman, *Women, the State and Revolution: Soviet Family Policy and Social Life, 1917–1936* (Cambridge: Cambridge University Press, 1993), 198–202.

[100] Estrin, *Ugolovnoe pravo*, 7.

only after Dostoevsky's Ridiculous Man has infected them, the Soviet codes were also *signs* of a distressing ideological fall from grace.[101]

The prosecutor's summation to the court in the Chubarov case drew upon this theme of crime as a legacy of the past. So, apparently, did the summations of the defense attorneys. It is crucial to realize, however, that the opposing sides were concerned with two different pasts. Kochergin's lawyer blamed pre-Revolutionary, bourgeois corruption for his client's actions: "The source of infection is not to be found on Ligovka, but on Nevsky. It is precisely from that bourgeois sowing machine that these seeds have fallen on a proletarian street and corrupted people."[102] One defense attorney even cited Leonid Andreev's "The Abyss" for the proposition that in their downtrodden moral condition, poisoned by capitalism, the defendants had been unable to resist "the power of the female body."[103]

While the prosecutors used distinctly Gothic rhetoric to urge the court to punish the defendants severely, they did not emphatically link Gothic imagery with a *bourgeois* legacy. Such an approach would have served to mitigate the defendants' individual responsibility since they might then have been said to have yielded to an extremely powerful enemy and tempter. Rather, the lead prosecutor simply referred to hooliganism as a phenomenon that had to be kept in the grave. He ended his speech to the court in the following manner:

> I think the sentence in the Chubarov case will be the funeral bell heralding the real destruction of hooliganism. We know from statistics that the number of cases involving hooliganism is falling, but hooliganism still produces acute explosions such as the Chubarov case.
>
> Comrade Judges! Act so that your sentence in the Chubarov case—however hard, however terrible, however cruel it may be—serves as a nail driven into the firmly boarded lid of the coffin in which hooliganism, the latest social disease, will be buried along with the Chubarov ringleaders deep in the Soviet earth.[104]

---

[101] Soviet judicial officials resisted the view that the promulgation of judicial codes was a sign—or symptom—of NEP. The deputy commissar of justice, Nikolai Krylenko, cautioned a group of students in 1923: "Many who cannot tell the difference between form and content still say that all of this raging torrent of legislative creativeness has been called forth exclusively by NEP. [. . .] NEP provided only the atmosphere, facilitating it is true and hastening [. . .] this inescapable phase of our court work, but it never did more than that. It never foreordained the content of that work." Cited by J. N. Hazard in his "Soviet Law: The Bridge Years, 1917–1920," in *Russian Law: Historical and Political Perspectives*, ed. William E. Butler (Leyden: A. W. Sijthoff, 1977), 239 (235–255).

[102] *Chubarovshchina*, 63.

[103] Ibid., 84.

[104] Ibid., 62.

The defense's citation of Andreev, the prosecutor argued in his final rebuttal, was perhaps appropriate, but the defendants were relying on the wrong Andreev text. The proper story to cite was not "The Abyss" but "Lazarus":

> [The defense] has called forth Andreev's shade. [. . .] Since Andreev has already been mentioned, let me take an image from him that is far more appropriate to the matter at hand.
>
> In one of Andreev's stories we find the image of Lazarus, who has been in the Other World. Instead of eyes he has terrifying black eye sockets. Whomever he looks upon with these sockets loses all his gaiety and dies.
>
> If Andreev's symbols are needed, let's take this one. These people have transgressed all the bounds of the permissible; they would look at our youth with the eyes of Lazarus, drawing to them today "Klop" [the nickname of one of the defendants], tomorrow "Blokha," and the day after tomorrow still others . . . The court will close these eyes, so that they will not turn a single additional life from the true path.[105]

Whose eyes in particular was the court trying to close? What was the precise nature of this hooligan revenant? To answer this question, we must first understand that the rape in Chubarov Alley was not only an uncanny projection of social desire, it was also, on a much more evident level, the materialization in the "real world" of a theme that had been appearing frequently in Soviet literature—the sharing of a single woman by a group of komsomol'tsy. In these fictitious representations it was usually a woman rather than a man who had several sexual partners (whether or not against her will). Men were bound together by their sexual contact with this single female; instances of female "bonding" through sexual contact with the same man were rarer. A theme that appeared more often than one might expect was that of a komsomolets impregnating a komsomolka and then trying to convince her that sleeping with many other komsomol'tsy would abort the pregnancy. Vadim Okhremenko's epistolary feuilleton "The Crime of Kirik Basenko" provides an example of this strangely frequent demand:

> Ekaterina!!!
>
> Quit being dumb and do what I told you. I've read a lot about the question of sex and know quite a bit about it, that even if you're three weeks pregnant it's not serious. If a woman sleeps with a few more men, this time simultaneously, all the seeds will be liquidated and even the first conception will be gone from her belly. I'm sending you this note with Mishka Onishchenko and I'm asking you for the last time not to dare to turn these guys down. Petro and Grisha will keep everything secret. They know how to keep their Komsomol word.[106]

---

[105] Ibid., 84–85.
[106] Vadim Okhremenko, "Prestuplenie Kirika Basenko," *Komsomol'skaia pravda*, 25 Septem-

There is an evident fascination as well as disgust with this topic. Writers emphasize that komsomol'tsy sharing the same women are bad komsomol'tsy, and often take pains to demonstrate the horrific consequences of such contacts, but they keep returning to the theme.

Questions of homoerotic desire aside, the reason for this fascination may rest in still another, perhaps unconscious, recognition of something familiar, originary, and unpleasant. No doubt the vicious attacks on utopianism by Marxists in the late nineteenth century arose in no small measure from their awareness of their philosophy's utopian origins and from their desire to purge themselves of this historical taint.[107] The consistency with which writers during NEP depicted sexual communality can perhaps be traced back to a desire to rid themselves of the phalansteries where they had been conceived. Zamiatin's *We* and Malashkin's "Moon . . ." may be read as preoccupations with the original sexual implications of the Crystal Palace, although these two works treating promiscuity as an undesirable phenomenon have very different goals. The sharing of women represented a relic of the past—not only of the philosophical past but also of an immature, prehistoric communism that may never have existed but whose image evoked disgust in the movement's founder and followers. In early 1927 *Komsomol'skaia pravda* published excerpts from a recently discovered manuscript by Marx on the question of sex and marriage:

> In its first form communism is only the *generalization and consummation* of private property. As such [. . .] it so overestimates the role and power of material property that it wants to destroy everything which is not capable of being possessed by all as private property. It wants to do away by force with talent, etc. In its eyes the sole purpose of life is direct, physical possession. [. . .]
>
> Private property continues to exist as the relationship of the community [as a whole] to the world of things. The institution of universal private property comes to replace that of [exclusive] private property, a development which finds expression in animal form by replacing *marriage* (certainly a form of exclusive private property) with the *communal ownership of women*, in which a woman becomes a piece of *communal* and common property. It may be said that this idea of the *communal ownership* of women unmasks [this stage of social organization] as a still completely crude and senseless [form of] communism. Just as woman passes from marriage to general prostitution, so the entire world of wealth (that is, of man's objective substance) passes from a relationship of ex-

---

ber 1926, 1. This tale was the uncredited source for F. Ermler's popular 1928 film, *The Parisian Cobbler*. For judicial parallels not involving komsomol'tsy, see A. Sh., "Strakh pered alimentami," *Izvestiia*, 12 December 1925, 5, and "Sud. Podmoskovnye 'chubarovtsy,'" 4.

[107] For an interesting discussion of Bolshevism's utopian pedigree, see Roger Pethybridge, *The Social Prelude to Stalinism* (London: Macmillan, 1974), 22–67.

clusive marriage with the owner of private property to a state of universal prostitution with the collective.[108]

Soviet ideology in the mid-1920s was preoccupied with rejecting this first
stage, with cutting itself loose from the coarseness of its roots. The idea of a
flawed, perhaps bestial embryonic phase, whether identified with War Communism, with a collective pagan past (Pil'niak's vision of War Communism),[109]
or with the teachings of Fourier, was particularly offensive to the ideology
that emphatically denied its emergence from it. The desire to bury the pha-
lanstery in all its extremely diverse forms may partially account for the intense hostility toward Kollontai, who in her views on sexuality and the style
in which she wrote was closer to Chernyshevsky (and Fourier) than most
contemporary writers on the subject. The connection of her articles on
Winged Eros—chaste when compared to literature such as Borisov's
"Vera"—with the type of depravity described by Malashkin or occurring in
Chubarov Alley initially appears ludicrous. But her ideal of sexual linkages
binding together an entire society may have been attacked—like the collective rape of Chubarov Alley—because, for all their differences, these two
"contributions" to Soviet communist discourse represented phenomena that
were too closely related to originary ideological desires. The communist utopia was seeking to establish itself as an island secure from contagion, while
Kollontai and the Chubarov case threatened to contaminate its ideal by reflecting its history and yearnings in a manner that it found both hideous and
perversely accurate.

For intra-Party political reasons, too, we may read the Chubarov case as a
tale haunted by the return not only of the bourgeoisie but of both a not too
distant (War Communism) and a more remote ("crude," originary communism) *communist* ideological past. In 1926 these pasts were associated most
especially with Zinov'ev's defeated faction, which had repeatedly asked,
"Where is the greatest danger?" and had argued that the most terrifying
ghosts were bourgeois, not War Communist.[110] The Chubarov case would

---

[108] D. Riazanov, "Marks i Engel's o brake i sem'e," *Komsomol'skaia pravda,* 12 February
1927, 2. I have used Martin Milligan's translation of this passage from the German (Karl Marx,
Economic and Philosophic Manuscripts of 1844 [New York: International Publishers, 1964],
133) as a basis for my translation of its Russian rendition in *Komsomol'skaia pravda.* The
manuscript was not published in German until 1932. A much longer, although still incomplete,
version of the manuscript was published in Moscow in 1927 in the third volume of *Arkhiv K.
Marksa i F. Engel'sa,* edited by Riazanov. While it may seem astonishing that a newspaper so
philosophically undistinguished as *Komsomol'skaia pravda* should have had the distinction of
printing a previously unpublished text by Marx, the paper was undoubtedly selected because the
excerpt fit into the discourse on sex in which *Komsomol'skaia pravda* played so important a
role.

[109] "and here, in front of everyone, rape, rape, rape! Thought, nobility, shame, stoicism—to
the Devil! Beast!" *Golyi god* (M.: Khudozhestvennaia literatura, 1976 [1921]), 149–150.

[110] See, e.g., "Rech' L.B. Kameneva," 1. and Bardin, "Gde glavnaia opasnost'," 64. To a

seem to be a refutation, in the era's prevailing Gothic discourse, of this
Zinov'evist position. But more was at stake. After all, why a gang rape
rather than a murder or other heinous crime? According to Nikolai Krylenko,
the deputy justice commissar, the rate of sex crimes stayed constant during
the entire NEP period.[111] Why, then, was there such interest in rape, and,
most particularly, gang rape in 1926 and 1927? Could it really have been
true that "reports of rape [were] being received from all quarters"?[112] When
gang rapes occurred, they were usually a rural phenomenon in which peasant
men attacked peasant women on holidays after excessive drinking.[113] Was
Zinov'ev's leadership of the Leningrad organization the only reason an atyp-
ical, urban gang rape was selected as the year's—indeed, the decade's—
representative sexual crime? In attempting to prove that "group rape has
risen out of the wave of hooliganism," a pair of legal commentators had to
admit that the number of gang rapes occurring in Russia was actually small.
In 1927 these two criminologists, V. A. Vnukov and A. O. Edel'shtein, wrote
that of 167 rape cases heard in the Moscow Criminal Court in the past three
years, only thirty-three convictions were of multiple defendants, and of these
most had involved only two defendants.[114] Why, then, did they claim that
"the gravity of these sexual offenses lies not in their quantity but in their
radical social danger?"[115] Although Vnukov and Edel'shtein protested defen-
sively that the participants in a gang rape were actually not part of a true
collective but rather members of a chance mob, the word "collective" continually invaded the criminologists' speech, and they were forced to admit that
what made gang rapists so interesting to study, and composed the essence of

---

certain extent, these arguments were a reprise of charges made by the Workers' Opposition, but
Zinov'ev's supporters did not seek to identify themselves with the earlier, defeated faction.

[111] *Khuliganstvo i prestuplenie*, 18. The prosecutor in the Chubarov case, Mikhail Pershin,
claimed in a 1927 article that sex crimes in the Leningrad Guberniia had actually fallen by half
in the first ten months of 1926 (presumably, statistics for the last two months were lacking).
"Polovye prestupleniia," 772–773. The only contrary statistical evidence I have found is provided by B. S. Man'kovskii, who writes that the number of sex crimes in the R.S.F.S.R., as
reported in the second and third quarters of 1924, 1925, and 1926, rose from 3,043 to 5,174 to
6,055 respectively. "Sovremennaia polovaia prestupnost'," 80. One wonders why Man'kovskii
chose those six months as a basis for his data. (The omission of the fourth quarter is understandable, since data for 1926 might not have been complete. But why should he omit the first
quarter?) Presumably, Krylenko, who was the chief assistant prosecutor of the R.S.F.S.R. as
well as deputy justice commissar, would have had access to as complete figures as anyone else.

[112] Ia. Bugaiskii, "Khuliganstvo," 139.

[113] V. A. Vnukov and A. O. Edel'shtein, "O kharaktere lichnosti pravonarushitelia i mekhani-
zmakh pravonarushenii v oblasti polovykh otnoshenii," in *Pravonarusheniia v oblasti seksual'nykh otnoshenii*, ed. E. K. Krasnushkin, G. M. Segal, and Ts. M. Fainberg (M.: Moszdravotdel, 1927), 65 (23–76); N. P. Brukhanskii, *Materialy po seksual'noi psikhopatologii* (M.:
M. & C. Sabashnikovy, 1927), 5.

[114] Vnukov and Edel'shtein, "O kharaktere," 61.

[115] Ibid.

their criminality, were the "collective mechanisms of their antisocial act."[116] They went so far as to call gang rape an "interpsychic act" (*mezhpsikhicheskii akt*) and proceeded to seek the explanations for the phenomenon in Freud's notion of the primitive horde, in Jung's idea of the collective unconscious, and in Frazer's descriptions of defloration rituals.[117]

Anywhere but in Marx. As we have seen, Marx had, as *Komsomol'skaia pravda* proudly revealed to its readers, rejected any association between modern and primitive communism. There were figures, however, in recent Soviet history who had laid the foundations for collective or "interpsychic" rape, the authors of War Communist discourse. In chapter 1 we have already explored the centrality of the collective body and rape to the rhetoric of the Civil War years. Bound together by their common muscles and thoughts, the united proletariat had bored into the earth, unconcerned with the soil's fertility, as it had built its tremendous phallic towers on the ravaged ground. In this context, we should again note the importance of Liubov' B.'s identification as a peasant woman. This urban gang rape of a peasant by a tightly knit proletarian band was a frightening replay of the War Communist years— and, perhaps, a farewell to (or working through of) that primitive utopian ethos as state, Party, and society moved forward to new forms of rigid social control.

Scenes of female humiliation have a long history in Russian culture as moments of symbolic importance. Until at least a few years ago Russian schoolchildren were still memorizing Nikolai Nekrasov's poem "Yesterday after Five O'clock" (*Vcherashnii den', chasu v shestom*), in which the sight of a peasant woman being beaten with a knout prompts the poet to tell his muse: "There is your sister."[118] Several times Gor'ky had used descriptions of humiliated and raped women as symbolic moments in his attacks on Russian backwardness.[119] In *The Pit*, his "progressive" pre-Revolutionary attack on the institution of prostitution, Aleksandr Kuprin had painted a vivid picture of how a woman looks when she has been "given" to more than a dozen men in the course of a night.[120] Finally, Artsybashev had also, we have seen, used the humiliation and rape of women in several contexts as a vehicle for expressing political and moral views.

In War Communist discourse, rape—in its metaphorical transformation— for the first time became a *positive* symbol: the assault on the earth was

[116] Ibid.

[117] Ibid., 65, 69–71.

[118] N. A. Nekrasov, *Polnoe sobranie sochinenii i pisem v piatnadtsati tomakh* (L.: Nauka, 1981–1990), 1:69.

[119] See his sketches "Vyvod" (1895), "Kak ee obvenchali," and "Ee medovyi mesiats" (both 1896) in his *Sobranie sochinenii v tridtsati tomakh* (M.: Khudozhestvennaia literatura, 1949–55), 2:5–7; 23:81–85 and 86–88.

[120] A. I. Kuprin, *Polnoe sobranie sochinenii*, 8 vols. (SPb.: Marks, 1912), 8:441.

essential to the building of an unprecedented, resolutely phallic and icono-clastic proletarian society. Possibly, this valorization of rape owed a debt to Futurist aesthetics. Long before the Revolution, Maiakovsky had been de-picting nature in a process of constant violation: either self-violation[121] or rape by the poet.[122] It is fascinating, therefore, to see Maiakovsky retreating from his earlier imagery in the wake of the Chubarov affair. "The Hooligan," published several days after the Chubarov story broke, does not revel in violence or épatage. Now the hooligan—a role Maiakovsky played with gusto in a pre-Revolutionary film with Lily Brik[123]—provokes a feeling of alarm that leads the poet, in keeping with the Gothic fears of the time, to open his work with portal imagery:

> Республика наша в опасности.
>
> В дверь
>
> лезет
>
> немыслимый зверь.

[Our Republic is in danger. / In the door / creeps / an unthinkable beast.][124]

---

[121] See, inter alia, his "Iz ulitsy v ulitsu" (1913):

> Лиф души расстегнули
> Тело жгут руки.
> Кричи, не кричи:
> "Я не хотела!"—
> резок
> жгут муки.
> Ветер колючий
> Трубе
> Вырывает
> дымчатой шерсти клок.
> Лысый фонарь
> сладострастно снимает
> с улицы
> черный чулок.

[They've taken off the soul's brassiere. / Hands burn the body. / Scream, don't scream: "I didn't want to!"— / Sharp / is the braid / of torture. / The barbed wind rips from the pipe a tuft of smoke-colored fur. /The bald lamppost / voluptuously removes /the street's / black stocking.] (Vladimir Maiakovskii, *Polnoe sobranie sochinenii v trinadtsati tomakh* [M.: Khudozhestvennaia literatura, 1955–1961], 1:39)

[122] See, inter alia, his "Kofta fata" (1914):

> Пусть земля кричит, в покое обабившись:
> "Ты зеленые весны идешь изнасиловать!"

[Let the earth, which, left in peace, has become like a woman, scream: / "You have come to rape the green springs!"] (Ibid., 1:59)

[123] On the connection between Futurism and hooliganism, see Neuberger, *Hooliganism*, 142–150.

[124] Maiakovskii, *Polnoe sobranie*, 7:180. Also in *Izvestiia*, 19 September 1926, 3. Note here

In former times Maiakovsky had delighted in references to intercourse, with the word "meat" flaunted in front of the reader as a sign of his healthy vulgarity and lack of inhibitions (Вся земля поляжется женщиной,/ заерзает мясами, хотя отдаться [The entire earth will lie down like a woman, / will wriggle her meat about, wanting to give herself]).[125] Now he can barely bring himself to look at the violated female body:

по переулочкам—луна.
Идет одна.
            Она юна.
——Хорошенькая!
            (За косу.)
Обкрутимся без загсу!—
Никто не услышит,
                    напрасно орет
вонючей ладонью зажатый рот.
——Не нас контрапупят——
                                не наше дело!
Бежим, ребята,
                чтоб нам не влетело!—
Луна
    в испуге
            за тучу пятится
от рваной груды
            мяса и платьица.

[Along the sidestreets—the moon. / A woman walks alone. / She is young. / — Good looking! / (By the hair.) / Let's do it without the marriage bureau!— / Nobody will hear, / in vain she shouts. / Her mouth is stopped with a stinking hand. / —They won't make a fool out of us!— / It's not our business! / Let's run, guys, / so that we won't get in trouble!— / The moon / all afright / steps back behind a cloud / from the torn heap / of meat and dress.][126]

Maiakovsky did, of course, "look" . . . otherwise he would never have written the poem. His gaze was riveted by the terrifying sight of a dream of paradise come true. The San-Galli Garden was a distortion of War Communism's proletarian Eden. Soviet ideology saw its own "childhood" fantasies represented in Chubarov Alley and recoiled.[127]

Maiakovskii's use of the word "*zver'*" (beast), which was the common parlance for the Chubarovtsy in the Komsomol press.

   [125] Maiakovskii, *Polnoe sobranie*, 1:187 ("Oblako v shtanakh").

   [126] Ibid., 7:181.

   [127] Maiakovskii was not the only former Futurist who in the wake of the Chubarov case sought to distance himself from the movement's association with hooliganism. In a 1926 bro-

Utopian texts describe their projects of desire as much by what they seek to render absent as by their portraits of the society they hope to build. By examining the objects, events, and phenomena that an ideology rejects with horror, we may learn much about its fundamental beliefs and anxieties. The execution of the Chubarov rapists was an attempt by the mentality that—more than any chronological boundaries or economic forms—constituted NEP to purge itself of its profound, essential insecurities. On the day after reporting the Chubarov sentences, *Komsomol'skaia pravda* wrote about a huge fire that had broken out on the premises of the Kooperator factory:

> On 29 December a fire erupted in the "Kooperator" factory and lasted for fifteen hours. Fire brigades were dispatched from all stations in the city. Several factory shops were consumed by the blaze. *Workers from the factory living in the San-Galli colony helped to extinguish the conflagration.* (The crime of the Chubarov hooligans occurred on the grounds of this colony.)[128]

---

chure entitled *For the Battle against Hooliganism in Literature*, Aleksei Kruchenykh criticized Il'ia Sadof'ev, a former member of the Proletkul't and a friend of Esenin's, for his 1924 poem "Listen," in which Red Army soldiers are urged to uphold Soviet power and preserve their ideological virtue by "publicly [or nationally] rap[ing]" the "coddled daughter" of a tavern keeper who has invited them in for wine and women. (А если жгуч избыток силы\И ждать возлюбленной не в мочь\То всенародно изнасилуй\Его изнеженную дочь). Calling the poem "a genuine example of Chubarovshchina" and terming the collection of verses in which it was later republished a handbook for hooligans who needed to defend themselves in court, Kruchenykh distinguished the Futurists' hooliganism from Sadof'ev's and that of the "Imaginist" group of poets with which Sadof'ev and Esenin had been associated:

> The "hooliganism" of the members of LEF—if the word "hooliganism" can even be stretched to apply to them—was a protest against the stagnation of pre-Revolutionary literature.
> The hooliganism of the Imaginists is a goal in and of itself, the sole content of the impoverished work of Johnny-come-latelies. [. . .]
> Imaginism has either ended quietly and gloomily, leaving broken noses and broken beer bottles behind as unpleasant traces, or it has degenerated into the brazen ideology of the law of the knife, of Chubarovshchina, and of hooliganism. (A. Kruchenykh, *Na bor'bu s khuliganstvom v literature* [M., 1926], 9–10, 20–22)

In part, Kruchenykh may have been using the Chubarov case to settle old scores; in 1919 Sadof'ev had published an article in the Proletkul't journal *Griadushchee* attacking the Futurists and asserting their inferiority to the Proletkul't. See N. I. Dikushina, "Zhurnalistika i kritika 20-kh godov," in *Istoriia russkoi sovetskoi literatury*, ed. A. G. Dement'ev, 4 vols. (M.: Nauka, 1967), 1:631 (617–658). Kruchenykh's comments explicitly acknowledge the responsibilities of poetic imagery for the crime in Chubarov Alley but deny that one of its sources was the group with which he had been most closely identified. His attack on Sadof'ev betrays a certain nervousness over the old question of "who is to blame."

[128] "Pozhar na zavode 'Kooperator' likvidirovan," *Komsomol'skaia pravda*, 30 December 1926, 2.

The entire affair should be read as a discursive act of self-purification,[129] doomed to fail because NEP could never purge the contradictions that defined it. In the short time remaining to the New Economic Policy, NEP's efforts to rid itself of its congenital disease would continue, although no other symbolic constellation capable of arousing the horror surrounding the Chubarov case was found. It was not until the period's end that the discourse concerning the contagion of "young, still untempered souls" (*ne uspevshie zakalit'sia molodye dushi*)[130] and of "workers as yet untempered in their class mentality" (*klassovo-nezakalennykh rabochikh*)[131] would change, reflecting new approaches to new and old fears. The Stalinist period would give birth to its own mythologies and discourses in which sex crimes would not play an emblematic role. But strangely, in the novel that became the Stalinist epoch's literary sign, Nikolai Ostrovsky's *How the Steel Was Tempered* (*Kak zakalialas' stal'*) (1932–1934), we meet in the hero a disconcerting echo of the Chubarov case. Slightly altered, the name of the executed Chubarov ringleader became that of the self-sacrificing fictional protagonist who was to serve for years as a socialist realist model for youth. Filed away within the unconscious of cultural memory, sounds that had signified a negative example for maturing communists[132] were reshuffled and, retaining their exemplary force, acquired positive meaning: "Pavel Kochergin" became "Pavel Korchagin."[133]

---

[129] See the remarks of the "social prosecutor" at the Chubarov trial: "The Soviet Court is doing the proletariat's will and clearing the way for a new form of everyday life and for socialist creation." *Chubarovshchina*, 7.

[130] G. Bergman, "Esenin—znamia upadochnykh nastroenii," 2.

[131] "Protiv chubarovshchiny," 1.

[132] See Prosecutor Pershin's remark at the trial that Pavel Kochergin's name was one which "will always be pronounced with a shudder and anxiety, with anger and cursing." *Chubarovshchina*, 84.

[133] N. N. Orlova suggests that Ostrovskii may have taken his hero's name from a minor, ideologically correct character named Pavel Korchagin in Arkadii Gaidar's 1930 novel *Shkola*, and it may be that the first metamorphosis of Kochergin's name occurred there. See her "Obrazy geroicheskogo vremeni (Po romanu N. Ostrovskogo *Kak zakalialas' stal'* i povesti A. Gaidara *Shkola*)," *Uchenye zapiski moskovskogo gosudarstvennogo bibliotechnogo instituta*, vyp. 9 (1962): 135 (128–162). In the transition from "Kochergin" to "Korchagin" the name undergoes a symbolic transformation from a threatening to a more nurturing object. *Kocherga* in Russian refers to a fireplace poker; *korchaga* means an earthenware pot. This transformation is in keeping with the two epochs' differences in ideological tenor.

CONCLUSION

As THE 1920s came to an end, the ideological terrors distinguishing NEP also drew to a close. With the inception of the First Five Year Plan, the Gothic anxieties haunting Soviet ideology began to evaporate like a mirage. The Party abandoned the distasteful necessity of economic coexistence and embarked with enthusiasm on monumental new tasks, leaving "small deeds" and disturbing ideological uncertainties behind. The discourse of the following years would in many respects go beyond even Enchmen's wildest predictions of maximized joyousness. The anxieties and everyday fears introduced by the ideological contradictions of NEP were happily exchanged for a second utopian childhood equally and unabashedly as violent as the first.

The *late* 1930s have come to be remembered as an extremely dark time. Retrospectively, accounts of the era have cloaked themselves in the Gothic, particularly when they have sought to gain emotional and narrative strength from the suggestion that "Stalin" might not, after all, be dead.[1] Yet the ideological discourse of the era was much less preoccupied with fear, in large measure, I suspect, because political restraint ceased to be a virtue. Tolerance of enemies was no longer encouraged nor was poverty a sign of ideological conviction. Liberated from the ideological terrors of coexistence and of indefinite political anticipation, Bolshevism was free to enjoy to the hilt the exercise of its own naked power and all of the material benefits that power could bring. To be sure, the transcripts of the purge trials are laden with charges of moral monstrosity, but the forces of evil were always shown to be reassuringly impotent, and the trials were not without their moments of carnivalesque exuberance in which prosecutorial viciousness relied for its effect more on laughter than on fear.[2] The level of fear in the daily life of Soviet culture may have been higher during the 1930s than at any other time in Russian history, but this fear was not ideological—it was focused more on personal safety than on historical legitimacy.

The final nail in NEP's coffin was surely the campaign for collectivization that swept through Russia until its implementers became "dizzy with suc-

---

[1] This suggestion is particularly poignant in Iurii Trifonov's *House on the Embankment* (1976). The "Gothic atmosphere" of the novel's treatment of Stalinism is noted by Thomas Seifrid. "Trifonov's *Dom na naberezhnoi* and the Fortunes of Aesopian Speech, *Slavic Review* 49 (1990): 614–625.

[2] The rhetoric of monstrosity is particularly marked in Andrei Vyshinskii's summation at the trial of Nikolai Bukharin and others in March 1938. *Report of Court Proceedings in the Case of the Anti-Soviet "Bloc of Rights and Trotskyites"* (M.: People's Commissariat of Justice, 1938), 625–697.

cess."[3] This brutal time in Soviet history, along with the First Five Year Plan that accompanied it, was, to a great extent, responsible for springing Bolshevism from the interior space in which it had been huddling and allowing it to stride out into the ideological storm, to fight with the storm's elements, and eventually, when "the second day" of constructing the Soviet state had passed, to take discursive solace in material abundance and the pastoral harmony of the kolkhoz.[4] Many historians have noted that the First Five Year Plan was perceived by Soviet citizens as a return to the ethos of War Communism, an ethos now strengthened, perhaps, through the sublation of its NEP antithesis. As far as sex and gender were concerned, the new cultural epoch *was* in many respects similar to War Communism. The Cultural Revolution of the end of the decade witnessed the abolition of the women's divisions and ushered in a "gendered [militaristic] language [that . . .] undoubtedly resonated with male youth far more than their female counterparts."[5] This language, however, did not tend toward the obsessive stigmatization of femininity that had marked the discourse of the previous era. In the course of the 1930s the female body and female physiology emerged from the veil of horror that had surrounded them during the 1920s. For the first time women became prominent in Soviet iconography.[6] The theme of rural abundance demanded that women be reconfigured and enlisted as ideological symbols of kolkhoz fecundity.[7] And in the rarefied world of Soviet endocrinology, experimenters in rejuvenation abandoned the idea of grafting testes or tying seminal vessels. Instead, under the direction of Aleksei Zamkov, doctors

[3] Stalin's famous phrase was immortalized in an article under this title published in *Pravda* on 2 March 1930. Reprinted in I. Stalin, *Sochineniia*, 13 vols. (M.: Gos. izd. politicheskoi literatury, 1949), 12:191–199.

[4] On the return to nature in Soviet literature of this period, see Katerina Clark, *The Soviet Novel: History as Ritual* (Chicago: University of Chicago Press, 1985), 98–113.

[5] Lewis H. Siegelbaum, *Soviet State and Society between Revolutions, 1918–1929* (Cambridge: Cambridge University Press, 1992), 222.

[6] Elizabeth Waters, "The Female Form in Soviet Political Iconography, 1917–32," in *Russia's Women: Accommodation, Resistence, Transformation*, ed. Barbara Evans Clements, Barbara Alpern Engel, and Christine D. Worobec (Berkeley and Los Angeles: University of California Press, 1991), 239–242 (225–242).

[7] Victoria Bonnell has recently shown that women's emergence in political iconography occurred in at least two steps. During the First Five Year Plan, women farmers on posters were basically proletarians in ideological drag; they had the thin, understated bodies of the ideal, masculinized communist woman of NEP. By the late 1930s, the female collective farmer "had begun to fill out and acquire a fuller, more rounded look. The large bosoms and corpulence of the [negative rural woman] of the 1920s did not return, but the trim and athletic look of the early 1920s also faded from the scene." "The Peasant Woman in Stalinist Political Art of the 1930s," *American Historical Review* 98 (1993): 63–72 (55–82). Bonnell relies on poster art for her conclusions, which are concerned only with peasant women; an analysis of popular films, as well as socialist realist painting, photography, and newsreels, might suggest that the ideal Soviet woman became increasingly buxom, although not less athletic, over the course of the decade.

experimented with injections of liquids prepared from the urine of pregnant women, a treatment administered to more than twelve thousand patients by 1934, including Gor'ky, Zetkin, and Kuibyshev.[8] We should not be blind to the gender switch in this glandular search for the fountain of youth.

By the time Stalin spoke to a group of "vanguard combine operators" in December 1935, reproduction was a contradiction-free, joyous event, the character of which was indicated even by an official stenographer's rendition of audience response:

> These days everyone here is saying that the material conditions of our work-ers' lives have improved significantly, that life has become better, more cheerful. This, of course, is true. But this results in the population's multiplying more rapidly than in former days. The death rate has gone down, the birth rate has gone up, and the rise in population is incomparably greater. This, of course, is good, and we salute it. (Cheerful animation [*veseloe ozhivlenie*] in the hall.)[9]

A month earlier, Stalin had criticized those who believed that "socialism may be strengthened only by means of leveling, by making the people live the life of poor peasants." "This isn't true," he had declared; "it's the petty bourgeois concept of socialism." Socialism, he proclaimed, could be built only on the basis of "prosperity" (*zazhitochnost'*).[10] From NEP's first sum-mer, the voice of "Communist" ("we should [not make] ourselves as poor as the most deprived") had emerged triumphant; this time it had no discursive opposition.

Some of our story's heroes, such as Andrei Platonov, would have a diffi-cult time accepting Soviet society under Stalin as War Communism redux. Platonov viewed Stalinist "happiness" as the triumph of the petty-bourgeois values whose reappearance had made NEP so troubling. In a series of re-markable stories written in 1935 and 1936, he captured the anguish of a communist forced to trade in utopian aspirations for brightly colored but worthless certificates of ideological deposit.[11] In one of these works, "The Potudan' River," Platonov gave his hero a name—Firsov—that he had used as a pseudonym only once before, when he had taken the side of Pletnev in

---

[8] Nik. Atarov, "Gravidan," *Nashi dostizheniia*, no. 3 (1934): 78 (74–80); A. Zamkov, "Gra-vidan v meditsine," *Novyi mir*, no. 8 (1935): 190–212; Mikhail Zolotonosov, "Masturbanizat-siia: erogennye zony sovetskoi kul'tury 1920–1930-kh godov," *Literaturnoe obozrenie*, no. 11 (1991): 93–99.

[9] I. V. Stalin, "Rech' na soveshchanii peredovykh kombainerov" (1 December 1935), in his *Works. Sochineniia*, 3 vols. (Stanford: Hoover Institution, 1967), 1:106.

[10] I. V. Stalin, "Rech' na pervom vsesoiuznom soveshchanii stakhanovtsev" (17 November 1935), *Works. Sochineniia*, 1:81.

[11] See, inter alia, "Reka Potudan'," in Andrei Platonov, *Gosudarstvennyi zhitel'* (M.: Sovetskii pisatel', 1988), 354–376; and "Sredi zhivotnykh i rastenii," in Andrei Platonov, *Techenie vre-meni* (M.: Moskovskii rabochii, 1971), 369–388.

the Voronezh debate on asceticism and had called upon communists to donate "everything necessary" to their starving brothers.[12] "The Potudan' River" is set in 1921 or 1922 and deals with a demobilized soldier's difficulty accepting the idea of sexual life and its more general context: everyday routine. The tale poignantly bids farewell to the mentality and sexual discourse of the early 1920s. The author and his hero abandon their dreams of War Communism and reluctantly embrace the pale promise of the Stalinist utopia and a communist version of Schopenhauer's "life of the species." Appropriately, the rejection of food and sexuality are paired; Firsov leaves his wife, ceases talking, drastically reduces his intake of food, and finds work cleaning outhouses—an occupation that raises the obsession with purity to a parodically literal plane.[13] Eventually, Firsov overcomes his denial of basic bodily needs, returns to his abandoned wife, Liubov', and consummates their marriage. Liubov' has tried to kill herself, and, significantly, Firsov arrives home shortly after learning that "blood flows frequently from her throat."[14] In keeping with the dynamics of the story, in which oral and genital functioning are consistently linked, this image of bleeding may be read as a reference to the resumption of menses and, within the context of "Revolutionary anorexia," to the rebirth of sexual desire. Looking back at the start of the NEP era from a distance of fifteen years, one of the greatest of Soviet writers was attempting to "work through" problems that had bedeviled the ideology of his youth. "The Potudan' River" is not only a moving story about love and sex but a brilliant piece of ideological mourning.

Boris Pil'niak experienced far fewer problems than did Platonov in reflecting the spirit of the new age. In a series of works written in the mid-1930s he celebrated his country's general "prosperity" and the new Stalinist order.[15] The extent of his transformation is evident in a 1935 story, "The Birth of a Human Being," which, like his earlier work, justifies sex on the basis of procreation and criticizes abortion. Through a communist's sexual biography, Pil'niak once again provides a thumbnail sketch of Soviet history: the hero's first spouse, an androgynous War Communist wife (presumably lacking "muffs"), yields her place to a dissolute NEP bride, who in her turn is later replaced by the ideal woman of the mid-1930s, a pregnant Soviet prosecutor.[16]

---

[12] Firsov (Andrei Platonov), "Kommunist! Pokazhi, chto ty kommunist," *Voronezhskaia kommuna*, 10 August 1921, 1.

[13] The outhouses may be a reference to Lenin's remark, made in the context of a caution against impatient utopian ideation, that eventually, "when we conquer on a world scale, I think we will build outhouses of gold on the streets of several of the largest cities of the world." "O znachenii zolota teper' i posle polnoi pobedy sotsializma" (6 and 7 November 1921), *Polnoe sobranie sochinenii*, 5th ed., 45 vols. (M.: Gos. izd., 1958–65), 44:225.

[14] Platonov, "Reka Potudan'," 374.

[15] See, inter alia, Bor. Pil'niak, "Kamen', nebo," *Novyi mir*, no. 12 (1934): 34–45.

[16] Boris Pil'niak, "Rozhdenie cheloveka," in his *Izbrannye proizvedeniia* (M.: Khudozhestvennaia literatura, 1976), 414–440. The story was first published in *Novyi mir*, no. 1

Pil'niak's story, which takes its name from a pre-Revolutionary work by Gor'ky, is worth a brief look, for it shows how the terrifying phantoms of the 1920s became harmless ghosts in the 1930s. En route to the "Klara Zetkin Maternity Hospital," Mariia Antonova (we learn her biblically resonant first name only after she gives birth) stops at a sanitarium that was formerly a gentry estate. The property is described as gloomy and unwelcoming; it even contains a large room "in the Gothic style" where Masons gathered.[17] This atmosphere fails to frighten the heroine. Unlike Kollontai's Vasia, Prosecutor Antonova can laugh at the terrors of the past. She writes in her diary:

> The room where the Masons met is a room like any other [. . .], dark, with Fascist swastikas, nothing special, dusty, . . . and in this room the Lady of the manor used to walk with terror, trembling and in horror. [. . .] Demons, the tokens of demons, and the affairs of demons used to surround the Lady on all sides; they used to climb out of dark corners, from under the bed, and through the windows. In the Lady herself two things had dwelled—God and the Devil—their tenancy duly registered, just as a passport is registered at a police station. The Lady had lived her life oppressed by these two deciders of destinies. [. . .] And with the Lady was her Lord, a Mason, a lieutenant, who slept with the chambermaid when [his wife] was pregnant.
>
> Yes, yes. It's all like that. All that had died! . . .[18]

Pil'niak's heroine wakes in the middle of the night, but her sensations are quite different from those of Gladkov's Polia.

> The child moved inside me at night, and I awoke. Words cannot convey this delight that is so strong as to become horror, this simultaneous feeling of life and death, this joy that becomes a physical sensation, this shame that makes me cry and that simultaneously makes me want to leap out of bed and call anybody at all on the phone and tell him that just now, five minutes ago, a new human being moved within me, one who has never been before, who is unique and who will live in a new epoch, in a classless society . . .[19]

Antonova's "horror" is closer to rapture, an inability to believe that life is as wonderful as it is. The Gothic has left its traces in Pil'niak's tale, but they have been purged of emotional affect. When writing about sex, he still refers to Gothic images and uses Gothic language, but fear no longer has a hold on

---

(1935): 111–126. For an interpretation of the story as implicitly critical of contemporary Soviet society, see Gary Browning, *Boris Pilniak: Scythian at a Typewriter* (Ann Arbor, Mich.: Ardis, 1985), 178–181. Mary Nicholas places the work in the context of Pil'niak's treatment of woman's voice, "Russian Modernism and the Female Voice: A Case Study," *Russian Review* 53 (1994): 530–548.

[17] Pil'niak, "Rozhdenie cheloveka," 418.

[18] Ibid.

[19] Ibid., 420.

the communist woman's psyche. Importing the poetics of Russian Formalism into our consideration of ideology, we might say that here NEP Gothic is being "parodied" by the new, Stalinist worldview.[20]

Antonova is "hard as stone," the product of the 1920s Komsomol. Before becoming a prosecutor, she taught herself to live on the basis of a single text: "I read *Komsomolka* [the affectionate name for *Komsomol'skaia pravda*] from cover to cover, because I was supposed to transpose into life everything that appeared in it. *Komsomolka* was my reference guide for everything that concerned my life and my work."[21] She remained aloof from the sexual debates of the 1920s: "My sexual affairs were my own private business, in which I did not allow anyone to meddle. They occupied little of my time."[22] Convinced that "the morality of the family was not only dead but stank with corruption," she never married and had two abortions.[23]

In the course of her stay at the sanitarium Antonova changes her attitude toward birth. Through her diaries and letters Pil'niak manages to marry Rozanov's and Schopenhauer's "life of the species" to the dictates of the Stalinist utopia's version of the communist family, just as earlier he had sought to marry Rozanov's love of procreation to the War Communist ethos and later to the widespread disgust with NEP. Walking through the grounds of the sanitarium, Antonova meets Sergei Surovtsev, a machine-tool builder, who is deriving great pleasure from hearing "fallen leaves" (*opavshie list'ia*) rustle under his feet. The leaves, which appear in the name of Rozanov's most famous book (*Fallen Leaves*), play an important role in the story, for the couple's courtship occurs as they walk through them and discuss "the influence of societal changes on crime."[24] Surovtsev's life experiences have taught him that reproduction and a close relationship with a women are an essential part of life:

> I am a communist, that is, a man of the collective,—and as soon as I am left
> alone within four walls or even in the forest, with fallen leaves underfoot, I
> become lonely and am terrified by my loneliness. When nobody else is around, I

[20] In the terms of Iurii Tynianov's famous essay, parody is the use of quotation in a context that radically undermines the intention of the quoted material's original use. See his *Dostoevskii i Gogol' (K teorii parodii)* (Letchworth: Prideaux, 1975 [1921]).

[21] Pil'niak, "Rozhdenie cheloveka," 420.

[22] Ibid., 426. Antonova's aloofness is surprising, given the frequency with which sex and the public significance of private life were discussed in the Komsomol press. Apparently, Pil'niak was a much less avid reader of *Komsomol'skaia pravda* than was his heroine.

[23] Ibid., 425. Pil'niak tells his readers why Antonova did not abort her current pregnancy. She discovered her condition only when she was already en route by train to Central Asia, where she was sent to conduct a series of interrogations. The primitive living conditions there and the intense demands of her work precluded Antonova's seeking an abortion until too late. (Here, as in "Old Cheese," Central Asia forces childbirth upon Woman, but the ideological trappings of this later pregnancy are completely different.)

[24] Ibid., 431.

am terrified, but I know that sometimes a person must be able to be alone and feel himself complete. And one ought not to feel alone when one is together with a woman, because at such a moment there arises that which gives a person the feeling of immortality.[25]

A lasting heterosexual relationship is no longer the epitome of terror and a symbol of isolation from the larger community. Rather, a loving rapport between a man and a woman comes to represent escape from isolation into a larger, intergenerational world. Antonova's friendship and blossoming love for Surovtsev teach her that birth is "an enormous joy and enormous happiness."[26] She comes to reject the mentality of the 1920s; in a letter that she sends to Surovtsev from the maternity ward, she diametrically opposes her experience of parturition to Nemilov's portrait of the horrors of birth:

> [A]t night, in the unending cries of the women [around me], the concept of time became confused, my idea of myself became confused, and it seemed to me that all this was me, and that yesterday, and today, and tomorrow—at all times—I am still giving birth and screaming,—all this has repeated, is repeating, and will repeat from one century to another, for the entire life of mankind. [. . .] And a new image of woman took shape in me, an image of a person who gives birth to another person, and I began to feel how unjust it is that we are awed by death but not by birth, awed by social warfare, while the birth of a man and of mankind is considered either a physiological act unworthy of attention or, as one idiot put it, the "physiological tragedy of woman!"
>
> And more. The feudal sense of family, of blood, and of roots has been lost. I fought them. In feudal times a woman came to her husband and was taken in by his family. That didn't happen to me. I have no family roots that might give me life. And it turns out that my family is not being perpetuated, but is just beginning. [. . .] My family has an advantage,—it does not look backward—but straight ahead.[27]

In this passage Nemilov's *Biological Tragedy of Woman* and the concomitant terror of repetition are negated by a formula that links the age-old process of birth with the insistence on forward movement always so important to Bolshevism. Rozanov's worship of sex has been fused with the natalist demands of joyous Stalinism. The horror of the "bad infinity" of the past has been replaced by confidence in the good repetition of the future. Elsewhere Antonova says to herself, "I need a man, a husband, a father to my child, [. . .] whose sex would be as sacred for me as mine for him."[28] This sanctity, however, was not quite what Rozanov had envisioned, for in the Soviet

---

[25] Ibid., 435.
[26] Ibid., 438.
[27] Ibid., 439.
[28] Ibid., 429.

1930s it entailed the virtual merger of prosecutorial and reproductive functions. Far more prophetic than Rozanov, it turned out, was that student who had exclaimed at that debate on sex in the Krupskaia Academy that it was essential to love and work like Dzerzhinsky.

The era's characteristic overcoming of the fear of repetition is noticeable also in the work of Nemilov himself. In 1932, he published an article in the popular science journal *Priroda* in which he apologized for his earlier enthusiasm for "rejuvenation." His recantation was odd; he had been, after all, only a tepid supporter of "rejuvenation," advising that the process be employed for animals only. Now, however, he claimed to have realized that his entire position—limited enthusiasm and all—had been ideologically and scientifically flawed:

> If [rejuvenation were possible], it would mean that life is in no sense a dialectical process and that the wheel of life might turn backward, like some sort of movie reel. If an old person can be made young, then there is no conformity to the laws that inevitably lead bourgeois government to socialism, and the social order whose stability is so vital to the bourgeoisie is not doomed by the course of historical process but can be rejuvenated and reborn. Somehow we have so far failed to pay attention to this social underpinning of the problem of rejuvenation, but it has enormous significance for the analysis of scientific work in that field and explains quite a lot there.[29]

It is significant, I believe, that Nemilov did not have this insight during NEP, when in his oft reprinted book he had been preoccupied precisely with the necessity of adapting oneself to the ever-present horror of a resurgent past. Now that the Gothic no longer commanded such a dominant position in Soviet ideology, Nemilov could take new comfort in the wisdom he gleaned from Engels in *The Dialectics of Nature*:

> If life is a dialectical process, then it cannot be absolutely reversed, and, in actuality, there does not exist a single scientifically supported observation that a live organism can entirely return to a stage of development through which it has already passed. Within the boundaries of that which a given organism represents [. . .] there cannot be a simple return to an already passed stage of youth, since that would contradict the most fundamental laws of nature.[30]

Nemilov proclaimed that repetition could occur only through transformation into something new. Using an example that was far more than incidental, he wrote: "There is no experimental action that might repeal the laws of the dialectic. An old organism can become new only through taking that path by

---

[29] A. V. Nemilov, "Lozh' i pravda v voprose ob 'omolozhenii,'" *Priroda*, no. 8 (1932): 721 (710–738).

[30] Ibid., 723.

which, let us say, a bourgeois government can rejuvenate itself by turning into a socialist one."[31]

The work of tracing genre patterns through the 1930s remains to be undertaken by other scholars, but my preliminary impression is that this was a far less Gothic time than the previous decade and that when Gothic narratives appeared they did so—as in Bulgakov's *Master and Margarita*—humorously and were, at least ostensibly, stories about the culture of NEP, tales grounded in the 1920s. The most Gothic moments in Bulgakov's novel occur in a darkened theater whose name bespeaks not only theatrical genre but also the heterogeneity that so marked NEP: The Variety (*Var'ete*).[32] Far more characteristic of the 1930s than Bulgakov's novel is Mikhail Bakhtin's fabulous essay on historical conceptions of time and space, a glorification of an ancient, precapitalist community in which nothing was concealed and everything was external.[33] That wonderful ancient world, where there was no place and no need to hide, was redeemed, according to Bakhtin, by Rabelais after a long protobourgeois era of collective decline and individual isolation. In

[31] Ibid., 726.

[32] Bulgakov's use of Gothic motifs merits extensive consideration; here I note only that in its criticism of Soviet realia, Bulgakov's work often displays an *oppositional* use of the Gothic: Gothic motifs are treated humorously or from a positive, familiar perspective. One might even read Voland's oft-repeated defense of "shadows" ("what would the earth look like if shadows disappeared from it? [. . .] Would you like to denude the earth of all the trees and all the living beings in order to satisfy your fantasy of rejoicing in the naked light?" Mikhail Bulgakov, *The Master and Margarita*, trans. Mira Ginsburg [New York: Grove Press, 1967], 368) as a *genre-oriented*, rather than strictly philosophical or broadly aesthetic, statement. For Bulgakov a light-hearted, almost domestic attitude toward the Gothic is part and parcel of an aesthetic stance that never tires of demonstrating its love for and ties to the past. (Bulgakov was hounded for his affection toward the past. In a satirical New Year's poem ushering out 1928, A. M. Argo went so far as to rhyme Bulgakov's name with "midnight gloom": И дальше грезится Татьяне/ Виденье сквозь полночный мрак:/Трусит верхом на таракане/Гробово-островный Булгак." Quoted in Viktor Losev, "'Rukopisi ne goriat,'" in Mikhail Bulgakov, *Velikii Kantsler* (M.: Novosti, 1992), 6 (3–22). Other authors, too, employed this loving embrace of the Gothic (and inversion of the genre's affect) to indicate opposition to the dominant, progressive discourse; an early use, predating NEP, is to be found in Zamiatin's *We*, with its images of the "Ancient House," and its focus on a society's fear of penetration and its conquest by the past. *We*, trans. Gregory Zilboorg (New York: Dutton, 1924). It may be that Zamiatin's much-vaunted prescience is amply displayed in his anticipating the generic discourse that would best pose a challenge to the spirit and representations of War Communism. He failed to foresee, however, that War Communism would be challenged in this way *by the Party*, and that, as a result, Soviet communism would remain both triumphant *and* profoundly terrified by the genre in which it had forced itself to speak. Only in the works of this "generic opposition" to which Bulgakov and Zamiatin, at least, belonged was the Gothic treated with exhilaration and a sense that in entering the world of the past one had, at long last, come home.

[33] Mikhail Bakhtin, "Forms of Time and of the Chronotope in the Novel: Notes toward a Historical Poetics," *The Dialogic Imagination*, trans. Caryl Emerson and Michael Holquist (Austin: University of Texas Press, 1981), 84–258.

many respects, one can read Bakhtin's essay on the chronotope as a scholar's utopian dream in which one of the goals of Stalinist community—total transparency—is attained without the accompanying violence frequently inherent in the beloved Marxist and Stalinist practice of "unmasking."[34] We should not be blind to the importance of corporality in Bakhtin's vision. The naked, accessible, continually producing and excreting Rabelaisian body is central to Bakhtin's communal utopia. The body holds no terrors in this world of blessed openness; even death is "cheerful" (*veselaia*) in Bakhtin's fairy-tale version of life in Stalin's violent and "cheerful" world.[35] The theme of incarnation was not a source of discursive anxieties in the Soviet Union after NEP, and in Bakhtin's essay on time and space we see how in that essay's time and place the body was transformed from a locus of terror into a refuge from fear.

This disjuncture of Gothic discourse and the ideology of the Stalin period is somewhat paradoxical; after all, in Soviet culture terms such as "terror" and "return of the repressed" more often refer to specific historical periods than to psychological phenomena, and it would seem that the late 1930s would be *the* period in Soviet history most likely to generate Gothic imagery. Stalinism became Gothic, however, chiefly in retrospect. The annihilation of NEP's economic diversity and of its reluctant, distasteful tolerance appears to have obliterated Gothic discourse as well, for that diversity and that tolerance had been essential to NEP Gothic's formation. The mentality of the years following NEP are best expressed not by the Gothic of Radcliffe or Maturin but by the formulation proposed by Marx in *The Eighteenth Brumaire*, where he claimed that in embracing the second—or, to be more precise, third—Napoleon's dictatorship, the French were demanding "*Rather an end with terror than terror without end.*"[36]

To what extent do moments like Stalin's address to the "vanguard combine operators" ("Life has become better, more cheerful") constitute Soviet ideology's tagging on a happy ending to its own version of the Gothic? If their bones could speak, few of the actors in this tale would claim that they lived happily ever—or even *long*—after. Much work remains to be done in the reconstitution of the narrative of early Soviet ideology, but we should

[34] For a more detailed treatment of this theme, see Anne Nesbet and Eric Naiman, "Formy vremeni v 'formakh vremeni': Khronosomy khronotopa," *Novoe literaturnoe obozrenie*, no. 2 (1993): 90–109. On Bakhtin's use of discourse as an "anaesthetic," see Mikhail Ryklin, "Bodies of Terror: Theses toward a Logic of Violence," trans. Molly Williams Wesling and Donald Wesling, *New Literary History* 24 (1993): 51–74.

[35] The link between Bakhtin's and Stalin's use of the word "cheerful" was first noted by Boris Groys in "Grausamer Karneval: Mikhail Bachtins 'aesthetische Rechtfertigung' des Stalinismus," *Frankfurter Allgemeine Zeitung*, 21 June 1989, 3.

[36] Karl Marx and Friedrich Engels, *The Marx-Engels Reader*, ed. Robert Tucker (New York: W. W. Norton, 1972), 505.

recognize that our understanding of the Terror in "real" life—terror that resides primarily outside of ideological discourse, terror with immediate, devastating effects on particular bodies, and terror that puts at stake the legitimacy of an individual existence rather than that of Bolshevik power— will necessarily remain incomplete until we have probed the depths of the discursive terror that preceded it.

INDEX

Note: page numbers followed by an "n" contain the relevant item *only* in the footnotes; if the item is found in both text and notes, no "n" has been appended.

About the Author

ERIC NAIMAN is Associate Professor of Russian and Comparative Literature at the University of California, Berkeley.